For Not To Be Taken
From the Room
reference COPY 10

AIDS
in the
Workplace

AIDS
in the
Workplace

Legal Questions and
Practical Answers

William F. Banta

Kullman, Inman, Bee, Downing & Banta
New Orleans—Memphis—Birmingham

Lexington Books
An Imprint of Macmillan, Inc.
New York

Maxwell Macmillan Canada
Toronto

Maxwell Macmillan International
New York   Oxford   Singapore   Sydney

Library of Congress Cataloging-in-Publication Data

Banta, William F.
    AIDS in the workplace : legal questions and practical answers /
William F. Banta.—Rev. and exp. ed. updated and expanded ed.
        p.   cm.
    Includes bibliographical references and index.
    ISBN 0-669-28056-9
    1. AIDS (Disease)—Patients—Employment—Law and legislation—
United States.   I. Title.
    [DNLM: 1. Acquired Immunodeficiency Syndrome—United States—
legislation.   2. Occupational Medicine.   3. Public Policy—United
States—legislation.   WD 308 B219a]
KF3570.B36   1993
344.73′ 0465—dc20
[347.304465]
DNLM/DLC
for Library of Congress   92-33947
                                                                   CIP

Lexington Books
An Imprint of Macmillan, Inc.
866 Third Avenue, New York, N.Y. 10022

Maxwell Macmillan Canada, Inc.
1200 Eglinton Avenue East
Suite 200
Don Mills, Ontario M3C 3N1

Macmillan, Inc. is part of the Maxwell Communication
Group of Companies.

Printed in the United States of America

printing number
1 2 3 4 5 6 7 8 9 10

To my mother, who taught me to read and write,
and to my father, who paid for the
remainder of my education.

Contents

Appendix D: Employer Policies, Procedures, and Checklists

Introduction

I was in the office of the human resources manager of a hospital client of our law firm, reviewing employment records pertaining to a civil rights charge she described as frivolous, when the hospital administrator abruptly pushed the door open. Another, more demanding issue had emerged that very morning which consumed the remainder of that day and a portion of the evening: a female registered nurse (RN) assigned to the emergency room had just informed the director of nursing that she was HIV positive.

The arrest of the RN's husband for selling illegal drugs the previous week had fed the rumor mill: "Did you hear that Charlene's husband was caught red-handed selling dope? He's no good and never has been." "Have you noticed how much weight he's lost recently? He looks god-awful. I'll bet he's gotten AIDS from shooting up all those drugs. Maybe he's infected Charlene." "Did you see the photographs of Charlene's husband in the newspaper last week? Boy, did he look bad. Either he's in withdrawal or he's got AIDS. I sure hope Charlene hasn't been sleeping with him." "Did you notice that scab on Charlene's right hand? She cut herself last week while treating a patient. I'd hate to have her blood get on me." "Charlene has been looking a little peaked lately. Maybe her jerk of a husband infected her with HIV."

The director of nursing had just spoken privately with Charlene, mentioning the rumors and asking pointedly whether Charlene was concerned about her HIV status. Charlene immediately broke into tears, sobbing that her husband had been diagnosed with AIDS six months earlier, and that her test for the HIV antibodies, conducted immediately after her husband's diagnosis, was positive. She reminded the director of nursing that she had three children, explained that her husband lacked insurance and was incurring substantial medical bills, and begged not to be fired.

The director of nursing sent her home for the remainder of the shift, with pay, and reported the matter to the hospital administrator, who now posed a series of questions to me: Should Charlene be removed from her job as an emergency room RN; if so, what action should be taken and how should it be explained? What obligations, if any, does the hospital have to identify the patients treated by Charlene during the last year, and to notify them of her positive HIV status? Does the hospital have a legal duty to disclose her condition to fellow employees, or does the law protect Charlene's privacy and prohibit disclosure to other personnel? What should the hospital do if some of Charlene's fellow employees refused to perform their duties when she was in their area or walked off the job? And if Charlene continues to work at the hospital, does the hospital have a duty to disclose her positive HIV status to patients with whom she comes in contact?

The questions were endless, easy answers elusive. As the discussion continued, the civil rights case seemed simple compared to the multiple and complex issues raised by a single employee carrying an infectious, fatal virus.

Charlene was an excellent worker with long seniority, had never been disciplined, had always been in excellent health, and had an almost perfect attendance record. The director of nursing captured the humane perspective of the problem when she spoke sympathetically about Charlene's personal situation: her mother was dead, her father had remarried and lived in another state; her husband was being treated for AIDS-related illness in another hospital, and if his health improved he faced a criminal trial and a probable jail term; medical and legal bills were accumulating; her children, aged two, ten, and fourteen, needed care and comfort; and she now feared that her job—her only source of income—was in jeopardy. The nursing director wanted to visit Charlene that evening, to express care and concern, and to assure her that she could continue in her job.

The hospital administrator was worried about talk in the community; he was afraid that his hospital would be labeled "the AIDS hospital," and that bad publicity would cause a drop in admissions. He also expressed concern about lawsuits against the hospital filed by patients Charlene had treated in the emergency room. He suggested placing Charlene on paid leave of absence for a month "to cool things off" and then offering her a clerical job at a lower rate of pay in which she would have no contact with the blood or body tissue of patients or fellow employees. With this approach, he argued, disclosure of her condition to others would be unnecessary, her privacy would be protected, talk in the community would "die down," and both Charlene and the hospital would be better off.

The human resources director, discerning the difficulty of replacing an experienced RN in the emergency room, first argued that Charlene could be reinstructed on the "universal precautions" prescribed by the federal Centers for Disease Control (CDC), and then given double gloves and special gear to wear while continuing to work in the emergency room. Then, remembering that some emergency room personnel had already expressed concern about working with Charlene, the director proposed that Charlene switch jobs with an RN assigned to a patient ward. Away from the emergency room Charlene would rarely come into contact with bleeding patients, and therefore would pose less of a threat. She saw no reason to inform employees about Charlene's condition, counseled secrecy, and concluded that any employees who refused to work with her should be fired.

I supplied the legal perspective, explaining that involuntary removal of Charlene from her position would probably violate state and federal laws protecting the handicapped, and that disclosing her HIV condition, without her informed, written consent, to patients and fellow employees could invade her right to privacy and breach the hospital's duty of confidentiality. I also emphasized, however, that if the risk of transmitting the virus from Charlene to patients during the performance of her duties was greater than remote, then leaving her in the emergency room position could constitute negligence. I suggested medical evaluation of the degree of risk Charlene posed, based, in part, on the latest findings of the CDC. Such a report would determine how to respond to the problems of possible disclosure of Charlene's HIV status to patients and fellow employees. I endorsed the idea of a transfer on the condition that it be voluntary, suggested medical evaluation of Charlene and counseling for her and her family at hospital expense, and advised that any employees refusing to work with her simply be sent home without mention of discharge.

As we attempted to resolve these issues over the next week, our discussions were hampered by a lack of written policy and no precedents to follow. While the hospital had a general infectious disease policy, it was unclear how it would apply to HIV situations. Realizing that decisions concerning Charlene would create precedents that would influence future, related issues, the administrator met with the medical director and key members of the board of directors several times during the ensuing days. Finally, Charlene voluntarily and gratefully accepted a transfer to a ward position, at the same rate of pay and without loss of any benefits. The medical director met with all personnel in the emergency room, to explain the latest findings issued by the CDC on transmitting the virus and to demonstrate the protective gear they were supposed to wear while working. With the written consent of Charlene, fellow employees in her ward were informed of her HIV status and urged to treat her empathetically. After review of the medical records of patients treated by Charlene during the past year, and a lengthy interview with her about any potential exposures, we decided not to inform any patients of her HIV condition. No lawsuits were ever filed against the hospital by Charlene's former patients. The hospital drafted and implemented a written AIDS policy.

This story of an actual situation presents, in capsule form, many of the legal issues, practical concerns, individual attitudes, and real-life tragedies of AIDS in the workplace. It raises a number of difficult questions about how an employer should proceed in these circumstances. It illustrates the medical, legal, and personnel aspects of the issues. It also spotlights a critical omission on the part of many employers: the failure to develop an AIDS policy that will facilitate the handling of AIDS-related issues that are likely to arise.

A survey of corporate executives found that they ranked AIDS as the third most important problem facing our country today (behind the federal deficit and drug abuse), but that over 50 percent of the companies where they were employed had no AIDS policy. In other human resources areas, managers have relied upon carefully crafted and well-implemented written policies to guide them through personnel problems and crises and to promote consistency.

Inconsistent treatment of similarly situated employees is evidence of improper conduct in the eyes of judges and arbitrators; uniform application of written policies, however, reduces the risk of costly legal challenge.

Since its discovery in 1981, AIDS has become of paramount interest to the American public. Realizing that AIDS has all the ingredients of a long-running soap opera—sex, drugs, and death—the media maintain a steady barrage of stories on the fatal syndrome and its impact on people. Medical, legal, and personnel associations and periodicals debate the issues. Legislatures, courts, and businesses are presented with novel situations. The following list of news stories indicates the pervasiveness of AIDS and the kinds of problems it is creating in our society:

- An Oakland HIV-positive man was arrested for assault with a deadly weapon after vowing to infect all the women he could through sex before he dies, and for throwing blood from a self-inflicted wound on another man.
- A judge sentenced a man to sexual abstinence for having sex with his girlfriend after learning that he had the HIV virus.
- A woman's application for life insurance was rejected because of a positive test for HIV. Later, she and her husband arranged for separate tests, which were negative. After being sued by the couple for emotional distress, the insurance company explained that its earlier report of a positive test result was "a clerical error."
- A man with AIDS killed a store clerk with a knife during a robbery. Arrested with her blood and the knife on him, he confessed. At the trial his attorney presented evidence that he was suffering from dementia caused by AIDS and argued that he lacked the necessary legal intent to kill. The jury acquitted him of first degree murder but found him guilty of second degree murder.
- The president of the National Hockey League sent a letter to all teams recommending voluntary and confidential HIV testing for all personnel because a young woman who died of AIDS-related causes had informed her doctor that she had sex with more than fifty professional hockey players.
- A toy manufacturer distributed a new game called "Bacteria

Panic" in which the player left holding a card marked "AIDS" is the loser. The game was quickly recalled following complaints that it was insensitive.

- The National Commission on AIDS reported that our prison system provides inadequate medical treatment for inmates with HIV infection and subjects them to unnecessary indignities that offend their basic human rights.

- A new Mississippi law requires all convicted sex offenders to be tested for HIV and mandates that positive results be reported to the victim, the victim's spouse, and the spouse of the person convicted of the sex offense.

- College clinics experienced a sudden surge in student testing for HIV following Magic Johnson's revelation that he has the HIV virus.

- *Ebony* magazine included a letter from "C. J. of Dallas" who claims she contracted HIV from a man and is now attempting to infect others by picking up men in bars and having sex with them.

- Concerned about their own safety, medical associations lobbied for and in some states obtained laws that allow physicians to test patients for HIV without the patient's consent in certain circumstances.

- Upon being diagnosed with AIDS, a teacher was reassigned from the classroom to the school office where he is supposed to write applications for grants. His lawyer, however, secured an injunction returning him to teaching duties which the court rules do not present a significant risk of harm to students.

As the number of people infected increases with the passage of time, fewer and fewer employers will remain untouched by the AIDS crisis. A job applicant who unknowingly contracted the virus from a sexual partner is hired. An employee who successfully completed a drug rehabilitation program more than a year ago begins displaying the symptoms of symptomatic HIV disease (at times referred to as AIDS-related complex). Another employee becomes extremely ill with a form of cancer that is connected to AIDS; eventually it is discovered that a blood transfusion he received after surgery seven years earlier was the means of transmission.

Questions that will be presented to these employers are many and varied. An employee, like Charlene, may test positive for HIV antibodies but be quite healthy—and as capable of performing job duties as ever—for many, many years. Some people exposed to the virus have developed AIDS within two years, while others continue to be AIDS-free eight years after exposure. Administration of AZT, DDI and DDC has been found to slow down the course of AIDS and to impede many of the illnesses that accompany it. Hence, an employee like Charlene who recently became infected may be able to perform all the duties of her or his job for many years, without impairment of any type. Thereafter, the employee may develop symptomatic HIV disease which could or could not affect her or his ability to perform work. Moreover, even an employee with full-blown AIDS may have long periods of relative health during which she or he could carry out all or some of their job duties. Each person with AIDS (PWA) has a different illness history. In an early stage of the disease, which could consume several years, a person with AIDS (PWA) might be physically capable of performing all job duties as usual, while in the late stages of illness the PWA could be entirely incapacitated for a long period of time. Between the early and late stages, there can be months and even years of widely fluctuating degrees of ability to perform work. One employee with AIDS can perform all essential duties but not some of the incidental ones. Another cannot do one physically demanding duty classified as essential but requests a reasonable accommodation so he can continue in his job. Still another claims that he can continue to perform all his duties but that he requires a special schedule because he becomes extremely tired and cannot work more than five hours per day. Complicating the issue even further is the significant percentage of AIDS patients who suffer deterioration of mental faculties at some point. Occasionally, this deterioration begins early and progresses quickly. But many PWAs remain as mentally alert as ever through the final stage of their illness. Hence, an employee with AIDS could be physically but not mentally qualified or vice versa to perform the duties of the job in question. There is no simple answer to questions involving what to do with a job applicant or an employee with an AIDS condition. Neither is there an established formula to apply for every case. While written policies can be extremely helpful, as I suggested above, the facts and circumstances of the physical and mental condition of every applicant and employee and the specific qualifications of the job in question must be thoroughly analyzed before reaching conclusions.

In preparing to draft or revise an AIDS policy, employers should pose and analyze numerous questions. Should it conduct its own tests of employees, like Charlene, who are rumored to be HIV positive? Should the employer offer or demand a thorough physical examination by the employer's doctor at the employer's expense? Suppose the employee refuses to be tested and declines the medical examination? May an employer, such as a restaurant, hotel, or hospital, take into account the anticipated loss of business if it permits an employee with AIDS to continue on its payroll? If the employee does not lose pay, benefits, or seniority, could he or she be involuntarily transferred to another nonpublic job or placed on leave of absence? Suppose fellow employees refuse to work with a person who is HIV infectious: could they be threatened with termination or, in the event of repeated refusals, discharged? Suppose a job applicant or employee confides to a manager that he or she is HIV positive, but emphasizes that the communication is confidential and none of his family, friends, or fellow employees is to know. Does the employer have a legal obligation to notify a spouse? Children? Employees who work with him or her? Patients or customers? If any disclosures are made, is the employer vulnerable to claims of invasion of privacy and breach of confidentiality?

Managers desiring to approach AIDS-related questions in the workplace with sound judgment, sensitivity, and an awareness of legal precedent are frequently confused by a myriad of state and federal laws, lack of past precedent, and conflicting advice from doctors, lawyers, and fellow managers.

Aside from questions of hiring, transferring, promoting, placing on leave of absence, and terminating persons with AIDS conditions, managers are concerned about the cost of caring for the several million people who will suffer from AIDS in the years to come. Who will pick up the tab for treating them? The lifetime cost of caring for PWAs is estimated to be approximately $80,000 per patient. As the number of AIDS patients skyrockets, so will the cost for their care. Approximately $100 billion dollars was expended in treating AIDS patients from 1986 through 1991. Employers attempting to contain rising insurance premiums may be tempted to exclude AIDS-related illnesses from coverage in return for lower premiums. Hospitals may refuse admission of PWAs who do not have insurance. As these types of situations develop, governmental regulations and new statutes will probably be used to achieve social objectives, including protection of PWAs from being discriminatorily deprived of insurance benefits and medical treatment.

This book reviews all the laws potentially applicable to AIDS in the workplace—federal, state, and local—and then analyzes various AIDS employment issues in a practical fashion, identifying the pros and cons of alternative approaches and recommending courses of action that are both consistent with legal cases and protective of legitimate business interests. Special chapters are devoted to the controversial subject of testing for HIV antibodies and the particular problems faced by health care facilities in their dual roles of caring for patients and employing physicians, nurses, technicians, and other personnel who have direct contact with the blood and body fluids of patients during the performance of their duties. A specific framework for analyzing employment issues involving AIDS is set forth, point by point. Moreover, a checklist for preventing AIDS claims and a list of thirty separate defenses to AIDS lawsuits are included. Appendix A includes various guidelines, rules, instructions, and standards on this topic issued by agencies of the federal government. Appendix B contains pertinent portions of the Americans with Disabilities Act, and sample letters, claims, and complaints alleging violations of federal and state laws. Policies especially appropriate for health care facilities constitute appendix C, while sample policies for other employers are included in appendix D.

AIDS
in the
Workplace

"I have AIDS. I was formerly a dentist in the Martin County area, and if you were my patient, I ask you to please read this letter."

> —Letter placed in newspapers by Dr. Acer, a Florida dentist, who later died, urging his patients to be tested for the virus. Investigators concluded that five of his patients had been infected with HIV during treatment.

"I blame Dr. Acer and every single one of you bastards. Anyone who knew Dr. Acer was infected and had full-blown AIDS and stood by not doing a damn thing about it. You are all just as guilty as he was. You've ruined my life and my family's."

> —Letter to Florida's Department of Health and Rehabilitative Services written by Kimberly Bergalis, one of the five patients who was infected by Dr. Acer. She died at the age of twenty-three.

"Because of the HIV virus I have obtained, I will have to announce my retirement from the Lakers today."

> —Earvin "Magic" Johnson, explaining his sudden departure from professional basketball at the age of thirty-three.

"I have AIDS. I am sorry that I have been forced to make this revelation now, at this time."

> —Arthur Ashe, who felt his privacy was invaded by the press which was writing a story about his HIV condition.

"The court finds under all circumstances of this case that the defendant's conduct was not merely inexcusably insensitive and illegal but was so outrageous that the sanction of punitive damages is warranted."

> —Decision of a federal district court judge in concluding that a lawyer had been illegally fired soon after his legal firm learned that he had AIDS. Plaintiff was awarded $65,000 for mental anguish and humiliation and $50,000 in punitive damages.

"In the case at bench, we deal with the ultimate in personal horror—the fear of a slow, agonizing, certain death."

—California's Second District Court of Appeal, in upholding a $5 million damage award to Marc Christian, from whom Rock Hudson withheld knowledge of Hudson's AIDS condition while the two were lovers. Christian was not infected.

"In terms of impact on our society, this disease will certainly be the most important public-health problem of the next decade and going into the next century. On an international scale, it threatens to undermine countries, particularly in Africa."

—Dr. David Baltimore, microbiologist who was awarded a Nobel prize in 1975 for his work on viruses

"To accomplish the tasks that loom ahead, we must, as a society, find a way to convert anger, fear, and indifference into informed action. We must deal effectively with discrimination and prejudice, overcome present governmental inertia, rededicate ourselves to maintaining a necessary intensity of research endeavor, educate the public to replace panic with an informed awareness of what is needed to prevent infection, and coordinate our resources to meet the urgent health care needs of the sick in cost-efficient ways that take full advantage of our powerful science. We must recognize our obligations to future generations in these tasks, for further indifference or misdirected efforts spells doom for millions."

—"America Living with AIDS," Report of the National Commission On Acquired Immune Deficiency Syndrome

"Everybody knows that pestilences have a way of recurring in the world; yet somehow we find it hard to believe in ones that crash down on our heads from a blue sky."

—Albert Camus, *The Plague*

1

AIDS in the Workplace

General Considerations

Since it was identified in 1981 AIDS has presented challenges to doctors, lawyers, business managers, hospitals, ministers, and sociologists, among others. The medical, legal, and ethical questions raised by this disease cut across the lines of all these disciplines.

Medical Facts

The person who becomes infected with HIV usually develops antibodies within six months. A significant percentage of the present HIV-positive population live and work day after day, free of any physical or mental manifestations of the virus, and often ignorant of their infection. Eventually, signs of symptomatic HIV disease appear. Approximately 50 percent of persons infected with HIV will develop symptomatic HIV disease or AIDS within ten years. Some scientists believe that all HIV-infected people will eventually contract AIDS. The progression from HIV infection to AIDS is basically a question of time, until an effective treatment is found.

Tests are available to determine if a person has developed antibodies to HIV. If a positive test is confirmed, the individual has been infected by the virus. Currently available drugs, such as AZT, may prolong conversion to AIDS conditions for several years. Hundreds of thousands of HIV-infected people are currently free of the symptoms.

Medical experts emphasize that one does not have to be concerned about casual workplace contact with people who are HIV positive, as the virus cannot be transmitted by touching, hugging, kissing, sneezing, or sharing toilets.

Social Considerations

AIDS-related issues have made a significant impact on the world in a very short period of time. The tragic fact that affliction with AIDS is always fatal generates concern and fear. While some institutions and governments have been slow to respond to AIDS, others have overreacted in terms of concerns about potential transmission of the virus. Ramifications of foundless fears include discrimination against HIV-infected people and homophobia.

AIDS is a pandemic, an epidemic involving multiple countries. According to the World Health Organization (WHO), 1.5 million cases of AIDS have surfaced in 138 different nations. WHO estimates that more than thirteen million people are currently infected with HIV throughout the world and that 120 million people will be carrying the virus by the year 2000. A WHO doctor estimates that someone in the world is infected with HIV every 10–15 seconds. WHO sponsors a "World AIDS Day" each year to educate people, prevent the spread of HIV, and encourage compassionate treatment of the afflicted. The Pan American Health Organization believes that there are more than two million HIV-positive people in North and South America and the Caribbean. The United States, with the highest number of reported AIDS cases among all the nations in the world, has recorded almost 250,000 people with the syndrome.

In some parts of Africa one-third of the adult population has been killed by AIDS.* Almost 70 percent of the cases of AIDS throughout the world are in Africa, which has only 12 percent of the world population. Hospitals in Zambia report up to 80 percent of their admissions are AIDS-related. Eighty percent of the new cases are occurring in developing countries where the main means of transmission is heterosexual sex. Since women are more likely to contract HIV during heterosexual encounters, their infection rates may surpass men by 2000. The spread of AIDS cases in Asia has also been phenomenal in recent years. It has been predicted that eventually 90 percent of all AIDS cases will occur in developing

---

*Central Africa is believed by many researchers to be the place of origin of the AIDS virus because a relatively high proportion of the population has it, and the green monkey carries a virus closely related to the HIV virus identified in humans. A virologist discovered HIV in the blood plasma of a man who donated it in Zaire more than twenty-five years ago.

nations. Hospitals in Russia, Georgia, and Ukraine are compelled by shortages to use the same syringes on many patients. The result is predictable: the rate of HIV infection is growing and the primary cause is tainted needles, not sex. Russian officials have adopted policies designed to stem the spread of the virus: foreigners who wish to stay longer than three months must produce certificates indicating that they are free of AIDS; and carriers of HIV who have sexual contact with another person are subject to a five-year jail term, even if the virus is not transmitted. Japan has authorized officials to ban or quarantine HIV-infected foreigners who are likely to behave irresponsibly. Further, Japanese doctors are legally required to report to officials the names of HIV-infected patients who are likely to spread the virus. Until the execution of dictator Nicolae Ceausescu, Romania reported that it had no cases of AIDS. Now it admits that hundreds of undernourished babies had been injected with blood from tainted needles. Approximately one thousand babies in two cities alone contracted AIDS from contaminated blood, tainted needles, or both! As part of its fight against AIDS France is considering legalization of brothels. Claiming that HIV could be transmitted if both partners had bleeding sores in their mouths, a commission in Italy declared that French kissing is a transmitter of AIDS. To prevent its citizens from infecting each other, Cuba isolates all persons with any AIDS condition. Copenhagen, known as a sexually tolerant, fun-loving city, embarked on an AIDS educational campaign. "Sex tours" to Bangkok and Manila have fallen off. Supposedly, the first Chinese person to die of AIDS was a hemophiliac who was injected with infected blood sent from the United States. While China has not publicly blamed the United States for its AIDS problems, Libya's Moammar Gadhafi has accused U.S. intelligence agents of creating HIV and spreading it around the world. A more responsible world leader, Pope John Paul II, has appealed for a cure of AIDS through science and love.

While 75 percent of the people throughout the world who are suffering from AIDS were infected through heterosexual contact, only 6 percent of PWAs in the United States contracted the syndrome in this manner. Though the rate of infection by heterosexual contact is increasing in the United States, some experts estimate the epidemic is now peaking both here and in Western Europe, while it increases at alarming rates in Africa and Asia.

In the United States, AIDS is the eleventh leading cause of death. Over one-half of the gay men in San Francisco and New York have HIV. The tragedy, however, is neither strictly male nor homosexual. Almost 10.5 percent of the total cases reported in the United States involve females, and each year more and more women are contracting AIDS, confirming the fear that the syndrome is being increasingly spread through heterosexual contact. Further, AIDS is having a disparate impact on minorities. Although blacks comprise only 12 percent of the population, they account for 30 percent of AIDS cases. Moreover, of the women who have AIDS, 54 percent are black, and of the children with AIDS, 55 percent are black. Death via AIDS is 3.3 times higher for blacks than whites. While Hispanics make up only 7 percent of the population, 17 percent of the PWAs are of that ethnic group. The numbers of males and Caucasians with AIDS are declining while the numbers of females and minorities with AIDS are increasing. These alarming statistics are especially upsetting in minority communities; one black politician overreacted by claiming that Jewish doctors were injecting the HIV virus into blacks. A survey by the Southern Christian Leadership Conference of over one thousand black church members found that 35 percent believed that AIDS was a form of black genocide.

In the United States male homosexual/bisexual contact is the source of 57 percent of AIDS transmissions; intravenous (IV) drug use accounts for 22 percent of transmissions; both homosexual and IV drug users 6 percent; and heterosexual contact accounts for 6 percent of transmissions. However, cases traced to IV drug use and heterosexual activity are climbing, while the number of homosexual cases is decreasing. Still, death by AIDS is 8.7 times more probable for men than women. With respect to sex as a conduit for the virus, a study of lower socioeconomic minorities (both homosexual and heterosexual) who were HIV positive concluded that the majority continued to have sex without informing their partners of their infected status. Federal and state governments have been criticized for failing to allocate sufficient funds for prevention and cure because of their view that HIV is largely a disease of homosexuals, minorities, drug abusers, and the poor.

In New York City AIDS is the number one killer of women aged twenty to thirty-nine. Nationally, black and Hispanic women account for 74 percent of the females with AIDS. While 49 percent of all women with AIDS contracted the virus through IV drug use, 29 percent became infected via sex, and 11 percent by means of contaminated blood transfusions. Tragically, 80 percent of the females with AIDS are in their childbearing years.

Just as AIDS has struck people across all geographical boundaries, it has claimed people of all ages. Babies are born with the virus after being infected in the womb by their mothers. Contaminated blood transfusions have infected hundreds of young children in the United States. The courageous life and death of Ryan White taught valuable lessons about AIDS to adults as well as children. Ricky Ray, one of three hemophiliac brothers infected with HIV, decided to seek judicial permission to marry his girlfriend due to his uncertain future; Ricky was fourteen at the time of this decision. The U.S. Department of Education has published a booklet, "AIDS and the Education of Our Children." Some scientists have predicted that the next high-risk group for AIDS is sexually active teenagers. One study concluded that three of every one thousand college students are infected with HIV. Colleges and high schools debate the wisdom of making free condoms available to their students.

The number of AIDS cases in the largest cities such as New York and San Francisco is still growing, but the virus is spreading faster in the suburbs and smaller towns. Presently, though, over 30,000 people in San Francisco are carrying the virus.

People from all walks of life are infected with HIV. Rock Hudson, Liberace, and designer Perry Ellis are only three of the many celebrities in the entertainment and fashion industries who have died from AIDS. People in other industries and occupations are also vulnerable. Jerry Smith, a former professional football player with the Washington Redskins, publicly announced that he had contracted AIDS. Race car driver Tim Richmond expired after being infected by a female friend. Roy Cohn, a renowned attorney, died of complications connected to the virus. Terry Dolan, founder of the National Conservative Political Action Committee, died at the age of thirty-six of complications from AIDS. The technical causes of some of these deaths are instructive: Ellis died of virus encephalitis (four months after his business partner and lover, who suffered from Kaposi's sarcoma, died of lung cancer); and Cohn died of heart failure.

Illustrating that AIDS is a problem affecting our entire society, people from all walks of life and backgrounds have contracted the virus: a twenty-three-year-old socialite in New York; a thirty-three-year-old professional basketball player in Los Angeles; a forty-six-year-old judge in Los Angeles; a Jesuit priest in Portland; a forty-three-year-old male star of pornographic movies who is rumored to have had sex with over 14,000 women; a superintendent of a public school system; a male bodybuilder who used a tainted needle to inject steroids; a six-year-old child infected by her mother; a Boy Scout infected through a tainted blood transfusion; and a prominent bisexual businessman. Statistically speaking, however, the HIV virus is much more likely to appear in communities with substantial numbers of people who use drugs or who are gay. While the percentage of homosexual cases is dropping each year, the majority of all persons with AIDS in this country have been homosexual or bisexual males.

AIDS has influenced most aspects of society in the last few years, including the media, the arts, public policy, and social behavior. The media has informed the world of public and private battles against AIDS. Publishers and broadcasters have reacted with new policies on listing AIDS as a cause of death, using sexually explicit language, and carrying advertisements for condoms.

Public interest groups and manufacturers of condoms were critical of the initial decision by television networks, *Time, Newsweek,* and *People* to refuse advertisements for condoms as a device to retard the spread of AIDS. Fox was the first network to accept such advertisements on the condition that they address the issue of preventing disease. *Newsweek* changed its policy and accepted an advertisement from a condom manufacturer that pictures an attractive young woman saying, "I'll do a lot for love, but I'm not ready to die for it." The copy for the ad read, in part, "AIDS isn't just a gay disease, it's everybody's disease. . . . Especially since the surgeon general recently stated: 'The best protection against infection right now, barring abstinence, is use of the condom.' " The stock of several condom companies rose in value in proportion to the increased interest in AIDS and skyrocketing sales.

The media has publicized and exploited the issue. Newspapers publish stories such as "AIDS Spreading to More Children." *People* magazine's cover announces: "First you find out your son is gay. Then you learn he's dying—EVERY PARENT'S NIGHTMARE."

People also had a long story on Alison Gertz, a twenty-four-year-old New York socialite who contracted HIV from a single sexual encounter with a young man who turned out to be bisexual. *Newsweek* ran cover stories entitled: "Future Shock—AIDS," "Sex in the Age of AIDS," and "Doctors and AIDS." *Time, U.S. News & World Report, New York*, and *Business Week* have all published cover stories on AIDS issues. *U.S. News*'s article, "OUTCAST—How AIDS Is Tearing Apart One American Community," discussed the only known PWA in a small town. The *New York Times* wrote about "Heterosexuals Spreading AIDS in Haiti." The *Times* of London did a story on married women and children who have contracted AIDS. The respected *Atlantic Monthly* had a sixteen-page article entitled "AIDS and Insects."

The art world has called AIDS to the attention of millions who have not yet been touched personally by the epidemic. Many plays have been written about AIDS, including *The Normal Heart, As Is, Beirut, Warren, Urban Blight, Tina Tuna Walk, Soul Survivor, Zero Positive*, and *Falsettos*. For the most part, they describe, from a PWA's perspective, the tragedy and comedy of contracting the syndrome and the inevitability of death. Harvey Fierstein, author of *Torch Song Trilogy* and *La Cage aux Folles*, wrote *Safe Sex*, a trilogy of plays dealing with the anger, fear, and frustration of being gay and worrying about AIDS. *Beirut* is about an internment camp for HIV-positive people. A film entitled *Longtime Companion* focuses on the impact of AIDS on seven gay men and one straight woman in New York from 1981 through 1989. A movie made for television, *An Early Frost*, depicts a son with AIDS returning to his family. *Our Sons*, another TV movie, is about mothers of gay lovers, one of whom has AIDS. A novel, *At Risk*, explores the tragedy and chaos imposed on a family when an eleven-year-old daughter contracts AIDS. Daytime soap operas often introduce AIDS themes. Television has broadcast news stories such as "AIDS, Lies, and Rumors," "To Live with AIDS," and "The Risk of AIDS in Medical Treatment."

The Museum of Modern Art in New York City exhibits blank canvasses and empty pedestals to symbolize the art that will never be created because of the early deaths of artists with AIDS.

Governments and community organizations have also worked to raise public awareness and encourage acceptance of and empathy for PWAs. One ad by the NO/AIDS Task Force offers a photograph of six racially diverse young men and women who appear very normal and healthy and the message, "You just can't tell from outward appearance who is infected with HIV." The CDC spent $4.6 million for a series of radio and television spots that urge people to protect themselves; one admonishes the audience to learn the correct way to use a condom. The Texas Department of Health paid $300,000 for English and Spanish versions of advertisements designed to warn sexually active heterosexuals of HIV risk. Parents and ministers in the rural South protested an AIDS educational film shown by numerous high schools called *Sex, Drugs, and AIDS*. Their complaint? The film promotes premarital sex and homosexuality. A few Chinese restaurants got involved in the campaign against AIDS by giving free condoms to their customers after every meal—in fortune cookies! Benetton, the clothing manufacturer, spent $80 million on an advertisement that features a real-life photograph of family members confronting a young man dying of AIDS and the caption: "United Colors of Benetton"; in response to criticism that it was exploiting AIDS, the company said that it preferred using news photographs to using staged situations with models.

The Vatican, which has been generally critical of homosexuality, sees AIDS as another reason to oppose it. A Vatican official has been quoted as saying that "AIDS cannot be ignored in any consideration of the moral and ethical issues raised by homosexuality." In recent years, though, the Catholic church has been a leader in caring for patients suffering from AIDS-related diseases. Episcopalians adopted a resolution to protect AIDS patients from discrimination. Fundamentalist minister and former presidential candidate Pat Robertson brought AIDS before the audience of his "700 Club" television show by touching a PWA and saying, "We rebuke this virus, and we command your immune system to function in the name of Jesus."

Eschewing traditional means of education, members of ACT UP, a largely gay group, use controversial approaches to make their points. They attack individuals and organizations that should, in their view, be taking action to combat AIDS. They have thrown condoms at Helen Gurley Brown, publisher of *Cosmopolitan* magazine; necked in the office of Senator Jesse Helms; staged a "die-in" at Dallas City Hall; and damaged property in Catholic churches.

A Names Project AIDS Memorial Quilt, with the names of four thousand men, women, and children who have died from AIDS, toured twenty cities, to remind citizens of the scope of this scourge. Various religious and community groups minister to those suffering from AIDS. *Project Inform* allows PWAs to obtain the latest data on experimental drugs and the location of support groups. The National Leadership Coalition on AIDS, established by Congress to advise it and the president, is a strong advocate for statutes, regulations, and programs to support the battle against AIDS. The AIDS TeleForum permits numerous service groups around the country to communicate with each other and coordinate their activities.

The public's fear of contracting AIDS through blood transfusions has stimulated the use of commercial (as opposed to community) blood banks that charge a fee to freeze blood for a donor's own use and accept donations from relatives. A company has made and is marketing to the public a videotape entitled "AIDS and the American Family." Advertisements invite people to use their Master Card or Visa to order the tape to "save your family."

Governmental officials have struggled with treatment of HIV-infected criminals. County judges in Alabama asked defendants with AIDS to enter pleas by telephone in lieu of personal appearance because bailiffs did not wish to have contact with them! The Federal Bureau of Prisons segregates HIV-positive inmates who display "predatory or promiscuous behavior." A report entitled "AIDS in Correctional Facilities: Issues and Operations" raises questions about such issues as mass testing of inmates, to whom results should be disclosed, isolation of HIV-infected prisoners, and distribution of free condoms to inmates.

Various levels of government, including legislators and police, have been required to face situations that were unimaginable prior to 1981. Many police jurisdictions now ignore laws on the books that prohibit distribution of hypodermic needles for injection of illegal drugs when community activists openly hand them out to drug addicts for the purpose of preventing the spread of HIV. Legislators debate whether real estate agents and sellers should inform a buyer that the property formerly belonged to a PWA (some states now have laws stating that AIDS is not a material defect that must be disclosed). Recognizing that emergency medical technicians sometimes hesitate to use lifesaving procedures such as CPR in treating patients whom they fear may have AIDS, New York City enacted a law requiring all public facilities (restaurants, hotels, theaters, and so forth) to have masks with one-way valves and rubber gloves on hand and readily accessible for emergencies. City councils receive complaints from residents adjacent to lakes and rivers that hospital garbage washed ashore, including vials of blood that test positive for HIV antibodies (in at least one situation children found and played with syringes). In an effort to stem the spread of AIDS, Illinois and Louisiana enacted statutes requiring couples to be tested for HIV antibodies as a condition to secure a marriage license. In the first year Illinois tested 155,458 people, only 26 of whom were HIV positive. Each positive case uncovered cost $209,270. Not surprising, considering such poor cost-effectiveness, Louisiana and Illinois then repealed those laws. Nevada is considering legislation that would promote the public safety and prevent AIDS transmission by repealing the right of counties to legally license prostitution. A school in Florida was sued for requiring a young girl with AIDS to stay in a glass cubicle specially constructed in the classroom. School boards across the country debate and adopt policies on dealing with teachers and students with AIDS conditions. When the U.S. Department of Health and Human Services proposed removing the ban on immigrants and foreign visitors infected with HIV from entering the United States because it was discriminatory and medically unjustified, thousands of telephone calls and letters in protest persuaded the Bush administration to continue the exclusion. The federal government acknowledges that transmission of HIV from immigrants to citizens is unlikely but justifies the ban on the ground that admission of infected people would create an economic burden for U.S. taxpayers. The military has decided to test every recruit and member for the virus in an attempt to keep AIDS out of the armed services.

While AIDS has had a pervasive effect on society at large, it has also transformed individual emotions and behaviors. Groups promote use of condoms and counsel less sex with fewer partners. Some homosexuals have moved to the Dakotas and Montana to escape the HIV-infested gay enclaves in San Francisco and L.A. *Newsweek* reported that AIDS and the publicity generated by it are changing the way women approach sex: sexually active women are not as promiscuous, and other women have become celibate. A survey by

Glamour magazine concluded that 47 percent of the women interviewed say they have changed their sex habits because of AIDS. *Time* ran a cover story on "The Big Chill—How Heterosexuals Are Coping with AIDS." A young lady dating a photographer with extensive contact with gay men in his work wrote to Ann Landers that she feared contracting AIDS, but that her fiancé rejected as insulting her request that he be tested for the AIDS virus. She wanted Ann to judge if she was reasonable in demanding a medical certificate. When he was dating, Donald Trump requested women to submit to an HIV antibody test at his doctor's office prior to a romantic evening.

Dating services and social clubs are responding to the fear of AIDS among sexually active people. The "Peace of Mind" club issues cards when members test negative. The AIDS FREE singles club charges a $500 initiation fee and requires all members to be tested four times annually at a fee of $90 per test. Members of some dating services are informed of other members' test results. The American Institute for Safe Sex Practices accepts into membership only people who present a medical certificate stating that an AIDS test was negative. Members whose names are kept in a computer list available to the membership, must be retested every six months. Private investigators are retained to perform background checks on boyfriends and girlfriends; one investigator's advertisement asked: "Do you know who you're dating? These days, it's important to know." A company called "Protection Connection" offers fast home delivery of condoms and spermicidal sponges. AIDS figured prominently in a New York criminal courtroom when the defendant, accused of murdering his homosexual lover, argued that the shooting was triggered by the lover telling him, immediately after two acts of sex, that the lover had AIDS.

With respect to the campaign to promote "safe sex" and utilize condoms, researchers have found that members of the low-risk group (monogamous heterosexuals who do not use IV drugs) have responded favorably, but members of the high-risk groups (particularly IV drug users) have not. The most sexually active people use condoms the least was the conclusion from a survey of adolescent sexual behavior.

A poll asked children between the ages of eight and seventeen to identify their worst fears. The top three fears identified were being kidnapped, nuclear war, and AIDS. Among adults, the top three health worries are cancer, AIDS, and heart disease—in that order.

Persons' fear for their own safety has led to angry and near-hysterical reactions against people known or suspected to be carrying HIV. Ryan White, a fourteen-year-old with hemophilia who contracted AIDS through a tainted blood transfusion, was barred from attending school in Indiana because of community fear that he would infect fellow students. But Ryan moved to another town, was welcomed to that community, and became a symbol of courage and hope to millions of Americans prior to his untimely death. In California, Ryan Thomas, a kindergarten student who had contracted AIDS through a tainted blood transfusion, was prevented from attending school after he bit another child. The parents of Ryan Thomas, in one of the first AIDS cases, sued and obtained an injunction requiring his readmission. He died at age ten.

Catholic priests all over the country have received inquiries and complaints from parishioners about the practice of common use of the cup connected with communion; some worshipers have brought small, individual cups to the communion rail for the purpose of preventing possible spread of the AIDS syndrome. The rector of St. Patrick's Cathedral in New York City denied the request of a couple who wished to be married there on the grounds that the groom had AIDS. The denial was overruled by the archbishop and the ceremony was performed.

In Los Angeles, paramedics paused before helping a heart attack victim because they thought—incorrectly—that he had AIDS. In New York City, a gay manager was fired when he announced that he would be absent to see his doctor—because of a false rumor that he had AIDS. "The prejudice and violence AIDS has inspired is a scourge almost as terrible as the disease itself," said a rabbi in San Francisco who has many AIDS patients in his congregation. "I'm reminded of medieval times when Jews were made scapegoats for the plague."

The fight against AIDS continues. Some look for cures, some work to expand care, some urge prevention through education. The U.S. government and other nations are expected to allocate millions of dollars. The Design Interior Foundation for AIDS has thus far raised $400,000 in funds, with considerable assistance from celebrities. Businesses and socialites who have raised millions of dollars over the years to fight cancer and heart disease and improve the zoo are now writing checks and attending balls to combat AIDS. Stars, such as Morgan Fairchild, have filmed educational messages for broadcast. Elizabeth Taylor and Madonna are two of the many celebrities who lend their names and talents to AIDS fund-raisers. The National Institute of Allergy and Infectious Diseases has awarded $100 million to fourteen universities and hospitals for conducting drug research to combat AIDS. The Robert Wood Johnson Foundation AIDS Health Services Program allocated $22.1 million among eleven cities and countries to develop more specialized or humane health services for AIDS patients. Nevertheless, the National Academy of Sciences laments that these and other programs are "woefully inadequate" and recommends that $2 billion be devoted to AIDS research and treatment. The President's Commission on AIDS recommends that $20 billion be spent over the next ten years, largely on treatment for drug abusers. Others, though, point out that the federal government is spending over two times the money on AIDS than on heart disease, the nation's biggest killer, and slightly more on AIDS than cancer, and argue too much money is being devoted to AIDS, which kills substantially fewer than either heart disease or cancer. The stocks of laboratory companies striving to develop a vaccine or drug to battle AIDS have been volatile, as investors respond to the financial implications of a possible cure. Federal funding for research, education, and prevention of AIDS expanded from $6 million in 1982 to $1.7 billion in 1991.

State and city governments, however, have been overwhelmed by demands for health care and education. A report issued by the U.S. Conference of Mayors explains that the budgets and resources of our largest cities are insufficient to meet the expanding AIDS-related needs of its citizens. Large cities are attempting to address escalating rates of HIV infection with creative programs. Washington, D.C., is considering free needle exchanges for intravenous drug users and distribution of condoms to high school students and jail inmates. Meanwhile, a major player has been more on the sideline than in the game: the federal government. The executive and legislative branches should formulate a *national strategy* to stop the spread of the virus, cure those who have contracted it, and promote fair treatment of the individuals and institutions wrestling with the issues described herein.

Ethical Considerations

For understandable reasons most of the information on AIDS focuses on the perspective of the PWA. But what about the concern of the emergency room nurse who is asked to treat an AIDS patient suffering from knife or bullet wounds? Or a patient undergoing a heart bypass operation with a surgeon or nurse who has symptomatic HIV disease? Or the employees at any facility who sincerely fear that they may be infected by a fellow employee with a confirmed case of AIDS? Do employees, customers, patients, and members of the public have the right to be apprised of AIDS situations involving them? Do employers have an ethical obligation to inform employees, patients, and customers that an employee with AIDS is on the payroll? Morally speaking, should employees be able to refuse to work with, serve, or treat people with HIV, symptomatic HIV disease, or AIDS for fear of contracting it themselves and spreading it to members of their family?

According to a survey conducted for the American Dental Association, 80 percent of the dentists who responded would refuse to treat patients with AIDS. Many frustrated PWAs with dental problems can confirm the accuracy of this study. Heart surgeons and orthopedic surgeons have irritated the American Medical Association and offended its ethical standards by refusing to operate on HIV-positive patients. Should professional dental and medical associations insist that members comply with ethical principles concerning treatment of AIDS patients and discipline those in violation?

What about another ethical obligation, the obligation to disclose? If a hospital administrator knows that a patient scheduled for surgery is HIV positive, should he or she notify the surgeon? Nurses in the operating room? Personnel in the intensive care unit? Nurses on the floor? Suppose the patient is admitted only for tests or observation: who should be notified then? Or suppose that a marital counselor is confidentially informed by the husband that he is bisexual and HIV positive: does the counselor's ethical obligation to inform the wife, who may be at risk, outweigh his or her ethical obligation to respect the privacy of the husband?

There are many questions, but few answers. The whole AIDS area is unclear and subjective. Gradually, the law will settle many key issues, but the fundamental tension between the rights of a person with HIV infection or AIDS and the rights of those with whom he or she may come into contact will continue to raise troublesome ethical issues.

Ethical questions also have arisen in research and treatment. One experimental drug called "azidothymidine," or AZT, has proved effective in blocking the reproduction of the virus. More specifically, although AZT failed to kill the virus upon contact with cultures in the laboratory, it did stop it from spreading. In England AZT was given to eleven symptomatic HIV disease and AIDS patients for six weeks. Infections cleared up, fevers and night sweats terminated, and most patients gained weight. Next AZT was used to treat PWAs at twelve medical centers in eight U.S. cities. However, in order to test AZT's effectiveness the responsible doctors established two groups of AIDS patients: one group was given AZT and the other a placebo. None of the PWAs knew which group they were in. And the only way to have a chance to be treated with AZT in 1986 was to be accepted into the study. Critics complained that human beings were being used as guinea pigs. Now AZT is widely available.

When AZT was approved by the Food and Drug Administration, the cost to the patient was over $200 per week. This expense was too high for many AIDS patients, and they were forced to go without the one thing that could prolong their lives because they could not afford it. Initially AZT was not approved under Medicaid, so only PWAs with substantial savings or superior medical insurance had access to it. Later, it gained approval and the federal government is now funding drug expenses for poor PWAs.

Various blood banks are carrying out a "Look Back" program designed to trace recipients of blood from donors later found to have HIV. The idea is to locate recipients of contaminated blood that was donated prior to 1985 (when blood banks began testing donations for the antibodies), inform them that the donor of the blood tested positive, and request them to submit to the test. Approximately 50 percent of those recipients who have been traced had themselves become infected with the HIV virus. Several recipients who were successfully traced and tested positive then secured counsel and sued the blood bank. Should blood banks be expected to continue tracing and notifying those who received contaminated blood, when such action may well lead to a lawsuit against them?

Throughout his illness, New York lawyer Roy Cohn said that he was battling liver cancer. After his death, friends and lawyers represented he had died of cancer. However, a week prior to Cohn's death, investigative reporters Jack Anderson and Dale Van Atta ran a story that quoted from documents surreptitiously obtained from the National Institutes of Health. These documents revealed that Cohn was being treated with AZT and must, therefore, have had AIDS. Was this ethical? The privacy and dignity of a dying man were violated, and for what valid purpose? On the other hand, *Women's Wear Daily* and *Variety*, which cover the fashion and entertainment industries, do not report that prominent people in those fields have AIDS.

Arthur Ashe and his wife were angry when a newspaper reporter called Ashe, told him that an informant had indicated that he had AIDS, and asked him for his comment. Ashe and his wife had wanted to shield themselves and their daughter from the publicity that such news would prompt, but they could not shield themselves from media appetite for "celebrity-AIDS" stories.

The death of Liberace also sharply illustrates the conflict between a patient's right of privacy and the public's right to know. While he was ill, Liberace's friends emphatically denied that he was suffering from AIDS. After Liberace's death his personal physician certified that the cause of death was heart failure brought on by degenerative brain disease. When the Riverside County coroner accused the doctor of "pulling a fast one on us" and announced that Liberace had actually died of cytomegalovirus pneumonia due to AIDS, the nation chose sides. One group argued as follows: It is important to record and examine each case of death due to AIDS; many states have laws against listing false causes on death certificates, and people—especially those who had contact with the deceased—should know the truth in situations in which the cause of death is an infectious disease. Accurate reporting allows health department officials to track and inform sexual partners. False reports, like that about Liberace, raise the question of how many AIDS-related deaths have been covered up in the past. The other side argues that a person who has suffered untold agony should be allowed a peaceful death, living out his final days with his reputation intact and no sensational stories pervading the media. The actual cause of death should be a private matter between the deceased and his or her family. In the case of celebrities, the public's motive for knowing is curiosity, a mere yen for gossip. What valid purpose is served by the coroner calling a press conference to inform the nation that Liberace had AIDS? Both sides in this debate make valid points. The best approach may be to enact laws that require physicians to accurately report both AIDS cases as soon as they are diagnosed *and* AIDS-related deaths to local health officials who, in turn, must report the figures to the CDC. But while the law should provide stiff penalties for physicians who prevaricate, it should also insist that the reports be sealed, confidential, and without public access.

Employers with successful human resources programs know that fair and sensitive treatment of employees is a critical factor for preventing labor problems and employment claims. Personnel principles often echo ethical standards about how to treat fellow human beings. Employer empathy for an injured or ill employee reassures him or her and also makes a favorable impression on fellow employees. Hence, should managers demonstrate compassion and concern for employees with AIDS by providing benefits that extend beyond what is legally required? Specifically, should employers pay a higher premium to fully cover all AIDS-related medical expenses in its health policy? What if the insurance agent points out that the premium will be reduced substantially if AIDS coverage is excluded or limited? Further, should management *create* a special job for an employee with AIDS who is unable to perform the essential duties of his or her regular job, for the purposes of allowing him or her to maintain his routine, see friends at work, and continue company coverage under its medical and life insurance plans? The tension between reducing costs and promoting employee interests stimulates many ethical questions involving AIDS in the workplace.

Legal Considerations

Since 1981 PWAs have often been denied access to restaurants and hotels, and have been evicted from their apartments. They have been isolated, transferred, forced to take unwanted leaves of absence, and terminated from the workplace. Some dentists and doctors have refused to treat them. A few children with AIDS have been refused access to schools; one grade-school child with the virus was only allowed to remain in the classroom if she stayed inside a glass cubicle that was specially constructed for her. A hospital limited the staff privileges of a male physician with AIDS. A judge required a defendant with an AIDS condition to wear a mask in the courtroom. Discrimination stalks PWAs even after death. A few funeral homes have refused to accept people who died of AIDS-related causes.

An array of laws can be utilized by PWAs to challenge practices or policies they perceive as discriminatory. Over the years numerous federal, state, and local laws have been enacted or interpreted to apply to AIDS employment situations. The federal Americans with Disabilities Act, effective July 26, 1992, grants disability status to applicants and employees with AIDS conditions and prohibits discrimination against them in hiring, training, promoting, compensation, termination, and other conditions of employment. Statutes in most states also recognize PWAs as handicapped and protect them from employment discrimination. A few states have enacted laws ordaining that if the seller of real property had an AIDS condition this information does not have to be communicated to potential buyers. In its report *America Living with AIDS* the National Commission on AIDS concluded that "Nearly one thousand bills related to AIDS were proposed in state legislatures in the first decade of the epidemic. It is the most litigated disease in American history."

The potential for lawsuits involving AIDS in the workplace is enormous. Here are a few possible causes of action against employers:

Violation of the Americans with Disabilities Act (ADA) for refusing to hire an applicant who announced in the job interview that he was HIV positive

Violation of the ADA for firing an employee perceived by the employer to be homosexual and a candidate for AIDS

Violation of the Rehabilitation Act (VRA) of 1973 (applicable to federal government contractors) and Employee Retirement Income Security Act of 1974 (ERISA) for terminating an employee soon after receiving a medical insurance claim form that identified said employee as having an AIDS condition

Invasion of privacy for insisting that an applicant or employee submit to a test for HIV antibodies or for asking whether he or she has the AIDS virus

Breach of confidentiality, libel, slander, and defamation of character for communicating an AIDS virus test result or medical report or other diagnosis involving AIDS to fellow employees, supervisors, or the public

Violation of the duty to warn other employees, patients, customers, sex partners, needle partners, or family members of the fact that the applicant or employee is HIV positive and capable of transmitting a deadly virus

Suit by a former employee with AIDS who claims that he was discharged solely for the purpose of avoiding extensive medical claims under the insurance plan, in violation of Section 510 of the Employment Retirement Income Security Act

Unfair labor practice charges with the National Labor Relations Board (NLRB) by former employees who allege that they were fired for collectively protesting the continued employment of a PWA in their area, which threatened their safety

Charges with the Occupational Safety and Health Administration (OSHA) indicating that their regulations for protecting employees from the HIV virus were violated

Worker compensation claims that the employees contracted HIV on the job

Claims that at the time of discharge a PWA was not given notice of his right to convert the group medical insurance provided by the employer to individual coverage, in violation of Consolidated Omnibus Budget Reconciliation Act (COBRA)

Claim of "perceived" handicap discrimination by an HIV-negative employee returning to work after a bout with pneumonia and enduring taunts, barbs, and discriminatory treatment from fellow employees who incorrectly thought his pneumonia was caused by AIDS

Most PWAs will allege discrimination due to handicap (ADA, VRA, or state laws) or sex (Title VII or state commissions). But any analogy between AIDS and civil rights is not appropriate. Courts and commissions must recognize a unique aspect of people with HIV that dramatically differentiates them from persons with bad backs, impaired hearing, or minority status: HIV is infectious and deadly.

Litigation of AIDS issues outside the employment arena should also continue to grow. Typical examples of suits involving AIDS are listed below:

- The U.S. Department of Justice sued an apartment complex, claiming that it violated the Fair Housing Act by refusing to rent to a PWA.
- A paramedic stuck by a needle protruding from a disposable container used for medical syringes filed suit against the manufacturer of the container, claiming breach of warranty and product liability. After the plaintiff testified that he had no evidence that the needle was tainted and his five tests for HIV antibodies were negative, the court dismissed the case, ruling that the paramedic could not recover simply because he feared developing AIDS.
- An inmate sued the government operating his jail, alleging that being forced to share razors with other prisoners had made him fear catching AIDS and pushed him into a nervous breakdown.
- A jury awarded Marc Christian $21.75 million because Rock Hudson concealed his AIDS condition from and continued his sexual relationship with Christian, even though Christian has repeatedly tested negative for HIV. The court later reduced the damage award.
- Hundreds of lawsuits have been filed against the American Red Cross and other blood banks by persons with HIV, who claim that contaminated blood was transfused into them.
- In France a court ordered the National Center for Blood Transfusions to pay $1 million francs to those hemophiliacs who were infected with HIV by means of tainted blood transfusions.
- A marine died of AIDS-related cancer a few weeks after receiving $3.8 million from the federal government, which he had accused of infecting his wife with the virus during a blood transfusion.
- A PWA sued a nail salon for refusing to give him a pedicure.

While legal challenges to employer decisions involving AIDS are expected to increase substantially in the future, it should be noted that, thus far, the number of claims is extremely low compared to the number of PWAs in the work force. Apparently, applicants and employees who perceive that they are victims of race, sex, or age discrimination are much less hesitant to file suit. Factors that explain the relatively low level of AIDS claims include the reluctance of PWAs to publicly declare their condition in a claim, the lack of interest on the part of plaintiff attorneys to prosecute these types of cases, and the humane and extensive efforts of employers to resolve employment decisions in a manner that is satisfactory to the applicant or employee with an AIDS condition.

When an HIV-infected applicant wishes to challenge a rejection or an HIV-infected employee wants to challenge a transfer or discharge, he or she normally consults a lawyer. After determining the facts as presented by the client, the attorney usually sends a letter to the employer threatening to file a legal claim and attempting to pressure it into a change of action that would benefit the client (see sample letter from plaintiff attorney to employer in appendix B, document 7). If the letter proves ineffective, a lawsuit could be filed in either state or federal court (see sample suits in appendix B, documents 8, 9, 10, and 11). If the employee is in a bargaining unit, and the union fails to vigorously push the claim, a charge could also be filed against the union with the National Labor Relations Board (see appendix B, document 12) or the union could be made a joint defendant with the employer in a lawsuit (see appendix B, document 11).

Business Concerns

What about the perspective of management, which has obligations to maximize profits, but also to protect the health of customers, clients, and other employees?

Suppose that a restaurant manager sincerely believes that allowing a PWA to continue working as a cook would discourage customers, reduce revenues, and jeopardize the health of customers and employees. Or suppose that the owner of a large barber shop determines that a community rumor that one of his barbers has tested positive for HIV is true and worries that his established customers will go elsewhere. What if a hospital administrator reasonably concludes that admission of AIDS patients at his suburban hospital would drive down other admissions? Word-of-mouth communications that a neighborhood restaurant has a PWA chopping carrots in the kitchen or that a shop has an infected barber shaving and cutting hair could have an almost immediate negative impact on revenue. And at least one hospital has suffered from unusually low admissions because it became branded as "the AIDS hospital." When businesses go into a tailspin or fail, people are adversely affected. Employees are laid off and investors lose money. How should the interests of institutions and people other than the PWA be considered and treated?

A business that is sued for illegal discrimination by a discharged PWA will find it nearly impossible to prevail in court if it uses the argument that it would have incurred substantial monetary losses and even have failed absent the removal of the plaintiff with AIDS. First, losses are speculative. The second hurdle is insurmountable: monetary losses cannot be invoked to justify discrimination against the disabled.

Does management have a legal duty or an ethical obligation to disclose information about AIDS in the workplace? Suppose a manager learns that its employee Fred has AIDS and allows him to continue in his regular job. Is there an obligation to tell other employees about Fred's condition? If the answer is yes, does the obligation extend to all personnel at the facility or only those who work closely with Fred? But what about Fred's right of privacy? If the answer is no, what if the employees learn through other sources about Fred's and management's failure to disclose the situation to them? Would their anticipated anger and frustration be justified? What if another employee later contracted the HIV virus (perhaps through sexual or drug contacts) and sued the company, claiming that he or she had contracted HIV in the workplace from Fred, and alleging that management violated its duty to inform him or her and other employees about Fred's condition?

Business has legitimate reasons to be concerned about the impact of AIDS decisions on other employees as well as its customers. The refusal of some or all employees to work with a PWA, causing disruption or total stoppage of operations, is only one of the many potential ramifications. Employees at a nonunion company could sign union cards and petition the National Labor Relations Board for representation because they are upset with how management handled an AIDS matter, and they believe that an outside, third party can assist them. Employees at a union company can file grievances on AIDS issues and process them to arbitration. And employees in both nonunion and union companies can submit health and safety complaints to OSHA or state health agencies.

The Service Employees International Union (SEIU) and other

labor organizations have disseminated written educational materials on AIDS to health care and other personnel, and are using the issue as a device to sign up new members. The SEIU suggests that employer-employee cooperation in developing infectious disease programs is the best approach to protecting the health of employees in the workplace. SEIU argues that some companies are too lax in their infection control policies. The threat of AIDS, unions feel, is important to thousands of employees; potential members are promised that union representatives will promote infection control committees (with union representation) and require management to develop policies to protect employees fearful of contracting AIDS from patients, customers, or other employees. The SEIU also promises education of all workers and strong opposition to mandatory antibody testing. Meanwhile, the huge AFL/CIO has adopted a resolution opposing the screening of workers for AIDS. The American Federation of State, County, and Municipal Employers (AFSCME) lobbied OSHA to issue stringent standards that would protect health care workers from exposure to communicable infections such as AIDS and hepatitis B. This approach demonstrates action to current members and assists campaigns for new members. Business, therefore, finds unions as well as government and the courts looking over its shoulder as it tries to resolve AIDS issues in the workplace.

Employers are also struggling with insurance issues. The insurance industry has a simple equation: HIV positive = insurance negative. Should a cap be placed on payments for AIDS-related illnesses? Would efforts to reduce premiums that adversely affect PWAs offend regulations or laws? When forced to choose, should employers favor cutting benefit costs or protecting HIV-positive personnel?

The best way for business to prevent government regulation is to recognize potential problems before legislators do and work to address them. Self-regulation or business-driven policing actions are needed for AIDS-in-the-workplace issues. The Citizens Commission on AIDS for New York City and Northern New Jersey issued ten principles for dealing with AIDS, which have since been endorsed by over six hundred corporations, unions, and nonprofit agencies. Recommended by the National Leadership Coalition on AIDS, all of these principles may not be appropriate for every employer, but all employers should study them and decide which ones should be adopted. The principles are:

1. People with AIDS or HIV infection are entitled to the same rights, benefits, and opportunities as people with other serious or life-threatening illnesses.
2. Employment practices must, at a minimum, comply with federal, state, and local laws and regulations.
3. Employment practices should be based on the scientific and epidemiological evidence that people with AIDS or HIV infection do not pose a risk of transmission of the virus to co-workers through ordinary workplace contact.
4. The highest levels of management should unequivocally endorse nondiscriminatory employment practices and education programs or information about AIDS.
5. Managers should communicate their policies and practices to workers in simple, clear, and unambiguous terms.
6. Managers should provide employees with sensitive, accurate, and up-to-date information about risk reduction in their personal lives.
7. Managers and co-workers must protect the confidentiality of employees' medical/insurance information.
8. To prevent work disruption and rejection by co-workers of an employee with AIDS or HIV infection, managers should undertake education for all employees before such an incident occurs and as needed thereafter.
9. Managers should not require HIV screening as part of preemployment or general workplace physical examinations.
10. In those special occupational settings where there may be potential risk of exposure to HIV (for example, in some health care settings) managers should provide specific, ongoing education and training, as well as the necessary equipment, to reinforce appropriate infection control procedures and ensure that they are implemented.

This study and analysis should extend to the question of whether a written policy for handling AIDS employment matters should be adopted and communicated to all personnel. Studies show that employers with one thousand or more employees are significantly more likely to have policies and educational programs. One survey found that less than 10 percent of all employers have formal, written policies. As the number of HIV-infected applicants and employees increases in the years ahead, many employers will be forced to face AIDS issues without the benefit of an implemented policy to guide them.

With respect to education, some employers have distributed literature to employees that describes in detail how to protect oneself and others from contracting AIDS; brought experts to the facility to explain facts about transmission of the virus, including how unlikely it is to happen in the workplace; and shown video presentations on the subject. General Motors and the United Automobile Workers Union jointly sponsored newspaper advertisements setting forth facts on AIDS: "It can't be cured now . . . but it can be stopped," was the theme. Trade associations and business groups provide members with seminars and material about AIDS and employment.

Business needs to be proactive instead of reactive. It should anticipate problems in this area, provide a policy for solving them, assist in educating its personnel, and advance the arguments behind its interests before legislatures and courts. Employers should realistically recognize that when the interests of business and applicants or employees with AIDS conditions conflict, they will usually lose. Thus the legislative body, court, or administrative agency weighing interests will normally determine that protecting PWAs from discrimination and elimination of benefits is more consequential than burdening employers with added costs.

2

Federal Laws

For the first decade of the AIDS epidemic, PWAs who believed that they were the victims of employment discrimination relied upon a host of well-entrenched federal and state laws enacted long before HIV was discovered, including the Rehabilitation Act of 1973, Title VII of the Civil Rights Act of 1964, and the handicap protection statutes of most states. The Reagan administration resisted pressure for new legislation specifically designed to protect job applicants and employees with AIDS conditions and suggested that the states should resolve such AIDS-related issues as discrimination, privacy, duty of disclosure, and confidentiality. When a bill was introduced in the U.S. Senate to establish a national program to combat HIV, provide major funding, ban discrimination, and distribute educational materials, conservative senator Jesse Helms sponsored an amendment that prohibited federal funding for material that encouraged homosexuality and that required any AIDS literature to promote monogamy. Senator Edward Kennedy sponsored legislation forbidding AIDS-related discrimination in housing and public accommodations, as well as employment, and authorizing funding for confidential HIV testing and counseling. A bill introduced by Representative William Dannemeyer mandated testing for certain groups, required that HIV test results be reported to public health agencies, and established knowledgeable transmission of the virus as a federal crime. Predictably, all of these bills stimulated acrimonious debate, but none of them were enacted into law.

Advocates of new legislation to protect PWAs from employment discrimination were greatly encouraged by the Americans with Disabilities Act (ADA), enacted by Congress and signed by President Bush in 1990, and effective as of 1992. Recognizing AIDS as a disability and protecting disabled applicants and employees from discrimination in the workplace, the ADA is enthusiastically embraced by PWAs as a friend. Most businesses, however, view the ADA with its numerous potential pitfalls as an enemy.

Americans with Disabilities Act

Effective July 26, 1992, for public and private employers with twenty-five or more employees and July 26, 1994, for those with fifteen or more employees, the employment provisions of the ADA prohibit managers from discriminating against job applicants and employees with disabilities. Before I discuss its specific application to applicants and employees with AIDS conditions, I will explain the law's basic concepts and doctrines.

Title I, which constitutes the employment section of the ADA, is included in its entirety in appendix B, document 1. The exact language Congress used in defining three of the more important terms or doctrines that will be applied in countless employment decisions and interpreted by numerous judges is as follows:

Qualified Individual With a Disability. The term "qualified individual with a disability" means an individual with a disability who, with or without reasonable accommodation, can perform the essential functions of the employment position that such individual holds or desires. For purposes of this title, consideration should be given to the employer's judgment as to what functions of a job are essential, and if an employer has prepared a written description before advertising or interviewing applicants for the job, this description shall be considered evidence of the essential functions of the job.

Reasonable Accommodation. The term "reasonable accommodation" may include . . . job restructuring, part-time or modified work schedules, reassignment to a vacant position, acquisition or modification of equipment or devices, appropriate adjustment or modifications of examinations, training materials, or policies.

Undue Hardship. In determining whether accommodation would impose an undue hardship on a covered entity, the facts to be considered include—

(i) The nature and cost of the accommodation needed under this Act;

(ii) The overall financial resources of the facility or facilities involved in the provision of the reasonable accommodation; the number of persons employed at such facility; the effect on expenses and resources, or the impact otherwise of such accommodation upon the operation of the facility;

(iii) The overall financial resources of the covered entity; the overall size of the business of the covered entity with respect to the number of its employees; the number, type, and location of its facilities; and

(iv) The type of operation or operations of the covered entity, including the composition, structure, and functions of the work force of such entity; the geographic separateness, administrative or physical relationship of the facility or facilities in question to the covered entity.

Before I leave definitions, I wish to point out the specific language chosen by Congress in describing "discrimination" and "defenses." Note particularly the defenses available to employers in cases that could involve AIDS:

Discrimination: No covered entity shall discriminate against a qualified individual with a disability because of the disability of such individual in regard to job application procedures, the hiring, advancement, or discharge of employees, employee compensation, job training, and other terms, conditions, and privileges of employment.

Defenses: It may be a defense to a charge of discrimination under this Act that an alleged application of qualification standards, tests, or selection criteria that screen out or tend to screen out or otherwise deny a job or benefit to an individual with a disability has been shown to be job-related and consistent with business necessity, and such performance cannot be accomplished by reasonable accommodation, as required under this Title.

The term "qualification standards" may include a requirement that an individual shall not pose a direct threat to the health or safety of other individuals in the workplace.

The Secretary of Health and Human Services, not later than six months after the date of enactment of this Act, shall review all infectious and communicable diseases which may be transmitted through handling the food supply; publish a list of infectious and communicable diseases which are transmitted through handling the food supply; publish the methods by which such diseases are transmitted; and widely disseminate such information regarding the list of diseases and their modes of transmissibility to the general public. Such list shall be updated annually.

In any case where an individual has an infectious or communicable disease that is transmitted to others through the handling of food, that is included on the list developed by the Secretary of Health and Human Services . . . and which cannot be eliminated by reasonable accommodation, a covered entity may refuse to assign or continue to assign such individual to a job involving food handling.

Congress and the president have required the secretary of the Department of Health and Human Services (through the Public Health Service) to review and issue a list of all infectious and communicable diseases that may be transmitted through the handling of food. The list, which must be updated on an annual basis to take advantage of the latest scientific and medical evidence, is intended to educate the public (including employers) on this subject. Congress believed that many people had mistaken beliefs concerning the transmission of HIV through food handling that could be corrected if they had access to objective data. Accurate, scientifically accepted evidence, not false perceptions, should dictate whether asymptomatic individuals should be allowed to remain in food-handling jobs. The appearance of a specific disease on the list does not mean that the restaurant, processor, or other type of food employer can refuse to hire or has the freedom to fire any individual infected with said disease. Instead, the employer must attempt to reasonably accommodate him or her, which could mean providing gloves or other special equipment; exempting the employee from some incidental food-handling duties, and so on. However, if an accommodation cannot be made on a reasonable basis, then the employer is free to refuse an otherwise qualified applicant or to transfer the infected employee to another position that does not involve food handling. The ADA does not permit an employer to automatically terminate employees with listed diseases. Finally, the act of the secretary in placing a particular disease on the list does not, of itself, establish said disease as a disability. Instead, that question must be answered by application of the regular criteria for determining whether the plaintiff is a "qualified individual with a disability."

Those food employers and consumers who thought that a primary purpose of the analysis and listing was to assist in the prevention of HIV transmission were disappointed when the first list was published *without* mention of HIV. Thus, this special section of the ADA is, thus far, inapplicable to applicants and employees in food-handling jobs. Hence, restaurants and food service employers may *not* discriminate against applicants and employees with AIDS conditions. The fear of an HIV-positive food handler transmitting the virus to customers or other employees is groundless, and does *not* justify failures to hire or decisions to fire. AIDS, then, will be treated under this law as are other disabilities, which makes it important for food employers to be familiar with the ADA's provisions, procedures, and potential liabilities.

Like Title VII and the Age Discrimination in Employment Act, the ADA is applicable to *all* employers with the requisite number of employees, even if they have no contracts with the federal government. The statute is also broadly constructed to be applicable to virtually every type of employment decision affecting both applicants and employees.

Geographically, the ADA grants protection to applicants and employees working for American companies in foreign countries unless achieving compliance with the act would cause the employer "to violate the law of the foreign country in which the workplace is located." Important procedural provisions include the right of plaintiffs to seek a trial by jury on claims of compensatory and punitive damages and the ability of successful claimants to recover attorney fees and expert witness costs from the defeated employer.

In terms of proof, the initial burden is on the applicants or employees filing the complaint to show:

1. That they have a disability *or* are perceived as having a disability *or* are related to or in association with a person who has such a disability (the latter two categories are particularly applicable to AIDS situations)
2. That they are "otherwise qualified" or able to perform the essential functions of the job, even if reasonable accommodation is required; and
3. That adverse employment action was taken based upon this disability or relationship

In order to satisfy the first element of proof—that the plaintiff has a disability, real or perceived—he or she must present evidence of a physical or mental impairment that substantially limits one or more major life activities *or* show a record of such impairment *or* demonstrate that he or she is currently being perceived as having such an impairment. The definition of "major life activity" is comprehensive and is expected to include such functions as caring for oneself, performing manual tasks, walking, seeing, hearing, speaking, breathing, learning, and working. Examples of conditions that would be classified as a handicap, thereby making the person disabled under the act, include tuberculosis, chronic bronchitis, dyslexia, and multiple sclerosis. Conditions that courts and agencies interpreting other handicap laws have found *not* to be a protected disability include being cross-eyed, acrophobia, and left-handedness.

Once the plaintiff satisfies the definition of disability, he or she must present evidence that he or she is qualified for the job in question. Employers are not obligated to create a new job for a recently disabled employee or to completely train a handicapped applicant; instead, he or she must possess the ability to perform the essential duties of the job in question. However, the law's intent becomes muddy at this point because the plaintiff's proof is deemed sufficient if he or she can show that a present lack of qualifications can be cured by means of reasonable accommodations (or job adjustments) by the employer. To protect employers (and create further ambiguity and complexity) the law next provides that employers may escape an accommodation obligation by proving that it would constitute an undue financial or other hardship. Hence, smaller companies have an advantage in their attempts to convince the investigator or the court that a particular accommodation would unduly strain the employer's resources; conversely, large corporations will experience difficulty in gaining judicial acceptance of this doctrine and defense.

Assuming that a plaintiff presents persuasive proof of being a qualified individual with a disability and demonstrates that he or she is either not in need of accommodation *or* able to perform if allowed a reasonable accommodation, and the employer fails to prove that the accommodation would be unreasonable or would require an undue burden on it, the final point to be addressed is whether the applicant was passed over for employment or the employee was transferred, demoted, or fired *because of the disability*.

The plaintiff must offer evidence that the employer's adverse action was motivated by his or her handicapped condition. Stated differently, there must be a direct nexus between the individual's disability and the employer's decision. If the employer can prove either a lack of knowledge concerning the handicap (this could be important in AIDS cases) or that knowledge of the individual's handicap played no role in the decision-making process (whether it be to hire, fire, place on leave, and so on), the employer should win the case. Therefore, it is critical for employers to carefully document all employment decisions that are based upon legitimate business concerns, such as a poor reference from a past employer, a spotty or otherwise suspect work history, or another applicant with superior qualifications as reasons for not hiring, for example, or excessive absenteeism, violation of written policy or past practice, fighting on the job, or customer complaints as reasons for firing.

As the above description suggests, there are shifting burdens of proof. Whenever employers are confronted with an employment decision involving a potentially disabled individual, help and advice should be obtained from counsel or the human resources department in answering these and related questions: (1) what proof does the individual have that he or she is disabled *and* that the employer had knowledge of the condition alleged to be a disability; (2) what evidence is available that will prove or disprove that the individual can perform the essential duties of the job in question (the employer's evidence on what specific duties are essential and which are not is significant; here the existence of written job descriptions can be critical); (3) assuming that the individual is not presently qualified to perform all essential duties, what accommodations are available to make him or her qualified; (4) can the employer prove that the desired accommodations are unreasonable and, if not (5) what evidence exists that could prove that the accommodations create an undue hardship on the employer?

As I have indicated, the prohibitions against discrimination apply to preemployment, as well as to employment, situations. In fact, preemployment issues abound. Improper discrimination includes limiting, segregating, or classifying an applicant in a way that adversely affects opportunities or status, because of his or her disability, as well as refusing to hire him or her. It covers preemployment inquiries, application forms and procedures, preemployment physical examinations, and all other forms and procedures connected to the preemployment process. More specifically, preemployment examinations and inquiries used to determine whether the applicant is a person with a disability or to ascertain the severity or extent of the disability are completely prohibited. However, preemployment inquiries regarding the applicant's ability to perform job-related functions are permitted. Medical examinations may be required by the employer only *after* an offer of employment has been extended, but prior to the commencement of actual employment. Offers of employment may be made conditional upon the results of such an examination, if (1) all entering employees are subjected to such an examination regardless of disability; (2) information regarding the disability is collected and maintained on separate forms and is treated as confidential (there are few exceptions here); and (3) the results of some examinations are used only in accordance with the ADA.

With respect to remedies, the most likely awards for successful plaintiffs are reinstatement, back pay, and attorney fees. The goal of ADA's remedies is to make the plaintiff whole without penalizing the employer. However, if the plaintiff can prove that discrimination by the employer was *intentional*, compensatory monetary damages over and above back pay and legal expenses are available. Moreover, if the evidence establishes that the employer engaged in a discriminatory practice "with malice or reckless indifference to the federally protected rights" of the disabled applicant or employee, punitive damages may be recovered. There are, however, important restrictions on the plaintiff's right to secure punitive damages. First, they are not available when the employer is a public entity. Second, they may not be awarded where the employer has demonstrated good-faith efforts to "identify and make a reasonable accommodation that would provide the individual with an equally effective opportunity and would not cause undue hardship on the operation of the business." Normally, employers who consult with the disabled applicant or employee in a sincere effort to ascertain an accommodation have an excellent argument to prevent punitive damages.

Of the several legal terms and doctrines inherent in this statute, the most difficult one to apply arises from the employer's duty to *reasonably accommodate* disabled employees, unless such accommodation causes an *undue hardship*. Hence, employers are obligated to make accommodations that enable individuals with disabilities to participate in particular programs, jobs, and activities, or to benefit from particular services, facilities, benefits, privileges, or accommodations. In short, employers must make reasonable adjustments to match a particular disabled person with a specific, desired opportunity. In general, an accommodation is any change in the work environment or in the way work is customarily done that enables an individual with a disability to enjoy equal employment opportunities. The term "reasonable accommodation" is not precisely defined in either the act or the regulations interpreting it. Employers will be required to make individualized determinations on a case-by-case basis as to whether "reasonable accommodation" applies to a particular set of circumstances.

An example of a "reasonable accommodation" set forth in the statute is that of "job restructuring." The employer may be required to restructure a job by reallocating or redistributing nonessential or marginal job functions. For example, an employer may have two different jobs, each of which entails the performance of a number of marginal functions. The employer hires a qualified individual with a disability who is able to perform some of the marginal functions of each job, but not all of the marginal functions of either job. As an accommodation, the employer could redistribute the marginal functions in such a way that all of them that the qualified individual with the disability can perform are made part of the position to be filled by the disabled employee. The remaining marginal functions that he or she cannot perform could then be transferred to the other position.

An employer is not required to reallocate essential functions. The essential functions of a job are by definition those that an individual who holds that job would have to perform, with or without reasonable accommodation, in order to be considered qualified for the job. For example, suppose a security guard position requires the individual who holds the job to inspect identification cards. An employer would not have to provide an individual who is legally blind with an assistant to look at the identification cards. In this situation, the assistant would be performing the job for the individual with the disability rather than assisting the individual to perform the job.

Reassignment to another vacant position is also listed as a potential reasonable accommodation. In general, reassignment should be considered when an accommodation within the individual's current position would pose an undue hardship. Reassignment is not available to job applicants. An applicant for a position must be qualified for and be able to perform the essential functions of the position sought with or without reasonable accommodation. Reassignment may not be used to limit, segregate, or otherwise discriminate against employees with disabilities by forcing reassignments to undesirable positions or to designated offices or facilities. Employers should reassign the individual to an equivalent position, in terms of pay and status, if the individual is qualified and if the position is vacant. An employer may reassign an individual to a lower graded position if there are no accommodations that would enable the employee to remain in the current position and there are no vacant equivalent positions for which the individual is qualified with or without reasonable accommodation. An employer is not required to accommodate an individual with a disability by promoting him or her to a higher paying job when the particular disability would not cause problems.

The obligation to provide reasonable accommodation does not extend to the provision of adjustments or modifications that are primarily for the personal benefit of the individual with a disability. In other words, if an adjustment or modification is job-related— specifically done to assist the individual in performing the duties of a particular job—it will be considered a type of reasonable accommodation. On the other hand, if an adjustment or modification will assist the individual throughout his or her daily activity, on or off the job, and is of primary benefit to the nonwork life of the individual, it will be considered a personal item that the employer is not required to provide. Accordingly, an employer would not be required to provide the employee with a disability with a prosthetic limb, wheelchair, or eyeglasses. Nor would the employer have to provide as an accommodation any amenity or convenience that is not job-related, such as a private hot plate, hot pot, or refrigerator that is not provided to other employees without disabilities.

Additionally, the ADA specifically provides that an employer may not compel a qualified individual with a disability to accept an accommodation, if the accommodation is neither requested nor needed by the individual. However, if a necessary reasonable accommodation is refused, the individual may not be considered qualified. For example, an individual with a visual impairment that restricts his or her field of vision but who is able to read unaided would not be required to accept a reader as an accommodation. However, if the individual were not able to read unaided and reading was an essential function of the job, the individual would not be qualified for the job if he or she refused reasonable accommodation that would enable him or her to read. Set forth below are examples of accommodations that are expected of employers:

- Allowing individuals to work part-time or modified work schedules when they are unable to work standard schedules
- Purchasing a telephone headset for $50 that allows a salesperson with cerebral palsy to write while talking
- Supplying a visually impaired receptionist with a light probe costing $45 that allows her to determine which telephone lines were ringing, on hold, or in use
- Providing a draft table, page turner, and pressure-sensitive type recorder for a sales agent paralyzed from a broken neck, at the cost of $300
- Purchasing a special chair to alleviate back pain for an employee with lower back difficulty

Once a request for accommodation is made by a qualified individual with a disability, the employer must make a reasonable effort to determine whether it is appropriate. The process of doing so is an informal, interactive, problem-solving technique, involving both the employer and the applicant or employee with the disability. A sincere consultation with the disabled applicant or employee is an important exercise for at least three reasons: (1) it may convince the disabled person that an accommodation is impossible; (2) it may lead to a discovery by the employer that an accommodation is reasonable and practical; and (3) in the event of a later legal claim by the applicant or employee, it provides the employer with a defense against requests for punitive damages. Here, then, is a four-part, problem-solving approach:

1. Analyze the particular job involved and determine its purpose and essential functions
2. Consult with the disabled individual to ascertain the precise job-

related limitations imposed by the individual's disability and how those limitations could be overcome with a reasonable accommodation

3. In consultation with the individual to be accommodated, identify potential accommodations and assess the effectiveness each would have in enabling the individual to perform the essential functions of the position

4. Consider the preference of the individual to be accommodated, and select and implement the accommodation that is most appropriate for both the employee and the employer.

Often, identifying the appropriate accommodation is not easy. For example, the individual needing the accommodation may not know enough about the equipment used by the employer or the exact nature of the work site to suggest an appropriate accommodation. Likewise, the employer may not know enough about the individual's disability or the limitations that disability would impose on the performance of the job to suggest an appropriate accommodation. Under such circumstances, it may be necessary for the employer to initiate a more defined, problem-solving process, such as the step-by-step process described above. This requires individual assessment of both the particular job at issue and the specific physical or mental limitations of the particular individual in need of reasonable accommodation. If consultation with the individual in need of accommodation still does not reveal potential appropriate accommodations, then the employer—as part of the process—may want to turn to outside technical assistance. Such outside assistance may be available from disability consultants, state or local rehabilitation agencies, or the Equal Employment Opportunity Commission, which has been designated by Congress to administer the act. Once the potential accommodations have been identified, the employer should assess the effectiveness of each potential accommodation and implement the choice that is most appropriate for the employee and the employer. Throughout this process the employer should make sure that all these efforts and analyses are well documented.

The duty to provide reasonable accommodation may at times conflict with the employer's personnel policies or the terms of a collective bargaining agreement. For example, a labor contract may reserve certain jobs for employees with a set amount of seniority. Thus, it may be a violation of the terms of the agreement to accommodate a less-senior person with a disability by allowing him to move into a job for which he is not entitled under the bargaining agreement. Under the ADA, the provisions of a collective bargaining agreement "may be considered as a factor" in determining whether the accommodation of assigning a disabled person without seniority to such a vacant position is reasonable. However, the terms of the labor contract would not be determinative on this issue.

As I noted, the "undue hardship" provision is specifically tied to the financial realities of employers trying to comply with the law. However, the concept of undue hardship is not limited to financial difficulty. It also refers to any accommodation that would be unduly costly, extensive, substantial, or disruptive, or that would fundamentally alter the nature and operation of the business.

Application of the ADA to AIDS in a preemployment context will be rare. Few employers can or should test applicants for HIV antibodies, and with the new restrictions on permitted preemployment medical inquiries, employers generally will not know whether the applicants they are interviewing and processing are HIV positive or negative. However, with the spread of HIV throughout the country and into heterosexual groups, it is more and more probable that employers will learn that an *employee* has an AIDS condition. The most likely method for the issue to surface is for an employee who has been absent or on medical leave to orally inform his supervisor that he has AIDS or to provide the human resources director with a letter from his doctor explaining the diagnosis. Frequently PWAs wish to continue working, to benefit from (1) medical insurance and the promise of disability and life insurance; (2) a secure, reliable paycheck; and (3) supportive relationships with fellow employees. Doctors have observed that PWAs who continue a routine of working fare better medically for longer than those who do not. Since many AIDS conditions fluctuate in terms of kinds and degree of illness, often employees (and their employers) face the prospect of a continuing cycle of illness increasing in severity, hospitalization, release for return to work, a period of relatively good health, a new medical crisis, and so on.

Are AIDS conditions "disabilities" within the meaning of ADA? While Congress explicitly referred to HIV as a condition that constitutes a disability during their deliberations, neither HIV nor AIDS are mentioned in the statute itself. Congressional history reveals the rationale for classifying HIV as a disability: substantial limitation on procreation and intimate sexual relationships. The Equal Employment Opportunity Commission, the federal agency that is administering ADA, has flatly stated that the HIV virus and AIDS are types of impairments that are usually disabling. However, the commission says in its regulations that HIV-infected individuals are not automatically classified as disabled; instead, there must be evidence that the impairment substantially limits a major life activity (Regulations, 29 CFR section 1630.2(L)(1991); see appendix B, document 2). It is expected that as suits are filed, most courts will treat all AIDS conditions as disabilities.

The next question is whether the particular employee with symptomatic HIV disease or AIDS is qualified to perform the essential duties of the job he or she has been occupying. If not, the matter of accommodation must be analyzed, and the employer must determine if he or she is capable of making one that is reasonable. For PWAs, possible accommodations could include restructuring the job from five eight-hour days to six six-hour days because the individual tires in the late afternoon; allowing the individual to leave work every other afternoon for medical treatment; reassigning a few nonessential but physically demanding duties of the job to another employee because the individual is becoming too weak to perform them; asking a fellow employee to assist the PWA with a few essential duties so that they can be completed in a timely manner; and transferring the employee to another vacant position with duties commensurate with the PWA's restricted abilities. Employers have the option of arguing that accommodations suggested by the PWA (or his or her spouse, parent, sibling, lawyer) are *unreasonable*. Or employers can argue that even though the accommodation is reasonable, the requested accommodation would create an undue financial or other hardship. Other statutory defenses provided to employers include a policy, test, duty, or employment standard— such as the abilities to drive a forklift down narrow aisles or accurately count bottles coming down an assembly line—that is job-related and necessary for the business which the PWA cannot accomplish, even with reasonable accommodation; and medical evidence that continuation of the PWA in his or her job would pose a direct threat to the health or safety of others in the workplace. Physical and mental manifestations of AIDS can be a challenge to the accommodation obligation. These include weakness, loss of energy, loss of memory, and blindness. The AIDS patient's alternating possession of and loss of physical and mental abilities complicates the employer's duty to reasonably accommodate.

Assume that an employer has concluded that an employee with an AIDS condition cannot be reasonably accommodated, or that the accommodation sought would constitute an undue hardship, or that the PWA's presence on the job threatens the health of others. What now? Since the employee is not being allowed to return to work, should the PWA be involuntarily placed on disability? Given a leave of absence? Terminated? Prior to making a final decision, the employer should consider the implications of each option. If the PWA is dissatisfied with the employer's decision, a legal challenge under the ADA or other laws is probable. If the employer is rejecting or ignoring a medical release to return to work, the PWA has a particularly strong position. If suit is filed, the PWA's attorney can be expected to review employment records and search management memories for light-duty positions allowed or special jobs created or duties reassigned in past situations. Evidence of any disparity between how the employer handled an employee who wished to return to work after an occupational injury and the PWA would bolster the plaintiff's case. If the employer "accommodated" ill, hurt, or disabled employees in the past, why not now with the PWA? Regardless, if the PWA's attorney can prove that the employer refused an accommodation that was reasonable and without undue hardship, the employer will probably lose the suit. The point, of course, is that a thorough analysis of the legal issues and ramifications must be made before implementing a decision to place someone on involuntary leave or to terminate him or her. The probability of successfully defending a claim of handicap discrimination should be computed. Often, once the odds are calculated and the implications of potential back pay, interest, attorney fees, and reinstatement are factored into the overall equation, prudent employers decide to accommodate, place on paid leave of absence, or take other action that is acceptable to the PWA.

To increase the probability of prevailing in the event of legal challenge, employers should (1) identify specific duties that must be performed for various jobs (that is, those that are "essential"; detailed job descriptions should be reviewed with their obvious relevance to ADA cases in mind); (2) adopt or strengthen policies and rules clearly grounded in business necessity and related to the jobs at the particular facility which could then be applied to all employees including those with AIDS conditions, for example, a strictly enforced "no-fault" attendance policy that provides set penalties for violations; (3) carefully document all analyses and considerations of accommodation; and (4) prepare records and documents revealing the burden or hardship that would have to be assumed for each possible accommodation.

Designated by Congress to investigate the claims of discrimination and otherwise administer the law, the Equal Employment Opportunity Commission (EEOC) has issued regulations pertaining to the interpretation and application of the ADA. They are set forth in their entirety in appendix B, document 2. While the regulations are helpful, the best insight into how the ADA is being applied to specific situations are the court cases interpreting the Rehabilitation Act, another federal statute protecting the handicapped which has been in effect since 1973.

The Rehabilitation Act of 1973

Unlike the broad ADA, this narrowly constructed law applies only to contractors with the federal government and other employers who receive federal financial assistance, and prohibits them from discriminating in employment on the basis of an applicant's or employee's handicap. Section 503 of this act applies to companies having contracts or subcontracts with the federal government in excess of $2,500, while Section 504 is applicable to *all* employer-recipients of federal financial assistance (primarily hospitals and schools). The Office of Federal Contract Compliance Programs (OFCCP), part of the U.S. Department of Labor, has been given the responsibility under Section 503 to monitor compliance with this law by contractors and subcontractors. It is the responsibility of that agency to audit employers to determine if their Affirmative Action Plan (AAP) is sufficient under Executive Order 11246 and to investigate any complaints from applicants or employees concerning companies covered under the executive order or Section

503. If an AIDS applicant or employee files a complaint of discrimination based upon handicap with the OFCCP, it must first determine whether the employer has sufficient connection with the federal government to satisfy the jurisdictional standards. A checklist for determining whether a private employer is a contractor within the meaning of the law and thus under the umbrella of the Rehabilitation Act of 1973 is presented in appendix B, document 3. Further, copies of the texts of Sections 503 and 504 appear in appendix B, documents 4 and 5.

The Department of Health and Human Services (DHHS) has overall responsibility for enforcing Section 504. Since there are no dollar limitations for jurisdiction, the first procedural question arising from an AIDS-related complaint is whether AIDS is a handicap. Individual claimants have the right to secure counsel and pursue private complaints in federal district court under Section 504 but not under Section 503.

Like the ADA, the Rehabilitation Act of 1973 has been recently amended to (1) make compensatory damages (where the employer engages in intentional discrimination) and punitive damages (when the employer discriminated with malice and reckless indifference) and expert witness fees available to successful claimants; (2) provide trial by jury of claims involving compensatory and punitive damages; and (3) protect U.S. citizens working in foreign countries for American employers.

Suppose an HIV-positive mechanic is not hired, refused promotion, involuntarily transferred, or fired by his employer. Assuming the employer's federal contractor status and court jurisdiction, what evidence is required to support the employer's claim under Sections 503 or 504? What defenses are available to the employer? What are the potential penalties that could be faced by the employer? Unlike the situation with the novel Americans with Disabilities Act, ample court cases and judicial interpretations of words and terms contained in this statute, adopted in 1973, exist to guide us.

The mechanic has the initial burden of proof, and therefore must present evidence that: (1) he is handicapped or is regarded as being handicapped; (2) he is otherwise qualified to perform the duties of his position; and (3) he was discriminated against solely because of his handicap.

The first inquiry, then, is whether people who are simply asymptomatic or who have symptomatic HIV disease or who are suffering from full-blown AIDS are within the definition of handicap. The statute defines a person with a handicap as one who has a physical or mental impairment that substantially limits one or more major life activities *or* has a record of such impairment *or* is regarded as having such an impairment. While the act does not refer specifically to HIV or AIDS, Section 7(8)(c) states:

> For the purpose of Sections 503 and 504, as such sections relate to employment, such term does not include an individual who has a currently contagious disease or infection and who, by reason of such disease or infection, would constitute a direct threat to the health or safety of other individuals or who, by reason of the currently contagious disease or infection, is unable to perform the duties of the job.

Once the plaintiff presents evidence of his or her HIV infection (and indications of symptomatic HIV disease), the burden shifts to the employer to show that the condition is not a handicap.

Theoretically, an employer argument that an HIV-positive employee without any indications of symptomatic HIV disease or AIDS is unprotected because he or she is as capable as ever of performing all job duties and not impaired in any way is solid. Despite the byzantine logic of this argument, federal agencies and courts are permitting the claim on the ground that he or she is "regarded as being handicapped." Thus, the OFCCP adopted a policy that HIV, symptomatic HIV disease, and AIDS (*all* HIV conditions) constitute handicaps within the meaning of Section 503, provided that the applicant's or employee's health condition does not pose a direct threat to the health or safety of others *or* prevent successful job performance. The "OFCCP Directive on AIDS," which explains how complaints are filed and processed, is included in appendix B, document 6. The mechanic, therefore, is highly likely to be classified as handicapped regardless of the specific nature of the AIDS condition.

The next question to be answered is whether the mechanic, notwithstanding his or her status of being handicapped or perceived as being handicapped, is "otherwise qualified" for the position in question. In the employment context, an otherwise qualified person is one who can perform the *essential duties* of the job in question.

Can the mechanic physically and mentally perform the duties in the job description? Would his or her presence in the workplace threaten the safety of fellow employees, the public, or patients?

In the seminal case entitled *School Board of Nassau County v. Arline*, 480 U.S. 273, 107 S.Ct. 1123 (1987), the Supreme Court ruled that people with contagious diseases (suffering from tuberculosis, Arline was fired as a third grade teacher) may be considered handicapped within the meaning of the Rehabilitation Act. The school board and the U.S. Department of Justice had argued that Arline's recurring relapses involving a communicable disease posed a threat to the health of schoolchildren and others, but the Court brushed this argument aside, saying:

> The fact that *some* persons who have contagious diseases may pose a serious health threat to others under certain circumstances does not justify excluding from the coverage of the Act *all* persons with actual or perceived contagious diseases. Such exclusion would mean that those accused of being contagious would never have the opportunity to have their condition evaluated in light of medical evidence and a determination made as to whether they were "otherwise qualified."*

Thus, the question of whether the mechanic's HIV status represents a health hazard and poses a threat to the safety of fellow employees or others is a challenge for the employer to meet. The employer must present objective evidence establishing a health hazard. The *Arline* court instructed employers and lower court judges to listen to and defer to "reasonable medical judgments of public health officials," and then to consider whether the employer can reasonably accommodate the employee.

In determining whether an HIV-infected plaintiff is "otherwise

---

*480 U.S. at 285. Returning to the first standard of proof—plaintiff must prove that he or she is handicapped—the Supreme Court specifically mentioned AIDS when it rejected the argument that persons with HIV were not handicapped because they were neither physically impaired nor suffering from other symptoms of AIDS:

> The argument is misplaced in this case, because the handicap here, tuberculosis, gave rise both to a physical impairment and to contagiousness. This case does not present, and we therefore do not reach, the questions whether the carrier of a contagious disease such as AIDS could be considered to have a physical impairment, or whether such a person could be considered, solely on the basis of contagiousness, a handicapped person as defined by the Act. (*Arline*, 480 U.S. at 282.)

qualified," the court would undoubtedly direct an individualized inquiry into whether he or she poses a significant risk to others. The inquiry would include an analysis of the nature of the risk, the duration of the risk, its severity, and the probabilities that the virus would be transmitted and cause harm (see *Arline*, 480 U.S. at 287). In answering these questions, specific testimony by medical experts and studies and reports by the CDC would be most relevant. The court recognized that the employer has the right to require the plaintiff to be able to perform the essential functions of the job in question; if he or she cannot perform all essential functions, the inquiry shifts to whether a "reasonable accommodation" would be appropriate. However, an accommodation is not reasonable if it requires fundamental changes in the job or imposes unreasonable financial or administrative burdens on the employer. The extent to which an employer must accommodate an applicant or employee with an AIDS condition is greater than most employers probably imagine. For example, it has been held to be insufficient that a handicapped person *may* at some point *in the future* be unable to perform job requirements or increase an employer's costs because of possible work-related injuries (*State Division of Human Rights v. Xerox*, 65 N.Y.2d 213, 491 NYS 2d 106 [1985]; *E. E. Black Inc. v. Marshall*, 497 F. Supp. 1088 [D. Hawaii 1980]). Hence, an employer may not reject out of hand an asymptomatic applicant simply because it knows that about the time he or she has been adequately educated and trained, at considerable expense to the employer, ever-increasing absences caused by a terminal illness and eventual death can be anticipated. Likewise, an employer cannot terminate an employee with symptomatic HIV disease for the purpose of avoiding the cost of carrying an employee who puts in fewer and fewer production work hours while simultaneously maximizing expensive insurance benefits.

The court concluded that there are circumstances in which an applicant or employee with a communicable disease could be removed from his or her position. The employer is allowed to present persuasive medical evidence that the employment of the mechanic would be a real and substantial threat to the health of other employees or that the mechanic cannot be reasonably accommodated. As the court observed, "A person who poses a significant risk of communicating an infectious disease to others in the workplace will not be otherwise qualified for his or her job and a reasonable accommodation will not eliminate that risk. The Act would not require a school board to place a teacher with active, contagious tuberculosis in the classroom with elementary school children."

The third inquiry to be addressed is whether the mechanic was discriminated against *solely* because of his handicap. The Eighth Circuit Court of Appeals observed that this is a higher standard than normally required in employment discrimination cases: "It is significant that the Section 504 plaintiff must show that handicap was the *sole* reason for the decision while the Title VII claimant pursuing a disparate treatment claim need only show that a protective classification was *a factor* influencing the decision" (*Norcross v. Sneed*, 755 F.2d 113, 117, note 5 [1985]). Inherent in this question is whether there was discrimination at all. Clearly, if the mechanic is not hired, harassed, demoted, or fired *solely* because of his medical condition, there has been discrimination. But what if he or she is given a lateral or upward transfer by the employer, without loss of pay or benefits? The employer in these circumstances should argue that the mechanic is unprotected and without redress because he suffered no discrimination or deprivation. The employee, however, could respond that loss of status or deprivation of the job he or she was trained to perform and enjoyed performing constitutes discrimination. This issue is so close that different courts can be expected to resolve it in different ways.

Various asymptomatic plaintiffs have successfully cleared the above hurdles, presented persuasive evidence, and prevailed in claims under this act. In Florida, Todd Shuttleworth was fired by his county employer shortly after he developed AIDS. Shuttleworth developed proof that he was fit to perform the essential duties of his job at the time of his discharge and filed a $15 million lawsuit in federal court for lost wages, medical and legal expenses, and damaged reputation. The matter was settled shortly before trial, with Shuttleworth being offered reinstatement to his former job and back wages and benefits estimated at $190,000, including medical costs not to exceed $100,000. Further, his life and health insurance were reactivated, and his attorneys were paid $56,000 in fees and expenses by his former employer. The court denied the plaintiff's request for damages connected to alleged emotional distress and mental anguish, however, on the basis that they are not available in Section 504 actions.

Agencies of the federal government have accepted numerous claims involving AIDS and processed them under Sections 503 and 504. Hence, employers within the coverage of this statute who take adverse action against an applicant or employee with an AIDS condition may face investigations and hearings before the OFCCP (Section 503) or DHHS (Section 504) and litigation in federal court. Potential penalties include all back pay, reinstatement, attorney fees, restoration of benefits, and—the most significant—deprivation of federal contracts, grants, or reimbursements. For hospitals with extensive Medicare and Medicaid reimbursements and corporations whose lifeblood are contracts with federal agencies, careful compliance with all aspects of this statute is critical.

The Ninth Circuit Court of Appeals ordered the reinstatement of a California teacher with AIDS, ruling that the teacher was handicapped, otherwise qualified to perform his job, and a victim of discrimination. Vincent Chalk, a teacher of hearing-impaired children, had been treated for AIDS in a hospital, but then was medically released for return to work. The school board first placed him on administrative leave pending further medical evaluation and then assigned him to office duties without loss of pay or benefits. Mr. Chalk's repeated requests to return to the classroom were refused on the ground that students would be placed at risk of acquiring HIV. The teacher then filed suit under the Rehabilitation Act and submitted medical evidence that his teaching duties presented no significant risk of harm to his students. The court awarded him monetary damages as well as reinstatement (*Chalk v. U.S. District Court for Central District of California*, 840 F.2d 701 [1988]).

In another California case "John Doe" was discharged from a hospital's alcohol and drug rehabilitation program because of his HIV-positive status. Claiming discrimination, he filed suit under Section 504. The court ruled that exclusion from a federally funded program because of fear of contagion violated the Rehabilitation Act (*Doe v. Centinela Hospital*, 57 U.S.L.W. 2034 [C.D.Cal. 1988]).

Not all such cases, however, favor plaintiffs. In *Leckelt v. Board of Commissioners of Hospital District No. 1*, 909 F.2d 820 (1990), the Fifth Circuit Court of Appeals upheld a hospital's termination of a homosexual male nurse for refusing to reveal the results of his HIV antibody test. Recognizing that the hospital had a compelling and substantial interest to protect its patients and employees from the spread of communicable diseases, the court concluded that the hospital was on solid ground in demanding that the nurse reveal the result of the test, be tested again, or be terminated. The particular position at issue and that employee's constant exposure to patients undoubtedly influenced both the hospital and the courts.

In dismissing a Section 504 lawsuit by a fire fighter with AIDS, the court observed that the plaintiff was "aggressive, distrustful and a lawsuit-promoting person." After learning that he had AIDS and receiving medical advice that he should no longer perform the rescue duties required by his job, the plaintiff tendered his resignation. Had it been quietly accepted, there probably never would have been a lawsuit. Instead, the fire chief rejected the resignation and assigned him a light-duty job which permitted continuation of salary and insurance benefits. Later the plaintiff began complaining that his new duties were demeaning and threatened a lawsuit. After failing to report to work, he was initially placed on paid leave of absence and eventually terminated. The court concluded that the employer properly accommodated the plaintiff's handicap and made a reasonable decision to discharge an unsatisfactory employee. The suit was dismissed (*Severino v. North East Meyers Fire Control District*, 935 F.2d 1179 [11th Cir. 1991]).

Employers functioning under the umbrella of the Rehabilitation Act must be mindful of the high probability that their treatment of applicants and employees with AIDS conditions may well be carefully reviewed at a later time by an agency investigation and a federal judge who will quickly determine that the plaintiff is both handicapped and otherwise qualified and then examine whether he or she was discriminated against solely because of the AIDS condition. In these circumstances, creating and maintaining documentation of action taken against the PWA *for reasons other than the AIDS condition* is extremely important.

The statute, the OFCCP Directive on AIDS, and the court cases leave several questions unanswered. Is a male employee who openly acknowledges his homosexuality and is rumored to have AIDS protected from discharge, even though he is, in fact, HIV negative? At what points does "reasonable accommodation" become unreasonable with a PWA on the payroll who is compiling an extraordinarily high absenteeism rate due to relapses and medical treatment? Suppose the cycle of relapse, treatment, and reinstatement occurs five or more times within a six-month period—when does the employer's burden of hiring temporary workers or temporarily reassigning work to compensate for the absences become too great? Assume that the PWA can perform the essential duties of his or her position for six or seven hours, but thereafter becomes exhausted and must rest when a full eight-hour day and overtime are required to completely fulfill the job's expectations. Or assume that a mechanic with AIDS is capable of performing all the essential duties except one that requires lifting and climbing. Do PWAs in these circumstances have to be accommodated? What if an applicant represents during the interview that he or she is physically capable of performing all of the described duties for a particular job and is hired, but the employer quickly determines that he or she is not fully capable? Since the PWA misrepresented his or her abilities, may he or she be fired? In *Russell v. Frank*, 1991 WL 97456 (D.C. Mass. 1991), the plaintiff concealed his schizophrenic condition in completing an employment application. Although hired, his mental disorder later became known, and he was fired for falsifying employer records. The court ruled that he was *not* handicapped within the meaning of the Rehabilitation Act and dismissed his claim, declaring that "Neither the statute nor the regulations require employers to suspend standards of employee honesty in the name of reasonable accommodation. The ability to tell the truth is an essential part of every job." Moreover, suppose a computer operator or executive is physically able to perform all essential duties but gradually develops dementia. Where will the line between reasonable and unreasonable accommodation be judicially drawn in cases of mental impairment? Suppose a PWA is transferred to a semi-isolated area or perhaps instructed to perform the duties of the job at home—without loss of pay or benefits. Has there been improper discrimination? With respect to remedies, should the parents or lover of a PWA who dies before his successful claim becomes final be eligible for receipt of monetary damages that would have been awarded to the plaintiff? Until the courts are actually presented with cases like these under the ADA and Rehabilitation Act, employers, the disabled, and their attorneys will have to speculate about the answers.

Title VII of the Civil Rights Act of 1964

This federal statute proscribes discrimination against an applicant or employee on the basis of sex, as well as race, color, creed, national origin, and religion. The Equal Employment Opportunity Commission (EEOC), which was created to administer this law, has jurisdiction over employers with fifteen or more employees. Claimants have the right to file a charge with the EEOC within 180 days after the alleged act of discrimination; an administrative investigation, determination, and possible conciliation are triggered by the charge. Regardless of the commission's conclusions, the individual claimant is given the right to file a lawsuit in a federal district court and to have his or her claims of discrimination fully presented to the federal judiciary. Class actions, where an individual applicant or employee claims to represent all others who are similarly situated, are not infrequent, and available remedies for successful claimants include back pay, interest, payment of the plaintiff's attorney fees, and injunctive relief.

At first blush it seems that a homosexual PWA or even a gay male *perceived* to have AIDS who suffers discrimination on the job could file an actionable charge of *sex* discrimination with his local EEOC office. There is, however, a serious, if not fatal, flaw in any attempt to apply this law to an AIDS situation in the workplace. The prohibition against sex discrimination contained in Title VII definitely prohibits adverse action against a male or female employee because of sexual *gender*, but the law is clear thus far that discrimination by employers based upon sexual orientation or preference is not prohibited.

Enterprising plaintiff attorneys may argue that because the vast majority of PWAs are male, any employment policy or practice that discriminates against them would have a disparate impact on men. Hence, discrimination on the basis of sex is established. Since homosexuality is a preference, however, any such claim would be highly vulnerable to dismissal by either the EEOC or a federal district court.

In a California case, three homosexual men and two lesbians filed suit against Pacific Telephone and Telegraph Company, alleging failure to hire, harassment, and discharge because of their sexual orientation. The male plaintiffs offered proof that alleged policies and practices on the job disproportionately and adversely affected men and argued that this was sex discrimination in violation of Title VII. The federal courts rejected all claims and dismissed the lawsuit. The appellate court concluded that "Title VII's prohibition of 'sex' discrimination applies only to discrimination on the basis of gender and should not be judicially extended to include sexual preference such as homosexuality" (*DeSantis v. Pacific Tel. & Tel Co.*, 608 F.2d 327, 329 [9th Cir. 1979]). The Federal Fifth Circuit Court of Appeals has flatly ruled that "discharge for homosexuality is not prohibited by Title VII or Section 1981" (*Blum v. Gulf Oil Corp.*, 597 F.2d 936 [1979]; see also EEOC Decision no. 76-115 [1976]). There may be an opportunity for legal redress under Title VII for an employee who believes he is being harassed on the job because of his status as a homosexual with an AIDS condition (*Joyner v. AAA Cooper Transportation*, 597 F. Supp. 537 [M.D. Ala. 1983]). The cases on the issue of sex discrimination, however, establish that gays who are fired, not hired, or forced to take leaves of absence because of an AIDS condition can expect that Title VII claims of discrimination due to sex will be soundly defeated.

Applicants and employees of Haitian and African descent who believe that they have been unfairly treated due to an AIDS condition may have a viable claim of national origin discrimination. The media have extensively reported that Haitians are a "high-risk" group concerning AIDS, and that large numbers of residents of certain portions of Africa have AIDS conditions. Suppose an employer refused to hire a Haitian or African immigrant because of the perceived connection between those areas of origin and AIDS. Even though the CDC removed Haitians from their list of high-risk groups, potential plaintiffs from Haiti and Africa could argue that they were discriminated against because of their national origin.

In a creative but unsuccessful effort to rely upon federal civil rights laws, an inmate sued his prison, alleging that officials violated 42 U.S.C. Sec. 1983 for failing to protect prisoners from exposure to HIV. Specifically, the plaintiff offered evidence that a minimum of five fellow inmates had tested positive for HIV antibodies and that homosexual activity occurred in the prison. The plaintiff wanted seropositive prisoners segregated. Officials, however, were able to show that their policies were not inconsistent with medical guidelines on transmission of the virus, and the court concluded that the plaintiff's fears were grounded on ignorance. One appellate court judge, however, decided that a colorable claim could exist with specific evidence that transferring infected prisoners from cell to cell exposed inmates to unreasonable danger of sexual assault (*Glick v. Henderson*, 855 F.2d 536 [8th Cir. 1988]).

Employee Retirement Income Security Act

A broad federal statute enacted in 1974, the Employee Retirement Income Security Act (ERISA) regulates employee welfare benefit plans, whether funded or self-insured. Such plans include medical, surgical, and hospital benefits, as well as benefits in the event of sickness, accident, disability, and death.

In passing ERISA, Congress decided to prohibit employers from discharging or otherwise discriminating against employees for the purpose of interfering with their right to claim benefits under an employee benefit plan. With the medical cost of treating AIDS patients high and going higher, cost-conscious employers are searching for ways to stem insurance premiums. Suppose that an employee with an AIDS condition is terminated, allegedly for the purpose of avoiding health care or medical claims to which the employee would be entitled under an ERISA-qualified plan. The definition of "benefit plan" is broad, including any health, disability, or life insurance policy or program. Employers who discharge employees who test positive for HIV antibodies or who present medical documentation of symptomatic HIV disease or AIDS for the purpose of preventing costly insurance claims and a subsequent increase in premiums could be in violation of this federal law.

The director of planning filed suit under ERISA against Cooper Investments, alleging that his employer fired him from his $40,000-per-year position two weeks after he acknowledged his AIDS condition. The employer informed him that he would have to pay his own health insurance premiums to continue the coverage, but then the carrier canceled the policy. The judge was asked to enjoin the company from allowing the coverage to expire. The court ordered the company to maintain the director's care by either obtaining insurance or absorbing his medical expense after finding that the discharge was motivated by the AIDS condition and a desire to avoid health care costs. Following the issuance of this temporary judicial order, the parties settled the case with a payment of $50,000 to the plaintiff (*Doe v. Cooper Investments*, WL 336658 DC Colorado) (1991).

In another case the HIV-positive plaintiff kept his condition a secret from fellow employees and supplied his employer with a false medical note. After being fired for performance problems, he filed suit under ERISA. The court dismissed the claim, ruling that management retained the right to terminate all employees performing below standard, including those with HIV. Further, the judge described the plaintiff as "manipulative and secretive" and suggested that the law should not protect employees who withhold information about medical illness from their employers (*Phelps v. Field Real Estate Company*), 57 Fair Employment Practice Cases 1508.

Insurance companies, faced with very substantial claims by AIDS patients, have refused to pay portions of them on the ground that the drugs administered or the treatment given was experimental. A New York court ordered Empire Blue Cross and Blue Shield to pay for a $150,000 bone-marrow transplant for a patient infected with HIV, even though this procedure is unusual in AIDS situations and unlikely to be successful.

Employers concerned about the skyrocketing premiums and adverse court orders in AIDS situations are using various techniques to contain costs. One approach is to eliminate or cap the benefit for AIDS. What if the employer changes policies and becomes self-insured *after* learning that an employee is HIV positive? H & H Music Company's original plan provided $1 million in lifetime benefits for employees with AIDS, but a few months after learning that John McGann had been diagnosed as having AIDS the company switched to self-insurance and placed a cap of $5,000 on AIDS-related benefits. McGann's suit under ERISA was dismissed, with the federal district and appellate courts ruling that the high cost of the generous plan had forced the company to make changes (*McGann v. M & H Music Company*, 946 F.2d 401 [5th Cir. 1991]).* Similarly, Storehouse, Inc., had a maximum cap of $1

*The Fifth Circuit Court of Appeals concluded:

ERISA does not broadly prevent an employer from "discrimination" in the cre-

million for medical treatment of AIDS conditions. After learning that Richard Owens and three other employees had AIDS and then paying more than $250,000 under that plan for Owens alone, the company modified the plan with a $25,000 cap for treatment of AIDS. Storehouse, Inc., thereafter voluntarily paid an additional $90,000 for treatment of Owens before stopping payments. Owens's suit was dismissed, the federal district court ruling that employers may modify policies on the basis of experience and costs (*Owens v. Storehouse, Inc.*, 773 F. Supp 416 [N.D. Ga. 1991]). Sections 501(c)(2) and (3) of the Americans with Disabilities Act seem to sanction this practice.

Targeting applicants or employees for special, less-attractive coverage or treatment will draw attention and legal challenge. Examples include rejecting an HIV-positive applicant to prevent insurance costs and premiums from increasing; excluding AIDS-related health problems from the disability or life insurance policies; and providing inferior coverage for AIDS patients. Circle K Corporation adopted a policy of terminating the medical insurance of its employees who become sick or injured due to AIDS, alcohol, drugs, or self-inflicted wounds. This effort to curb costs was explained as a decision not to insure ramifications of certain "life-style decisions." While the discriminatory policy did not violate state laws because the company was self-insured, adverse publicity and pressure motivated Circle K to reverse the decision. Other companies have reduced group life insurance coverage (or failed to increase it) due to higher premiums

---

ation, alteration, or termination of employee benefits plans; thus, evidence of such intentional discrimination cannot alone sustain a claim under Section 510. That section does not prohibit welfare plan discrimination between or among categories of diseases. Section 510 does not mandate that if some, or most, or virtually all catastrophic illnesses are covered, AIDS (or any other particular catastrophic illness) must be among them. It does not prohibit an employer from electing not to cover or to continue to cover AIDS, while covering or continuing to cover other catastrophic illnesses, even though the employer's decision in this respect may stem from "prejudice" against AIDS or its victims generally. The same, of course, is true of any other disease and its victims. That sort of "discrimination" is simply not addressed by Section 510. Under Section 510, the asserted discrimination is illegal only if it is motivated by a desire to retaliate against an employee or to deprive an employee of an existing right to which he may become entitled. (F.2d at 530, 531)

caused when young employees die from AIDS within five years of their hiring. Disability insurance is another benefit that asymptomatic employees in their twenties and thirties need and use but which becomes more expensive as they do.

Employers considering self-insuring health coverage should be aware that while self-funded plans are generally exempt from state laws and regulations, Section 510 of ERISA establishes that they cannot terminate or in any way discriminate against a particular HIV-infected employee regarding his or her medical benefits after learning of a particular health condition. However, there are considerable advantages to self-funding in the area of reducing financial loss. Options that are available:

1. Exclude coverage of HIV-related illnesses that develop in the future.
2. Have a general provision that denies coverage for *all* preexisting conditions (this could stimulate claims in HIV cases where the development of antibodies and conversion to symptomatic HIV disease or AIDS can be lengthy, but a policy or practice of rejecting all claims for preexisting conditions of all illnesses undercuts an argument of discrimination).
3. Increase the probationary or other waiting period before coverage is triggered.
4. Limit lifetime maximum coverage for specific conditions; adjust the cap for AIDS conditions to lower levels when justified by experience and cost.
5. Add stop-loss insurance to limit claim exposure.

While state laws pertaining to benefit regulation must be studied for application to particular employer plans, bear in mind that most are probably preempted by ERISA.

Occupational Safety and Health Act

This federal statute, enacted in 1970, requires employers to provide a safe working environment for their employees. The Office of Safety and Health Administration (OSHA) of the U.S. Department of Labor has the responsibility to administer it.

In general, employers have the duties under this act to comply with all promulgated standards and regulations and to furnish a workplace "free from recognized hazards that are causing or are likely to cause death or serious hardship." Moreover, a provision in the statute prohibits employers from retaliating against employees who refuse to perform assigned work that they reasonably believe poses a danger.

Suppose a group of employees files a complaint with OSHA to the effect that their employer has violated this law by allowing an employee with AIDS to work with them and expose them to the virus. More particularly, suppose a hospital employee is exposed to HIV by means of a needle stick, but declines the hospital's offer to be tested for the virus with the statement, "Why should I go through the test every month for the next twelve months? Even if I am positive, there's nothing I can do about it." The employee then is allowed to continue his or her duties, and fellow employees file a charge with OSHA, alleging an unsafe working environment in that they are possibly being exposed to the virus as they continue handling the same needles, working with the same laboratory specimens, and otherwise having contact with a potential HIV carrier. Is allowing employees in these situations to continue in their regular jobs "hazardous" within the meaning of OSHA?

Under current law, the probable answers to all these hypotheticals are negative. Hospitals, however, should be certain to apply all appropriate infection control procedures and satisfy all such standards; failures in this area would make one vulnerable to OSHA charges by employees or others. OSHA's rules and proposals concerning protection of health care personnel from being infected with HIV are reviewed in chapter 7 and set forth in appendix A, in documents 4, 6, and 9 (A–D).

OSHA's bloodborne pathogen standard covers approximately five million employees in hospitals, nursing homes, medical offices, law enforcement agencies, funeral homes, and correctional agencies. Employers under this standard must write and make available a written exposure control plan, train employees about its provisions, and maintain required records. Details for such a plan are provided in chapter 7.

National Labor Relations Act

The National Labor Relations Board and U.S. Supreme Court have recognized the right of employees to protest working conditions by refusing to work, circulating petitions, or engaging in other concerted activities. A decision by their employer to discipline or discharge them for engaging in such a protest is an unfair labor practice (Section 8[a][1] violation) and would result in reinstatement of all employees with full back pay plus interest. The NLRB has no jurisdiction over public employees, so this section is applicable only to nonpublic situations.

Known as "protected concerted activity," this doctrine applies to action taken by two or more employees without union initiative, activity, or involvement. The only two requirements are that the employee action be concerted (usually involving at least two employees) and carried out for the mutual aid or protection of employees. Examples of protected concerted activity include circulating a petition to protest a decision to work on a holiday; refusing to work scheduled overtime; walking off the job to display dissatisfaction with machinery not being properly maintained; and leaving job stations and gathering in the break room because it is too hot, too cold, raining, snowing, or the vending machines are broken again. A recent case involved a truck driver who refused to drive because of his belief that the fleet of trucks was not properly maintained, and therefore that it was unsafe for all truck drivers (the doctrine can be applied in this case even though only one person protested because the protest involved a condition affecting a group of employees).

Over the years hundreds of managers and supervisors have run afoul of this doctrine because of their sincere belief that employees had engaged in insubordinate acts and therefore deserved to be disciplined or fired. Supervisors feel embarrassed, chagrined, and undermined when employees they had previously disciplined or fired for disobeying instructions to work overtime in the dark or to perform electrical work when it was raining file charges with the NLRB and eventually achieve reinstatement with full back pay and interest. Further, Section 502 of the National Labor Relations Act extends protection to employees in situations where their safety is threatened by "abnormally dangerous" work conditions.

Since 1981 hundreds of employees throughout the country have threatened to stop working with fellow employees who have AIDS. In New York City, for example, thirty-nine sanitation workers refused to work with a PWA, with the result that all thirty-nine were suspended without pay for one day. One hundred and fifty tons of garbage were not collected that day, but when the PWA was reassigned to another position (watchman on the 12:00–8:00 A.M. shift), the other employees returned to work. Paul Cronan, a repairman for New England Telephone Company, was fired shortly after contracting AIDS. A $1.5 million lawsuit resulted in a settlement providing for his reinstatement approximately one year later. However, on his first day back at work a sign was painted on the wall—"Gays and bisexuals should be taken to an island and destroyed"—and twenty-nine of forty-four fellow repairmen refused to work because of his presence! Cronan complained that he was "treated like a leper." A few nurses have refused to treat AIDS patients for fear of contracting the syndrome and transmitting it to their families. While rare, some laboratory technicians and other medical personnel have refused to handle needles used to inject AIDS patients. Food service and housekeeping employees have announced that they will neither deliver food to nor clean the hospital rooms of AIDS patients.

Almost always, the manager or supervisor who gave the instruction or possesses the overall responsibility becomes enraged when employees refuse to work with a fellow HIV-infected employee. This reaction is particularly true of doctors who expect nurses and other hospital personnel to place the medical treatment of patients above and beyond any concern for their own personal safety. Doctors and health care administrators take the position that hospitals are inherently hazardous in that the potential for contracting disease always exists. But, they feel, as long as established precautions are taken, the risk is minimal and necessary; hence, any hospital employee who refuses to follow orders or carry out normal duties vis-à-vis AIDS patients should immediately be fired.

It is inevitable that the NLRB and the courts will handle numerous cases concerning the question of whether concerted activities by employees refusing to work with or treat PWAs is "protected." Employers will undoubtedly argue that while such a refusal by a group of employees may be concerted, it should be deemed "unprotected," because the interests of the PWA, compliance with the law, and application of the employer's normal rules and policies in the assignment of work should override unfounded concerns for health or safety on the part of the protesting employees.

Part of the difficulty with this doctrine is that the employer's representative often feels that he or she must make a quick decision on the spot: either fire the employees or allow them to continue their protest. Managers believe that if the activity is truly protected and concerted, they must allow the protest to continue or face sanctions from the NLRB; on the other hand, if they conclude that the employee protest is unprotected, then they believe that they should immediately discipline or discharge the employees or their authority will be undermined. However, the best approach to defusing the situation and resolving possible protected concerted activity problems is usually neither to punish nor to allow the protest to continue. Instead, employees withholding their services should be told very clearly and definitely, in front of witnesses, that they must either return to work and carry out their duties or leave the employer's premises. No law or regulation requires employers to allow employees who refuse to work to stay on the employer's property. A nurse refusing to treat a PWA, a maintenance crew refusing to repair a machine manned by a homosexual rumored to have AIDS, the clerical staff refusing to work with a bookkeeper whose brother has a confirmed case of AIDS—all should be ordered to perform the duties they were assigned *or* to leave the employer's premises. If they refuse to leave, they should be told that they are subjecting themselves to disciplinary action, up to and including discharge, for violating the order to vacate the premises. Security or the police should then be called. If disciplinary action becomes necessary, now the manager can invoke their refusal to obey an order to leave the employer's property and sidestep the issue of a protest connected to AIDS.

In 95 percent of the cases, if the matter is handled well, the employees will obey orders to leave the employer's property. Once the employees have left, the employer has the legal right to hire permanent replacements for the protesting personnel. If permanent replacements are hired and in place before the protesting employees return to work, the employees can be legally told that their positions have been filled in their absence with permanent replacements, and if they wish to seek reinstatement to their former positions, they must complete an application for reinstatement by leaving their names, addresses, and telephone numbers. The employer is not required to discharge the permanent replacements to make room for the protesting employees. Instead, the employer's only obligation is to offer the protesting personnel who have declared their desire for reinstatement an opportunity to fill openings for which they are qualified that accrue in the future, prior to hiring from the outside. This obligation to employees on the reinstatement list is indefinite.*

It is important, then, for supervisors, department heads, and managers who may be faced with employees' refusal to work in an AIDS situation to be trained *not* to make snap decisions, *not* to fire employees, and *not* to allow demonstrations or refusals to work to continue in the workplace. Instead, the human resources manager or other appropriate manager should be called, regardless of the day or hour, and approaches to the AIDS problem that incorporate these principles should be taken.

Set forth below are a series of AIDS-related situations in the work force involving the doctrine of protected concerted activity. Included in each is a situation presenting the problem, an assessment of whether the protest is protected or unprotected under an NLRB law, and a suggested response for management. In dealing with real AIDS situations in the workplace, remember that there is no substitute for advice from a labor lawyer fully apprised of applicable laws and pertinent facts.

Example 1

Situation. A group of twenty production employees sign a petition demanding that a janitor, a male homosexual, be fired. When presenting the petition to the superintendent, the group leader, Don, says that the janitor is rumored to have AIDS and that none of the production employees want to use bathrooms cleaned by him. Don adds that if the janitor is still in that job the next morning, the

---

*To prevent a replacement from later claiming that he or she had an employment contract with the company on the basis of his or her being told their services would be "permanent" in duration, inform the newly hired employees that they are "regular" and not temporary.

twenty petitioning employees and probably others too will walk out.

Protected Concerted Activity? No. A demand by employees that another employee be removed from a job should not be and is not protected under U.S. labor laws. There is no evidence in this case that the health or safety of the employees has been threatened in any way. A rumor that the janitor has AIDS is insufficient to demonstrate a legitimate employee concern.

Management Response. The superintendent and the personnel manager (two managers) should ask Don to join them in an office and address him in the following manner: "If you or other employees have detailed information on any illness the janitor may have and how it may threaten the health or safety of others, please pass it on to us. At the present time there is no evidence that either the janitor has AIDS or that the health of you or others is threatened by him in any way. In these circumstances, you and the others must follow the regular work schedule—if you don't you'll be subjecting yourselves to being permanently replaced." Then go to the production floor and individually give the same message to others who signed the petition. Begin reviewing applications so you can quickly contact, interview, and perhaps hire twenty or more employees if a walkout occurs.

Example 2

Situation. Edna, a housekeeping employee at a hospital, informs the department head that she will not clean room 5B because its current patient is being treated for AIDS. When the department head points out that the hospital has been treating AIDS patients for several years and neither she nor any other housekeeping employee has ever refused, Edna replies that her husband has just learned that she cleans the rooms of AIDS patients from time to time and last night he ordered her never to do it again, because of a fear that she might contract it and transmit it to him and their five children.

Protected Concerted Activity? No. Once again the NLRB should dismiss an unfair labor practice charge, if filed. Here, the activity is not concerted: only Edna is refusing to perform a duty assigned to numerous housekeeping employees. There is no indication that others have authorized Edna to speak for them; Edna (or her husband) may argue that she is expressing concern that affects or threatens other employees, but in those circumstances the NLRB should conclude that the activity (refusing to perform assigned duties) is definitely not concerted and probably not even protected (there is no indication that simply cleaning the room of an AIDS patient is infectious).

Management Response. The department head and personnel director should meet with Edna and tell her something like this: "Your assigned duties will continue to include the rooms of AIDS patients, and you'll be expected to clean those rooms in the same manner as the rooms of other patients. We hope you'll agree to this; if you refuse to carry out your duties, you'll be guilty of insubordination and subject to being permanently replaced."

Example 3

Situation. The office manager discovers most of his clerical staff discussing a newspaper article about a male politician in town who has just resigned from his office with the announcement that he is suffering from AIDS, which he contracted through injecting illegal drugs. The wife of the politician, Shirley, works as the office manager's secretary. One of the clerical workers tells the office manager: "It has been proven that AIDS is transmitted through sexual contact. This means Shirley may well have AIDS. And she's here every day, getting water from our drinking fountain, using our rest rooms, and serving you coffee and lunch. What are *you* going to do about it?"

Just then Shirley walks up and says: "Last week the children and I were tested for the AIDS virus, and I just learned that while the results were all negative for the kids, my test was positive. The doctor assures me that I don't have AIDS now and may never have it. I feel fine and want very much to continue working. My husband is expected to die before the end of the year, and with the loss of his paycheck, medical bills, and four children, I really need my job."

One of the clericals shouts: "Well, that's not good enough for me. Any of us could catch AIDS from Shirley and then give it to our husbands, just the way her dopehead husband gave it to her. I'm going to the break room and won't return to work until Shirley leaves and never comes back." The other clerical staff follow her to the break room, leaving the office manager and Shirley.

Protected Concerted Activity? Probably not. There is no indica-tion that AIDS can be transmitted through casual contact in the workplace. Even if Shirley eventually develops AIDS, the CDC and almost all doctors say that she will not infect other staff members or her boss by carrying out her office duties and having normal contact with them. And to date, she does not have AIDS. On the other hand, the employees are definitely engaged in concerted ac-tivity, and have a sincere concern about the health and safety of themselves and members of their families. Medically, their fears are unfounded, but they neither understand nor believe that. The NLRB would probably conclude that the concerns of the clerical staff were unreasonable and their refusal to work unprotected.

Management Response. Education is in order here. Send Shirley home with pay, after expressing sympathy and concern. Then meet with all the clerical staff, bringing in a nurse or doctor if appropriate (as well as educational materials) for the purpose of informing them of basic facts about AIDS and answering their questions. At the end of the session, explain in no uncertain terms that Shirley will return to work the next day and that all of them will be expected to report and work as scheduled; those who do not will be subject to being permanently replaced. (Consider moving Shirley to a work location that is at least partially isolated from the other clericals, but only if she accepts the transfer voluntarily.)

Example 4

Situation. When a nurse inquires about the past or present medical problems of a patient in the emergency room who was injured in an automobile accident, the patient reports that he has AIDS. Word spreads to the other five nursing personnel on duty in that depart-ment, all of whom refuse to treat the accident victim, who is bleeding profusely. All five nurses refuse orders from both doctors and the department head to assist in treating the patient.

Protected Concerted Activity? Probably yes. The refusal is ob-viously concerted, so the only question is whether it is protected. The hospital can argue that it should not be, because nurses have an obligation to carry out orders in emergency treatment situations, and that danger is remote because they have followed universal precautions; however, the NLRB could note the risk of blood splashes and other exposure to the virus and rule the refusals to be protected.

Management Response. Be certain that the orders to assist in treating the AIDS patient are clear and understood, and that the refusals are definite, heard by witnesses, and documented. Then send the nurses home. Do *not* allow them to treat other patients or to be transferred to another area. Hire permanent replacements as soon as possible (this may be difficult to accomplish in a short amount of time). Follow NLRB rules concerning permanent replacements and applications for reinstatement. Obviously, educational efforts are very much in order.

Example 5

Situation. A plant manager places a notice on the bulletin board of a manufacturing facility stating that effective the next day all employees are subject to random testing for HIV antibodies. The following morning 50 percent of the employees on the first shift walk around the plant with petitions protesting the AIDS test instead of reporting to their machines. The manager announces over the loudspeaker system that all employees are ordered to their machines and that any who do not comply will be fired. The announcement is repeated three times. Ten minutes later the manager appears on the plant floor with security guards, informs the twenty-five protesting employees that they are fired, and orders them off the property.

Protected Concerted Activity? Yes. The HIV antibodies test has just become a condition of employment, and employees have the right to register their objection to this new employer demand by withholding their services and informing others of their protest. The activity is obviously concerted. While the employer could argue that it should be unprotected because it occurred during working time, interfered with work by employees who began their assembly assignments as scheduled, and generally disrupted operations, the NLRB would probably dismiss all these arguments.

Management Response. The manager made a series of mistakes. The decision to test production and maintenance employees randomly in a manufacturing facility is founded neither on logic nor on the law. The Americans with Disabilities Act and possibly the Rehabilitation Act and state handicap statutes have probably been violated. Aside from the law, it is poor employee relations to implement any new policy with a one-day notice. In this case of a controversial rule, there should be a minimum hiatus of thirty days between the announcement and the implementation. Moreover, meetings with employees to explain the rationale and inviting their questions and comments would be in order. The policy of testing employees for HIV suggests poor judgment. Finally, the manager should have reminded employees of the rule prohibiting solicitation while they are supposed to be working and should have instructed them to report to their machines. Assuming that reminder is ignored, the employees roaming the plant with petitions should be ordered either to report to their job stations to begin work or to leave the company's property. Those who continue the protest should be escorted off company property. No one should be threatened or told they are fired. The message should be put simply: if you do not intend to work, you must leave. After escorting them out of the plant, apply the rules and procedures for protected concerted activity.

The Constitution: Equal Protection and Due Process Clauses

Persons with AIDS conditions on the payrolls of the federal, state, or local governments could consider suits under the Fourth, Fifth, or Fourteenth Amendment to the U.S. Constitution. The Fourth Amendment prohibits government employers from subjecting their employees to unreasonable searches and seizures; the Fifth Amendment protects applicants and employees from being deprived of "property" without due process of law by the government; and the Fourteenth Amendment extends individual protections in the first ten amendments to state and local government employees. Specifically, the Fourteenth Amendment prohibits states from depriving its citizens of "property" without due process of law, or from denying them equal protection of the laws.

Since the equal protection clause essentially means that similarly situated people must be similarly treated, a policy or practice by a governmental employer that discriminates against AIDS applicants or employees may violate the Constitution. Any exceptions to the rule of uniform treatment must be grounded on legitimate public interests, such as promotion of safety or health. Further, the Fourth Amendment's protection of citizens from unreasonable searches and seizures already has been applied to void job firings for positive drug test results, and it is at least equally applicable to tests for HIV antibodies. The public employer drug cases balance the degree of intrusion into the individual's personal life against the validity of the rationale behind the test to determine if it is "reasonable" and thus constitutional. A similar approach to HIV tests should be anticipated.

The city of Willoughby, Ohio, implemented a mandatory blood-testing program as part of the annual physical examination for fire fighters and paramedics that was designed to ascertain the presence of HIV. An employee with ten years of seniority filed suit, challenging the test as an unreasonable search and seizure, an unwarranted invasion of privacy, and a denial of due process. The court, however, refused to enjoin the testing program and dismissed the lawsuit, stating that "The protection of the public from the contraction and transmission of AIDS by fire fighters and paramedics is a compelling government interest. Stopping the spread of the deadly AIDS epidemic is a compelling government interest" (*Anonymous Firemen v. City of Willoughby*, 779 F. Supp. 402 [D.C.N. Ohio 1991]).

The sensitivity of HIV issues suggests that privacy rights will be vigorously argued by plaintiff attorneys. Hence, "invasion of privacy" claims could be filed by (1) patients whose blood is tested for HIV antibodies upon admission to a public hospital either without their informed consent or under circumstances of coerced consent; (2) a nurse at a public clinic who is required by policy to report exposures to HIV but fails to do so because she does not want to know if she contracted it, and who is subsequently disciplined by clinic officials who discover her breach of policy; (3) a fireman who refuses to administer mouth-to-mouth resuscitation to a victim of smoke inhalation who lives in a gay area and who is eventually fired after protests by a homosexual community group; (4) a public school teacher who is absent excessively, loses weight, and develops blotches on her face, and who is fired because her principal demands that she be tested for HIV antibodies, but she refuses; and (5) city-employed emergency medical technicians who are singled out in a new city council ordinance that requires them to declare, in writing, whether they have communicable diseases or have been exposed to any and, if so, to be thoroughly examined by a city hospital doctor— such examination including a blood test for HIV antibodies.

While the U.S. Constitution is void of language expressly recognizing a right of privacy, the Supreme Court's decision in *Griswold v. Connecticut*, 381 U.S. 479 (1965), has been argued to implicitly establish such a right. However, that case concerned birth control— not employment—and employers should maintain the position that there is no individual employee right of privacy available to public employees.

State and local government employers should be especially sensitive to lawsuits grounded on constitutional theories.

COBRA

A final federal law applicable to AIDS situations is the Consolidated Omnibus Budget Reconciliation Act (COBRA), which requires employers with twenty or more employees to offer to any employee who quits or is discharged (for reasons other than gross misconduct) the opportunity to convert group medical insurance and continue its coverage for up to eighteen months. Departing employees who accept the offer must assume the entire cost of their insurance, but this is a substantial benefit for PWAs fighting high doctor and drug bills. Employers have the same obligation of offering continued insurance coverage to a spouse or dependents if the employee dies.

The penalty for employers who fail to comply is stiff: a $100 per day excise tax paid to the Internal Revenue Service and/or a $100 per day penalty payable directly to the employee. These penalties can be reduced or waived in certain situations. Moreover, the employee still has the right to force the employer to offer the COBRA coverage!

3

State and Local Laws

Until recently, managers concerned about labor laws needed only to bear in mind federal statutes and how they are interpreted by federal commissions and federal courts. During the last ten years, however, states, counties, and even cities have exercised legislative discretion by enacting statutes and ordinances to protect job applicants and employees from employment discrimination and by creating human rights commissions to administer their laws. Greater protection at governmental levels beneath the federal level has been extended to cover such areas as maternity, age, sexual preference, and AIDS. In fact, AIDS is a subject that has generated considerable debate in local legislative bodies. Hence, prudent managers with multistate and multicity facilities must become aware of all state and local laws that may pertain to AIDS before making decisions or drafting policies on this topic.

Many large companies with far-flung facilities have made the mistake of carefully crafting personnel policies for their entire empires that are totally consistent with state laws in their headquarters areas but violate state, county, or city laws where plants or warehouses are located. Human resources managers and house counsel for corporations with multistate operations must engage in a continual review of local labor and employment laws in the areas of each facility to ensure conformity between policy and practice, on the one hand, and legal requirements, on the other hand. Often headquarters-generated policies will have to be amended for local operations.

States

Several states have enacted legislation specifically pertaining to AIDS. For example, Florida, Wisconsin, California, and the District of Columbia all prohibit or restrict the use of results from the HIV antibody test in employment decisions affecting either applicants or employees. California and Wisconsin also mandate that such test results are confidential and prohibit their disclosure in order to protect the privacy of the afflicted employee.

Here is a brief summary of some of the statutes enacted by various states that deal with AIDS and employment. Note the different perspectives and motivations of the legislators who were able to enact their bills into law:

Arizona establishes a legal cause of action for employees who have been exposed to HIV on the job; explains proof required in these suits by employees against their employers.

California prohibits the use of results from blood tests for HIV antibodies in determining suitability for employment.

Delaware amends employment discrimination statute to classify AIDS as a handicap.

Florida explicitly prohibits discrimination against applicants or employees who have AIDS conditions; also prohibits employers from requiring applicants or employees to submit to tests for HIV antibodies as a condition of employment.

Illinois requires public health officials to give notice of possible exposure to patients undergoing an invasive medical or dental procedure by a health care professional who is seropositive. Health care providers must be notified if they treat patients who are HIV positive.

Iowa classifies a diagnosis of symptomatic HIV disease as a disability under the state's antidiscrimination statute; also classifies requiring an HIV antibody test as a condition of employment or terminating an employee because of the results of voluntary HIV antibody test as an unfair employment practice.

Kentucky prohibits requiring an HIV antibody test as a condition of hiring, promotion, or continued employment unless the employer can show a valid, bona fide occupational qualification; also prohibits employers and labor organizations from discriminating against all persons with AIDS.

Louisiana requires a hospital to notify within forty-eight hours any fire fighter, or other individual who provides emergency services to a patient who is subsequently diagnosed with AIDS; moreover, the hospital and employer must take measures to ensure confidentiality. A physician or other individual reporting the death of any patient with HIV or other contagious disease must notify the coroner of the nature of that disease; failure to comply will result in conviction of a misdemeanor and a fine of up to $5,000. When a physician with actual knowledge that a patient has AIDS admits him or her to a hospital, including the emergency room, the physician must inform the hospital of that condition. Hospitals and nursing homes must adopt rules and procedures, consistent with CDC guidelines, to protect the public from being infected with HIV by health care providers. To protect health care providers from contracting HIV from patients, there is a specific exception to general consent requirements: when it is suspected that a hospital physician or employee has been exposed to a patient with HIV, tests for that virus can be conducted on previously drawn blood or other body fluids without the consent of the patient; in situations where no previously drawn blood has been collected, the hospital may order, without consent of the patient, that blood or body fluids be drawn to conduct the necessary test. However, these test results will not become part of the patient's medical record, although any positive test result must be reported to the patient as well as to the physician or employee who was exposed.

Maryland requires that whenever an employee of a correctional institution is exposed to an inmate in a manner that could transmit HIV, the inmate must be tested, and the employee must be notified of the result of that test.

Nevada mandates that employers of prostitutes are liable for damages when the employer knows or should know that his prostitute employee had tested positive for HIV.

New Mexico prohibits employers from requiring employees to submit to a test for HIV antibodies as a condition of hiring, promotion, or continued employment, unless a bona fide occupational qualification exists.

North Carolina prohibits employers from discriminating against current employees with AIDS, but allows employers to reassign or fire employees with AIDS conditions *if* their continued employment poses a significant risk to others or *if* the employee is unable to perform his or her job.

Ohio grants immunity to employers of PWAs from liability or damages arising out of the transmission of the HIV virus from an infected employee to another employee or person, unless the transmission results from reckless employer conduct.

Oregon frees an employer from responsibility for providing the employee with "reasonable accommodation" under Oregon's Rehabilitation Act if the employee does not provide the employer with the results of HIV antibody tests.

Rhode Island prohibits employer discrimination against PWAs; also prohibits a test for HIV antibodies as a condition for employment unless a statutory exemption exists or unless there is a clear and present danger of transmission of the virus to others.

Texas ordains that municipalities, counties, and other political subdivisions that provide health coverage to its employees cannot exclude or limit insurance coverage for AIDS; orders health care facilities to require their employees to complete an AIDS education course; indicates that the state's employment discrimination statute shall *not* be interpreted to apply to AIDS, which will fall outside the definition of "disability" *if* there is a direct threat to the health or safety of others or *if* the person is unable to perform the duties of his or her job.

Vermont prohibits discrimination by employers against applicants and employees with AIDS; proscribes testing for HIV antibodies.

Washington amends state's employment discrimination statute to include AIDS and protect PWAs.

States have been particularly active in considering laws that involve AIDS and health care facilities. Generally, there are two types of these laws: disease-specific laws expressly pertaining to HIV and AIDS; and general laws pertaining to all communicable or infectious or sexually transmitted diseases, which are applicable to HIV without specifically referring to the virus. Hospitals, clinics, and nursing homes must be sensitive to these laws enacted by legislatures and to regulations interpreting them released by administrative agencies.

States can be expected to continue debating hundreds of laws involving AIDS during the next several years.

Most states, however, are using existing laws to protect PWAs from discrimination or amending antidiscrimination laws to define AIDS as a disability or handicap.

The Washington State Human Rights Commission has specifically recognized AIDS as a disability under that state's discrimination law and has proposed policy guidelines for preventing discrimination against PWA's in employment. One guideline stresses that the agency "does not currently recognize any job classification where a diagnosis of AIDS would prevent the hiring of any person who has the syndrome" and indicates that employers are obligated to "reasonably accommodate" disabled persons, including PWAs, unless their disabilities prevent proper performance on the job. On the other hand, the U.S. Court of Appeals for the Fifth Circuit has ruled that a Texas law prohibiting employment discrimination against the handicapped does not protect an employee with AIDS (*Hilton v. Southwestern Bell Telephone Co., 936 F.2d 823* [1991]).

PWAs protesting alleged discrimination under state statutes have won the vast majority of cases. Thus, a Massachusetts Superior Court concluded that AIDS is a handicap within the meaning of that state's antidiscrimination law, and then found in favor of a repair technician with New England Telephone who claimed he was forced to disclose a diagnosis of symptomatic HIV disease to a supervisor after a series of medical absences. The plaintiff testified that he eventually quit, after unsympathetic co-workers threatened to lynch him. The employer's first defense was that the plaintiff was technically not suffering from AIDS and therefore was not handicapped. However, the court ruled that the definition of "handicapped" includes individuals with HIV "who are not a threat to co-workers, but whose co-workers erroneously consider them unemployable." Specifically, the court ruled that an employee with symptomatic HIV disease "would be handicapped regardless of whether he was presently suffering any adverse physical effects of AIDS. It is the potential to contract other illnesses that constitutes the handicap." After that ruling gave the plaintiff the right to have his case heard on the merits, the case was settled, short of trial, with the plaintiff being reinstated to his former position (*Cronan v. New England Telephone Company*, 41 FEP cases 1273 [Mass. Sup.Ct. 1986]).

California's Fair Employment and Housing Commission (FEHC) decided that the Raytheon Company discriminated against a PWA by refusing to allow him to return to work. After the FEHC concluded that AIDS was a handicap, it proceeded to shoot down Raytheon's defense that the reason for not reinstating the PWA was that HIV could be transmitted in the workplace (*Raytheon Co. v. California FEHC*, 46 FEP cases 1089 [Cal. Sup.Ct. 1988]).

Wisconsin's Department of Industry, Labor, and Human Relations took the same approach when it held that Racine's school district violated prohibitions against handicap discrimination when it adopted a policy that discriminated against individuals with AIDS conditions. Once again, the school district's belief that HIV could be transmitted by a teacher or other employee to fellow employees was found to be false, and AIDS was classified as a handicap (*Racine Education Association v. Racine Unified School District*, ERD No. 8650279 [DILHR 1987]).

After observing a male waiter painting his fingernails during work time and using the women's bathroom, the owner of Sebastian's Restaurant terminated him. The waiter filed a claim, arguing that his termination was triggered by a rumor that he had AIDS. The West Virginia Human Rights Commission agreed with the waiter and ordered him reinstated and compensated in the amount of $50,000, on the grounds that the waiter had suffered humiliation, embarrassment, and mental distress (*Isbell v. Sebastian's Restaurant* [1988]). The West Virginia Supreme Court of Appeals has specifically ruled that an HIV-positive person (without symptomatic HIV disease or AIDS) is protected, as handicapped, under that state's Human Rights Act. Since such individuals are not physically or mentally impaired in any fashion, employers may wonder why they are considered handicapped. West Virginia courts have answered that HIV severely limits an individual's ability to socialize, which is considered a major life activity, and as a result HIV-positive individuals are handicapped (*Benjamin R. v. Orkin Exterminating Co., Inc.*, 390 SE 2d 814 [W.Va. 1990]).

A judge interpreting the Minnesota Human Rights Act relied upon a different theory to conclude that an asymptomatic person is handicapped and therefore protected. He found that HIV is a contagious infection that limits two major life activities, the abilities to engage in sexual intercourse, and reproduction, and ruled that an HIV-positive employee was due $70,000 in fines and damages. The judge was unconcerned that the two "major life activities" were totally unrelated to job duties (*Minnesota v. DiMa Corp.* [1990]).

The Oregon Civil Rights Division has decided that an employer's exclusion of AIDS treatment from health insurance coverage constitutes unlawful sex discrimination because of its disparate impact on males, the group most likely to be afflicted with AIDS. In *Griffin v. Tri-County Metropolitan Transportation District*, an Oregon employer was found to have improperly discriminated against a dispatcher because he was HIV positive; after concluding that the dispatcher was a victim of handicap discrimination, the jury awarded him $255,000 in monetary damages and $245,000 in other damages.

In Texas a hotel and restaurant was found to have violated that state's Human Rights Act by firing a waiter with AIDS. The plaintiff was awarded $60,000 in lost wages and $19,500 because the employer had failed to inform the plaintiff of his right to continue his insurance as required by COBRA (*Gardner v. Rainbow Lodge, Inc.* [SD Tex. 1990]).

In *Cain v. Hyatt* (734 F. Supp. 671 [E.D. Pa. 1990]), Hyatt Legal Services was found to have unlawfully terminated the plaintiff (an attorney) due to an AIDS condition, in violation of the Pennsylvania Human Relations Act. After concluding that AIDS constituted a handicap within the meaning of that state's law, the court awarded the plaintiff over $42,000 in back pay, $65,000 for mental anguish and humiliation, and $50,000 in punitive damages.

The Connecticut Human Rights Commission ruled that an employer violated that state's statute against handicap discrimination by terminating an employee who was *perceived* to have AIDS (*Chro v. Respondent, Connecticut Human Rights Commission* [1989]).

In New York, many cases have established that PWAs are physically handicapped within the meaning of both New York City's Human Rights Act and New York State's Human Rights Law (for example, *Shawn v. Leggs Co.* [1989]; *Barton v. New York City Commission on Human Rights*, 542 NYS 2d 176 [1989]; *People of the State of New York v. 49 West 12 Tenant's Corp.* [1983]).

A graphic artist in Virginia filed suit against his company, claiming violation of the state's handicap law, when he was first placed on mandatory leave of absence and eventually terminated, allegedly to protect other employees.

There have been at least two suits in Louisiana, one by a waiter fired after he allegedly disrupted the hotel by announcing to fellow employees and guests that his roommate had AIDS, and another by the credit manager of a television station who claimed that he was physically and mentally able to perform his job after his symptomatic HIV disease progressed to AIDS, but who nonetheless was fired. (See the lawsuits filed in state court in these two cases in appendix B, documents 9 and 10.)

Since most states have laws protecting the handicapped and some states, as noted, have special statutes dealing specifically with AIDS, considerable litigation on this issue at the state level can be anticipated.

A number of issues remain unresolved by laws or cases. Suppose, for example, a job applicant is not presently impaired in any way, but the employer has medical proof that he is HIV positive or is in an early stage of AIDS. The employer rationally concludes that eventual impairment and an early death are inevitable. Anticipating extensive absenteeism, a short return on training time and cost, heavy use of health insurance, and finally a life insurance payment, all within the relatively near future, may the employer refuse to hire or promote the person? In *State Division of Human Rights (New York) v. Xerox Corp.*, the court rejected the employer's argument that an obese job applicant was unacceptable because his physical condition would deteriorate. Similarly, in *Chrysler Outboard Corp. v. Wisconsin Department of Industry*, the court addressed the claim of an applicant who was denied employment because he had acute lymphocytic leukemia. Relying upon a report from its medical consultant that the applicant's condition posed a high risk of infection from minor injury, a risk of prolonged recuperation, and risk of complications from the disease, all of which would result in lost time, the employer rejected the applicant. The court, however, concluded that the disease was a handicap and observed that "the employer's contention that the complainant may at some future date be unable to perform the duties of the job is immaterial."

Plaintiff attorneys, always resourceful, are not limited to statutes specifically covering AIDS, handicaps, or sexual orientation. In Michigan, a man who had been employed for fifteen years was terminated two days after discussing his AIDS condition with an executive of his company. He was allowed to retain health insurance coverage but deprived of life insurance, he alleges. His attorney has sued for $10 million, claiming breach of employment contract and intentional infliction of emotional distress, as well as discrimination against the handicapped.

State court tort actions should be anticipated in an environment where jokes and rumors about AIDS are endemic. A hotel was sued by an employee who claimed that he suffered severe emotional distress due to false gossip at work about his PWA status. Wishing to avoid publicity, the employer quietly settled the suit for a substantial sum. Defamation, slander, and libel are possible causes of action against an employer whose agents maliciously and falsely state, orally or in writing, that an employee has AIDS. In Pennsylvania, a hospital, a church, and a minister were sued by a patient who alleged that hospital employees had falsely told the minister that the patient was suffering from AIDS, and then the minister repeated the erroneous information to others, including several members of his congregation. The suit seeks damages for emotional distress, embarrassment, lost wages, and medical expenses.

A woman at O'Hare Airport in Chicago attempted to board a plane without a boarding pass. When the American Airlines agent refused her passage, causing her to miss the flight, she allegedly grabbed his arm. The agent then supposedly kicked her in the shins and bit her. When the agent later tested positive for HIV, the woman's lawyer filed suit for $12 million against American Airlines for negligently hiring a PWA and failing to safeguard its passengers from exposure to employees with contagious diseases.

The obligation, if any, of an employer to inform an applicant, an employee, or others of an AIDS condition is an issue certain to receive considerable attention. In *Dornak v. Lafayette General Hospital*, 399 So. 2d 168 (La. 1981), the plaintiff was referred to the hospital's physician for a preemployment physical examination after completing her application for employment as a nurse's aide. The hospital hired her but failed to disclose that her chest X-ray had revealed tuberculosis. When she later experienced persistent coughing and other symptoms, she was examined by her personal physician, who diagnosed her tubercular condition and determined that the X-ray in her personnel file had revealed it earlier. The plaintiff filed a tort action, claiming that the hospital was negligent in not telling her of the tuberculosis and asserting that she would have secured medical treatment for the condition during the almost three years between the preemployment X-ray and her doctor's diagnosis. The Supreme Court of Louisiana ruled that the hospital breached its duty to disclose the result of the X-ray. Specifically the court said:

> While we do not consider that the hospital had any obligation to give plaintiff a pre-employment physical examination, once it undertook to do so and subsequently employed her, she was entitled to and did rely upon the expectation that she would be told of any dangerous condition actually disclosed by that examination, especially considering the fact that she was employed by the hospital to perform duties placing her in contact with co-employees and hospital patients.

Here is a question to ponder: what if an HIV-positive female applicant or employee submits to a blood test in conformity with the employer's physical examination policy and then—ignorant of her condition—infects her baby (by breast feeding) and husband (during sexual intercourse). Would the infected third parties have a cause for action against the employer for failure to promptly disclose the infectious condition to the woman? It seems definite that if an employer tests an applicant or employee for antibodies to HIV, any positive result should be communicated immediately to the person. This information should be provided even if the applicant is not hired. Note, though, the court's emphasis in the case cited above about placing an employee with a "dangerous condition . . . in contact with co-employees and hospital patients." While there appears to be a legal duty to disclose a dangerous condition to the employee, is there a corresponding obligation to inform coemployees and patients?

Marc Christian, homosexual lover of Rock Hudson, sued the Hudson estate for $14 million, alleging that Hudson continued to have sex with him after Hudson's AIDS condition was diagnosed, thus subjecting Christian to fears that he will eventually contract the disease. A sympathetic jury awarded him several million dollars more than he sought, but the judge reduced the damage award. An appellate court approved a $5 million payment to Chrisitan *even though he never developed the virus*! The gravamen of the suit was that Hudson had a legal duty to disclose that he had AIDS. Christian was allowed compensation for his *fear* that he *could* become infected.

Apply this concept to the employment arena: Suppose that a patient or customer learns that an employee who treated or served her has AIDS, or that an employee who had worked closely with another employee for a long period of time discovers that this co-worker has AIDS. Now suppose that the patient, customer, or employee discovers that the employer had knowledge of the employee's condition and allowed the ill employee to continue his or her duties without notifying others. Perhaps a hospital permitted an asymptomatic surgeon to continue operating or a food service worker who delivers trays to the rooms to stay in her position after developing symptomatic HIV disease. Or a restaurant or hotel agreed to an HIV-positive waiter's or chef's request to keep working. In each case the employer felt it was on sound ground in permitting continuation of employment. After all, the CDC advises that the risk of transmission is slight, and lawyers warn that removal of an HIV-positive employee could lead to a claim of handicap discrimination. Regardless, the patient, customer, or fellow employee now fears that the virus may have been transmitted to him or her and could sue to secure compensation for that fear, under the concept endorsed by the Christian court. Thus, an employer is in the proverbial Catch-22 situation. If it permits the employee to continue performing the same job, without notification or restriction, it is vulnerable to a duty-to-disclose suit. If it notifies all patients or customers, its business could be adversely affected and the employee could sue for breach of privacy and confidentiality. If it restricts the duties of the employee, it could be sued for handicap discrimination!

The employer's defenses in a duty-to-disclose suit would be that AIDS cannot be communicated through casual contact, that the doctrine should be inapplicable in AIDS situations, and that a superseding obligation to maintain confidentiality concerning the PWA was operative. Such disclosures, if made, could stimulate discrimination against and harassment of the PWA.

Suppose the PWA was a surgeon or nurse involved with invasive procedures, or a laboratory technician regularly handling blood, and a patient or fellow employee actually contracted HIV. These circumstances would certainly strengthen a plaintiff's case. In fact, a plaintiff could argue that the legal duty of the employer goes beyond disclosure to the actual removal of the infected employee from those and similar jobs. However, there is no precedent for such a strong ruling, and plaintiffs in these cases would have a heavy burden of proof. Any employer considering disclosure of an employee's AIDS condition to fellow employees, patients, or others should consider the very real possibility of claims against it for breach of confidentiality, improper communication of medical records, libel, slander, and defamation by the PWA. An employer weighing the risks of disclosure should conclude in most situations that the probability of losing a suit is significantly higher if disclosure is made. Where feasible, an employer that decides that disclosure is appropriate in a particular case should obtain an authorization for such disclosure from the employee with AIDS.

There is no substitute for a precise and careful analysis of the facts in every situation where the rights of an employee with an AIDS condition may conflict with those of fellow employees or others. The most probable place for this tension between two rights to occur is a health care facility. Suppose Tom is a patient with an advanced case of AIDS at Riverview Hospital. Not only is he positive for HIV, he is contagious with respect to a variety of secondary infections, including rubella, brought on by his impaired immune system. A severe shortage of nurses caused by the hospital's inability to recruit replacements and unusual absenteeism causes Riverview to assign Cathy, on an overtime basis, to the ward in which Tom and other PWAs are located. Suppose further that Cathy is pregnant. Probably Cathy would not be asked to directly care for Tom, and the hospital would disclose Tom's conditions to her if she was working in the general area of his room. Now suppose the reverse of this situation—Tom, still a PWA and slowed down, but not stopped, by contagious secondary infections including rubella, is the nurse and Cathy—pregnant—is the patient. Once again, Tom should—in the view of many—be removed from Cathy's ward. In fact, Tom would probably be removed from all patient care duties. If, however, Tom worked in a small office where he had no contact with patients, and doctors treating his secondary infections certified that the few employees with whom he has contact were not endangered, there would be no cause for either disclosure or removal.

The probability of persons with AIDS in its later stages developing secondary infections injects an important factor in the equation. Serious contagious infections such as rubella may dictate removal of the employee from a particular job, while pneumonia and cancer can be handled by means of disclosure to fellow employees. Thus, there are situations where removal of an employee with an AIDS condition is necessary, other situations where disclosure of an AIDS condition is appropriate, and many more situations where neither action should be taken; in the latter cases, the employee with HIV, symptomatic HIV disease, or AIDS should be allowed to continue working without any action or publication concerning his or her condition. It is impossible to rigidly apply previously adopted procedures or rules in these situations. Instead, management should analyze the rights and the facts in the specific situation, rely heavily upon medical evaluations, and document the decision-making process. (See chapters 6–8 for more detailed recommendations about how to analyze these situations in health care settings.)

As I have suggested, separate from special statutes on AIDS and interpreting HIV as a condition falling within the scope of handicap discrimination laws, there are a number of torts contained in established state laws that could easily be applied to AIDS in workplace situations. These include *negligence, negligent hiring*; infliction of *mental anguish* and *emotional distress*; *slander, defamation*, and *libel* (oral or written communications stating that an applicant, employee, or ex-employee has HIV, symptomatic HIV disease, or AIDS); *invasion of privacy*; *breach of confidentiality of medical records* (a personnel manager or clerk shows an employee's customer, patient, or other member of the public medical records describing the AIDS diagnosis of an applicant or employee); and *duty to disclose* (employees working side by side with a PWA claim that their employer should have notified them about the medical condition of the employee with AIDS).

Examples of negligence suits involve doctors, hospitals, and a law firm. Mount Carmel Medical Center and a doctor were found guilty of negligence and malpractice involving an Ohio woman who was infected with HIV during a blood transfusion. She had donated her own blood prior to breast reduction surgery, but after the operation an employee allegedly administered blood from the regular inventory without her doctor's permission. The tainted blood transmitted HIV to her. A jury awarded the woman $12 million in compensatory damages. In Toronto an unmarried woman tried repeatedly to have a baby through artificial insemination. On her thirty-fifth attempt to become pregnant, she was infected with HIV during the procedure. Suing her doctor for malpractice, she claimed he should have discussed the possibility of AIDS with her and warned her of the risk of infection. A jury agreed and awarded her $883,000. A real estate developer was irate because his law firm failed to respond to a motion for summary judgment, with the result that he lost a multimillion dollar foreclosure case. In his suit the developer claimed that the firm was negligent for allowing an attorney with symptomatic HIV disease to handle the case (*Move v. Schantz, Schatzman, and Aaronson*). An attorney with the firm was quoted as saying that the infected attorney "just totally missed it and became totally disabled because of the disease."

The latter case illustrates the dilemma in which employers can find themselves. If they allow an employee with symptomatic HIV disease or AIDS to continue with his or her regular duties and errors of commission or omission are made, due to the impaired physical or mental state of the employee, then they could be liable for negligence. If, however, employers transfer or terminate an HIV-infected employee to avoid errors, prevent transmission, or improve efficiency, they are vulnerable to claims of discrimination against the handicapped and possible violation of special laws protecting individuals with AIDS conditions.

When workplace rumors surface that a particular employee has AIDS, employers must take care to prevent supervisors or managers from repeating these rumors or discussing them with anyone. While production, maintenance, warehouse, clerical, and related employees are not legal agents of the company, managers, supervisors, and executives are. This means that when a first-line supervisor states to another employee, a neighbor, or a relative that "Fred Jones, our mechanic, is homosexual and has AIDS" or "My secretary contracted HIV from her dope-dealing husband," and the statement is later proved to be false, then the employer may be guilty of defamation. In *McCune v. Neitzel*, 457 N.W. 2d 803 (1990), the defendant told several people in a small town that the plaintiff had AIDS. They, in turn, relayed that false information to others. After suing for slander, the plaintiff testified that as a result of these rumors he stopped seeing friends and family and began abusing alcohol. After trial the jury found that the plaintiff had been slandered and awarded him $25,350.

While some lawyers may not be interested in representing PWAs, a few firms and several organizations are actually seeking such cases. The American Civil Liberties Union (ACLU) has been very active in this area, filling numerous suits in federal and state courts. It is anticipated that the National Association for the Advancement of Colored People (NAACP)—largely because a disproportionate number of PWAs are black—will also become involved. These organizations, primarily interested in making or changing the law, are expected to continue prosecuting cases through the various levels of courts, even after a plaintiff's death, to achieve their goals. A sample suit filed by the ACLU in state court against an employer that discharged an employee with AIDS can be found in appendix B, document 10.

Finally, with different states taking varied and sometimes contradictory approaches to AIDS situations, employers must be careful of a special area of the law called "conflict." Suppose Ted, a resident of Indiana, works at a restaurant in Chicago that is owned by a large corporation based in California. Ted, fired after the manager hears a rumor that he has AIDS, wants to sue. The law of which state or city would apply? The answer could be critical, as different states have different, sometimes contradictory, legal concepts, doctrines, and statutes.

In concluding this section on state laws, I should note that states have adopted workers' compensation antiretaliation statutes applicable to disabled employees. Since PWAs frequently become disabled and sometimes file for workers' compensation, employers should be aware that attempts to terminate them may be challenged under a state law protecting employees who file for workers' compensation from retaliation.

Cities

Counties (parishes in Louisiana) and cities have not hesitated to place their oars in this turbulent water. Among the cities that have enacted ordinances involving AIDS and employment (most expressly prohibit discrimination against applicants or employees with AIDS conditions) are Austin, Texas; Kansas City, Missouri; Toledo, Ohio; and Los Angeles, San Francisco, West Hollywood, Heyward, Santa Clara, and Sacramento, California. The city attorney for West Hollywood has said, "The West Hollywood law is broad enough to allow us to find discrimination under certain circumstances involving people telling jokes about AIDS!" The Los Angeles and San Francisco ordinances move considerably beyond most employment discrimination laws, which provide for compensatory damages only, by allowing claims for punitive damages. Jessica's Nail Salon has been formally charged with violating criminal provisions of West Hollywood law for canceling a pedicure appointment with a PWA. Conviction could lead to a jail sentence of six months, a fine of $1,000, or both. The small business's defense is that blood accidentally drawn from a PWA during a pedicure could infect others. Contra Costa County enacted an ordinance that prohibited discrimination in employment and housing against people who are HIV infected or those that may be perceived as being at risk for becoming infected with the AIDS virus. The law was challenged as being preemptive of California's state law which also forbids employment discrimination against individuals with AIDS conditions. However, the state law does not protect those who may be perceived as at risk for AIDS, and appellate courts upheld the county law (*Citizens for Uniform Laws v. County of Contra Costa*, Cal. S. Ct. [1991]). The Austin ordinance proscribes AIDS-based discrimination in housing, as well as in employment and public accommodations. The liberal mayor of Boston avoided controversy with the conservative city council by issuing an executive order that protected all city employees with AIDS conditions from discrimination in hiring, promotions, and employee benefits.

The Legal Aid Society of San Francisco has filed a complaint with that city's Human Rights Commission alleging that Neiman-Marcus violated the ordinance protecting PWAs by terminating a salesman one month after he was diagnosed as suffering from AIDS. The specific claims are that the department store refused his request for unpaid medical leave (which would have allowed insurance coverage to continue), harassed and humiliated him, and communicated his condition to other employees, thereby violating his right of privacy. The company's position is that the salesman had used all of his sick days; the medical plan he selected could not be converted into a private policy; the regular approach for resolving medical problems was employed in his case; and that therefore there was no violation of the law.

The New York City Human Rights Commission has a special AIDS discrimination unit for investigating and processing complaints. Chattanooga is using AIDS as a justification for increasing its regulation of adult movie and entertainment facilities. Citing the threat of AIDS and the need to protect public health, a new ordinance requires special licenses and permits for such facilities and regulates how they are operated. Courts, which in the past have frequently nullified attempts to regulate these establishments as violative of the First Amendment, have thus far approved laws like these as valid exercises of the city's power to protect and promote public health.

Employment-at-Will

The employment-at-will doctrine concerns employees without an employment contract who are on the payroll at the discretion of their employer, and who can be fired "at will" for good reason, bad reason, or any reason, as long as the reason is not proscribed by law. This means that any plaintiff protesting a termination by filing a lawsuit in state court should have that claim dismissed unless a specific statute or employment contract can be identified that protects him or her. For example, a minority man might claim that he was fired because of his race; a woman would argue that she was terminated because of her sex; a sixty-eight-year-old, long-service employee could claim that he was forced into retirement because of his age; a young female could say that she was constructively discharged (forced to quit) because of sexual harassment in the office; or a newly hired vice-president, fired after a disagreement with the president, could claim that a letter describing his annual salary and benefits constitutes an employment contract.

Over the years, numerous lawsuits have been dismissed by judges because terminated employees were unable to connect their termination to a particular type of discrimination that was protected by law. However, during the last ten years a serious erosion of the employment-at-will doctrine has taken place. The Texas Supreme Court carved out an exception to the employment-at-will doctrine in that state by ruling that a plaintiff would have the right to go to trial on a claim that he or she was terminated for refusing to perform an illegal act. Other cases have given protection—absent special statutes—in circumstances when whistle-blowing employees were fired after they reported illegal conduct at their companies to the authorities. Employment contracts, covenants of fair dealing, and requirements of good faith have been implied in several states to give an unfairly discharged employee his day in court. The employment-at-will doctrine has almost become a memory in California, but still remains strong in most southern and midwestern states.

It is suggested that employees with HIV, symptomatic HIV disease, or AIDS who are not hired or are terminated by an employer that makes no attempt to accommodate them may have an opportunity to create additional exceptions to the employment-at-will doctrine. In their efforts to represent applicants and employees with AIDS conditions, creative plaintiff attorneys and organizations like the ACLU can be expected to exploit the softening of the employment-at-will doctrine that has occurred in recent years. Judges, impressed with the inequity of an employee summarily fired simply because he has developed AIDS or has tested positive for the HIV antibodies, may imply a covenant or stretch a doctrine to protect the plaintiff and provide an opportunity for recovery of special damages.

Multiple Claims

The ACLU and plaintiff attorneys will not limit themselves to a single federal, state, or local law when filing a legal challenge on behalf of a PWA. To the contrary, they should be expected to use the shotgun approach of listing every conceivable law to support their claims, hoping that the court will agree that at least one pellet has hit the jurisdictional mark. Appendix B, document 7, presents a letter mailed to the administrator of a hospital by an attorney representing a terminated PWA. The letter threatens suit under three separate laws, one state and two federal. Note the involvement of both the ACLU and Lambda, an organization formed to promote the legal rights and interests of homosexuals. A formal complaint alleging violations of both federal and state laws can be found in appendix B, document 8.

Of considerable interest is the AIDS Civil Rights Project, administered in San Francisco by the National Gay Rights Advocates, which provides a full-time lawyer to assist those claiming AIDS discrimination. Advice, information, and technical expertise on filing and processing AIDS-related claims is available. Further, legal pleadings, law review and other articles, and general data on AIDS from across the nation are placed in a computer database that is available to claimants. Many major cities have AIDS task forces that advise PWAs, help them find medical care, and provide lawyers in the event a suit is desired.

Jurisdiction or Coverage

Regardless of whether the law is city, county, state, or even federal, questions always arise of whether it covers the particular applicant or employee filing the claim (jurisdiction over person) *and* the particular conduct of the employer in failing to hire, terminating, demoting, or placing the charging party on leave of absence (jurisdiction over subject matter).

While it appears that most, if not all, of the laws discussed thus far would, directly or indirectly, be applicable to persons with symptomatic HIV disease or AIDS, suppose that the person filing the charges has neither but has tested positive for the antibodies to the HIV virus. If not impaired in any way, should he or she be covered because his employer ascertained that he or she is HIV positive and took action adverse to him? The hotel case (appendix B, document 9) raised the question of whether the roommate of a PWA should enjoy the protection of a law designed to help people with AIDS conditions. Finally, should homosexuals and drug addicts who are perceived by their potential or actual employers to be candidates for AIDS be able to take advantage of these laws, assuming they are not hired or are fired because of their homosexuality or drug addiction?

With respect to subject matter jurisdiction, an employer's action in refusing to hire or in discharging a PWA would probably be covered by the statutes. Suppose, however, that the employer merely transfers the PWA to another job, which has less exposure to customers, patients, or employees, without a reduction in wages. Should a suit with those facts be dismissed for lack of jurisdiction or be allowed to go to trial on the merits? Assume that an employee with AIDS at a hospital is placed on involuntary leave of absence with full wages for four weeks, half wages for the next four weeks, and one-quarter wages for the next two weeks, pursuant to that employer's disability policy. Should the employee have the right to legally address his or her irritation with being taken off the job because of the affliction? Assume further that a PWA is placed on leave and assigned to a company's employee assistance program (EAP), just as victims of alcohol and drug abuse have been in the past, with the right to be reinstated in the future. Once again, is he or she entitled to a day in court?

Finally, should the prohibition against discrimination be interpreted to prohibit asking an applicant or employee if he or she has AIDS? Or should the statute be triggered only if the employer takes action that involuntarily deprives the person of employment at his or her regular wage rate? Employers may argue that questions about and tests for HIV are meant to assist them in making legitimate decisions about job placement, and not to discriminate impermissibly. Bear in mind the requirements of the federal Americans with Disabilities Act in dealing with this issue.

These and related questions will be debated in courts and administrative hearings for years to come. It is anticipated that those with the HIV virus and others perceived by employers to be candidates for AIDS will be given protection under various laws already enacted. PWAs transferred or demoted, as opposed to discharged, will also be protected as long as they can show that they were adversely affected by their employer's actions.

Potential Remedies

Until recently, the typical approach by a court or administrative agency in an employment discrimination case was to make the victim "whole." That is, the plaintiff was given restitution and returned to the situation he or she had prior to the illegal act of discrimination. Managers who made decisions that turned out to be illegal did not go to jail, and their companies were not punished with fines. Thus, the remedies were completely compensatory, not penal. Specifically, victims of employment discrimination would be reinstated to regular jobs or placed in the positions for which they applied, with full back pay plus interest. Restoration of benefits—including insurance coverage—was also accomplished. The victims—whether they had been terminated, demoted, or transferred—were restored to their former positions, without monetary loss. Their attorneys' fees were often reimbursed by the losing employers. The Civil Rights Act of 1991 dramatically changed this situation by adding compensatory and punitive damages as potential remedies in federal disability suits. Now plaintiffs can profit and defendants can be monetarily penalized in these cases. And in the most significant change of all, juries now determine these issues.

There is a practical problem with litigating AIDS cases. Due to the seemingly inevitable delay in litigation, cases often consume at least one or more years between initial filing and final resolution. It is highly probable that during the time the case is being processed through the legal channels, the PWA will die or at least become permanently incapable of performing the duties of his or her former job. In these circumstances, is the back pay in dispute computed from the time the victim was deprived of employment until death or until the date at which he or she would have become physically unable to work? And assuming that the PWA has died, to whom should the award of back pay, compensatory damages, and punitive damages be presented? While these questions will be debated for some time before they are finally resolved, courts are expected to require that damage awards be paid to family members of a deceased PWA. In extreme cases a judge may issue a temporary injunction, compelling the employer to reinstate the plaintiff pending the trial and decision. Permanent injunctions prohibiting persons with AIDS conditions other than the plaintiff from being discriminated against may also be issued, with the court retaining jurisdiction for a year or two to be certain that the discrimination is not repeated.

Public Health Laws

Almost all statutes and ordinances dealing directly or indirectly with AIDS in the workplace are designed to protect the victims of alleged discrimination. But what about the public? Every state's workers' compensation law emphasizes the state's general duty to protect and promote the health of its citizens. Many states also have special health and safety laws. Of course, Congress enacted the Occupational Safety and Health Act (OSHA) at the federal level many years ago. Is there a legal obligation on the part of employers to be certain that persons with AIDS conditions do not work in sensitive jobs, such as an operating room, an emergency room, or a blood bank? Should states, in exercising their power to protect public health, require employers to disclose, at least to employees in the same department, the fact that a particular employee has contracted AIDS or to remove employees with HIV, symptomatic HIV disease, or AIDS from certain jobs?

As I noted previously, Louisiana passed a law requiring hospitals to notify emergency medical technicians of patients they had treated who turned out to be HIV positive. New York City health officials closed the Mine Shaft, a notorious gay bar where promiscuous sex was reportedly common, for the purpose of protecting public health. Laws proposed—but not enacted—in some legislatures are intended to prevent gays from donating blood; prohibiting people with AIDS from working in health care jobs; and quarantining all AIDS patients. Most states require both hospitals and doctors to report names of PWAs to health authorities. Further, Colorado law requires doctors and hospitals to report the names and addresses of all individuals testing positive for antibodies to HIV to the Colorado Board of Health. Colorado also has delegated to state and local health officials the authority to take "restrictive measures" against people with HIV or AIDS who are "an imminent danger to public health."

There is a strong precedent for states exercising their broad police powers to control communicable diseases and protect the public's health. Here is what some states have done to limit the spread of AIDS: in Georgia convicted prostitutes may be required to submit to tests for the HIV antibody; in Florida a prostitute with AIDS was ordered by a court to wear an electronic monitor that signaled the police if she went more than two hundred feet from her telephone; and in Texas the threat of AIDS has been invoked as a rationale for retaining the law prohibiting sodomy.

When the state's interest in promoting safety conflicts with an individual's rights to privacy and protection from discrimination, where should the line be drawn? The courts will have ample opportunity to draw that line as they attempt to balance the various interests in AIDS cases.

Nursing employees who regularly treat PWAs at San Francisco General Hospital demanded special equipment for carrying out their duties. The hospital denied their requests for gowns, masks, and gloves, and then transferred the protesting nurses to other positions. They then filed complaints with the California Health and Safety Commission, alleging multiple violations of the regulations promoting the health and safety of employees. After consideration of the complaints, the commission approved the hospital's actions and rejected the nurses' claims. In another indication that the laws on this issue will not always work exclusively for persons with AIDS, a bill was introduced in the U.S. Congress that would legally ensure the right of health care workers who treat AIDS patients at federally funded hospitals to wear the type of protective clothing demanded by the nurses at San Francisco General. A second bill provides that hospitals knowingly permitting health care personnel with AIDS to continue working will be ineligible for federal funds; since the vast majority of hospitals are heavily dependent upon Medicare and Medicaid reimbursement, this bill, if enacted, would be a strong stimulus to regularly test personnel for HIV and carefully observe those who are positive for signs of AIDS. It should be anticipated that numerous attempts will be made in the near future at all levels of government to pass laws designed to prevent the transmission of HIV and protect employees, patients, customers, and the public from being infected. Few, though, will be enacted.

Insurance

A complex, sensitive issue tied to AIDS in the workplace is insurance. Suppose an employer has a generous health insurance policy, disability insurance that pays full salary for ten weeks and half salary for twenty weeks, and a group life insurance policy with a $50,000 benefit. Typically, a PWA has medical costs and claims between $50,000 and $100,000; uses up all disability benefits because of his or her inability to work during the later stages of the syndrome; and eventually dies. The typical AIDS-infected employee would thus use to the full all forms of insurance benefits associated with his or her employment. One such employee in a small business or many in a larger one would have an adverse effect on the employer's rates, with the result that the premium would escalate or—more probable—the policies would not be renewed.

The Department of Health and Human Services estimates that the cost of treating AIDS will be $10.4 billion by 1994. Currently, the average annual cost of treatment is in excess of $75,000 when inpatient, outpatient, home care, and drug costs are totaled. The Health Insurance Association of America (HIAA) reports that a few employers have experienced medical insurance claims of $300,000–$500,000 for individual AIDS patients, and points out that since the insurance industry did not even know about AIDS until recently, revenues had not been set aside for these claims. Many insurance companies are attempting to specifically exclude from coverage medical problems related to or caused by AIDS. If employers accept these terms, probably for the purpose of retaining the remaining coverage at the same premium, PWAs will be left without insurance, and hospitals will either refuse to admit and treat them or be forced to extend uncompensated care. Another approach insurance companies utilize is to deny claims for illnesses during the early years of the policy on the ground that they are caused by a "preexisting condition."

Life insurance companies believe (probably correctly) that PWAs have purchased and will continue to purchase policies in large amounts after learning that they have the syndrome. A study disclosed that a disparate percentage of AIDS death claims were filed within two years of the issue of a policy. Specifically, 33 percent of the AIDS claims involved policies purchased within the previous two years, while only 1 percent of total claims occurred within two years of a policy's date of issue. One hundred and twenty-five of the AIDS-related policies had a death benefit of $100,000 or more, and three were in the amount of $1 million each.

Some companies require the HIV antibody test before issuing large policies. A few ask AIDS-related questions on their application forms, and, depending on the answers given, then require the antibody test before issuing the policy. Suppose an insurance company asks questions related to AIDS and requires the test only of male applicants who are unmarried and living in urban areas with significant numbers of homosexuals, such as New York, Boston, San Francisco, Los Angeles, Houston, and New Orleans? Should the company be able to use data on sexual orientation, use of drugs, living arrangements, and type of occupation in determining insurability? The National Association of Insurance Commissioners has recommended that these and related questions concerning the applicant's "sexual orientation" not be asked, but has approved inquiries regarding past diagnosis and treatment of sexually transmitted diseases. Transamerica Occidental Life Insurance Company requires HIV antibody testing for large policy applicants in selected states. Some argue that just as men and women pay different rates for the same life and health insurance because premiums are based on risk, people in high-risk AIDS groups, such as gays, should pay higher premiums than heterosexual males.

These approaches of insurance companies often fly in the face of laws, including one in California that prohibits testing for HIV antibodies unless the individual consents to the use of blood tests to determine insurability. Wisconsin has a law specifically prohibiting insurance companies from using HIV antibody test results in making decisions on policy coverage. The California Insurance Department has rejected a request by Blue Cross of California to offer group health insurance policies that would exclude coverage for AIDS and other sexually transmitted diseases. The District of Columbia Council approved a bill prohibiting insurance companies from denying coverage to people testing positive for exposure to HIV. Groups are campaigning against efforts by insurance companies to exclude coverage for AIDS-related medical problems. For example, the National Gay Rights Advocates filed a sex discrimination lawsuit against Great Republic Life Insurance Company, alleging that it denies coverage to unmarried males in certain occupations—including florist, hairdresser, and antiques dealer—and requesting damages in the amount of $10 million. The same group has sued a health maintenance organization (HMO) for allegedly refusing to accept applications from residents of San Francisco because of the higher probability of their contracting HIV.

More litigation involving insurance and AIDS is anticipated. William Horner was distressed to learn that the claim he filed for medical costs connected with his AIDS condition was rejected by his insurance company on the ground that AIDS was a "preexisting condition." Horner filed suit, alleging unlawful denial of benefits, and obtained a settlement that reinstated his medical coverage. However, he died two weeks after the settlement became final.

Another area for litigation may arise as insurance companies challenge laws that limit or prohibit them from testing applicants for HIV antibodies. The insurance industry feels that it should be able to approach AIDS in exactly the same manner as other illnesses and diseases, including requiring a medical test for its existence at the time application is made for coverage, with premiums keyed to the risk. Wisconsin, which has expressed a strong desire to protect PWAs from discrimination, considered a regulation that would permit insurers to use a series of HIV antibody tests in writing individual life, health, and accident policies. The restriction would be that the testing of applicants must include both an initial screen and a more sophisticated (and expensive) confirming test. It is expected that, after considerable debate, most states will enact regulations allowing insurance companies to test under regulated conditions. (See the section on ERISA in chapter 2.)

4

Unions, Arbitration, and Compensation

In addition to their concerns about federal and state laws, courts, and commissions, employers with employees who belong to unions should be worried about union representatives and labor arbitrators looking over their shoulders. Moreover, issues involving AIDS and both workers' and unemployment compensation are likely to surface.

Unions

Under the National Labor Relations Act, unions have a legal duty to fairly represent their members. After all, one of the primary reasons why members pay dues is for union agents to represent them against management when they need help. A member of the bargaining unit with symptomatic HIV disease or AIDS who is transferred, involuntarily placed on leave, or discharged naturally expects his or her union to speak and act for him or her. A union that fails or refuses to process a grievance by a PWA risks an unfair representation claim. Technically, the aggrieved employee member would be filing two claims in one suit: a claim against the employer for lack of just cause in taking adverse action because of AIDS, and another claim against the union for failing to vigorously argue the case. The union, as well as the employer, would be vulnerable to an award of damages including back pay, interest, and the employee's attorney's fees. An example of a complaint that could be filed in Federal District Court under Section 301 of the National Labor Relations Act against both the employer and union is found in appendix B, document 11. A sample unfair labor practice charge that would be filed by a member against his or her union with the National Labor Relations Board (NLRB) is in appendix B, document 12.

From a legal standpoint, unions have the rights to refuse to process specific grievances and to dismiss employee claims short of arbitration as long as they are not acting in an arbitrary manner. But practically speaking, it is easier and considerably less expensive for a union simply to speak up for the protesting employee, present the case to management, and if necessary to an arbitrator, and let the neutral third party decide the issue. Hence, employers with union personnel should expect arbitration on almost any issue involving involuntary action against an employee with an AIDS condition.

But unions also have a strong duty to protect the health and safety of their membership. Suppose that 90 percent of the membership signs a petition seeking union assistance in removing a PWA from the workplace. Union representatives could take a page from management's book, attempt to educate their members on how AIDS is transmitted, and point out that the risk of casual infection is near zero, but many members, swayed by their emotions, are still likely to dismiss facts and press for removal. One or more members could retain an attorney or approach the NLRB with an argument that the union is breaching its duty of fair representation. If the union represents the interests of most members of the bargaining unit and presses management to remove the afflicted employee, it and its officers are open to a legal claim by the PWA. If the union relies on factual information indicating that the employees' fears are groundless, and instead supports the right of the PWA to continue in his or her regular job, the union and its officers are vulnerable to angry members, who may withhold their dues, replace current officers at the next election, resign (in right-to-work states), or even attempt to decertify their union under NLRB procedures. In other words, unions have strong practical incentives to satisfy the majority of their members. The conflict between legal obligations and practical incentives will present many dilemmas on this issue.

What if employees walk off the job to protest a PWA being allowed to continue working? Management can be expected to contact the union officers immediately, point to the ban on strikes in the current collective bargaining agreement, and ask the union to order its members to return to work. If the union accedes to the employer's demand, members may employ some or all of the tactics described above, including attempts to replace officers or even the union. Indeed, employees may file a claim against the union, charging that it is failing to defend and support their efforts to protect their health and safety. If, on the other hand, the union supports the illegal strike—either actively or passively—it almost surely will be sued by the employer for both an injunction requiring a return to work and for damages for lost revenue due to the unauthorized shutdown. While Section 502 of the National Labor Relations Act allows individuals or employee groups to ignore no-strike clauses and walk off the job when they have a good faith belief that dangerous conditions are present in the workplace, the U.S. Supreme Court has ruled that such strikes must be supported by ascertainable, objective evidence that the conditions are abnormally dangerous. It is highly unlikely that employees concerned about fellow employees with AIDS could satisfy this standard.

The admission of AIDS patients to a nursing home in Philadelphia was substantially delayed due to protests and problems raised by the union representing the health care employees. A union official threatened to strike the home if the problems could not be resolved. Specifically, union officials sought assurance that their members would not be exposed to AIDS, and that if any of them contracted the HIV virus while caring for patients, the employer would assume full financial responsibility. The president of the local union explained that while some employees at the home did not object to caring for the AIDS patients, the majority did object. The pragmatic union officials decided to represent the majority of their constituency.

Unions, as well as employers, will have confusing issues and conflicting demands to resolve concerning AIDS. Union officials can expect claims and lawsuits from members dissatisfied with their responses or lack of responses to AIDS-related conditions and decisions.

An example of union efforts to improve infection control procedures at health care facilities is the petition filed with OSHA by the Federation of Nurses and Health Professionals requesting emergency, temporary standards to protect health care workers from AIDS and other infectious diseases. Similar petitions were filed with

OSHA by the Service Employees International Union, the National Union of Hospital and Health Care Employees, and the Hospital and Health Care Employees Union. The petitions emphasize that health care personnel are subject to a higher degree of risk of being exposed to HIV and of subsequently developing AIDS, and therefore special standards and procedures designed to protect them should be issued and enforced by OSHA. Specifically, the unions argue that exposure of health care personnel to HIV could be prevented if OSHA would issue standards requiring health care facilities to follow the infection control procedures recommended by the CDC.

Another approach for unions wishing to promote the health, safety, and protection of its members from HIV is to propose special policies and procedures for infectious diseases in general or AIDS in particular. During negotiations for a new contract, the union could demand data from the employer about rules, policies, medical records, and other information relating to the transmission of communicable diseases. Since health and safety are conditions of employment within the meaning of Section 8(d) of the National Labor Relations Act, the employer would normally be obligated to produce records that are pertinent to bargaining subjects and negotiate in good faith on union proposals for special policies, rules, or standards. For example, the union may demand medical records of employees who have an AIDS condition. The employer would probably object on the grounds of private property and employee rights to privacy and confidentiality. In at least one NLRB and court case involving a medical issue other than AIDS, the employer was ordered to turn over the requested medical data after removing names and other information that might identify specific employees.

Unions can also be expected to try to protect their members from employer efforts to infringe upon the civil liberties of employees in the name of preventing HIV transmission. Thus a union may propose a contractual provision prohibiting the employer from testing for the HIV antibodies. Or unions could object to and attempt to block employer efforts either to interrogate members about exposure to HIV or to require submission to the test. The American Federation of Government Employees filed an unsuccessful suit against the U.S. State Department and the U.S. Information Agency, challenging a policy requiring HIV antibody testing of applicants, employees, and dependents of employees.

The AFL-CIO recognized the double and sometimes conflicting obligations of unions in its Resolution No. 84, distributed to potential and actual union members: "The AFL-CIO recognizes that unions have the dual concern of seeking to protect the health and safety of workers occupationally exposed to AIDS and the rights of workers who are AIDS victims and individuals who may be at high risk."

To be sure, some unions have publicly recognized their duty to properly represent members of the bargaining unit and in other ways have expressed concern for members with AIDS. The National Treasury Employees Union issued a position paper announcing that it will "aggressively" represent members with AIDS conditions who have problems with discrimination, breach of confidentiality, and HIV antibody testing. Moreover, the union stated that it would adamantly oppose HIV antibody testing in facilities in which there was no proof of job-related hazards. Finally—and dramatically— the union informed its members that refusals to work with fellow employees based upon fear of transmission would not be viewed as protected and would not be defended by the union. Local 2, Hotel and Restaurant Employees Union (San Francisco), negotiated into its master collective bargaining agreement with hotels a clause that creates a special fund for HIV-infected union members and their families. Hotels are contractually required to contribute up to $5 per month, per employee, into the fund which will dispense money to buy drugs, provide home care, and otherwise support members of the bargaining unit who develop AIDS. Other unions have purchased and distributed informational booklets on HIV subjects and in other ways sought to educate their members.

Labor Arbitration

Assume that an employee at a union facility is transferred to either another job or to an isolated area of the facility, placed on involuntary leave of absence, or terminated. Understandably upset, the employee can trigger a legal process against his or her employer without calling a lawyer or spending a penny. All he or she has to do is file a grievance. The employee's union, rather than risk his or her wrath and a possible claim for failing to prosecute, will almost certainly process the grievance to arbitration.

Thus far, very few arbitration awards have involved AIDS in the workplace. United Airlines decided to place a flight attendant afflicted with AIDS on an unpaid leave of absence. The male attendant, who wanted to continue working, filed a grievance protesting the action with his union, which took the issue to arbitration. The company argued that the health and safety of passengers and other employees justified its decision, but the arbitrator disagreed, ruling that United had violated its collective bargaining agreement and that the attendant must be given back pay for all the work days he had missed. However, the arbitrator extended partial credence to United's position in concluding that the attendant was not eligible for reinstatement until he successfully completed a physical examination given by a qualified doctor.

In another case, the arbitrator expressed concern that a nursing home employee grievant with AIDS might transmit the virus to others and criticized CDC guidelines as inadequate. He ruled that the proper course of action was to place the infected employee on medical leave of absence until it expired, and then on suspension until he no longer had a communicable disease. The arbitrator acknowledged that he was, in effect, prohibiting the grievant from returning to work, but he also nullified the previous decision to discharge the employee and reinstated his insurance and other benefits.

A nursing home discharged an HIV-positive employee, pursuant to its policy for controlling communicable diseases. The union argued that CDC infection control guidelines protected the patients and the grievant should be reinstated. The arbitrator, however, agreed with the employer that CDC guidelines were insufficient and that its own policy drafted pursuant to state laws for nursing homes was appropriate. The arbitrator then ruled that the HIV-positive employee should be suspended (not terminated) and that the employer should pay his medical bills (*In re Nursing Home*, 88 LA 681, 1987).

A machine operator admitted he was incapable of performing his regular duties, which included standing and occasional lifting. The union's physician declared that he could "do any type of job except those requiring lifting or prolonged standing." The company replied that no such jobs were available and urged the grievant to seek treatment and file for disability. Two weeks later the grievant gave the company a note from another doctor that lifted all activity restrictions; it was, however, disregarded because the company questioned its authenticity. The grievant was not allowed to return to his job. A week later the union's doctor reported that the grievant had AIDS. Thereafter he was terminated. The grievant never filed for disability pay because he did not think he was eligible, and he was concerned that such a claim would damage his chances for reinstatement. He did, however, file a grievance that was processed to arbitration. After finding the above facts, the arbitrator upheld the grievance, set aside the discharge, and placed the employee on leave of absence for these reasons: (1) grievant's admitted inability to perform the full range of his duties could not constitute just cause for summary discharge that day since there was a possibility of recovery; (2) the company erred in not verifying the doctor's note lifting activity restrictions; and (3) the union doctor's report that the grievant had AIDS did not address his ability to perform the duties of his job. The arbitrator held that if the grievant were capable of doing his job, he should be permitted to return provided that reinstatement posed no additional health threat to the grievant or to his co-workers. The health issue must be resolved by a medical AIDS specialist. The discharge was then converted to an involuntary medical leave of absence, and the grievant was given back pay (*In re The Bucklers, Inc. v. Local 517-S, Production Services and Sales District Council, AFL-CIO, 90 LA 937, 1987*).

Numerous cases involving involuntary, adverse treatment of employees with an AIDS condition will be presented to arbitrators in the future and it is anticipated that they will follow this approach:

1. The overall question is whether the employer had *just cause* to treat the employee as it did. Almost all collective bargaining agreements expressly provide that the employer must have just cause to support disciplinary action against a member of the bargaining unit. Arbitrators are certain to imply a just cause standard if a contract lacks one. If there are special contractual clauses or policies on the topics (transfers, demotions, or leaves of absence, for example), then the issue might well be confined to whether the contract was violated. The distinction between a just cause discipline case and a dispute over the interpretation of contractual language is important because the burden of proof is on the employer in the

former case and on the union in the latter. It is anticipated that most arbitrators will place the burden of persuasion on the employer to justify its action in AIDS cases.

2. What is the specific evidence regarding the employee's medical condition? Is he or she simply positive for antibodies to HIV but mentally alert and physically fit? Or is he or she suffering from dementia? Perhaps a serious physical ailment has disabled the employee. If there is an impairment, is it temporary or permanent? Is the employee presently physically and mentally capable of performing the specific duties of his or her job? Did the employee present a doctor's letter confirming this fitness? Was there medical testimony or evidence about the employee's condition? What objective evidence does the company have that the employee could not satisfactorily perform his or her duties? (The opinions of managers are virtually worthless, but job descriptions and testimony by managers on what duties are essential and which are incidental will be of high value).

3. Would there have been a medically documented danger to employees, customers, or patients if the employee had been allowed to continue working in his or her regular position? What objective evidence of the health and safety danger does the employer possess? (Again, documentation and the evaluations of experts are far superior to the subjective opinions of managers.)

4. What was the grievant's length of service? The longer the length of service, the more sympathetic to the grievant the arbitrator will be.

5. What is the past work record of the grievant? The better the work record, the more likely that the arbitrator will be supportive of the grievant. On the other hand, if the employer can show numerous writeups, perhaps a disciplinary suspension, and extensive absenteeism or tardiness prior to the grievant's AIDS illness, the employer's position is slightly bolstered.

6. How have other employees in similar but non-HIV situations been treated? Has a published rule or policy been violated? If so, has it been applied uniformly? If it is clear, for example, that the grievant violated the "no fault" attendance policy, and all others with the same absenteeism record were discharged in the past, the employer's position is strong.

In almost all cases involving involuntary action against an employee with symptomatic HIV disease or AIDS, the employer will carry a heavy burden of proving that its decision to transfer, place on leave, or terminate was justified by legitimate business considerations. The arbitrator's sympathy will be with the grievant, and absent compelling, objective evidence of the physical incapacity of the PWA or risk of infection to others, the grievance will likely be sustained.

It should be noted that unions do not represent either applicants or newly hired employees still in their probationary period. In fact, most collective bargaining agreements specifically state that probationary employees may be discharged without regard to the grievance and arbitration provisions of the collective bargaining agreement. Thus, a union employer's decision not to hire an applicant with HIV or to fire an employee who has not completed the probationary period and who has developed AIDS could not be grieved or reviewed by an arbitrator. However, as I previously noted, that person probably has other available forums.

The grievance and arbitration processes are not limited to employees with AIDS conditions. Instead, other employees—upset with having to work alongside, serve, treat, or otherwise have contact with people who may be contagious—will be voicing their displeasure by pressuring employers to protect them from contracting HIV. Union employers will frequently find themselves attempting to explain to bargaining unit members that under federal and state law the employer was obligated to reasonably accommodate the PWA and allow him or her to continue working side by side with them. Some employees may reject the explanation, protest (refuse to work), be discharged, and then request their union to accept and process their grievances. An example of this type of claim occurred with *AFSCM v. The State of Minnesota*, an arbitration case involving the discharge of a prison guard who refused to carry out his regular duty of "pat searching" an inmate with a confirmed case of AIDS. The grievant guard persisted in his refusal after consultations with several superiors and attendance at an educational session, during which a prison nurse told the guards that HIV cannot be contracted through casual contact. Eventually, he was terminated, whereupon he filed a grievance, and the case was presented to an arbitrator. The guard explained his refusal by testifying that he was "scared to death" of becoming infected, despite the nurse's explanation. Showing sympathy for the guard's sincere—but incorrect—concerns for his health, the arbitrator ordered that the guard be reinstated without back pay. Thus, an employer that provided education for its employees, rejected the hysterical and factually unfounded claims of an insubordinate employee, and gave the employee numerous opportunities to change his mind, had its decision reversed by an impartial third party!

In an unusual case, an insurance salesman had an employment contract with his employer that provided arbitration as a means of resolving certain disputes. After he contracted AIDS he was discharged. The company said that its decision to discharge the salesman was based on nonperformance, while the salesman claimed that the reason assigned was a pretext and that the decision was truly motivated by his AIDS condition. While the matter was pending, the salesman died. After hearing evidence from both sides, the arbitrator awarded over $16,000 to the estate, representing the salesman's back pay from the date of his discharge until his death.

Workers' Compensation

Every state has a law granting special compensation to employees who miss work due to injuries or illnesses contracted on the job. These laws also impose upon employers a general obligation to protect employees from hazards or unsafe conditions in the workplace. What if an employee files a workers' compensation claim, alleging that he contracted HIV from an employee, patient, or customer in the workplace? Suppose a group of employees required to work in the same department as a PWA file a claim requesting the state's department of labor to order the employer to take special precautions to prevent the spread of the virus?

With respect to the former case, the employee should be eligible *if* he or she can prove that he or she was exposed to and infected by HIV at the workplace. The obligation should be on the afflicted employee to establish a causative link between the job and the virus. A worker in California filed a claim against his construction company, alleging that he contracted symptomatic HIV disease while in a hospital because of a work-related injury. The connection between the employee's work on a construction site and the AIDS condition may seem strained to some, but it is nowhere near as tenuous as the relationship between work and AIDS raised in the Morrison Knudsen case. An employee of Morrison Knudson was not allowed to take his family with him while on duty in Zaire. After contracting HIV, apparently from prostitutes in Africa, he filed a workers' compensation claim. A hearing officer in California ruled that the company condoned sexual encounters with prostitutes by barring spouses from accompanying work crews, concluded that AIDS was a job-related "injury" in this situation, and awarded the employee disability in the amount of $197.12 per week.

Other kinds of possible claims by employees who contract HIV could be made. While workers' compensation is generally inapplicable to preexisting conditions, a claimant may argue that a particular condition was aggravated during employment. For example, suppose that Harry develops AIDS while working at ABC Company. After extensive absences, he is fired. Then he applies for a job at Baptist Hospital and is hired. With an impaired system of immunity, Harry is highly vulnerable to diseases. Soon Harry comes down with pneumonia and files a compensation claim against Baptist. The hospital's defense would be that AIDS was a preexisting condition, and that Harry's claim should therefore be dismissed. However, as real cases I have already discussed indicate, the judge may find a way to award compensation to Harry, perhaps by ruling that the condition was "aggravated" at Baptist. Actually, the hospital may be fortunate that Harry filed a workers' compensation claim instead of a lawsuit in tort alleging (1) failure to test for or inquire about HIV; (2) violation of the hospital's duty to inform him that infections abound in the hospital; and (3) negligent hiring. The potential monetary recovery is much higher in tort than in workers' compensation cases. Since workers' compensation is the *exclusive* remedy for work-related injuries, the hospital may not contest the coverage in these circumstances.

A nurse in San Francisco filed a claim alleging that her ulcer was caused by stress from worry that she would contract AIDS from the patients for whom she was caring. The hospital acknowledged that she was temporarily disabled by stress due to working with AIDS patients, and the claim was settled for $5,000.

These and related issues under these statutes are bound to be litigated.

Unemployment Compensation

To extend monetary protection to people who are deprived of their jobs, every state has procedures for unemployment compensation. Those who lose their jobs because a plant is shut down, or a department is eliminated, or a general layoff takes place, are obviously eligible to file for and receive unemployment money. Almost all states, however, take the position that employees who are terminated for misconduct, who voluntarily leave their employer, or who are physically or mentally incapable of performing the duties of the job are ineligible for this compensation.

PWAs who are forced by illness to quit work may be eligible for medical compensation under their employer's disability or medical policies, but they ordinarily would be ineligible for unemployment compensation because of their inability to perform the duties of their position. If the PWA is physically and mentally able to perform the duties of his or her job at the time of discharge, he or she may be ruled ineligible for unemployment benefits because he or she voluntarily resigned. Of course, sympathy for the PWA may motivate the referee or commission to award the compensation. Consider the case of a healthy, capable partner of a homosexual PWA who voluntarily quit his job for the purpose of caring for his dying partner. Should that employee be eligible for unemployment compensation? The California Unemployment Insurance Appeals Board ruled in the affirmative from its Office of Appeals in San Francisco, concluding that the claimant left his job "with good cause" and therefore compensation must be paid.

5

Testing for HIV

No labor relations issue is currently more controversial than employment testing, including drug, alcohol, performance, stress evaluation, and so-called honesty tests. Criticism and scrutiny have caused Congress to virtually outlaw polygraph tests and have stimulated applicants and employees who fail the wide array of tests employers now require to consider legal challenges. Of the available tests, none stimulates more intense debate than the screens for HIV.

All agree that testing for HIV antibodies is valuable for identifying contaminated blood, preventing it from getting into community blood supplies, and enhancing the safety of transfusions. Recognizing that the same test can be utilized to identify *people* who are carrying the virus, the U.S. Public Health Service has recommended that all persons in high-risk groups undergo periodic testing for the purpose of counseling those with positive results to reduce the spread of HIV to others, particularly sexual or needle partners. The federal government's definition of "high risk" includes homosexual and bisexual men and IV drug users. Several doctors have advocated widespread testing for the purposes of learning who is infected and providing them with counseling and treatment. General acceptance of HIV antibody testing as part of routine health care would certainly benefit public health. Because the incidence of HIV among young adults who contract it through heterosexual sex is rising dramatically, the U.S. surgeon general has suggested voluntary mass screening at all major universities. Some states anonymously test all newly born babies for HIV antibodies to determine the extent of exposure to the virus. Health care officials are concerned that a significant portion of the semen donated to sperm banks is not tested for HIV. Obviously, testing can be a valuable weapon in our nation's war against AIDS.

The true controversy concerns testing by employers to screen job applicants and employees for the virus. The U.S. Department of Health and Human Services has announced that there is no need for routine HIV testing. The CDC says that employment testing is unwarranted because HIV is not transmissible in the workplace, and argues that such testing would discourage people from seeking counseling and testing and thus thwart efforts to fight the disease. The U.S. surgeon general has said that mandatory testing is unwise, because the people who most need treatment would avoid the test. A congress of scientists, epidemiologists, and civil libertarians met and labeled required testing impractical and an invasion of privacy. Civil rights and gay rights organizations are highly critical of testing applicants or employees for HIV under any circumstances.

A few local jurisdictions have proscribed AIDS testing in employment on the grounds that it invades the privacy of applicants and employees and leads to discrimination. However, several employers—both public and private—have adopted mandatory testing for HIV in some capacity. The Pentagon tests recruits for all the armed services, and any with confirmed positive readings are rejected. Further, the army, navy, air force, and marines have a program for mandatorily testing all 2.1 million current military personnel; those having positive results are referred to medical treatment or to limited service and medical observation programs, depending on the circumstances. Millions of men and women have been screened for HIV by the military thus far, with millions more to be tested in the future. (Interestingly, the rate of HIV infection in the military is lower than that in the general population.) The U.S. State Department tests foreign service applicants, employees, and their families for the virus.* Positive applicants are rejected, while employees and their dependents who are carrying HIV are

---

*Local 1812, American Federation of Government Employees, filed suit on behalf of their affected members, challenging this new testing policy, alleging that it violates the Constitution, the Administrative Procedure Act, the Privacy Act of 1974, the Vocational Rehabilitation Act of 1974, and the Foreign Relations Act of 1980. However, the suit was dismissed and the right of the State Department to ascertain fitness for duty was upheld.

restricted from working abroad. Applicants for the federal Job Corps program are also being tested. In the private sector, only a few employers are utilizing mandatory testing in selected situations.

According to a poll, the public enthusiastically endorses employment testing for AIDS: 87 percent believe that high-risk groups should be tested, 71 percent think that it is a good practice for sensitive jobs, such as health care workers, and an astounding 52 percent agree that *everyone* should be tested. Another poll concluded that people believe that all patients who enter a hospital (74 percent), all job applicants (37 percent), and all employees in all industries (34 percent) should be tested. A third poll found that 42 percent of the public was in favor of testing job applicants for HIV. Thus, while there are some exceptions, the battle line has been drawn, with public health officials and gay and civil rights organizations on one side, and the public on the other. According to a survey, less than 3 percent of employers utilize HIV testing in any fashion. The vast majority of employers have not embraced HIV antibody testing because (1) it can cause legal problems, (2) it is costly, and (3) often it is preferable for a variety of reasons, not to know that any applicant or employee is infected with HIV.

Types of Tests

There are various types of HIV tests. Testing for HIV is never easy and can be unreliable. Unlike the urinalysis screen for drugs, AIDS testing is an invasive procedure, relying upon a sample of blood drawn from the person. The most popular test thus far is enzyme-linked immunosorbent assay (ELISA), which detects antibodies produced after HIV is transmitted. However, ELISA, which was developed to screen blood donors, is quite sensitive and has been heavily criticized for inaccurate readings. ELISA should be regarded as simply a preliminary test with an unacceptable percentage of false positives, that is, the result is positive but the person does not actually have the antibody. A positive result from ELISA or similar tests must be subjected to confirmation by a more sophisticated test, usually the Western Blot. Only when a reliable test like the Western Blot produces a positive result should a decision be made that affects the employment of the person being tested. Determinations of whether an applicant should be rejected or an employee transferred cannot and should not be made on the sole basis of preliminary test results.

All HIV tests are based on a simple idea: a substance known to attract and bond with HIV antibodies is added to a blood sample. Confirmation of this occurrence during a laboratory examination of the blood sample yields the conclusion that the person being tested has developed antibodies to and is therefore carrying HIV.

I need to strongly emphasize that no currently available test identifies AIDS, or even HIV. Tests can only establish whether the person tested has developed antibodies to HIV. The blood of a person who has recently contracted the virus but has not yet manufactured antibodies would produce a negative result. Typically, there is a four-week or longer hiatus between developing the virus and manufacturing enough antibodies that can be detected. Thus false negatives, in which a person tests negative but is actually carrying HIV, are more than a possibility.

No AIDS test, including the Western Blot, can predict whether a person testing positive will ever develop symptomatic HIV disease or AIDS. It is quite probable that an applicant or employee with a confirmed positive result does not have AIDS, will not develop symptoms within the next five years, and is currently without any type of impairment. However, a person with HIV is infectious, and will remain infectious with the virus until he or she dies.

While a few localities have enacted laws to prohibit testing in the workplace, cost is a more persuasive deterrent for public and private employers. ELISA, the preliminary search for HIV, has an average cost of $70.00 per person. Since the number of false positives with ELISA is unacceptable, a second ELISA test should be administered if the first is positive. Those who also fail the second should be administered a third, confirming test—usually the Western Blot, which costs around $90.00. Finally, those with repeated positive results should be subjected to a clinical examination, usually consisting of skin tests and cell analysis in a hospital. Obviously, this procedure is much more expensive, and the total cost for complete testing of those with positive results can be very high. However, the overwhelming majority of tested applicants and employees are negative on ELISA. The extra costs are only incurred for the small number of people who test positive with that screening device. The small but growing number of employers who utilize ELISA and like tests believe that their costs are a small price to pay to secure knowledge of HIV status.

Arguments Pro and Con

The arguments in favor of and against HIV testing are frequently emotional, subjective, and polemic. At one end of the spectrum, a law professor at the University of Nebraska favors mandatory HIV testing for the entire population of the United States as the first step toward stopping the spread of AIDS. At the other end of the spectrum, the American Medical Association opposes any form of mandatory testing, stating that "The best evidence available indicates that mandatory testing would be counterproductive because of the possibilities of false positives and breaches of confidentiality." An organization staking out part of the vast territory between those extremes is the American Nurses' Association, which "opposes the routine serologic screening of health care workers for the HIV antibody," but which supports employer testing "to document on-the-job exposure to HIV after an occupational accident." The National Education Association first approved and then voted to oppose mandatory testing of teachers for HIV. The president of the Association of Life Insurance Medical Directors says life insurance companies should be able to test all applicants because of the drop in life expectancy for those who test positive and to prevent discrimination against all homosexuals.

Gay and civil rights groups urge a ban on testing in the workplace. They fear that identified carriers will not be hired, or will be fired, blacklisted, branded unemployable or uninsurable, and possibly quarantined. They argue that thousands of carriers who are presently without physical or mental impairment and may never develop symptomatic HIV disease or AIDS will be discriminated against, without valid reason. A representative of the Lambda Legal Defense Fund has said, "AIDS is not airborne. It is not waterborne. It's not foodborne. People who wish to protect themselves can do so if they have the correct information." On the other side of the fence, William F. Buckley has advocated a compulsory form of marking to identify all AIDS carriers: "Everyone with AIDS should be tattooed in the upper forearm to protect common-needle users, and on the buttocks, to prevent victimization of other homosexuals."

As I previously noted, the tests can identify carriers. Without a test, a person could work as a nurse, laboratory technician, or surgeon for years without symptoms of medical problems and without knowing he or she possessed the potential for infecting people. These carriers could have multiple sex partners, transmitting the virus to many others who, in turn, infect still others, all the while ignorant of their condition. Women could become pregnant and not realize they had HIV until their babies develop AIDS.

There is little agreement and some indecisiveness on what testing, if any, should be done. William Masters, well-known researcher on human sexuality, and presidents Reagan and Bush are among those arguing that the test should be a requirement before a marriage license can be issued. However, Illinois and Louisiana enacted such legislation, found it to be quite costly in relation to the few positive results obtained, and then dropped the marital test. The surgeon general advocates that women contemplating pregnancy be tested because scientists estimate the probability that an infected mother will transmit the infection to her child is between 20 and 30 percent. Pediatricians who have unsuccessfully treated babies and children born with HIV, and helplessly watched them die, have strongly encouraged that women be tested for exposure to the virus before becoming pregnant. The CDC first proposed mandatory testing for all persons applying for a marriage license, seeking admission to a hospital, or being treated at a venereal disease or drug-withdrawal clinic. However, after a conference and debate among various health officials, the proposal was withdrawn. Various hospital associations support the medical consensus against mandatory testing, but encourage voluntary testing. Georgia's proposal for mandatory testing of all convicted prostitutes was challenged as unconstitutional by the ACLU.

The problems most frequently raised by critics of testing are lack of validity and improper procedures. Hospitals, doctors, and nurses have acknowledged testing routinely extracted blood for HIV antibodies without the consent of the patient—informed or otherwise. At times positive results have been reported to the individual in a formal written report or a terse telephone message, without the benefit of counseling. Laboratories have been accused of inaccuracy and sloppy practices. A study at a medical center revealed that almost 90 percent of the tests for HIV were performed without the consent of those tested or acceptable reasons.

A college student in Michigan secured a test for HIV antibodies after his homosexual partner admitted to promiscuity. The result was reported as positive. The young man then dropped out of school, abandoned his career, and became depressed. Two years later he was tested again, this time with negative results. The original sample was then retested, and this time it too was negative. The state health department, which acknowledged mixing up the tests, was then sued by the man. In another case an Indiana woman was tested for HIV after failing to respond to medical treatment. After the initial screen was labeled positive, a confirming test on the same sample was performed, which also was positive. The woman's boyfriend left her, friends shunned her, she was evicted from her trailer, and she planned her funeral. Thirteen months later another blood sample taken in connection with her continuing medical problems tested negative for HIV antibodies. This prompted a retest of the first sample, which was also negative. A legal claim was then filed. A laboratory in Ohio had mixed up tests with the result that a Vietnam veteran was erroneously informed that he was HIV positive. His fiancée broke off their engagement and he contemplated suicide before the lab discovered—twelve days later—that it had mistakenly given him the same code number as another patient.

The issue of testing without consent has also surfaced in the courtroom. A Seattle man applied for life insurance and signed a *general* blood test authorization form that included no reference to AIDS or HIV. When the company informed him the test for HIV antibodies was positive, he became angry and sued, claiming damages because the test had been conducted without his permission. A Pennsylvania court ruled that a doctor did not illegally invade the privacy of a couple by screening their blood for HIV because the engaged male and female had executed a *general* consent form relating to blood tests.

To be fair, the questions of test validity and integrity should not be resolved without consideration of the fact that most testing follows proper chain-of-custody procedures and is accurate. Researchers at Walter Reed Army Institute studied 135,187 HIV antibodies tests that had been performed on military personnel and concluded that there was only one false positive.*

Prior to examining the specific pros and cons concerning testing, consider what is virtually undisputed:

1. All persons donating blood *must* be screened for HIV antibodies. Those with positive results should be rejected as donors. (Currently only 1 in 10,000 donors is testing positive; donors were not tested for the virus prior to April 1985.)
2. All women contemplating pregnancy should be encouraged to be tested.
3. Persons worried that they may have contracted HIV from a sexual or drug experience or a blood transfusion prior to 1985 should be encouraged to submit to the blood test and they should encourage their partners to do the same.
4. Health care workers or others exposed to contaminated blood or semen through an accident such as a needle stick or blood splash should be encouraged to report the incident and voluntarily submit to the test.
5. The present ELISA test occasionally has false positives, and no decision or action should be made or taken with a positive result until a confirmation is secured from the Western Blot.
6. Since there is a time gap between exposure to HIV and the production of antibodies, those who test negative after possible infection with HIV should be retested at monthly intervals for at least twelve months following the initial test.
7. The test results should be treated with the utmost confidentiality—access must be severely restricted.
8. It is desirable to have numerous, reputable places for people who wish voluntary testing, which should be accessible and inexpensive; the government should subsidize the cost and consider making it free of charge for the purpose of encouraging testing on a voluntary basis; finally, anonymous tests should be widely available for those concerned about breaches of confidentiality.

---

*While critics and studies of these tests tend to focus on false positives, what about the incidence of false negatives? If the initial screen indicates negative for a person who is actually positive, the confirming test is not performed and the individual continues living with the incorrect belief that he or she is HIV-free.

There are arguments that hospitals and clinics should test all new patients, schools all students, and employers all applicants and employees. Most of them, social in nature, concern prevention and treatment of this fatal virus. I will now briefly review the major arguments in favor of mandatory testing:

1. Testing can be of enormous help in *preventing* the transmission of HIV and reducing the predicted numbers of people who will be afflicted. If a carrier is not tested he or she may infect hundreds of others through sex and IV drug use without realizing it. Those identified as positive can be given immediate counseling and advice on the critical need for responsible behavior. Their cooperation can be solicited in tracing other possible victims.* Spouses and lovers of those who test positive have a right to know the truth about their own possible danger. Hospital workers who treat people in the emergency room, frequently coming into contact with their patients' blood, would greatly appreciate knowing whether the patients are infectious. Studies suggest that significant numbers of homosexual males almost immediately curtailed sexually promiscuous behavior upon learning detailed data on the transmission of HIV. Accordingly, the virus in homosexual communities has been dramatically reduced in several large cities. Learning that one is infectious would hopefully increase the use of condoms, which in turn would stem the spread of the deadly virus. Widespread testing in various situations would also help researchers determine the extent to which HIV is spreading into groups other than homosexuals and IV drug users, and would allow the focus to be on the virus and its cause, instead of on AIDS, the syndrome which frequently does not develop for five or more years. Hence, testing of all applicants or newly hired employees during physical examinations would be helpful to the individuals, their families, and the communities in which they live. For the same reasons, mandatory testing of all newly admitted patients to hospitals and clinics would be a public service.

*The Heterosexual Contact Tracing Program in San Francisco has identified hundreds of people who had sexual relations with those infected by HIV. Those notified are given the opportunity to be tested. The organization uses the same approaches for tracing and identifying that are utilized with other sexually transmitted diseases. The names of all contacts are kept confidential. Tracing is not considered feasible for male homosexuals because so many have had numerous partners.

2. Testing opens the door to *treatment*. Several drugs seem to be effective in slowing the destruction of the immune system, and certain drugs can be administered that reduce the chances of opportunistic infections ravaging the body. This extends the hiatus between contraction of HIV and development of symptomatic HIV disease or AIDS—a worthy achievement. None of this can be done unless the person and his physician have knowledge of HIV.

3. The individual with symptomatic HIV disease or AIDS is provided with *knowledge* that is valuable in planning the remainder of his or her life. If the individual is simply positive for HIV, he or she may want to continue with his or her job and life-style but secure frequent medical evaluations. If the individual has symptoms, he or she may decide to check into a clinic that does substantial work on AIDS-related problems and benefit from the best, most up-to-date treatment. If the individual has full-blown AIDS in an advanced stage, he or she may elect to go home for a reunion with his or her family. Or he or she may not do any of these things—the individual would be free to decide. But without the test, the individual lacks the opportunity to make these critical decisions until his or her secondary illness is so advanced that he or she sees a doctor and AIDS is finally diagnosed.

4. With the resurgence of tuberculosis (caused by an airborne agent) HIV-positive persons with weakened immune systems should know their status so they can avoid places where tuberculosis is frequently transmitted (hospitals, clinics, prisons).

5. There is *precedent* for mandatory testing. History establishes that when epidemics such as syphilis and tuberculosis strike, testing has been heavily utilized, especially before a cure is found. Today donated blood and organs, of course, are carefully screened for various infections, including the HIV virus. Also, since AIDS is a sexually transmitted syndrome, why not utilize the same medical and legal measures that have been effective for gonorrhea and syphilis?

6. The cost is dropping as testing becomes more extensive. Mandatory testing is usually not desirable for employers in the narrow sense. But viewed broadly, testing can lead to prevention and treatment as indicated above and thus benefit the community.

Opponents of mandatory testing vigorously argue that:

1. It violates an individual's right to privacy. Some people who

are at risk or who have been exposed wish to be tested and others do not. A few who have been tested decide not to pick up the results because they do not want to know. These are *individual* choices that should not be interfered with by an employer insisting, as a condition of employment, that an applicant or employee be tested and sharing knowledge of the result with managers, their secretaries, and God knows who else. The concern about confidentiality and the discrimination and other adverse ramifications that often follow breach of confidentiality are strong arguments, standing alone, against any type of mandatory testing.

2. It is violative of the Fourth Amendment's right to be free of unreasonable search and seizure. (This principle is especially effective for governmental employers.)

3. It does not determine whether the person has or ever will have AIDS; all it does is identify HIV-positive people who may never develop AIDS.

4. The tests are sometimes inaccurate: there are both false positives *and* false negatives. Further, they show negative for a recently infected individual who has not yet produced antibodies.

5. Since as of yet there is no cure or vaccine, the test is useless. Regardless of whether the result is positive or negative, there is nothing useful or significant that has been accomplished or can be done. (Until effective treatment of syphilis became available, for example, mandatory testing was not helpful.)

6. It is impractical. Mandatory testing of large groups of people would be too expensive, difficult, and time consuming.

7. Persons identified as positive may have extremely unhealthy psychological reactions to that news, including depression and contemplation of suicide. Thus, the test has social and psychological ramifications, as well as medical and legal ones.

8. Mandatory testing would require identification of those who are positive and keeping a record of their location. It may motivate tracing of past sex and drug partners. In these circumstances, the concept of confidentiality could easily be compromised with the result that HIV-positive people would be branded, discriminated against, and possibly quarantined. The discrimination could involve housing, insurance, and employment. Thus, people with the HIV virus who are very healthy and may

never develop AIDS could be the victims of unfair and discriminatory treatment.*

9. Fearful of discrimination and harassment in the event of a positive result, homosexuals and drug abusers—the very people who could benefit the most from testing, counseling, and treatment—would find ways to avoid the tests.

10. Employers are better off not knowing the HIV status of their applicants and employees. Those who are positive are protected from discrimination by federal and state handicap laws. So employees generally cannot take action based on the knowledge, assuming they had a mind to. Knowledge may prompt a duty to disclose the condition to family members, fellow employees, or patients which, if accomplished, could cause a breach of confidentiality suit by the HIV-positive employee. When viewed strictly from the employer's perspective, there are major disadvantages to that knowledge.

11. Employers which hire substantial numbers of employees would find the testing policy to be costly.

12. Testing will divide our society into two groups—those positive and those negative—with conflict and antipathy between the two developing to a greater degree every year.

One Company's Testing Policy

A company based in Dallas that is heavily involved in oil and gas, began testing its food service applicants and employees. The twenty-person employee unit in question serves food to an oil and gas workforce of over one thousand. All applicants were required to take screening tests, and any who turned up positive were not hired as food service workers. "We're not going to hire someone as a food service worker who has any infectious disease, not just AIDS."

*Both Roy Cohn and Liberace wished to die without their AIDS condition becoming known, but their HIV status was publicly reported. The breaches of confidentiality in their situations seriously concern opponents of mandatory testing. A confidential list containing the names of five hundred people who were tested for AIDS was reported missing from a health clinic in Washington, D.C., leading to speculation of theft, blackmail, breach of confidentiality, and discrimination.

Employees with positive test results were referred for medical assistance, but not fired. A series of three tests were administered to detect communicable diseases, including AIDS. The same procedures were followed regardless of whether the identified condition was AIDS, hepatitis, tuberculosis, kidney ailments, or parasites. The overall goal was to protect the people being served. In response to company policies like this one, a representative of the CDC reiterated that office's position that there is "no evidence that AIDS is spread through food." Criticism from several quarters and the probability of handicap discrimination claims prompted the company eventually to drop its HIV testing policy.

Few companies have implemented a testing policy. There are simply too many pitfalls, practical and legal. Any action adverse to the interests of the applicant or employee taken by the employer after learning of a positive result is likely to cause a valid claim of handicap discrimination. Knowledge by an employer that a particular employee on its payroll is HIV positive can present difficult situations. Surveys show that employees, customers, and patients want to know if a person with whom they have contact has HIV and would be angry if the employer knew but did not inform them. Employers that decide to determine the HIV status of their applicants and employees should have a clearly legitimate objective that overrides the numerous disadvantages. Moreover, any employer making the decision to test should treat the results as extremely confidential; discuss both medical and employment considerations with those who test positive in a sensitive and caring manner; provide counseling; and make a definite, sincere effort to accommodate those with the virus, taking into consideration the marked distinctions among those who have the virus, symptomatic HIV disease, and AIDS.

How to Implement Testing policies

Most employers will not use HIV antibody testing because, for their particular operations, it is unnecessary, expensive, and likely to produce more problems than it solves. For employees who do decide to adopt testing, consider this advice.

With respect to applicants, explain to them most clearly that a test for HIV antibodies will be done as part of their preemployment physical examination. Require them to execute a simple "consent form" giving the employer or its agent the right to conduct the test. Such a form signed either by an applicant or by a newly hired employee recognizes the right of the employer to require HIV testing during his or her employment, and pledges the individual to co-operate upon penalty of discharge. (See the sample consent form in appendix D, document 8.)

There should be a hiatus of several weeks between the announcement of a new HIV testing program to employees and its implementation. A significant number of employees may resent the idea of the testing policy and resist it, especially if it involves random tests. Ample opportunity for questions, comments, and discussion should be afforded employees before they are required to give blood to be tested for antibodies to HIV.

Serious employee relations problems can emanate from implementation of mandatory testing. It is significantly less troublesome to adopt testing for applicants than for employees. Also, testing employees only after an accidental exposure to infected blood or upon reasonable cause to believe the employee is HIV positive would be less likely to offend personnel. Random testing of employees is especially sensitive from an employee relations perspective.

It must be remembered that blood testing is an invasive procedure. To protect against lawsuits alleging a battery or other tort, it is important to secure a release executed by the person, waiving all rights to sue, *before* the test is administered. If an applicant refuses to sign, he is not considered for employment. If an employee refuses to execute, he should be reminded of the message previously given to him that submitting to the test is a *condition* of his employment. Any who continue to refuse should be discharged for violation of the employer's policies.

Conclusions

Many states have laws requiring hospitals and doctors to report to the state board of health the names and addresses of all individuals who test positive for the HIV virus. This is a reflection of the threat of AIDS to the health of the general public. A few states prohibit employers from testing, reflecting concerns about confidentiality and privacy.

Numerous people and groups have a legitimate interest in knowing whether any person is HIV positive: the individual himself, anyone with whom he or she has a sexual experience or shares a needle, the individual's family, and, not incidentally, the employer, potential or actual. Identification will not necessarily lead to discrimination, but it can and should stimulate education, counseling, and prevention. Legislatures and courts should recognize the important distinction between securing data and using it. Determining whether a potential or actual employee has the virus can be a valid exercise; it is what the employer does with that determination that should be scrutinized and regulated. For example, hospitals having knowledge of a positive HIV test result could decide more effectively about the placement of an applicant or employee. Often the person with an AIDS condition may agree that a nursing job at the ward desk instead of in the emergency room would be more appropriate.

Testing can be a valuable tool for identifying carriers, leading to treatment and counseling, and making more intelligent and effective decisions regarding their status. Numerous categories of people should be tested as a matter of course: prostitutes and drug users convicted of crimes (the test result would be provided to the judge prior to sentencing); individuals seeking treatment at clinics for sexually transmitted diseases; and prisoners convicted of sex crimes, both before entry into prison and prior to their release, come immediately to mind.

Since the legal validity of mandatory testing is uncertain at best, there should be immediate and extensive encouragement of voluntary testing. Centers for testing that are administered or subsidized by the government should be established and publicized in all major cities. Because of the genuine concern for confidentiality, procedures for anonymous testing should be set up. Counselors should be trained and dispatched to the testing centers to advise those who test positive. With a syndrome that has killed thousands, threatened millions, and frightened everyone, testing should be viewed as a small, positive step toward identifying those who have the potential for developing AIDS, giving them an opportunity to receive appropriate medical evaluations and treatment, and counseling them to abstain from conduct that would spread the deadly virus.

AIDS and Health Care

Conflicting Interests of Employer,
Employee, and Patient

In excess of one million Americans are currently infected with HIV. Another million are likely to become infected in the next few years. During this decade the majority of these people will become ill and enter hospitals. Still others will apply for admission to nursing homes. These admissions and their inherent legal and moral issues will, almost inevitably, stimulate new legislation, spawn lawsuits, and raise intractable problems.

Financial Factors

A practical question that will have to be faced is how hospitals and nursing homes will be able to absorb the huge influx of patients afflicted with AIDS-related medical conditions. Hospitals in urban areas with significant HIV populations, such as San Francisco and New York, can expect to be overwhelmed. As the number of AIDS cases continues to spread to middle and rural America, the capacity of many health care institutions to accept and treat these patients will be challenged.

The American Public Health Association states that AIDS patients are accounting for five million hospital beds per year, with a price tag of $3.5 billion. A Public Health Service study predicts that the annual cost of treating AIDS will soon reach $60 billion! The average lifetime cost of medical care for a person with AIDS is over $100,000. The annual cost of caring for one person with AIDS is $38,000, and the annual cost of caring for a person infected with HIV but without AIDS is $6,000. While inpatient care is the major cost factor in the total medical bill for all patients with AIDS, drugs, home care, outpatient clinic, and physician costs are also heavy contributors. As persons with AIDS live longer and longer, and AIDS spreads into nonurban and heterosexual populations, more and more nursing homes and hospitals are being asked to accept AIDS cases. While these admissions may seem to solve present problems of surplus beds at many nursing homes and hospitals, who will pick up the tab?*

As employers and their insurance companies rewrite policies and restructure programs to limit their losses in this area, AIDS patients become more and more dependent upon Medicaid and other forms of federal or state assistance. Approximately 40 percent of all AIDS patients receiving health care are on Medicaid. However, the federal and state governments, in their efforts to balance budgets, are generally restricting reimbursements at every opportunity. Hospitals with an increasing or a relatively large number of admissions of AIDS patients are therefore at financial risk. The American Hospital Association has warned of "hospital death by AIDS" resulting from unpaid bills relating to treatment of AIDS patients. "Hospitals," a trade magazine, has run an article entitled: "AIDS—A Timebomb at Hospital's Door." The problem is compounded by insurance companies that either exclude treatment for AIDS-related problems or increase premiums to the point that corporations agree to exclude or cap AIDS coverage for the purpose of cost control.

Studies confirm that urban hospitals are bearing a disproportionate burden in terms of providing treatment for AIDS patients and absorbing monetary losses associated with AIDS care. The National Association of Public Hospitals reports that its members lose almost $8,000 for each AIDS patient they admit because reimbursement provides only 64 percent of their actual costs. Continuation of the current trend will bankrupt many public urban hospitals and eventually force a higher rate of HIV admissions to other facilities. An alternative, of course, is the infusion of large amounts of financial aid from governments to public urban hospitals

---

*Worldwide, $3.5 billion is spent in treating AIDS each year. However, over 90 percent of that total is expended in industrialized nations while the majority of new cases are occurring in poor, undeveloped countries. In Africa, with its alarming spread of HIV infection, only $400 is spent per patient per year.

and nursing homes for the targeted purposes of treating AIDS-related problems and caring for AIDS patients.

The city government in San Francisco, for example, contributed over $13 million in one year to San Francisco General for the purpose of relieving the financial stress resulting from that hospital's efforts in treating AIDS patients. A study in that city concluded that lifetime hospital costs per AIDS patient range from $29,000 to $60,000; other studies have found even higher figures. At present, too many PWAs who could be effectively treated at home, in hospices, in nursing homes, or at other sites are in hospitals due to the lack of outpatient services and alternate facilities. Hospitals should display leadership by initiating ideas for alternative care and case management in their communities and by working closely with local leaders to develop other facilities that can provide adequate care. But until changes are made, public, urban hospitals can expect to absorb heavy financial losses for many of the PWAs they treat and nonpublic hospitals should brace themselves for admissions of PWAs who can no longer be absorbed by the public sector.

In an effort to avoid financial and other risks associated with treating AIDS-related diseases, a children's hospital in an eastern state announced a policy of testing all patients for HIV, and transferring or refusing admission to those who tested positive. The administrator of this for-profit private hospital, which does not receive any federal funding, was quoted as saying, "They cannot come here. They can go elsewhere." However, after suffering a barrage of criticism from various medical and legal organizations, and studying a newly enacted state law protecting the handicapped, the hospital decided to suspend the testing program and nonadmission policy.

American Medical International (AMI) attempted an approach that many providers cheered: it opened a private hospital in Houston devoted exclusively to the treatment of AIDS patients. AMI intended to handle both paying and nonpaying patients, but the hospital was soon overloaded with indigents who had been under the care of private doctors until their medical insurance and financial resources were exhausted. The next year, after incurring over $7 million in losses, AMI closed the new hospital's doors and its patients were transferred to other hospitals in the area.

In theory, the medical code of ethics demands that all patients should be admitted to a hospital and treated regardless of their ability to pay. But this ideal is being tested by the practical problems raised by a large volume of uncompensated AIDS cases: if a hospital accepts too many of such cases, it could lose so much money that it would be forced to close.

Safety Aspects

There is no issue more critical than safety. Do patients and health care personnel infected with HIV pose a threat to the health of other patients and hospital personnel? If so, is the threat serious or remote? What are the different interests of hospital and nursing home managers, their employees, and their patients? Where these interests are contradictory, what should the employer do?

A significant number of patients and employees in health care facilities are *ignorant* of their HIV-positive status. A survey found that 14,000 people acknowledging recent homosexual activity or IV drug use had not been tested despite their high-risk status. A report by the CDC concluded that between 1 and 7.8 percent of the people admitted to urban hospitals are ignorant of their HIV infection. Thus, an automobile accident victim, ignorant of the early stages of erosion of his immune system due to AIDS, is unwittingly exposed to the diseases that abound in hospitals. Or a health care worker, without knowledge of her HIV-positive status, could contract a disease from the patients she is treating. For example, new stains of tuberculosis, immune to drugs, are attacking people weakened by HIV. Because the germ that causes tuberculosis is passed from tuberculosis patients to other people who are in close proximity to them (such as health care workers in hospitals or nursing homes), the disease can spread quickly. While the majority of the estimated ten million Americans who are infected with the TB germ will not become ill, those already infected with HIV are at high risk to develop active TB.

Approximately six thousand health care personnel across the country are known to have developed AIDS since 1981. Thousands more are HIV positive, and of these, many are unaware of their infected status. The vast majority are performing their regular duties at hospitals, clinics, and nursing homes every day, treating thousands of patients who are ignorant of their provider's infection. The CDC estimates that there is a statistical probability that at least one hundred patients may have been infected by HIV-positive surgeons and dentists during invasive procedures.

Does an infected health care employee have an *obligation* to inform his or her employer *and* all patients of his or her condition? Can a hospital *require* employees who develop the virus to disclose their infected status? Should a hospital periodically perform an HIV test on employees who regularly have contact with patients? If a hospital has knowledge that one of its employees is HIV positive, must it inform all patients treated by that employee? Are fear of *discrimination* against the employee and *remoteness of risk* to the patient valid reasons for not disclosing HIV status? Do *all* patients have the right to know that the doctor, nurse, or dentist treating them is carrying the HIV virus? Or should there be a duty to disclose only in certain circumstances?

Approximately fifty health care workers have contracted HIV during treatment of infected patients. Does the risk of infection give hospitals the right to test all patients for the virus upon admission and disclose the results to personnel involved in their treatment? When a facility learns that a particular patient is HIV positive, should it respect the privacy of the patient and maintain confidentiality *or* show concern for the safety of its employees by entering the condition on medical records and placing a notice on the patient's door?

If regular testing of patients or employees is adopted as a device to promote safety, who should pay the substantial costs and exactly to whom should the results be disclosed?

What about the perspective of the PWA? Does he or she have a right to a certain standard of treatment or should providers have the right to refuse treatment? Should the ill person with AIDS be protected against disclosure of his or her condition by a doctor or nurse to others? What if a male orders his doctor not to disclose his HIV-positive test result to his wife? Should someone who is HIV positive but free of symptoms have the right to make routine visits to the dentist or doctor or seek treatment in the emergency room for a wound without disclosing his or her infected status? Should a health care worker who is a carrier of the virus be protected against transfer or discharge by antidiscrimination laws? Suppose he or she has developed AIDS, can only perform some of the duties which involve physical contact with patients, and is frequently absent?

Legal Issues

Ramifications of these interests, often in conflict with each other, include lawsuits. Hospitals must be concerned with potential legal claims by all patients and employees. Claims can be based on refusal to treat, negligent treatment, discrimination, lack of informed consent, failure to counsel, breach of confidentiality, and violation of duty to disclose. Non-AIDS patients can allege that they were tested for HIV without giving their consent; that they were infected with HIV through contact with an HIV-positive employee; or that they received contaminated blood during a transfusion. AIDS patients can claim that they were refused admittance, or that they were confined in a segregated facility; that they were the victims of malpractice, discriminatory treatment, or negligent testing, or that their condition was revealed to third parties without consent. An employee can sue to protest mandatory testing for HIV, a discriminatory transfer or termination, failure to protect from patients with the virus, or breach of confidentiality and invasion of privacy.

A New Orleans hospital was sued for $43 million by a couple who claimed that their hemophiliac child contracted HIV during surgery. It can be difficult for a hospital to defend itself against this type of suit in which the HIV-positive plaintiff claims he is not homosexual, abstains from intravenous drugs, and was exposed to the virus while being treated at the defendant hospital. Employees, as well as patients, are potential plaintiffs.

Another hospital in the South was sued for $12 million by a janitor who claimed that he was infected with HIV when he tried to pick up contaminated needles and was stuck in the hand and fingers. Numerous "needle stick" cases have been filed across the country by aides and other hospital personnel who were accidentally stuck and possibly infected. At least one plaintiff acknowledged that she had tested negative several times after a stick but based her claim for damages on the emotional anguish and worry associated with the stick and possible infection.

Diagnosis of HIV, symptomatic HIV disease, and AIDS can incite malpractice claims. For example, suppose a healthy homosexual or drug abuser visits his doctor for a physical, is pleased when he receives a negative HIV test report, but soon becomes ill and discovers that he has been asymptomatic for years. Perhaps the original test yielded a false negative; or the laboratory mislabeled the result; or the doctor misread the report. Suppose further that the patient, who had reason to believe he was free of HIV, infected sex or needle partners during the period between the original examination/test and the correct diagnosis. Potentially infected third parties may also have legal claims against the doctor and laboratory. The reverse of this situation has also occurred: a number of patients have been told that they are HIV positive because of a false positive HIV antibody test. Some of the patients have sued the doctor, hospital, or laboratory responsible for the incorrect test result, claiming mental anguish and other damage.

Blood banks and hospitals have been repeatedly accused of negligence by plaintiffs arguing that they contracted HIV through a tainted blood transfusion. An Arizona jury awarded $28.7 million to a five-year-old boy who was infected by means of an unauthorized transfusion. An Ohio woman received an award of $12 million because the contaminated blood she received had not been tested *and* the transfusion had been unnecessary. However, most transfusion suits have been dismissed either because the plaintiff failed to prove any negligence or the defendant showed that it followed acceptable medical standards at the time of the incident. Many states have "blood shield statutes," which protect hospitals from strict liability and breach of warranty claims by requiring proof of fault by agents of the hospital during the transfusion. To prevail in a negligence case, the plaintiff must prove that the hospital violated a standard of care *and* that this misconduct was the proximate cause of his or her injury. One hospital was sued when its blood department personnel informed a pregnant donor that she had tested positive for HIV. A second blood sample was also reported as positive. After consulting doctors at the same hospital, the donor decided to have an abortion to prevent passing HIV to her baby. Later the hospital discovered that the two tests were actually negative and that the positive HIV status reports were caused by erroneous paperwork. After being informed that she was not HIV positive, the donor sought legal counsel (*Johnson v. U.S.*, 735 F. Supp. 1 [D.D.C. 1990]).

A woman alleged that a Wisconsin hospital negligently exposed her to the AIDS virus when she was inseminated with infected sperm. The defendant admitted that the donor of the sperm was HIV positive, and the plaintiff argued that a proper test should have been performed before the insemination. The pregnancy was terminated. In still another case, a female mental patient asserted that she was raped in a hospital by a fellow patient suffering from AIDS; her $6 million suit against the hospital, two doctors, and the rapist-patient also claimed that the hospital interfered with the police investigation.

A breach of confidentiality lawsuit involved a hospital in Akron, Ohio. An employee learned that a fellow employee—an EKG technician—had been admitted to the hospital as a patient. When she checked the hospital's computer to ascertain his room number so that she could visit him, she learned that he was HIV positive. She passed this information on to the employee's supervisors. When the ill EKG technician discovered that his supervisors were aware of his HIV status, he sued the hospital and three employees who had learned of his HIV infection for violating his right to privacy, requesting $250,000 in damages. The jury dismissed all allegations and refused to grant any damages. It was deemed significant that while the employee-defendants had reported the plaintiff's HIV condition to their supervisors, they had not disclosed the information to anyone else.

Practical problems can be caused by preventing or solving legal ones. After a nursing home in a rural community refused to accept an AIDS patient from a nearby hospital, the patient's family complained to the U.S. Department of Labor. Fearful of being deprived of essential Medicare and Medicaid funds if found guilty of discriminating against the handicapped, the home quickly settled the case and accepted the HIV-infected patient. Within a month almost 30 percent of the other patients had been removed from the home by their families because of their fear—medically groundless—that their relatives could somehow be infected with the virus by the PWA.

AIDS Patients: Segregate or Integrate?

Should hospitals and nursing homes isolate AIDS patients in special areas or integrate their treatment with that of other patients? What risks, practical and legal, arise from placing a patient with AIDS in the same room or ward with non-AIDS patients? Which approach, segregation or integration, presents the greatest potential for legal claims?

There are special considerations in the treatment of AIDS-related medical problems. It therefore seems logical to place these patients in the same area and to train health care personnel assigned to the care of AIDS patients to master the protocols connected with their treatment. More than a few hospitals have segregated AIDS patients on a certain floor or in a specific ward. Such segregation is not designed to prevent them from infecting non-AIDS patients (there is no evidence of this ever occurring). And the intent is certainly *not* to make them feel second-class or inferior. Instead, segregation is based on the theory that nurses and other personnel exclusively treating patients with AIDS-related problems will be more skilled and effective and less apt to expose themselves to risk. Moreover, the AIDS patients themselves can be given better protection from the infections of other patients: the AIDS patient with a deteriorating immune system is not exposed to other patients on a floor or in a ward or room who are suffering from communicable diseases. Enhancing care and decreasing exposure, of course, promotes health and prevents claims—two worthy and not mutually exclusive objectives.

AMI's short-lived hospital in Houston intended exclusively for the care of AIDS patients had an entire staff of personnel well trained and highly experienced in administering drugs, communicating with patient and family, and generally handling the special problems connected with HIV-infected people. But the New York City Task Force on Single Disease Hospitals issued a report criticizing such single-disease facilities and recommending that AIDS patients be integrated into hospitals' systems of care. The report cited fears of bias and a low quality of care associated with segregation. Moreover, isolation of AIDS patients in a single area clearly communicates to staff, other patients, and perhaps visitors that they are suffering from medical problems connected to AIDS, which may in itself breach a duty to maintain confidentiality. Critics of the report contend that none of these problems are necessary ramifications of separate units for AIDS patients.

In deciding which approach to take, hospitals should consider *Jane Doe v. Howard University Hospital,* where an HIV-positive patient seeking treatment for phlebitis was segregated in a private room pursuant to hospital policy for all HIV patients. After a series of events, during which the depressed patient took a drug overdose, the plaintiff sued for $2.7 million in compensatory and punitive damages, alleging discrimination (segregation due to HIV status), negligence, and malpractice. The case was thereafter settled, with an undisclosed monetary payment to the plaintiff. The allegation that HIV segregation is illegal seems suspect; the presence of malpractice and negligence claims clouds the issue and may have motivated the hospital to settle.

Hospitals that segregate PWAs must monitor staffing, equipment, and drugs in the AIDS and non-AIDS areas to ensure equality and prevent claims of discriminatory treatment.

Conflict of Interests

Health care facilities sometimes feel caught between the proverbial rock and the hard place. Full compliance with legal and ethical principles can cause practical problems. For example, administrators facing financial and competitive pressures fear that being labeled as the "AIDS hospital" or the "HIV nursing home" in some communities can stem admissions, stimulate withdrawals, and threaten financial ruin. Obviously, education is the antidote to the ignorance that motivates such unnecessary patient decisions.

Practices that promote patient treatment and confidentiality at the expense of employee safety can cause practical problems such as reduced employee morale, high turnover, and union activity. If a hospital with a reputation for treating significant numbers of AIDS patients does not test patients for HIV (even after an employee has been exposed to his or her blood), or provide special equipment to its employees, and never informs employees about the HIV status of the patients they treat (relying exclusively on universal precautions), some employees at some time can be expected to express their concern, protest, refuse a specific assignment, or otherwise take action that will cause the employer problems.

In attempting to resolve AIDS issues, health care employers must consider multiple factors, some of which contradict others. For example, as I have indicated, the obligation to care for seriously ill, uninsured AIDS patients often flies in the face of fiscal responsibility. A possible duty to disclose the HIV status of a patient or employee is contravened by the need to maintain confidentiality.

An already complex area is further complicated by the dual roles that hospitals and nursing homes play: they are both providers of care to patients and the employers of health care personnel. When seriously injured or ill people appear at their door, hospitals must treat them, regardless of HIV infection. But when treating AIDS patients, these employers must also be concerned about employee safety. And when employees contract HIV but are able to work, hospitals—to a far greater extent than any other employer—must consider patient or customer safety. As more and more AIDS patients are admitted and thousands of people ignorant of their positive HIV status seek treatment for other medical problems, hospitals become a potential breeding ground for the virus, which can be transmitted from patient to employee and employee to patient.

The legal obligations to patients may contradict the legal rights of employees; the converse is also true. For example, an HIV-positive nurse in the emergency room may feel firmly that any effort to transfer her to another position would violate state and federal laws protecting the handicapped; but the hospital has legitimate interests in treating patients safely, satisfying certain standards of care, and avoiding costly lawsuits. Or nurses could demand to be informed of the HIV status of the people they treat, while these patients could object to disclosures, claiming that they would violate the hospital's duty to maintain confidentiality.

Health care facilities are being asked to carefully examine the various interests of patients and personnel, as well as their own institutional interests, and to resolve the potential conflicts in a manner that will reduce the risk of litigation. In the next two chapters I will present issues that should be anticipated and analyzed.

7

Aids and Health Care
Protecting the Patient

What is the risk to a patient of contracting HIV from a doctor, dentist, or nurse during treatment? Do patients face a significant risk of becoming infected with HIV during their stay in a hospital?

It is important to recognize that the person inside the hospital who is most at risk is the patient or employee with AIDS. With the immune system deteriorating, he or she is in an environment that presents significant opportunities for contracting diseases, many of which could be fatal.

Patients at Low Risk

Among the noninfected people in the hospital, the patient has the least risk of contracting HIV. Picking it up from a fellow patient or visitor is virtually impossible, absent aberrant behavior or a transfusion of tainted blood. A report from the American College of Surgeons offers the general assurance that there is no evidence of casual-contact or environmental transmission of HIV in hospitals, and specifically states that patients cannot contract the virus by occupying a hospital room that was recently used by a PWA. Transmission from a doctor, nurse, technician, or other hospital employee is possible only if the patient is exposed to infected body fluids.

One means for patients to contract HIV while in a hospital is the transplant. In a rare incident multiple organs and tissues were removed from a donor who was murdered. After two tests for HIV antibodies proved negative, thirty different hospitals transplanted them for fifty-nine patients. However, three of the patients later died of AIDS-related complications, and scientists concluded that the young man was HIV positive but had not yet developed antibodies at the time of his death. Despite this incident, the CDC reassures the twenty thousand people waiting for transplants that the risk of receiving HIV from a transplanted organ or tissue is extremely small.

A Nashville study investigated patients who had been operated on at three hospitals over a long period of time by a surgeon who eventually died of AIDS-related causes. Of the 2,160 patients on which the surgeon had operated, 264 had died in circumstances unrelated to AIDS. The attempt to reach the remainder was only partially successful, with 1,037 refusing to be tested for HIV, 616 being tested, and the others not responding. The study concluded that only 1 patient had contracted HIV, and he did so through his own high-risk activities rather than through the surgery. Commenting on this study, a representative of the CDC found support for the concept that the risk to patients treated by HIV-positive health care personnnel is quite low.

Most disturbing, however, was the disclosure that a Florida dentist infected five of his patients during the course of surgery. The case became public when a former patient, twenty-two-year-old Kimberly Bergalis, threatened a malpractice suit. The dentist then sent a letter to all his former patients, informing them that he had AIDS and suggesting that they be tested for the HIV virus. The CDC investigated the case, interrogating Miss Bergalis, her parents, and her friends in an attempt to identify sex, drugs, or a blood transfusion as the means of infection. But Bergalis was a virgin, she never used IV drugs, and she had never had a blood transfusion. The CDC was forced to conclude that the virus was transmitted to her while she was being treated by her dentist. Laboratory examination of both his particular strain of virus and hers corroborated that theory. Later it was concluded that four additional patients of the same dentist, all of whom developed AIDS complications, had been infected by him. Investigators failed to identify the cause of the transmission: was the dentist's blood somehow mixed with that of the patients, or was contaminated equipment the culprit? It has recently been alleged by a friend of the dentist that he might have deliberately infected some of his patients to publicize AIDS. Kimberly Bergalis fulfilled her threat to sue and secured a million dollar settlement from the malpractice insurer of the dentist shortly before her AIDS-related death at age twenty-three.

Statistically, the overall odds of a patient contracting the HIV virus from a health care worker are extremely low. While approximately 6,500 of these personnel are known to have AIDS, this figure represents only 0.1 percent of America's 4.5 million health care workers.* But how many unreported cases are out there and what is the number of health care workers who are HIV positive, short of developing AIDS but still very capable of infecting patients? The motives for a health care employee to conceal the AIDS condition are numerous. It has been reported that the Florida dentist who infected five patients prior to dying from AIDS kept his HIV-positive status and bisexuality a secret for years because he feared loss of his 1700 patients and financial disaster. Hoping eventually to sell his practice, he continued working without disclosing his HIV status for three years after diagnosis. Others who are asymptomatic maintain secrecy because they fear reporting their condition will lead to a loss of job and insurance as well as discrimination and harassment.

In 1991 the CDC, motivated by the Kimberly Bergalis case, completed a study that estimated that a range of 13 to 128 patients had been infected with HIV during invasive procedures by surgeons and dentists. Morever, the CDC concluded that between 12 and 122 patient deaths could have occurred as a result of these infections. These statistical calculations are based on the number of dentists and surgeons estimated by the CDC to be infected with HIV (1248 and 336, respectively) and to have infected their patients (10–100 and 3–28, repectively). The CDC's estimates of infected workers by specific job area: surgeons, 336; nonsurgeon physicians, 5,096; nurses, 9,592; dentists and dental hygienists, 1,248; and others, 22,680; total, 46,520. Still, this estimate represents only 1 percent of all health care personnel.

The CDC report concludes that surgeons cut themselves 2.5 times for every 100 procedures, and that in 33 percent of these situations the patient comes into contact with the surgeon's blood. But even when an HIV-infected surgeon cuts himself and his blood mingles with that of the patient (usually by means of an instrument), the virus is rarely transmitted. It is statistically probable that for every one thousand times such mingling occurs, the patient is infected in three or fewer cases.

*The breakdown of cases of health care workers with AIDS reported to the CDC: surgeons, 47; nonsurgeon physicians, 703; nurses, 1358; and dental workers, 171.

At the 1991 International Conference on AIDS, a physician explained his calculation that the risk of HIV being transmitted from surgeon to patient was 1 in 48,000, or approximately the same as the probability of the patient being killed in an automobile accident on the way to the hospital. The CDC calculates the overall odds of a patient contracting HIV from a surgeon at 2.4 to 24 in 1 million. To put this figure in perspective, the CDC also offers these probabilities: contracting hepatitis B from a surgeon: 2,400 in 1 million; death from anesthesia: 100 in 1 million; death from penicillin: 10–20 in 1 million; and infection of wound during surgery: 10,000–147,000 in 1 million.

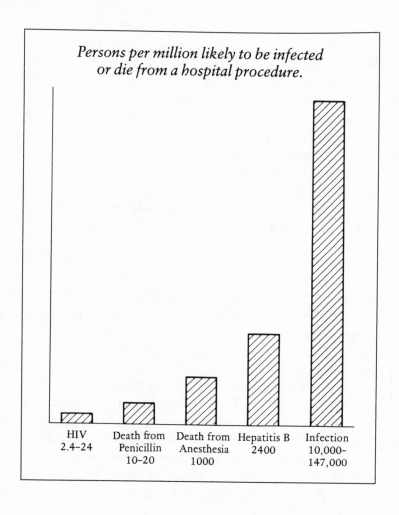

Persons per million likely to be infected or die from a hospital procedure.

| HIV 2.4–24 | Death from Penicillin 10–20 | Death from Anesthesia 1000 | Hepatitis B 2400 | Infection 10,000–147,000 |

Practice Restriction

These dramatic statistics, alarming to some and reassuring to others, frame two critical issues: restriction and disclosure. Should HIV-positive health care workers be restricted in the performance of their duties to decrease the small risk of their transmission of the virus to patients? Thus far, the majority of medical experts reply in the negative. Arguing that the risk to patients is remote, especially when the HIV-positive employee takes proper precautions, such as wearing recommended gear, most medical experts conclude that it would be unfair to impede the careers of infected but educated and experienced pesonnel who may not contract debilitating AIDS for a long time, if ever. But a minority of experts believe that even a small probability of infecting patients is too high. Kimberly Bergalis had her life irreversibly changed and significantly shortened because a health care worker presumably following acceptable standards infected her with HIV during treatment. How many more Kimberlys must there be before requirements are instituted that go beyond gear? Kimberly's parents feel that the dentist should have ended his practice as soon as he learned of his HIV status.

But if a health care facility attempted to restrict a doctor, nurse, or other HIV-positive employee from performing regular duties for the purpose of preventing patient exposure to the infection, it is vulnerable to a claim by the employee. When a public hospital in Illinois suspended the staff privileges of a surgeon with AIDS, the ACLU filed suit, claiming handicap discrimination. The suit was eventually settled, with the plaintiff-neurosurgeon accommodated and his privileges restored. The agreement purportedly protected the safety of his patients with restrictions such as double-gloving. The surgeon died a few months after the settlement.

A hospital's right to bar a surgeon with AIDS from performing surgery was upheld by the New Jersey Superior Court in *Behringer v. The Medical Center at Princeton*, N. J. Superior Ct (1991). Balancing the rights of an HIV-infected surgeon to practice against those of his patients to be free from risk, the trial judge concluded that the hospital made a "reasoned and informed response" when it barred the physician from performing surgery. This opinion also upheld the hospital's policy of requiring infected surgeons to disclose their infection to the patient and to secure the patient's consent prior to performing any invasive procedure. However, the court did acknowledge that requiring informed consent could be "de facto prohibition from surgical practice." In rejecting Dr. Behringer's allegation that revoking his surgical privileges was discriminatory, the court found the ban justified since the physician's continued practice created a "reasonable probability" of harm to his patients.

While the court supported the hospital's policy regarding restriction of privileges, it found the hospital liable for failing to protect Dr. Behringer's confidentiality as a patient, emphasizing that access to Dr. Behringer's chart was practically without restriction to hospital personnel. According to the opinion, the infected status of this physician was widely known throughout the hospital and even the community within hours of the diagnosis. The court noted that "All that was required was a glance at the chart, and the written words became whispers and the whispers became roars." The opinion sharply criticized the hospital's failure to protect Dr. Behringer's confidentiality and awarded damages to his estate in an amount to be determined at a later hearing.

Two of the doctors at a small clinic in California prohibited their third partner, a gynecologist, from treating patients after he developed AIDS. Arguing that his condition did not threaten the safety of patients or staff at the clinic, the gynecologist sued his two partners for discrimination and breach of contract.

Westchester County Medical Center in New York rejected an HIV infected applicant for a pharmacist position on the ground that his preparation of IV solutions posed a risk to patients. After the pharmacist filed complaints with both the New York State Division of Human Rights and the U.S. Department of Health and Human Services, the hospital offered a compromise: he would be hired and given full pay and benefits but be restricted from preparation of IV solutions. The offer was rejected, the matter litigated, and the pharmacist prevailed after a trial. The hospital was ordered to hire him without restriction and provide him with full back pay. *John Doe v. Westchester County Medical Center.*

The American Medical Association (AMA) issued a position statement after the Florida dentist case became public. The AMA suggested that doctors who perform invasive procedures or who otherwise are at risk of becoming infected during the performance of their duties should *voluntarily* and periodically submit to testing and from time to time determine their HIV status. However, the testing is not mandatory. The AMA's approach is that physicians who are HIV positive should be able to continue their medical careers *but* in a capacity that does not pose an identifiable risk to their patients. Thus, infected doctors are encouraged to *voluntarily* restrict their practices to procedures and treatments with a very low probability of transmitting HIV. Stated differently, surgeons and dentists are expected to terminate their specific practices and transfer to other medical occupations. Some HIV-infected dentists and physicians have criticized the recommendations and complained that they are the targets of a witch hunt. Arguing that no surgery is risk-free and that the AMA has been slow to restrict surgeons with substance abuse problems, most medical personnel infected with HIV are unlikely to comply with their recommendations. Like the AMA, the American Nursing Association is opposed to mandatory testing of nurses.

The CDC issued guidelines in 1991 that also rely on self-policing. All health care workers who perform exposure-prone procedures are encouraged (not required) to be tested for HIV antibodies. Examples of high-risk procedures include abdominal, gynecological, and heart surgery; tooth extractions; and root canals. Still, the CDC concludes that the risk of an infected health care worker transmitting the virus to a patient during an invasive procedure is small. And *if* the health care worker voluntarily submits to the test and it turns out to be positive, then he or she can continue to perform the exposure-prone work if his or her HIV status is disclosed to the patient and a medical review committee, both of whom grant approval. Without the informed consent of the patient, the health care worker is asked to voluntarily restrict his or her practice by avoiding exposure-prone procedures. While these are, technically, only *recommendations* by the CDC, public health officials of each state are required to *certify* to the U.S. Department of Health and Human Services that CDC Guidelines *or their equivalent* have been adopted. Failed or flawed certification could cause loss of federal public health funds. Pertinent portions of these recommendatons are located in appendix A, document 7.

The American College of Surgeons, the American College of Physicians, and the American Academy of Orthopedic Surgeons, as well as the American Dental Association, criticize the CDC guidelines as unworkable and unfair. Arguing that we lack sufficient scientific knowledge to determine which procedures are "exposure-prone" and that its infected physician and dentist members would be forced to stop practicing, most medical associations are totally opposed to this approach. The New York State Health Department completely rejected the CDC guidelines and issued its own policy that protects the confidentiality of infected health care workers and allows them to continue in their jobs without disclosure. All of this opposition persuaded the CDC not to issue a list of exposure-prone procedures. However, in 1992 the CDC reaffirmed the guidelines and directed state health departments to implement them.

A report by Congress's Office of Technological Assessment (OTA) criticized testing of health care workers. Finding that the risk of transmission from provider to patient was too small to justify *mandatory* testing, the OTA also suggested that *voluntary* testing is ineffective "since health care workers' fear of disclosure, potential discimination and loss of livelihood may provide a disincentive to seek appropriate counseling and testing."

I believe that only an insignificant percentage of physicians, dentists, and other health care workers who regularly perform invasive or other exposure-prone procedures will initiate testing of themselves. A survey of 196 health care workers either HIV positive or at high risk for contracting it corroborated the OTA report by concluding that the CDC guidelines motivates them to hide their condition and avoid testing. Fear of losing their jobs or privileges makes them reluctant to inform employers or patients. Periodic, mandatory testing of surgeons, dentists, and other health care professionals whose specialities pose the greatest risk of infecting patients, and the report of results to the proper representatives of hospitals and clinics is preferable to ineffectual voluntary testing and an honors policy of self-disclosure of positive results to patients and practice restrictions. If the medical associations and federal government will not promote mandatory testing in these limited circumstances, health care facilities should do it on their own.

Right to Know

Do patients have the right to know about an employee's positive HIV status prior to treatment? The AIDS-related death of a prominent breast cancer surgeon in Baltimore made his patients feel frightened and betrayed because he had informed neither them nor his hospital of his condition. Two weeks after his death it became known that he had operated on 1,800 patients at Johns Hopkins Hospital while infected. The hospital then sent letters to the patients, advising them of their surgeon's HIV status and soliciting calls from any who were concerned. Almost all of those responding accepted the hospital's offer of testing. In another development a Baltimore law firm advertised its availability to represent patients operated on by HIV-infected surgeons. However, thus far there is no evidence that any of the 1,800 patients were infected by the cancer surgeon.

After contracting the HIV virus, a thirty-nine-year-old family doctor in Minnesota continued all aspects of his practice, including such invasive procedures as delivering babies and conducting rectal and gynecological examinations. He did, however, notify state health officials of his HIV status, who permitted him to continue practicing without restriction despite an unrelated skin condition that caused open sores on his hands. Six months after diagnosis and unrestricted practice, the doctor inexplicably decided to send a letter to selected patients, informing them of his HIV condition and urging them to be tested.

As soon as Northwestern University learned that one of its dental students was HIV-positive, it contacted the 125 patients he had treated, reporting the exposure and suggesting a test. When a Missouri dental school dismissed an asymptomatic student, who then filed a handicap discrimination claim, the court noted the graduation requirement involving invasive procedures and ruled that the infected student was not "otherwise qualified" (*Doe v. Washington Un.* 780 F. Supp. 628 [E.D. Mo. 1991]).

When two Pennsylvania hospitals learned that an obstetrics-gynecology resident had contracted HIV after being accidentally cut by another physician during surgery, they decided it was appropriate to give formal notice of potential exposure to 442 patients who had been treated by the resident. While voluntarily withdrawing from participation in surgical procedures at the two hospitals, the infected physician attempted to judicially enjoin the disclosure of his HIV status. He argued that the exposures were only potential or speculative and that the notice would violate his right to privacy. The court ruled, however, that the physician's asymptomatic condition

was a public concern because of his participation in invasive procedures and permitted the notice. Thus in this case the patient's
right to know prevailed over the provider's right of privacy (*Milton
S. Hershey Medical Center and Harrisburg Hospital*, Penn. Super.
Ct. [1991]).

In one survey 86 percent of the people who responded said that
they should have the right to know if a health care employee treating
them is HIV-infected. Another survey concluded that HIV-positive
doctors should be required to disclose their condition to patients.
There are reports of people refusing to be treated by or canceling
appointments with dentists and physicians for fear of contracting
HIV. Disclosure of HIV status could calm nervous patients. However, such disclosures could have negative ramifications, including
patient decisions to change dentists or doctors and a plethora of
frivolous suits against the professional *and* health care facility. For
example, in Dallas, a pediatrician with AIDS was the defendant in
a lawsuit and was attempting to sell his practice. A reporter read
the court's file and reported his AIDS condition. His practice was
instantaneously destroyed despite assurances by medical authorities
to parents that it was safe for their children to be examined and
treated by the infected doctor. Horror stories such as this are the
main motivation behind the position of the Canadian Dental Association (and many individual practitioners) that infected members
are *not* obligated to inform their patients of their condition.

Princteon Medical Center proposed a special consent form for
Dr. Behringer to use in explaining his HIV-positive status to patients
and agreed that he could perform surgery on any who signed it. Dr.
Behringer, however, refused to exercise this option, and even the
judge observed that requiring informed consent could be tanta-
mount to a "de facto prohibition from surgical practice." Providers'
fears that disclosure will drive away patients are well founded. A
survey that found that 80 percent of the participants believed that
infected doctors should inform their patients of their HIV status
also concluded that 55 percent would switch doctors if they learned
their physicians were HIV positive! If patients are informed, will
their response be reasonable and consistent with medical knowledge
or emotional and discriminatory against the health care workers
and hospital? Should the anticipated answers to this inquiry affect
its resolution?

The issue of disclosure should turn on the degree of risk to the patients, not their anticipated response to the notice. Courts are in the process of establishing a legal principle that physicians are required to provide their patients with sufficient information to permit the patient to make an informed and intelligent decision about whether to submit to a particular medical procedure. A case that involved alcohol abuse articulated a doctrine that could easily be applied in an HIV situation. After experiencing bladder and bowel dysfunction following lumbar surgery, the patient sued, claiming that the physician should have disclosed his abuse of alcohol. In his defense the surgeon pointed to the general consent form signed by the patient prior to surgery, but the court labeled that form as bland and inadequate and ruled that the physician's failure to disclose his chronic alcohol abuse created a material risk that, if disclosed, could have motivated the patient to have elected a different cause of action (*Hidding v. Dr. Randall Williams* 579 So. 2d 1192 [La. 5th Cir. 1991]). While litigation on when treatment of a patient by an asymptomatic HIV-infected physician becomes a material risk has yet to make its way through the courts, it is probable that invasive procedures will be so labeled. And if HIV-positive surgeons are obligated to disclose their condition to patients prior to invasive procedures as a matter of law, it must follow that hospitals may require such disclosure as a matter of policy.

Proposed Policies

Since neither federal laws nor state regulations nor the AMA and the CDC directives have solved these problems, it is incumbent upon individual health care facilities to address them with carefully crafted policies and uniformly applied procedures. In responding to questions of practice restriction and patients' right to know, hospitals should differentiate among health care positions and procedures. A ward clerk and a radiologist are in different situations from an emergency room nurse and a heart surgeon. Taking a biopsy or removing a spleen would be differentiated from serving food or checking blood pressure. Documented, careful analyses of these issues resulting in a written policy tailored to the particular hospital or nursing home will bolster defenses to any lawsuits.

I propose the following *general rule*: while all health care providers should be required to immediately report HIV infection to their employers, the vast majority should be neither restricted in job duties nor required to disclose their status to patients. On balance, the disadvantage of restriction and disclosure far outweigh their advantages. Patients incur numerous risks of infection simply by entering a hospital. It's not fair to prevent well-trained and able health care workers from carrying out their duties simply because of a remote possibility that they may transmit HIV to patients. The costs associated with such restrictions and exclusions are greater than any marginal improvement in the degree of safety that would be realized. There is simply no legitimate reason to restrict the duties of an infected boiler room mechanic, pharmacist, or business office clerical worker. Neither is it necessary to inform a patient that the housekeeping employee who cleaned her room or the food service assistant who transported her meals from the kitchen to her room is HIV positive. It would also be inappropriate to reveal that a fellow patient is infected. Indeed, disclosing HIV status of patients in the same room or employees indirectly connected to care would likely stimulate breach of confidentialilty/invasion of privacy claims against the hospital by the patient or employee whose status has been revealed. And those claims would have a higher probability of success than any duty to disclose suit.

However, the *exception* to this rule should be triggered when the specific occupation or procedure causes the provider to have contact with the patient's blood or other body fluids. After all, HIV is a blood-borne virus. Heart surgeons necessarily engage in invasive procedures and have considerable contact with the blood of their patients. The same point is true for emergency room and operating room nurses and dental surgeons and technicians. The determining question to be posed is: is the risk of transmission from provider to patient identifiable? The standard of "identifiable" risk is realistically located between the extremes of "significant" risk and "remote" risk.

An emergency room doctor on the West Coast continued treating patients for more than two years after developing AIDS. The hospital, fearing loss of admissions if his condition became known in the community, pressured him to maintain secrecy. Eventually the hospital reversed its position and the doctor's AIDS condition was disclosed. In "safty-sensitive" jobs such as emergency room physician, the risk of infection is not significant. But neither is it remote. Because the doctor's contact with blood is routine, the risk is identifiable. In situations like this, improvement in safety and reduction of risk outweigh the negatives of restriction and exposure.

State departments of health are suppose to assist hospitals in performing an analysis of all occupations and procedures, assigning a level of risk to each. One question to ask in performing the analysis is, does performing this procedure present a recognized risk of percutaneous injury to a health care worker and, if so, is there a greater than remote chance that the employee's blood will contact the patient's body cavity, tissues, or mucus membranes? Certain surgical and dental procedures would automatically be classified as "identifiable." Then hospitals should mandate that HIV-infected employees who currently hold the relatively few jobs or who have occasion to perform procedures where the risk is classified as "identifiable" be restricted regarding the job or procedure and/or required to disclose the HIV status to patients. Normally, practice restriction or transfer to a lower risk job should be preferable to patient disclosure. This realistic recognition of the different degrees of risk is an exercise that should be encouraged but not required of health care employers.

Suppose a hospital is informed that a ward nurse has been infected with HIV. Should the hospital, like Johns Hopkins Hospital with the breast cancer surgeon, send a certified letter revealing the nurse's HIV status and suggesting testing or counseling to all patients she treated over the years? Such a response—almost sure to stimulate legal claims—does not seem appropriate or necessary in those circumstances. But notice would be appropriate if the HIV-infected employee was an emergency nurse who had documented exposure to the blood of specific patients in the performance of her duties. Again, an analysis of all relevant factors, including the employee's specific job duties, the procedures he or she performs, and his or her degree of exposure to bleeding patients, must be performed.

Some argue that goverments or health care employers should protect patients by adopting criminal laws or stringent policies that prohibit health care personnel from performing invasive procedures when they are HIV positive. The U.S. Senate initially voted eighty-one to eighteen to enact a law making it a crime for HIV-infected health care workers to perform procedures that could transmit the virus without first obtaining the consent of the patient. This reactionary legislation, debated in the emotional atmosphere prompted by the Kimberly Bergalis story, was wisely abandoned. Health care employers are far more capable than any government agency of implementing policies that protect patients without unnecessarily compromising the privacy or other interests of providers. Hospitals and nursing homes should be left the discretion to study the situation and adopt policies and procedures that are appropriate for their particular facilities.

Another intelligent policy for protecting patients is to require all employees who regularly handle blood or who are exposed to blood in carrying out the duties of their positions to be periodically tested for HIV. Submission to these tests, administered every three or six months, would be a condition of employment. When positive results are confirmed, the employee's job should be restricted or the employee should be transferred to a job in which he or she had no contact with patients' blood. Hospitals, which could use this testing policy to improve its defense to potential lawsuits, would pay for the tests.

In chapter 5, I offered general information on testing for HIV and evaluated the advantages and disadvantages of mandatory testing. Here I would like to present some specific arguments—pro and con—relating to a personnel policy on testing for a health care facility. First, employees are likely to resent the periodic procedure and demand that testing of patients be conducted to protect personnel. Second, a negative result is not a certainty: a test conducted on a recently infected employee who has not yet developed the antibody would be a negative (for some several months expire between infection and antibody), and an employee could become infected soon after the test and continue as an operating room nurse until three or six months later when the next test is conducted. Third, false positive results do occur, although these are rare when the initial screen is confirmed by the Western Blot. Fourth, regular testing of an appreciable number of personnel is costly. Yet the vast majority of infections would be discovered by a rational testing program. As a result of such a program, infected employees would be restricted from duties involving an identifiable risk (thus preventing potential exposures and lawsuits), *and* the health care worker would discover that he or she has a serious problem that needs medical evaluation and treatment.

A number of testing programs, however, are improper from both legal and ethical perspectives. A few hospitals, in the past, have tested *all* applicants for HIV antibodies and either rejected all who were positive or assigned them to positions unrelated to the handling of or exposure to blood. Another improper approach is to test only those applicants who appear to the personnel office or doctor who performs the preemployment physical to fit a high-risk category: homosexual or IV drug user. All of these programs have at least four factors in common: (1) the applicant is not informed that an HIV test will be performed and therefore does not give consent for the test *or* a general consent is solicited with "HIV" buried in the fine print the patient seldom reads or questions; (2) applicants who test positive are neither informed of that fact nor counseled about their condition; (3) these procedures offend federal and state laws protecting the handicapped; and (4) the whole approach lacks ethical validity.

I suggested that any testing program involving patients or employees should satisfy these minimum standards: (1) specific notice of an HIV test should be explained to the individual both orally and in writing; (2) he or she should execute an informed consent that is witnessed; (3) any sample that tests positive under ELISA must be tested again by the same procedure; (4) any individual having two ELISA positives on the same sample should have a different sample of blood submitted to the Western Blot examination; (5) only after the individual tests positive under both ELISA and the Western Blot should the result be deemed positive—any other results, including "inconclusive," should be considered short of positive; (6) all inconclusive and final positive results should be reported to the individual; and (7) those with inconclusive and final positive results should be counseled concerning the ramifications of their condition.

Patient Legal Claims

Hospitals should anticipate lawsuits alleging that the plaintiff was infected with HIV while being treated or that the plaintiff is suffering anxiety from the possibility of becoming infected after treatment by an HIV-positive provider. For example, when Milton S. Hershey Medical Center sent notice to 442 former patients of an HIV-positive physician, informing them that they had been potentially exposed, two patients filed a class action lawsuit, alleging negligence and lack of informed consent and claiming that the husband of one had suffered loss of consortium. Damages of over $100,000 were sought *even though neither plaintiff had contracted HIV!* (*Wolgemuth v. Hershey Medical Center* [1991]). In these cases the burden is on the former patient to prove a nexus between the treatment and infection. Still, hospitals have a dilemma: if they inform all patients that a particular provider is infected, as Hershey Medical Center did, the probability of such suits skyrockets, and also the employee may sue for breach of confidentiality. If, however, no such disclosures are made, and a patient later learns that he or she was treated by an HIV-infected provider, the hospital could be hit with claims of duty to disclose and negligence. The number of suits alleging that a former patient was infected during treatment has been low but will dramatically increase as laws and policies requiring disclosure are enacted.

The best approach for avoiding liability in this area is to prevent such suits by restricting the duties of health care personnel with an identifiable risk of transmission. As I already suggested, each health care employer should perform an analysis of each job classification and determine whether the risk of an HIV-positive employee in that job transmitting the virus to patients is remote or identifiable. Disclosure of HIV status to patients will promote litigation, but identifying HIV-positive workers and restricting their practice will prevent it.

A number of potential legal claims involving AIDS can be initiated by patients against hospitals and doctors; the claims can involve accusations of negligent testing, duty to disclose HIV status, invasion of privacy, breach of duty of confidentiality, discrimination, and malpractice. In an example of the last cause of action, a Boston jury awarded $750,000 to a young female infected by her former lover, an IV drug user, after her doctor repeatedly misdiagnosed the symptoms she reported to him.

The right of a plaintiff infected with HIV by means of a blood transfusion to learn the identity of the donor has been litigated. In

California an appellate court rejected an attempt by recipients of tainted blood transfusions to depose anonymously donors thought to be HIV-positive as violative of the state's HIV confidentiality statute (*Irwin Memorial Blood Bank v. Super. Ct. of S.F. County*, 229 Cal. App. 3rd 151 [1991]). However, the Supreme Court of Louisiana ruled a similarly situated asymptomatic plaintiff had a legitimate need to discover the identity of the donor that outweighed the donor's right to privacy (*Most v. Tulane Medical Center*, 576 So. 2d 1387 [1991]).

With respect to discrimination cases, the Dallas Gay Alliance filed suit against the Dallas County Hospital District, alleging that it represented a class of AIDS patients at Parkland Hospital who were being provided inadequate and discriminatory treatment. The allegations, however, were not supported by persuasive proof, and the suit was dismissed by the federal district court (*DGA v. DCH*, 719 F. Supp. 1380 [N.D. Tex. 1989].

An example of an invasion of privacy/breach of confidentiality claims is a New York case in which the plaintiff, after being diagnosed as HIV positive, was sitting in a waiting room at the defendant's hospital. A nurse asked the plaintiff if a photographer could take his picture; the plaintiff, who testified that he thought the photograph was for internal or research purposes, orally consented. A few days later the plaintiff's picture showed up in the newspaper (the photographer's employer)—silhouette only—in connection with a story on AIDS. The court concluded that the plaintiff consented to the picture, pointed out that he was not recognizable in the paper, and dismissed the suit (*Anderson v. Strong Memorial Hospital*, 542 N.Y.2d 96 [1989]).

8

Aids and Health Care

Protecting the Provider

Does a doctor or nurse have the right to refuse treatment to patients with AIDS? Should a food service or laundry employee be able to ignore the rooms of patients infected with HIV? Should health care personnel whose job duties involve physical contact with patients and their body fluids be tested for HIV at any time? If so, should the tests be mandatory or voluntary? If tested, should any of those who test positive be restricted in their job assignments to protect fellow employees, as well as patients? On the subject of testing, should patients admitted to hospitals and nursing homes be tested for HIV and the results reported to the personnel treating them? What steps, if any, should hospitals and nursing homes take to protect their personnel from exposure to HIV in the performance of their duties? Why have the vast majority of lawsuits against hospitals involving AIDS been filed by employees, not patients?

Risk to Health Care Workers

Health care personnel incur a far greater risk than patients. Doctors and nurses who unavoidably have frequent contact with blood and other body fluids of patients in the emergency and operating rooms and other personnel who handle needles, bandages, and equipment used to treat HIV-infected patients are repeatedly exposed to possible infection. The CDC explains that, of the 150,000 cases of AIDS reported in the United States since 1981, approximately 6,500 involved health care workers. However, an extremely small percentage of them acquired the virus occupationally. While the CDC acknowledges that many accidental exposures of hospital workers are not reported, of those that have been investigated, the overwhelming majority can be explained by nonoccupational risk factors. Among the remainder, some health care workers became infected through documented sticks and splashes but other cases of infection cannot be explained. As the CDC learned in its investigation of Kimberly Bergalis and her dentist, the precise means of transmitting the infection is sometimes elusive. That failure to identify the specific cause is especially worrisome to administrators concerned about the safety of their personnel.

Health Care Workers Occupationally Infected

An editorial in the *Journal of the American Medical Association* agrees with the CDC's estimate that hundreds of HIV-infected surgeons are currently practicing in this country. How did they contract HIV? How many, if any, picked it up through contact with the body fluids of a patient at the hospital, as opposed to other means?

We know of several examples of health care personnel who were infected with HIV during the performance of their duties. The surgeon in Nashville, referred to in chapter 7, who apparently did not infect any of the 2,160 patients he operated on prior to his AIDS-related death, believed that he had contracted the infection while operating on an HIV-positive patient. A thirty-year-old surgeon died in London of AIDS-related complications shortly after performing 338 operations in Britain. It was determined that he had contracted the virus during a five-year stint in Zimbabwe. Upon being advised of his AIDS condition, Dr. David Collings said, "That is one of the risks of doing surgery in Africa."

The opportunity for transmission from patient to health care worker is especially apparent in surgery. A survey by the CDC concluded that surgeons came into contact with the blood of patients in one of every five operations that involved an incision. The specific means of contact are a needle, scalpel, or other object that touches patient blood; blood splashing in eyes, mouth, or nose; and skin touching or gown/shoes being soaked with blood of patient.

Health care workers other than surgeons who come into contact with the blood and other body tissues of asymptomatic patients are also at risk. A cardiologist at Johns Hopkins Hospital was infected with HIV when a tube holding a patient's blood specimen shattered, cutting his finger. He died of AIDS-related complications seven years later at age thirty-six.

A nurse at a Wisconsin hospital is convinced that HIV was transmitted to her during an attempt to resuscitate a patient. After receiving instructions from a doctor to remove a malfunctioning intraveneous tube from the patient's arm, she grabbed some gauze, removed the tube, placed the gauze against the opening with her finger, and applied pressure for ten minutes. It was later determined that the patient, who died, was HIV positive. When the nurse, a mother of three, made a blood donation a few months later, she learned that she had HIV. She concluded that the patient's blood had soaked through the gauze and mingled with hers through small cuts caused by gardening. This explanation of transmission has been accepted by the CDC. She was placed on worker's compensation and accepted a confidential settlement with the hospital of all potential claims.

In 1991 a female nurse in Sacramento, California, became the first health care worker in America to die of AIDS complications after contracting the virus through employment. When it tested 265 of its personnel working in twelve laboratories that perform research relating to AIDS, the National Cancer Institute found one employee who tested positive. Since it did not appear that he engaged either in high-risk sexual behavior or IV drug use, and since he worked with high concentrations of the virus, an occupational transmission was suspected. Two employees at the National Institute of Health contracted HIV through their job duties. One was infected by a needle stick, but the other was the victim of "inapparent exposure"—no spill or stick—during the handling of the virus or while cleaning spills or touching contaminated surfaces, despite the use of gloves (scientists suspected a hole in a glove). On the bright side, a study concluded that no other personnel (of more than two hundred) regularly engaged in various laboratory duties involving HIV has been infected at work.

In New York Dr. Veronica Prego sued the hospital where she was employed and two other doctors for $175 million, alleging that she had contracted HIV by pricking her finger with a contaminated needle carelessly left among soiled refuse on a patient's bed. That Dr. Prego had developed AIDS was uncontested, and there were indications that she had less than a year to live when the trial started. The hospital, denying any negligence, pointed out that the two doctors were not present when Prego picked up the needle, and argued that her sole remedy was worker's compensation. However, Prego's attorneys successfully withstood procedural arguments and got the case to trial, which promoted the hospital to settle for $1.35 million.

A judge in New York awarded $5.3 million to a nurse infected with HIV during a struggle with a prison inmate patient while guards failed to intervene. The patient yanked out IV needles, kicked several hospital workers, and hit a nurse carrying an IV needle that then stuck the plaintiff (another nurse) in her hand. *Jane Doe v. Faxton Hospital.* In a similar incident, a policeman assigned to a public hospital was called to the emergency room where he helped subdue an HIV infected patient who bit him. Here, however, the plaintiff did not develop HIV and his claim was for the acute anxiety and emotional distress he allegedly developed from fear of contracting AIDS. Still, he recovered $1.9 million in damages. *Johnson v. West Virginia University Hospital, Inc.* 413 S.E 2d 889 (West Virginia Supreme Court 1991).

Is workers' compensation the exclusive remedy for hospital personnel in these circumstances? In *Peters v. New York City Health and Hospitals Corp.*, the New York Supreme Court, King's County, ruled that a nurse who suffered an accidental needle stick inflicted by a co-worker could not pursue damages for alleged emotional distress (a tort). Instead, she was relegated to a workers' compensation claim. However, unlike the situation with Dr. Prego, the plaintiff was not tested for HIV, and there was no evidence that she was HIV positive. Hospitals, of course, will logically try to argue that state court tort suits by infected employees seeking huge compensatory and punitive damages are preempted by workers' compensation statutes.

There is ample opportunity for exposures in health care facilities. OSHA conducted a survey of 329 hospitals to determine the extent of employee exposure to blood and other potentially infectious body fluids. It found that in one year alone there were 360,964 accidental needle sticks and 65,811 cuts by instruments other than needles reported by hospital personnel. Despite such high numbers for only a few hospitals, the CDC has emphasized their finding that the general probability of a health care employee contracting HIV through work is extremely low: a 1 in 500 chance. First, most workers are never exposed to the virus. Second, few of those who are exposed convert to positive status. A CDC study of orthopedic surgeons found that only 2 of the 3,420 tested were infected, and that these 2 were members of high-risk groups. At least 50 percent of the orthopedic surgeons who tested negative had operated on HIV-positive patients. Another study conducted by the CDC's Cooperative Needle Stick Surveillance Group, which involved more than 300 hospitals, concluded that the risk of a health care employee developing HIV following an exposure was substantially less than 1 percent. Specifically, the group studied 1,449 health care employees exposed to tainted blood through needle sticks (80 percent), cuts (8 percent), splashes (5 percent), and open wounds (7 percent). Sixty-six percent of the exposures occurred in the rooms of AIDS patients, with the others happening in operating rooms, intensive care units, or laboratories. Only 4 of 1,449 became infected with HIV. All 4 of the seropositive exposures occurred through needle sticks. It also should be noted that the study found that 37 percent of the exposures could have been prevented if personnel had followed recommended safety procedures.

San Francisco General Hospital, which treats significant numbers of AIDS patients, studied 270 employees who cared for them on a daily basis and were involved in more than 340 needle stick and splash incidents: not one tested positive for HIV. However, at a time outside the study period, at least one employee at that hospital became HIV infected after a deep, unavoidable needle stick.

Studies aside, the CDC has documented approximately fifty actual transmissions from patient to provider. Since many exposures are never reported and some exposures not fully investigated, it is likely that there have been substantially more. Though the actual numbers are low and the probability slight, health care workers are being infected with HIV by their patients. This fact should be of serious concern to health care facilities, their administrators, and their medical staffs.

Certain Jobs at Higher Risk

While additional studies will certainly be welcome, future evidence will likely bolster the present conclusion: the general risk of health care personnel contracting HIV through the performance of their job duties is near zero. Adherence to established standards and the use of special gear and equipment, including self-sheathing needles, reduce the general risk to remote. But a few health care jobs have a far greater risk than others. Heart surgeons and their team members are necessarily exposed to extremely large quantities of tainted blood when they operate on HIV-positive patients. A study discussed in the *New England Journal of Medicine* found that emergency room workers face a higher risk than other hospital personnel, principally due to the work they perform on patients whose HIV status is unknown. It was found that 119 of the 2,302 (5.2 percent) patients treated in the emergency room of one inner-city hospital were HIV infected. Positive test results were reported to the personnel prior to treatment for 27 of these patients, and special precautions were taken. But 92 patients who later proved to be seropositive had to be treated prior to testing; insufficient special gear and precautions were taken with this group.

Universal precautions, of course, legally require health care workers to treat all patients as if they are infected with HIV. This doctrine, embraced by the CDC and OSHA, is sound logically, but can be weak practically in urban emergency rooms that frequently treat gunshot and knife wounds. Patients come through the door with bleeding that requires immediate attention. Often doctors and nurses simply have no time to don all the gear that is required with every patient. When a patient is in critical condition, a medical team cannot take the time to secure a blood sample, send it to the lab, and wait for the test result. Often bleeding is arrested and invasive treatment completed before gown and goggles are remembered, and certainly long before personnel learn if the patient is infected.

Moreover, the law in several states prevents HIV testing unless the patient provides "informed consent." How is a nurse in the emergency room supposed to secure consent, informed or otherwise, from an unconscious patient who is bleeding profusely from three gunshot wounds and is in dire need of immediate and prolonged attention? Government officials who draft guidelines and judges who issue decisions in this area should spend several hours in the emergency room of a public urban hospital on Friday or Saturday night, observing the immense amount of patient blood on the equipment, the floor, and the hands, faces, and feet of the doctors and nurses working feverishly to save lives. The high volume of trauma cases and the large quantity of blood dramatically illustrate the risks regularly incurred by emergency room personnel.

Operating on an HIV-positive patient also presents a higher risk. Contaminated blood has to be washed off surgeons and nurses at the end of long, delicate procedures. Experienced surgeons have suffered cuts from patient bones, often sharp as glass, as well as the instruments they use, despite the presence of gloves and their exercise of extreme caution. Biopsies are taken, organs cut and sewn, and intravenous tubes implanted. The exposure to possible infection is almost continuous. The risk is real.

Obstetricians, almost always exposed to large quantities of blood while delivering babies and performing hysterectomies, are concerned about the increase in HIV status among females. Many doctors are now using surgical staples instead of needle and sutures and placing sharp instruments in a basin instead of handing them to another doctor or nurse.

In addition to surgeons, obstetricians, their assistants, and emergency room personnel, other job classifications that are at a greater risk than other health care employees because of their regular exposure to blood and body fluids include: phlebotomists, emergency medical technicians, laboratory technicians, X-ray technicians, intensive care and operating room nurses, dentists, and dental technicians. Health care facilities should analyze the question of whether special efforts should be expanded to protect them.

Ramifications of Risk

The rare but highly publicized cases of health care personnel becoming infected with a deadly virus have caused considerable concern in the medical community. A nationwide survey of residents found that 65 percent would design their practices to avoid AIDS patients; 52 percent do not want to be known as AIDS specialists; 50 percent believe doctors should have the right to refuse to operate on an AIDS patient; and 73 percent would withhold lifesaving treatment from an AIDS patient if the risk of becoming infected were even 1 in 100. Another nationwide survey of practicing physicians found that 50 percent would not treat AIDS patients if they had a choice. A third survey limited to internal medicine and family practice physicians reached the same conclusion: one-half would not accept or treat HIV-positive people if they were free to refuse them.

There have been more than a few cases of doctors refusing to treat patients in AIDS situations. A surgeon in Delaware determined that a man admitted to the emergency room needed surgery, but refused to perform it and transferred the patient by helicopter to a Washington, D.C., hospital because he suspected that the man was homosexual, and his HIV status could not be immediately proven. A study concluded that some doctors stigmatize gays and have negative attitudes regarding persons with AIDS as opposed to other diseases. Coroners have acknowledged delaying autopsies of people who die of AIDS-related complications.

Citing the necessary exposure to large quantities of blood, some heart surgeons have declared that they will not perform complex operations, such as coronary bypasses, on individuals who test positive for HIV. Ninety percent of the surgeons responding to a survey conducted by *Surgical Practice News* voiced that position.

The American Medical Association (AMA) and the American Bar Association (ABA) each have a specific position on this issue. The ABA believes that providers should not refuse to treat or limit treatment of an individual because of actual or perceived HIV status. The AMA states that "A physician may not ethically refuse to treat a patient whose condition is within the physician's current realm of competence solely because the patient has been infected with the AIDs virus. . . . When an epidemic prevails, a physician must continue his labors without regard to the risk to his own health." Moreover, the American College of Physicians has ruled that the refusal of a doctor to care for a patient with an AIDS condition is "morally and ethically indefensible." But it does not appear to be illegal.

At the turn of this century two of every one hundred medical students died of tuberculosis they had contracted from their patients. Though TB was not as deadly then as HIV is now, it was far more transmissible. Perhaps yesterday's medical community was more willing to place the welfare of the patient before its own welfare.

Many hospitals have incorporated into their medical staff bylaws a provision that requires doctors to abide by the AMA's Principles of Medical Ethics. Hence, a hospital may be in a position to discipline physicians who refuse to treat AIDS patients. A few state medical societies, however, have adopted policies allowing such refusals if another competent doctor is available and willing to assume care of the patient. The Associated Medical Schools of New York issued a policy statement that its doctors must unequivocally accept care of AIDS patients, indicating that those who refuse will be dismissed. The surgeon general has rebuked health care personnel for discrimination against AIDS patients and has said that those who refuse to treat them are "worthy of contempt and condemnation."

Applications for admission to medical school are down, and training programs at some hospitals are not full. Spouses of surgeons at public urban hospitals have expressed extreme worry about their husbands or wives contracting HIV in surgery and then unwittingly transmitting it to them during sexual intercourse. AIDS is blamed as one of the reasons hospitals, especially in urban areas, cannot secure the quality and quantity of doctors they need. Interest in internal medicine is especially low, reports the *Washington Post* in an article entitled "When Fear of AIDS Infects the Healers: Students Reconsider the Risks of Medicine."

A few urban hospitals have reported that some RNs regularly assigned to treat AIDS patients have accepted job offers at competing health care facilities. Their motive was neither higher pay nor better benefits, but instead a promise of freedom from treating AIDS patients. In the current, tight labor market for RNs, this attitude can cause a serious staffing problem.

Instead of quitting, health care workers who do not want to risk exposure to the HIV virus have the option of refusing to work. Actual cases of such refusals include a food service worker who left the tray at the door of an AIDS patient's room; a housekeeping employee who would not change the sheets of an AIDS patient; and a technician who balked at entering the room of an AIDS patient to hook up the television. A fire district in Colorado compiled a list of residents with infectious diseases, including AIDS, and adopted a policy of not responding to calls for first aid for anyone on the list.

In Indiana a medical laboratory fired a technician who refused to test vials of body fluids carrying warning labels about AIDS. Arguing that her refusal to perform her assigned duties was grounded in a concern for safety and protected by OSHA, the technician sued the lab. The court, however, concluded that her refusal was not justified and dismissed the suit (*Stepp v. Review Board of Indiana Employment Security Divisions*). The human rights commissions of several cities have accepted hundreds of complaints from PWAs that dentists and doctors have refused to treat them. When a Manhattan dentist refused to perform a root canal on a patient previously diagnosed with AIDS, the New York City commission on Human Rights investigated, found a violation of the public accomodation-equal access provision, and recommended a fine of $7,500. AIDS activists applaud this and similar cases because of the difficulty HIV-infected people sometimes experience in obtaining medical care.

The antidote for ignorance, of course, is education. Attitudes can often be changed with information. The AMA is trying to educate physicians and the public with a magazine advertisement in which a doctor says, "The first principle of medical ethics is to offer compassion and respect for human dignity. For me, this pledge includes the illegal alien dying of AIDS." The AMA has also arranged for a special insurance policy that will pay $500,000 per year to physicians who contract HIV. The annual premium is $900. Aware of student concerns, some medical schools have purchased disability insurance protecting them against HIV and other diseases to which they are exposed during their work. All students are automatically covered and have the option of continuing the policy by picking up the premium after graduation. Many hospitals arrange for infectious disease professionals to address their personnel concerned about handling containers of the virus or treating AIDS patients. Published policies that mandate discharge for refusing to perform assigned duties can also be effective. However, actually terminating a health care worker for refusing to treat a PWA may stimulate a wrongful discharge suit against the hospital.

The National Labor Relations Board has a protected concerted activity doctrine that permits *two or more* employees who act in concert to refuse to perform a job duty that threatens their safety.

However, the threat must be legitimate and the fear well founded. The refusal of most health care personnel to go into the room of or to touch a patient with AIDS should not qualify, but desk nurses temporarily working in the emergency room who refuse to treat a PWA may qualify under this doctrine. (See chapter 4 for a more comprehensive discussion of concerted activity.)

A drastic solution for preventing personnel from being exposed to the virus is to discriminate against infected patients or residents. Such action, though, is not even an option for hospitals and nursing homes that receive Medicare and Medicaid funding, and which therefore fall under the jurisdiction of Section 504 of the Vocational Rehabilitation Act of 1973 and Title VI of the Civil Rights Act of 1964. The U.S. Department of Health and Human Services (HHS) investigates all claims of refusal to admit HIV-infected patients, for they have handicapped status. HHS has ordered nursing homes in several states, including Texas and Louisiana, to discontinue admission procedures that discriminate against patients with HIV or risk losing federal reimbursement.

After being sued under Section 504 of the Vocational Rehabilitation Act by the American Civil Liberties Union and Lamba Legal Defensive Fund, a gay legal group, a hospital in California ended its policies of demanding that patients seeking admission to its chemical dependency program be tested for HIV and denying admission to any applicants who tested positive.

Beth Israel Hospital in Boston was sued when a surgeon on its staff refused to perform ear surgery on an HIV patient. Alleging discrimination against the handicapped in violation of Section 504 of the Vocational Rehabilitation Act, the suit by the estate of the deceased plaintiff survived summary judgment because Medicare and Medicaid payments to the hospital for plaintiff's treatment triggered federal jurisdiction.

Discrimination is not the solution. But administrators and other managers must be sensitive regarding their employees' fears and empathize with personnel who are regularly exposed to body fluids potentially contaminated with the virus. Safety is a condition of employment to which most employees attach considerable significance. Thus two related questions must be addressed: Should patients be tested for HIV, with positive results reported to personnel

164 · *Aids in the Workplace*

treating them? Are universal precautions sufficient, or should the facility purchase and require additional gear or adopt special policies designed to protect its personnel?

Testing Patients

Should all patients be routinely screened for HIV upon admission? If so, is there an obligation to notify employees treating them or patients located in the same area of their positive status? If not, and, for example, a nurse contracts HIV from a patient admitted for treatment of a gunshot wound, is the hospital liable? Would not the opportunity for voluntary testing—at least at urban hospitals—be helpful to the patient as well as the hospital?

Involuntary testing of patients for the purpose of refusing admission to those who are test positive is not acceptable. Federally funded hospitals would face strenuous legal challenge, and others would incur strong criticism and isolation in the medical community. Legitimate reasons for testing patients were set forth in chapter 5. More specific advantages are set forth below.

In hospitals where HIV-infected patients and employees are rare, a massive testing of all admissions would be unnecessarily costly and otherwise inappropriate. But an urban hospital in which 5 percent or more of its patients are ignorant of their HIV-positive status does present an appropriate testing situation. A blind study could be conducted to determine if an appreciable number of HIV-infected patients are being admitted or applicants are being hired. Urban hospitals with a blind or other study confirming a positive patient admission rate of 5 percent or higher would be performing a community service to conduct HIV testing of all patients upon admission. Those who learn of their positive status then would be in a position to seek medical counsel and perhaps begin drug treatment to reduce the advance of the infection. And hospital personnel treating them would know that they should exercise extra caution in performing functions connected with their body fluids. Testing all admissions for HIV can be an efficient and valuable exercise.

The above approach suggests that the patient's HIV-positive status should be communicated to hospital personnel assigned to his or her treatment. However, since the probability of infection is extremely low to zero, others—including fellow patients—should *not* be informed and the records containing the test result should be handled *confidentially*. Hospitals should be in full compliance with regulations and standards relating to the protection of patients and employees from transmission of infections for several critical reasons, including the possible need to defend HIV-related claims.

The prestigious *New England Journal of Medicine* recommends that all patients (and health care employees) be routinely tested for HIV, partially because of the benefits of early diagnosis and treatment.

If hospitalwide, mandatory testing of all patients is deemed unnecessary for a particular facility or improperly intrusive, consider a policy that would encourage all patients to consent. Those who refuse would still be admitted, but would be treated as PWAs. This approach could be supplemented with a requirement that all candidates for surgery be screened for HIV. Patients whose treatment involved handling of body fluids could also be added to the list. Most employees would welcome such policies as attempts to protect them.

It is advisable for all hospitals to obtain written consent to test for HIV from all patients at the time of admission. While this point may appear to be obvious, some hospitals have been performing these tests without the knowledge or consent of patients. One study confirmed that 34 percent of the hospitals surveyed only rarely obtained consent prior to testing patients for the HIV antibody. Forty percent reported that they gave the test results directly to the physician without recording them on patient records, regardless of whether consent was given, and only 27.5 percent used patient consent forms.

In a Pennsylvania case, three plaintiffs alleged that a physician tested their blood for HIV without their permission. Suing for negligence, invasion of privacy, and emotional distress, the plaintiffs acknowledged being informed of the positive results of their tests, but claimed it was improper to test without permission and assurances of confidentiality and counseling (*Doe v. Wils Eye Hospital*).

Suppose there is no admissions testing policy and an employee accidentally sticks himself with a needle used to draw blood from a patient. Concerned about the possibility of HIV transmission, the hospital and the employee request the patient to be tested, but he or she refuses. A frustrated, worried employee must now undergo a series of blood tests over an extended period of time to determine if he or she became infected with HIV through the needle stick. From the perspective of employee relations, it is critical to have a policy requiring the patient to provide a blood sample to be tested in these situations. Sympathetic legislatures have, in some states, enacted laws permitting hospitals to use a patient's previously drawn blood after an employee experiences an exposure; if none is available the hospital is legally authorized to secure a postexposure blood sample *without the patient's consent*! (See the summary of Louisiana's statute in chapter 3.)

After initially stating that hospitals should not screen patients (or employees) for HIV, the CDC revised its guidelines, and now advises that the decision to test patients should be made by physicians and individual hospitals. However, the CDC issued a list of specific procedures that hospitals that test are encouraged to follow:

1. Obtain consent prior to test
2. Inform patient of test result
3. Treat testing records confidentially and limit their access to employees directly involved in caring for the positive patient, or as required by law
4. Provide patient who is positive with needed care; assure he or she will not be denied care due to test result
5. Evaluate effectiveness of testing program in reducing employee exposure to blood and other body fluids of positive patients and determine impact of testing on patients.*

There are a number of reasons why all hospitals should adopt a written policy on patient HIV testing. First, the number of HIV-infected patients admitted to health care facilities is increasing every year; many of the patients are ignorant of their positive status and revealing it through a testing program gives them otherwise lost opportunities to obtain counseling and treatment to inhibit the infection; these, in turn, can improve the health of the HIV-positive patient and reduce the probability of him or her infecting others through sex or IV drug use. Second, testing will enable the hospital to inform health care workers who are assigned to care for the

---

*"Recommendations for Prevention of HIV Transmission in Health-Care Settings," contained in appendix A, document 7. With respect to the prerequisite of consent, sample forms are included in appendix C, documents 11–13.

infected patient, and to monitor their required use of special equipment; the hospital thus promotes their safety and protects them from exposure to this deadly virus. Third, hospital, clinic, and nursing home employees are generally fearful of contagion, and this testing policy represents an effort to control an infectious disease. Fourth, without a written policy, uniformly administered by the hospital, the hospital would have to rely on the judgment and opinions of various doctors and department heads, resulting in inconsistent decisions. Fifth, defenses to potential legal claims are much improved. Sixth, the community, including potential patients, is assured that complex issues involving AIDS have been anticipated and analyzed. As I have indicated, many state legislatures are considering bills designed to protect health care workers. At the very least, employers of health care workers who are potentially exposed to HIV in the course of their duties should adopt policies to promote their safety.

Turning to substance, the overriding question regarding testing is whether it should be mandatory or voluntary. With respect to admissions, hospitals with an actual or estimated HIV positive admission rate of 5 percent or higher should embrace mandatory testing. A study revising the figure below 5 percent would cause conversion to a voluntary program wherein all patients would be advised of their opportunity for an HIV antibody test and encouraged to take advantage of it. However, regardless of the percentage of positive admissions, patients should be advised that a condition of their admission is their consent to this test *if* a health care employee or fellow patient is accidentally exposed to their blood or other body fluids; by obtaining informed, written consent for the test in the stated circumstances *at the time of admission*, there is no need to secure consent again in the event of a later exposure. Legally, there could be problems with a mandatory testing program. First, hospitals must be certain that no local law prohibits testing for HIV antibodies. Second, hospitals cannot refuse to treat an emergency patient who refuses to consent to the test. Third, hospitals and physicians under the jurisdiction of the Vocational Rehabilitation Act and the Americans with Disabilities Act may not deny admission to or limit treatment of HIV infected patients who are regarded as handicapped (see chapter 2). With these admonitions, hospitals should adopt policies that adhere to the CDC guidelines, comply with federal and local laws, reassure personnel, and identify carriers of a deadly virus.

The specific components of an HIV patient testing policy must address two objectives that sometimes seem mutually exclusive: protect the health of the provider and promote the interests of the patient. To address the rights of the patient the policy should: (1) require that a written, informed consent form be presented to the patient at admission, and that the consequences of signing or not signing the consent form are carefully explained by trained staff instructed to solicit questions and ensure understanding; (2) prohibit testing without consent; (3) restrict access to test results to doctors and nurses directly responsible for that patient's care; and (4) mandate immediate notification of results to and counseling for patients with positive findings.

To protect the health of hospital personnel the policy should: (1) require mandatory tests upon admission for all patients in hospitals with an appreciable number of seropositive patients (5 percent or higher), and strongly encourage all patients to voluntarily submit to testing in all other hospitals: (2) inform all patients upon admission that as part of the hospital's protocol for infection control, they must provide written consent to test for hepatitis B, HIV, and other communicable diseases and viruses in the event of an exposure to a hospital employee or patient; (3) require that test results be entered on the patients' records so that nurses—as well as doctors—involved in caring for them have knowledge of those who are infected; (4) mandate that patients who refuse testing upon admission should be treated as if they are HIV positive; and (5) require that coded *caution* signs relating to body fluids be posted on the doors of positive patients.

Regardless of whether hospitals decide to mandate or encourage patients to be tested upon admission, all should consider *requiring* candidates for surgery and critical care to consent as a condition for performance of the treatment. The reason, of course, is the relatively high risk of exposure to blood with these procedures.

If a testing program is implemented, hospitals must be certain to comply fully with applicable state laws regarding confidentiality, informed consent, and disclosure. Many states require physicians and providers to report cases of HIV to public health officials. Some laws require counseling of patients testing positive and limit disclosure to certain people, such as spouse, sexual partner, or needle-sharing partner. A few laws specifically authorize disclosure to emergency medical technicians and other health care workers who have treated the patient.

This type of testing program can be costly to health care employers but the benefits set forth above far outweigh the costs.

Universal and Special Precautions

The Occupational Safety and Health Administration (OSHA) requires providers to use universal precautions, that is, to treat all patients as if they are infected with HIV. Some hospitals have decided that this approach makes economic as well as safety sense. It is less costly to purchase the extra gear and require its use for all patients than to screen every patient, at hospital expense, for the presence of HIV. OSHA estimates that nationwide application of universal precautions costs hospitals $195 million per year, while the University of Iowa College of Medicine says that the cost of using masks, gloves, gowns, and other protective gear for all patients is $336 million per year. Both figures are significantly less than the $2.6 billion it would cost to screen all patients at all hospitals for HIV. For suburban hospitals, where the incidence of HIV is thus far quite low, following universal precautions is a valid approach. But urban hospitals with an HIV patient admission rate of greater than 5 percent may want to supplement their universal precautions policy with a patient testing program.

. Hospitals should document the training they provide their personnel concerning use of universal precautions. Documentation can serve several purposes, including response to an audit by OSHA. Employees should be given the opportunity to put on and take off the protective gear and become accustomed to moving and working in it on hospital time. Literature promoting universal precautions should be distributed to personnel and posted on the bulletin board. Employees should be told that compliance with universal precautions is a condition of their employment, and personnel who fail to do so are subject to disciplinary action.

As a practical matter, there are limits to this legal doctrine. Employees in the emergency room at one hospital all began wearing masks, gloves, gowns, and goggles after a meeting with administration during which universal precautions were explained. There was much talk among personnel about the concept and gear during the first week, with one employee reportedly showing up with a bulletproof vest. Another had to be counseled about consuming ten to fifteen minutes in putting on gear he fabricated at home which restricted his mobility. However, during the weeks thereafter, interest plummeted, and the safety equipment was discarded as unrealistic and unneccessary. Gloves continued to be used, but masks, goggles, and gowns were seldom seen.

Even when health care personnel are motivated to wear the gear, the hectic pace and pressure with trauma cases make it unlikely that full compliance will always be achieved. A survey of emergency room personnel at one hospital asked how often they comply with universal precautions in the following situations: procedures where risk of splashed blood is minimal—60 percent; invasive procedures with significant risk of splashed blood—16 percent; and patients with profuse bleeding—19.5 percent. Hence, personnel are taking the fewest precautions in situations where they face the greatest risk. Hospitals should institute internal compliance programs to prompt their personnel to use universal precautions.

An orthopedic surgeon at San Francisco General Hospital insisted that her team wear the following protective gear: double shoe covers, knee-high boots, reinforced gowns, hats and masks, space suit-type helmets, goggles or glasses, a filter system that prevented breathing aerosolized blood particles, and triple latex gloves. Viewed as an alarmist and an extremist and criticized for overreacting and contributing to misconceptions about transmission of the virus by some, she eventually left her position. However, she wrote a book about the need for protection from the virus, some of her ideas have been adopted by orthopedists, and she has been asked to address groups in the medical community that are anxious to discuss her views.

At the other end of the spectrum are physicians who seem to ignore universal precautions. It is difficult for hospitals to insist that their other personnel comply fully with saftey policies when doctors freely violate them. Another practical problem is the occasional shortage of disposable gloves and other gear. However, several medical supply companies are creating and marketing new products designed to protect health care personnel.

Hospital are advised, guided, and regulated by the federal government for the purpose of protecting health care personnel from exposure to HIV. Various federal agencies have published guidelines, regulations, recommendations, enforcement procedures, and educational materials concerning AIDS. Thus the CDC has issued "Universal Precautions for Prevention of Transmission of HIV. . . in Healthcare Settings," and "Recommendations for Preventing Transmission of HIV. . . during Exposure-Prone Invasive Procedures", and OSHA has published a standard for health care employers and a set of instructions for this agency to follow while inspecting hospitals for compliance with its rules for health care workers potentially exposed to HIV. Health care employers are obligated to be aware of and in compliance with standards and rules designed to reduce the probability of occupational exposure to HIV and other bloodborne diseases.*

Here is a brief summary of pertinent provisions of the CDC guidelines:

- Wear *gloves* prior to contacting all body fluids and blood-soiled items; change them after treating each patient.
- Wear protective *gear*, including masks, eye wear, gowns, and aprons, during procedures likely to contain splashing of body fluids.
- Place *needles* in puncture-resistant containers for disposal—at no time touch used needles with your hands; dispose of used needles immediately after use—do not attempt to recap.
- Use mouthpieces, resuscitation bags, and other ventilation devices.
- Employees with open scratches or wounds should not engage in direct patient care.

---

*See appendix A, documents 1–9; *Update. Universal Precautions for Prevention of Transmission of HIV, Heptatis B Virus and other Bloodborne Pathogens in Health Care Settings*, 37 Morbidity & Mortality Weekly Rep. 377 (1988); adopted by OSHA—52 Fed. Reg. 41,818 (1987). *Occupational Exposure to Bloodborne Pathogens*, 54 Fed. Reg. 23,042 (1989), and *Work Practices by Healthcare Workers*, 13 O.S.H. Rep. (BNA) 765 (1983). OSHA Proposed Rule on Heptatis B and HIV (AIDS) Virus, 52 Fed. Reg. 45438 (1987). Department of Labor/Department of Health and Human Services Joint Advisory Notice—Protection against Occupational Exposure to Hepatitis B Virus (HBV) and Human Immunodeficiency Virus (HIV) (1987). OSHA #31202 Pamphlet: Worker Exposure to AIDS and Hepatitis B (1982).

• *Wash* hands and skin immediately if contaminated with body fluids.

OSHA put legal teeth into the CDC's concept of universal precautions by issuing Standard 1910.1030 (Bloodborne Pathogen), which covers all employers with personnel subject to occupational exposure. Any jobs with "occupational exposure," for example, a manufacturing plant's in-house nurse or a shipyard's private fire department, bring employers within the standard's jurisdiction. Here is a summary of its major provisions:

1. Employers must write and have available a written Exposure Control Plan that determines whether an exposure has occurred and establishes a procedure for evaluating the circumstances surrounding these incidents.
2. The plan, which must be accessible to employees, must be periodically reviewed and updated to reflect new procedures affecting occupational exposures.
3. Personnel must be given training concerning the plan and its procedures.
4. Engineering and work practice controls to eliminate or at least minimize employee exposure must be studied and adopted. Examples include use of puncture-proof containers and work practices such as hand washing to reduce contamination. Of course, protective equipment such as gloves, gowns, and masks must be provided to employees at the employer's cost.
5. Hazards of the workplace must be communicated to employees. This requirement includes warning labels on containers and signs indicating restricted areas.
6. Medical records must be made available to affected employees and maintained for thirty years after termination of employment. Records pertaining to training must be preserved for at least three years after the sessions.

The overall goal is to protect personnel who are exposed to infectious blood, fluids, or other materials in the normal performance of their duties. Educational sessions and protective equipment are supposed to prevent exposures to HIV, but employees who experience an "occupational exposure" must be given the opportunity for testing and counseling.

Compliance with the standard is a challenge. To assist hospitals in their efforts to understand the obligations and interpret the requirements, the American Hospital Association issued "OSHA's Final Bloodborne Pathogens Standard: A Special Briefing." It explains the components of an exposure control plan and suggests specific procedures for achieving compliance with all aspects of the standard (see appendix A, document 8).

Employers covered by the standard should anticipate inspections by OSHA to determine whether they are in compliance. Insight into policies and procedures followed by OSHA investigators while conducting such inspections is available in "Enforcement Procedures for the Occupational Exposure to Bloodborne Pathogens Standard." OSHA has also published various fact sheets to educate health care personnel about how to protect themselves from exposures and why it is so important to report exposures as soon as they occur. Use of these sheets by employers in communication plans can be of assistance in securing compliance with the standard, gaining a favorable result in the event of an inspection, and defending against claims of noncompliance with the standard. See appendix A, document 9 (A–D).

OSHA's authority to enforce these requirements is derived from the "general duty" clause of the act establishing it.* A hospital in Connecticut was cited for failing to implement an effective training program on blood-borne diseases and failing to provide employees with protective equipment. A Massachusetts hospital was fined over $23,000 for failing to abate hazards previously cited by OSHA, which included failure to ensure that immunology lab workers wear proper eye protection while working with blood; failure to ensure containers of hazardous material were equipped with covers; failure to remove hazardous waste as often as necessary; and failure to use hazard tags to identify containers with such waste. Other citations included failure to require employees to wear cleaning gloves impervious to bleach, failure to require the wearing of goggles, and failure to provide information and training to an employee. Another hospital was hit with a penalty of $39,000 for failure to provide

---

*OSHA monitors the employers' general duty "to furnish to each employee employment and a place of employment which are free from recognized hazards that are causing or likely to cause death or serious physical harm to employees" (29 U.S.C. Sec. 654[a] [1]).

protective equipment in the toxicology lab and failure to require use of protective eye equipment in the chemistry lab. Over five hundred inspections of hospitals have been conducted pursuant to employee complaints, referrals, accidents, or routine audits.

The Service Employees International Union (SEIU), American Federal of State, County, and Municipal Employees (AFSCME), and other unions have complained that OSHA has been late and lax in adopting and enforcing mandatory guidelines for the protection of health care employees. AFSCME has been critical of federal government estimates of the risks of infection to hospital workers. The union contends that the risk of contracting HIV from a needle stick is much more serious than OSHA acknowledges. From the perspective of at least some health care personnel, it appears that hospitals and hospital associations are less than enthusiastic about statutes and administrative rules designed to protect them, while unions are promoting efforts to protect them. Hospitals should look for and create opportunities to communicate their sincere concern, purchase all necessary protective gear—which should never be in short supply—and educate personnel on the need to comply with universal precautions.

A major function of hospitals is to enforce the policies they have adopted. For example, most health care facilities instruct their personnel to dispose of used needles in specially provided boxes; this instruction is consistent with a CDC guideline recommending *against* any attempt to recap needles (a practice that has caused numerous needle sticks). Despite these efforts by the CDC and hospitals, a survey of Michigan hospitals found that between 25 and 50 percent of used needles are recapped. Providing boxes, instructing against recapping, and educating on the need to protect themselves from HIV infections are insufficient. Health care facilities must also monitor compliance with their instructions and rules and take disciplinary action against those in violation.

Nursing homes and hospitals must be certain to comply with any applicable state laws enacted to protect their personnel. For example, Maine has a statute providing that health care workers who are accidentally exposed to the blood or body fluids of an HIV patient may file a suit in state court to secure an order *requiring* that the patient to submit to HIV antibody testing. The burden is on the health care employee to prove that an exposure occurred and that it creates a significant risk of HIV infection. In Louisiana the hospital may test the blood of the patient in these exposure situations *without* the consent of the patient. In cases involving litigation under these statutes, hospitals should seriously consider having their attorneys represent the interests of occupationally exposed employees.

Health care employers have both legal and practical motivations to adopt effective policies that protect the health and safety of their personnel. In the face of CDC studies and OSHA instructions and standards, a hospital or home that fails to administer a sound employee protection policy may be guilty of negligence. Irrespective of federal statutes and regulations, it is well established common law that employers may be liable for occupationally contracted diseases caused by its negligence. Hospitals and nursing homes are legally obligated to become informed of hazards in the workplace, to warn employees of hazardous conditions, and to furnish protection from such dangers. Hospitals must adhere to, as a minimum, standard practices for protecting employees and preventing infection; those that continue to follow old practices and policies in this area are vulnerable to the standard rising as new data becomes available and other hospitals adopt more sophisticated approaches. Thus, what was standard practice yesterday may be ruled negligence tomorrow.

From a practical perspective, employees at a health care facility that fails to fully comply with federal government recommendations and falls behind protection policies and practices in the industry are more apt to have low morale, sign union cards, and quit.

Health care facilities should integrate employee protection policies and procedures with the CDC guidelines, the OSHA Bloodborne Pathogen Standard, state laws, *and* their own policies on infection control. Risk management programs should be continuously searching for new products and equipment to shield employees from exposures. Educational programs on procedures and protective gear should be held periodically. Written policies should be regularly updated and expanded for controlling HIV. As part of that program the content of all jobs should be analyzed for probability of exposure to HIV. Do the duties and functions of each involve exposure to blood, body fluids, and tissue? Are there opportunities for sticks, splashes, and soakings? If so, what is the degree of risk?

To determine the degree of risk, the employer should analyze the *frequency* of exposure, the *volume* of blood or body fluid with which the person in the position has contact, and the concentration of the virus. Medical assistance is necessary for this exercise which should be well documented.

Then the jobs determined to involve risk should be assigned a category or class that will resolve questions involving special precautions, testing of patients and disclosure (for protection of employees), and practice restriction or disclosure (for protection of patients). I suggest the following three categories:

1. *Identifiable Risk*: Safety-sensitive positions; special precautions required; test patients and disclose results to employees directly treating them; special training of employees to minimize exposure; also practice restrictions for employees who are HIV positive or disclose their HIV status to patients.
2. *Low Risk*: Universal precautions sufficient; no special testing of patients but disclose known HIV-positive status of patients to employees in these jobs who are directly treating them; special education and training of employees to minimize exposures is advisable; neither practice restriction nor disclosure of employee HIV status is necessary.
3. *Remote Risk*: Universal precautions sufficient; no testing of patients but disclose positive HIV status to employees directly treating them, when known; special training, practice restriction, and disclosure of HIV employee status to patients unnecessary.

This special policy, of course, is designed to prevent the employee from being infected by the patient and vice versa. In category 1 jobs, prudent practices dictate that patients who refuse to be tested (as well as those who test positive) be reported to all employees and treated as infectious. Also "special precautions" in the form of gowns, two sets of gloves, and goggles should be mandated.

The documentation involved in analyzing and assigning the risks should be preserved for assistance in defending the facility against possible legal claims.

Duty to Disclose Patient Status to Employees

Inextricably inherent in any discussion of testing, informed consent, and protection of patients and employees is the legal doctrine of "duty to disclose." When a hospital has knowledge that a patient is HIV positive, must that information be disclosed to employees treating him or her? When a hospital knows that a health care employee has contracted the virus, must that knowledge be conveyed to patients being treated by him or her? Should the hospital inform the spouse or other members of the infected employee's family?

One hospital nurse complained about the fact that she had been caring for a particularly ill patient for several weeks before she learned that he had AIDS. The nurse became very emotional, worried about the numerous contacts she had with the patient and his body fluids, and demanded to know why she was not informed. Attorneys and administrators can easily dismiss this complaint with an explanation of universal precautions, but that does not really answer the plaintive cry of a health care worker who simply wanted to be advised of the HIV status of the patient so she herself could take extra precautions.

A Nebraska nurse was told to inject a particular patient with insulin. During the process she accidentally pricked her hand with the needle. Soon thereafter she was informed that the patient was positive for HIV, and that she had been exposed to the virus. While the nurse has not yet become seropositive, and may never do so, she filed a lawsuit, claiming that she has suffered emotional disturbance and shock to her nervous system as a result of the incident, and that the hospital was negligent in failing to inform her that the patient was suspected of having AIDS (*O'Calloghan v. Stone*).

A Pennsylvania nurse participated in an invasive diagnostic procedure on a patient without wearing protective gloves, even though she had a small cut on one hand. Informed the next day that the patient had AIDS, she became upset that the hospital had failed to disclose the AIDS condition prior to the treatment and eventually filed suit for $20,000, claiming emotional trauma. An HIV antibody test was negative and the suit was dismissed (*Halverson v. Brand*, 569 A.2d 927 [Pa. 1990]).

From the perspective of the patient, studies confirm that the public wants to know. Patients believe their hospitals should inform them that a health care employee treating them is positive for HIV. Should not employees be given the same notice, especially when the risk of infection from patient to employee is significantly higher than the reverse?

The legal doctrine of duty to disclose often runs directly contrary to the hospital's duty to maintain confidentiality. Frequently the hospital must make a choice: maintain the confidentiality of a patient's HIV status and risk offending an employee treating him *or* disclose the fact that the patient is carrying the virus for the purpose of protecting personnel and risk a suit for breach of confidentiality. The same choice must frequently be made with HIV-positive personnel who continue their duties of treating patients.

One hospital attempts to balance these competing interests by testing all patients upon admission and assigning the few who are positive to its floors and units with all other patients. When a unit has an HIV-positive patient, all personnel on all shifts assigned to that unit are informed that an undisclosed patient is infected. Thus the employees exercise extra care and the patient's confidentiality is not compromised.

The doctrine raises ethical issues as well as legal ones. Informed by his doctor of HIV-positive status (acquired through furtive homosexual experiences), Mr. Jones has a counseling session with his minister and then instructs the doctor and the minister not to divulge his condition to anyone, including his wife. What obligation, if any, do the doctor and the minister have to notify Mrs. Jones? States are entering this sensitive terrain with statutes that are grounded in common sense. Thus, New York permits doctors to disclose HIV-positive test results to spouses, sexual partners, and needle-sharing partners of the patient *if* they reasonably believe the contact will not be warned by the infected patient. This approach protects doctors from legal liability when they are taking steps to protect the health of individuals at significant risk. Courts should extend this concept to disclosures by nonmedical people with definite knowledge of an infected person who communicates an intent not to disclose his or her condition to those at definite risk.

Legislatures and courts should assert themselves in this area and clarify the rights and obligations of the parties so that individuals may act to protect others without fear of triggering a legal claim and resulting liability. Warning people at risk of acquiring a deadly virus is a legitimate interest of the state, one that normally outweighs the interest of maintaining confidentiality. For example, a large number of states require physicians and other health care providers to report cases of HIV to public health officials; compromising confidentiality to promote health and safety is often the better choice.

In some situations, though, the balancing of interests is a delicate exercise. A scientist refused to comply with a Colorado law requiring him to disclose the names of HIV-positive people to the state health department because he was running an AIDS drug research program financed by the federal government and the volunteers participating in the experiment had a right to confidential treatment of their names and status. For its part, the state wanted the names to help it track the virus, locate others who could be or had been infected, and stem its spread. Further, the data on each infected individual was maintained by the state on a special, self-contained computer and violation of the law mandating disclosure was a fine of up to $300. It is suggested that, once again, the interests of warning and protecting others and stopping the spread of HIV are superior to those of the persons with AIDS who desire anonymity.

In attempting to resolve these seemingly intractable issues and to draft policies covering them, hospitals and nursing homes must determine if any state laws dictate disclosures. For example, some states require hospitals admitting patients subsequently discovered to have certain infectious diseases, including HIV, to notify persons involved in treating or transporting the patient of that diagnosis. Most of these statutes have a provision requiring that the notification be made in a manner that tends to protect the confidentiality of the patient and the health care personnel treating or transporting the patient.

Protection of the health of hospital and nursing home personnel directly involved in patient care is an interest superior to that of the privacy of those particular patients. Thus, whenever a health care facility become knowledgeable of a patient's HIV-positive status, it should disclose that information to personnel *directly* involved in the treatment. These employees should be reminded of their obligation to maintain confidentiality, and the records revealing HIV status must be restricted.

Responding to Employees Potentially Infected with HIV

Testing

Suppose a hospital or nursing home administrator receives information that an employee may be HIV positive. The source could be unfounded rumors reported by fellow employees or others in the community, which should be rejected out of hand. Sometimes, though, the information is more substantial, such as an official report of a needle stick, blood splash, or other exposure to the virus. Or the employee himself or herself might advise the administrator that a sexual partner has been diagnosed with AIDS. Health care employers should have policies requiring employees exposed to infectious diseases (occupationally or otherwise) to report that fact.

What action, if any, should the hospital or nursing home take? Is testing appropriate? If so, should the test for the HIV antibodies be mandatory or voluntary? Should the employee be removed from the job in question? If so, should he or she be transferred or terminated? What are the legal risks presented by each of these issues?

As I noted earlier, the *New England Journal of Medicine* advocates routine testing of employees as well as patients. Knowledge of HIV status can be beneficial to all concerned, including the hospital. However, a federal court in Nebraska enjoined a public mental health facility from carrying out a mandatory HIV antibody testing program for all personnel. The ruling affected four hundred staff members at the facility which provides residential, vocational, and other services for the mentally retarded. The court held that the testing program violated the Fourth Amendment's prohibition against unreasonable searches and seizures, pointing out that "the risk of transmission of the disease from the staff to the clients . . . is minuscule, trivial, extremely low, extraordinarily low, theoretical, and approaches zero" (*Glover v. Eastern Nebraska Community Office of Retardation* 686 F. Supp. 243 [D. Neb. 1988]).

While nonpublic hospitals are not subject to Fourth Amendment rulings, such hospitals should recognize that viewed practically, preemployment testing of all applicants for HIV antibodies is generally inappropriate. Obtaining the knowledge that an otherwise perfectly healthy applicant for a health care position is HIV positive triggers complex legal issues. Failing to hire the applicant because of his or her HIV status would be construed as improper discrimination against the disabled. Rejecting the infected applicant for being "unqualified" or for other reasons can still stimulate a disability claim, with a government agency or court finally deciding what truly motivated the decision not to hire. And hiring and placing a new employee known to have HIV infection in a patient care position may present a "duty to disclose" situation. For example, a hospital's knowledge that an infected nurse was assigned to care for a patient who later becomes a plaintiff is evidence the plaintiff's attorney will use against the hospital. Further, testing clericals, food service, laundry, and maintenance personnel can cause far more problems than it solves. In almost all cases, the hospital's legal status is enhanced when it is ignorant of the HIV status of its applicants and most of its employees.

To be sure, there are specific situations in which mandatory testing of certain personnel becomes appropriate. Periodic testing of health care employees regularly exposed to blood and other body fluids in the performance of their duties helps to prevent infection *and* litigation. Surgeons, emergency room doctors and nurses, and others who are involved in invasive procedures should be tested. Any employee who has had a definite exposure to the virus in the performance of his or her duties should also be tested. In these cases, a test can benefit the employee, protect his or her family, and protect patients and employees at the hospital. If the test is performed immediately after the exposure and turns out to be positive, the hospital can use this evidence to defend itself should the employee file a claim against it; antibodies to HIV do not develop immediately, and thus their presence in the employee's bloodstream signifies a prior exposure, arguably one that took place outside the hospital. If the test is initially positive or the employee converts later in the testing program to seropositive status, he or she needs counseling and treatment. Further, the spouse or sexual partner should be notified. Finally, the hospital then can analyze the entire situation, including the employee's specific job duties and its own infection control policy to determine if the employee should continue all of the duties connected to his or her job.

A male nurse at a Louisiana hospital had a friend and roommate who was admitted as a patient to that hospital and later diagnosed as suffering from AIDS. The duties of the nurse included making rounds, doing assessments, giving medication both orally and by injection, starting IVs, changing dressings, performing catheterizations, and giving enemas. The administrator of the hospital determined that, in order for the hospital to comply with its guidelines and recommendations on the treatment of employees who are HIV positive, the hospital had to know the nurse's HIV status. When the nurse was asked to take the test, he explained that a test had already been performed. He initially indicated that he would provide the result to the hospital, but over an extended period of time repeatedly refused. He was then discharged for failure to comply with the hospital's infection control policies. The ACLU filed suit on his behalf, claiming that the hospital violated Section 504 of the Vocational Rehabilitation Act of 1973, the Louisiana Civil Rights for Handicapped Persons Act, the Fourteenth Amendment, and the Fourth Amendment.

The primary issue was whether the hospital could lawfully require the nurse to reveal his HIV test result. The federal district court dismissed all claims, but the plaintiff took the case to the U.S. Court of Appeals for the Fifth Circuit. That court carefully reviewed the CDC guidelines that were in effect at the time, which called for continuing consultation between the health care institution and the employee's personal physician to determine, on an individual basis, what job assignments the employee was capable of performing. The court agreed that the hospital had a right to require that pertinent facts about the nurse's health be revealed so that it could monitor his condition and determine whether additional precautions or job modifications would be necessary. Ultimately, the court concluded that because the hospital had the right to require such testing to ensure infection control and health and safety in general, it was justified in terminating the nurse. Specifically, the Fifth Circuit held that the plaintiff failed to prove any of the three elements of a federal law handicap claim: he was regarded as handicapped; he was discriminated against solely because of his perceived handicap; and he was "otherwise qualified" to perform the duties of his position (*Leckelt v. Board of Commissioners of Hospital District No. 1*, 909 F.2d 820 [5th Cir. 1990]).

Two federal laws have potential application to AIDS employment issues. The Vocational Rehabilitation Act of 1973 applies to employers possessing contracts and grants connected with the federal government. The Americans with Disabilities Act applies to all employers with fifteen or more employees, regardless of their contact with the federal government. It should be anticipated that judges interpreting each law would view an applicant or employee suffering from AIDS as "handicapped." It is also probable that an applicant or employee who is HIV positive but showing no signs of any debilitation would be perceived as handicapped and thus be protected. Further, a majority of states have special laws protecting handicapped individuals from employment discrimination which, if tested, would probably be interpreted to protect those with HIV, symptomatic HIV disease, and AIDS.

While plaintiffs who feel they have been discriminated against because of an AIDS condition have several laws upon which to base their claims, as the *Board of Commissioners of Hospital District No. 1* case demonstrates, hospitals are not without defenses. It is important, however, to study these laws to determine whether any facet of an HIV-AIDS policy, such as testing employees exposed to the virus, can be interpreted as a violation of the laws' intents.

One question to answer is whether testing of an employee following an exposure should be mandatory or voluntary. Hospitals deciding upon the latter course have found, in some situations, that health care workers exposed to HIV refuse the hospital's offer of free testing and counseling. Some say that they simply do not want to know whether they are HIV positive, while others seem to fear possible loss of job despite assurances to the contrary. Thus hospitals should strongly consider mandatory testing of health care workers exposed to the virus either in or out of the workplace.

Some fear that mandatory testing will dissuade employees from reporting an exposure. But a carefully crafted policy will require employees to report exposures and submit to testing, with those who violate either rule becoming subject to disciplinary action. As with other AIDS-related issues, the type and location of the hospital and the particular job in question must be analyzed before decisions . can be made on what policy, if any, to adopt in this area.

Evaluating an HIV-Infected Employee

Suppose a test has confirmed that a hospital worker is infected with HIV. Armed with this knowledge, what options does the hospital have? Any action taken in these circumstances, including the option of no action, is fraught with possible adverse legal and practical consequences.

Terminating the employee would be a blatant violation of federal and state laws that protect the disabled. Transferring the employee to a new position that is outside of patient care, at the same pay and benefits, may be appropriate in certain situations. However, in most situations, HIV infection alone, from a legal standpoint, is not sufficent reason to force an employee to assume another job. Exceptions to this general rule may involve operating or emergency room nurses and others with substantial exposure to wounds and body fluids of patients when the risk of transmitting the virus is *identifiable*.

If the hospital takes no action as far as the infected employee is concerned, does it have a duty to inform patients, fellow employees, or family members of the employee's HIV status? In most situations, the answer is no. But these questions and the lack of clear statutes and court cases to answer them demonstrate the dilemma. If the hospital transfers the employee to protect the patient, the hospital can be sued for handicap discrimination. On the other hand, if the hospital leaves the employee in his regular job, to ensure compliance with handicap discrimination laws, it may be subjecting itself to later suits from patients or fellow employees who claim that they contracted the virus from that employee. The plaintiff's attorney would argue that the hospital had knowledge of the employee's HIV status and was negligent in failing to remove this threat to his client's safety.

It would be helpful if hospitals and nursing homes were provided clearly drafted guidelines for dealing with infected but healthy and capable employees which, if followed, would shield them from suits. Recognizing that the current ambiguities place hospitals in a confusing state, the American Public Health Association proposed that the U.S. Department of Health and Human Services establish these standards for HIV-infected providers:

1. Responsibility is on health care employees to seek testing voluntarily if they are engaged in high-risk activities.
2. Policy should be adopted stating whether HIV status is reportable to the employer.

3. Policies protecting confidentiality of the provider's medical condition should also be adopted.
4. Determine, on the basis of scientific knowledge, whether an HIV-infected provider poses a risk to patients in the course of invasive procedures.
5. Responsibility is on the employer to accommodate the needs and protect the livelihood of health care providers with a blood-borne infection.
6. Responsibility is on the employer to ensure that an infected provider's skills are used to the maximum extent possible, and that an infected worker's medical treatment needs are accommodated in the manner that any other illnesses would be handled.

Health care facilities faced with an HIV-positive employee must perform a careful, reasoned analysis of whether the performance of his or her duties threatens the safety of patients or fellow employees. Is there an identifiable transmission? A group of representative physicians associated with the hospital can be enlisted to analyze the latest medical data concerning HIV infection. This analysis and conclusions regarding policy that follow it should be documented.

Medical Records

Hospitals and nursing homes have another set of unique legal and ethical issues created by their status as custodians of medical records. Almost every state has a statute requiring licensed hospitals to maintain accurate and complete medical records for each patient. While this information is vital to the patient and his or her physician, it is also important to the facility and the community at large. However, allowing improper access to the records of patients who are infected with HIV can lead to breach of confidentiality, violation of statutes protecting the privacy of patients, and serious lawsuits. The proper collection, storage, and dissemination of patient medical information is a challenge that all medical facilities must address.

Approximately thirty states have enacted laws that prevent disclosure of HIV status without the patient's consent, specify limited access to a patient's records, and provide penalties for wrongful disclosure. Moreover, courts have recognized "unauthorized disclosure of medical records" and "invasion of privacy" as torts or general causes of action and have permitted claims for compensatory and punitive damages. Some courts have recognized a state constitutional right to privacy and ruled that the *families* of patients whose records have been wrongfully disclosed have rights of privacy separate from those of the patient. Defenses to these suits include consent (an executed form is helpful) and need to know (for example, the health care employee to whom the disclosure was made is involved in treating the plaintiff and needed to know his or her HIV status).

The problem would be manageable if the only issues were tight control of patient records when HIV is involved, highly restricted access to those records, and utilization of carefully crafted consent forms. However, juxtaposed against unauthorized disclosure is the legal claim of duty to disclose. Several states have enacted statutes recognizing the doctrine of "need to know." Further, some statutes require hospitals and nursing homes to report cases of AIDS to state medical officers; Colorado has imposed criminal sanctions for failure to comply. The goal of these laws, of course, is to promote public health by stopping spread of the virus. Moreover, as I have often indicated, there are legitimate reasons for a policy that mandates disclosure of a patient's HIV status to the health care personnel directly involved in the patient's treatment.

The problem of unauthorized disclosure of medical records is complicated by the advent of computers. Access to the data contained in them is frequently quite open. Suppose a business office clerical worker happens to learn through the hospital's computer that a patient who is a neighbor is HIV positive. Suppose further that the clerical worker informs other neighbors of this development and the patient and his family are persecuted and socially ostracized by fellow townspeople. And next suppose that the patient decides to sue the hospital for breach of confidentiality. As the example suggests, data on a patient's HIV status is sensitive and in the wrong hands can lead to practical and legal problems for health care facilities.

Computer records dramatically increase the probability of unauthorized or wrongful disclosure. Multiple terminals throughout the hospital usually mean that employees unconnected to the care of the patient can gain access to the patient's records. Traditionally, of course, the patient's file is maintained on a clipboard located in the patient's room or at the unit desk down the hall. Restricting access to this paper file to authorized medical personnel is relatively simple. But special policies are required to prevent wrongful disclosures of computer-generated HIV data.

Hospitals should take the following recommended steps to secure computer-based medical data:

1. Adopt special policies that recognize this concern, attempt to protect the data from improper dissemination, educate employees on the importance of avoiding prohibited disclosures, and provide for punishment of personnel who violate them.
2. Use locks on cabinets where sensitive disks are stored.
3. Restrict access to the medical records department.
4. Install line-of-sight barriers to prevent reading of display by others while an operator is using the computer.
5. Require any computer user who requests data about a patient to identify himself or herself, and evaluate and record the name and position of the person making the request before access is granted.
6. Identify patients in the computer by Social Security numbers instead of names.
7. Grant different levels of access to employees using the computer system.

Public hospitals should be particularly careful about unauthorized disclosures of HIV status. In a federal court case a policeman was informed by a man he stopped and arrested that the suspect was HIV positive. Later the policeman disclosed this information to a woman in their relatively small community who, in turn, informed others. This led to the removal of children from the school where the man's child attended and stories in the local newspaper and on television, with one report mentioning the name of the man. The suit filed by the wife (not the man himself) was upheld: the court recognized that she held a privacy right that had been invaded by the policeman, and that through its policeman the town had violated federal civil rights laws as well as committed an intentional infliction of emotional distress.

In another case, the plaintiff, who received a serious head injury at work, was seeing a doctor in connection with his worker's compensation claim. During the examination the patient volunteered that he was HIV positive and warned the doctor's nurse to carefully sterilize the instruments used to examine him. The nurse informed the doctor, who, in turn, told the worker's compensation insurer. The patient then filed suit against the doctor and the insurance company, alleging violation of a state constitutional right of privacy and a state law declaring that HIV test results were confidential. The court concluded that the nurse and doctor had improperly used information about the patient's HIV status that was properly conveyed to them for the purpose of preventing transmission of the virus. The patient had a reasonable expectation of privacy, and the health care providers violated his legal rights.

It is especially important for health care providers that employ computers to store and disseminate patient data to review their current practices and determine whether new polices are required.

Policy Checklist

Health care employers should review the following policy recommendations regarding patients and personnel, and then analyze whether any or all are appropriate for their particular facility. The answers will vary according to the type (hospital, nursing home, clinic), the size, the ownership (public or private), the location (urban or rural), the percentage of HIV-positive patients and personnel it probably has, and the past practice of the facility.

Patient Recommendations

1. Inform patients at the time of their admission that they are required, as a condition of admission, to report any infectious disease they know or suspect they have, including HIV, and to supply informed, written consent to disclosure of any positive condition to their physician, the director for infection control, and health care personnel who will be directly treating them.

2. Inform patients of hospitals with an appreciable number of seropositive admissions (5 percent and higher) that they are required, as a condition of admission, to execute a form consenting to various tests, including a test for HIV antibodies. Encourage patients at all hospitals to voluntarily consent to HIV testing.

3. Inform all patients being admitted for *invasive procedures* that they must, as a condition of their admission, supply informed, written consent to a test for the HIV virus and to dissemination of that test result to the director for infection control for the hospital, the doctors assigned to them, and other health care personnel directly involved in their treatment (but never test without an executed consent form).

4. Inform all patients that they are required, as a condition of admission, to execute a form consenting to testing for HIV antibodies in the event of employee exposure to their blood or body fluids through an accidental stick, splash, or other means.

5. Inform any patient of a provider's HIV-positive condition *if* the risk of the patient's being exposed to that employee's blood or body tissue during the performance of his or her duties is identifiable. The duty to inform is in force even if the provider's HIV status does not become known to the facility until *after* the patient's possible exposure.

6. Never refuse treatment to a patient infected with HIV because of that status.

Personnel Recommendations

1. All employees are required to report all exposures to infectious diseases, including HIV, to the facility's director for infection control in writing, providing data and description, regardless of whether said exposure occurred on or off the job. Employees who observe an accidental exposure or otherwise become aware that a fellow employee has been exposed are required to report that knowledge to the director for infection control.

2. All personnel must agree to a mandatory testing program for the HIV virus following exposure to HIV, whether said exposure occurred on or off the job. The facility will absorb all costs associated with the tests, which normally are conducted throughout the year following the exposure. Any employee refusing to take the test is subject to discharge for violation of the policy.

3. Those personnel in a position that has an *identifiable* risk of exposure to the blood and other body fluids of patients during the performance of their duties must submit, as a condition of their

employment, to periodic, mandatory testing for HIV (usually two or four times per year).

4. Options for a facility to consider regarding placement of an employee who is HIV positive or who has developed AIDS: (a) continuation, without restrictions, in regular job as long as employee is able to perform its essential duties; (b) continuation in regular job with restriction of duties to prevent exposure to blood and other body fluids of patients or employees and monitoring of performance and medical condition; (c) transfer to another patient care position in the department with duties unrelated to exposure or handling of blood or other body fluids (no invasive procedures); (d) transfer to non-patient-care job in another department; or (e) place on medical leave of absence. In determining which option to select for a particular situation, consider degree of risk; federal, state, and local laws; past practice; medical evaluations of the infected employee; and the ability of the facility to accomodate the employee's disabilty.

5. Generally, providers infected with HIV should not be restricted in their job duties or required to disclose their status to patients. Practice restrictions should be triggered only by an analysis that determines that the risk of transmission to a patient or a fellow employee is *identifiable*. If the employee opposes such restrictions, the facility, in its discretion, may obtain the employee's written consent to disclose his HIV status to patients he is directly treating. HIV-positive employees may not continue working in positions where the risk is *identifiable* unless there has been either practice restriction or disclosure to patients. Infected employees who oppose restrictions and job transfers and refuse patient disclosure will be counseled on the facility's policy, be given an opportunity for reconsideration, and—in the event of continued refusals—discharged.

6. Personnel engaged in patient procedures where the risk of transmitting the HIV virus is moderate or low must comply with universal precautions and wear all protective gear provided them. Personnel engaged in patient procedures where the risk of transmission is *identifiable* must take special precautions and wear special gear.

7. Treat all reports about the positive HIV status of employees and patients as confidential; restrict access to records containing this information.

8. Personnel, including staff physicians, who refuse to treat HIV-

positive patients are subject to discipline, including dismissal and suspension of privileges.

9. Information on patients who are HIV positive will be reported to all employees directly involved in their treatment by means of notation on the medical records and a coded (caution) sign on the door; employees privy to this sensitive data must maintain it on a confidential basis; and access to the patient's records must be restricted. Breaches of confidentiality and unauthorized releases of medical record data subject employees to disciplinary action.

To be effective, policies must provide a penalty. Thus, employees who violate these policies should be reminded of possible penalties, counseled on their rationale, and the need to achieve compliance. Repeat offenders should be disciplined, and if necessary, terminated.

There are five stages to policy development: (1) study past practice and any existing policy on the topic; (2) list objectives; (3) draft the new policy; (4) implement the new policy; and (5) administer the new policy.

Considerable effort must be expended in the policy development process, including implementation and administration. Appointing a risk manager or other administrator to perform a central review function and training all managers concerning proper administration of the policy will promote a necessary ingredient for successful policies: uniform application. The sensitive nature of these topics makes close attention to all phases especially important. Appendix C includes sample policies, checklists, bulletin board notices, forms, and other materials relating to health care facilities and AIDS.

Conclusions

Health care facilities have different, sometimes conflicting, roles in the battle against AIDS. They must treat AIDS patients and protect them against the ubiquitous, opportunistic diseases within their walls. They must protect their employees from the infectious, fatal HIV virus being carried by some patients. And they must assist their communities in efforts to prevent and treat AIDS-related problems through educational programs, voluntary testing on site, counseling HIV-positive persons, securing alternative care for AIDS patients, and lobbying for additional funding to pay for prevention and treatment.

To date, the number of lawsuits involving AIDS issues that have been filed against hospitals and nursing homes has not been overwhelming. It may be that potential plaintiffs are hesitant to divulge their status as a homosexual or a drug user. One would like to believe that another reason is that health care employees are strictly adhering to universal precautions and are being extremely careful about breach of confidentiality, with the result that opportunities for claims are few. However, the potential for increased litigation in this area is enormous. Most of the suits thus far have been filed by employees, as opposed to patients. The new Americans with Disabilities Act should stimulate many more employee suits in the future. Further, plaintiff attorneys are just beginning to learn of the available causes of action in these cases, and plaintiffs are becoming less hesitant to step forward. Finally, with the continuing spread of HIV beyond the homosexual and drug communities, more people will be tested and learn of their HIV status. When they do, suits involving HIV instituted by patients as well as employees will follow.

Preventing time-consuming, costly litigation and improving the probability of securing an early dismissal of suits that are filed, short of trial, are worthy goals. Analysis of the issues raised herein and implementation of proper policies are strategies for achievement of these goals.

Analyzing AIDS Problems

Preventing and Defending AIDS Claims

Framework for Analysis

As the number of HIV-positive persons in the workforce climbs each year and the cases spread throughout the nation to men and women of all races and ethnicities, the probability of an employer encountering a personnel problem involving AIDS increases. It is relatively easy to subscribe to general employment doctrines such as "don't discriminate against the disabled" or "treat PWAs as you do other employees," but it can be very difficult to solve specific problems involving real people and businesses. An employer with an AIDS problem wants to obey whatever laws may apply and treat the infected employee with kindness and sensitivity, but there are practical, often countervailing, factors, such as productivity and profit to consider. What should an employer do? Upon what factors should the decision be based? The decision-making approach I offer here is based on a risk and impact analysis. What is the risk that a particular course of action involving the PWA violates a law? High, low, or unclear? How severe is the penalty? What are the anticipated ramifications of ignoring the AIDS condition and either hiring the applicant or leaving the employee in his or her regular job? Will the employer be exposed to legal claims or adverse employee response?

Advocates for PWAs can and will argue that any type of discrimination against their clients should be illegal. Yet, as I have indicated, employers must weigh many possible variables when considering options for dealing with AIDS-related problems. Variables include:

(1) whether the person is merely a carrier of the virus and otherwise free of any type of impairment, is beginning to display signs of symptomatic HIV disease and suffering mild mental or physical incapability, or has an advanced case of AIDS with periods of complete physical impairment and/or dementia; (2) what industry is represented by the employer (manufacturing, banking, construction, or health care?); (3) what is the exact job in question (and its specific duties) (crane operator, surgeon, file clerk, or janitor?); and (4) are doctors in agreement about the PWA's physical and mental ability to perform work, or are their opinions in conflict? In these circumstances of widely fluctuating, individual situations and competing interests, it would be improper and unfair to employers for legislatures or judges to adopt per se rules that are rigidly applied to all scenarios. For example, the courts generally uphold the principle that PWAs should not be discriminated against, but at least one judge permitted a hospital to suspend the staff privileges of a surgeon who was infected with HIV.

"Discrimination" has become an ugly word in the employment arena. Somehow it is a positive trait to be "discriminating" in the selection of clothes, cars, spouses, and friends, but a negative trait to discriminate against applicants and employees. Yet every day employers discriminate against hundreds of employees—legally and with legitimate reasons. Thus, a personnel manager discriminates against twenty qualified applicants for a secretarial position by selecting the twenty-first applicant who typed slightly faster than the others. A supervisor discriminates against two warehouse employees for fighting on company property by firing them. A department head, ordered to reduce her staff by five, discriminates in favor of a less senior but more talented computer operator, with the result that older, more experienced operators are laid off. These employees are legitimately discriminated against because they are not the most appropriate, productive workers for the job.

People with AIDS conditions should not be categorized with other groups that have been extended special protection by our laws. While our society, through its legislatures and courts, has good reasons to forbid employers from discriminating against a person of color because of race, a female because of her sex, or a senior citizen because of age, the legislatures and courts are wrong to give all the people with various AIDS conditions the same across-the-board protection because of the critical differences between race, sex, and age, on the one hand, and AIDS, on the other. The medical facts that people with HIV are capable of infecting others with the fatal virus, that those with symptomatic HIV disease and AIDS will become physically and perhaps mentally impaired in the future, and that applicants and employees with an advanced AIDS condition will die within the relatively near future require that AIDS employment problems be considered differently. The fatal virus they are carrying can render them unsafe and unproductive in performing certain duties.

Many employers yearn for simple rules to help them handle all AIDS problems. Unfortunately, simple, rigidly applied rules often produce complex, unacceptable results. As H. L. Mencken said, "For every problem there is one solution which is simple, neat— and wrong." It is preferable to articulate an approach for resolving problems with AIDS in the workplace that takes all interests into consideration and yields solutions that are responsible and defendable.

The following eight points comprise a suggested framework for employers to use to analyze the risk and impact of options involving an applicant or employee with HIV, symptomatic HIV disease, or AIDS.

1. Is there a statute or ordinance (federal, state, or local) that directly applies to the situation? Does it clearly prohibit taking any action against the applicant or employee? Usually, the "action" would be rejection, in the case of an applicant, and transfer to another job, enforced leave of absence, or even—in highly limited circumstances—termination, in the case of an employee.

If the answers to these two questions are yes, no further analysis is required; the law must be obeyed. If, however, there is sincere and serious doubt about whether the law in question applies to the particular situation facing the employer, then the employer should pursue two further inquiries. First, how valid are the defenses? Defenses can be *procedural* (for example, the claim is filed too late, and therefore barred by a statute of limitations) and *substantive* (a judicial precedent or legislative history or a well-entrenched, uniformly applied policy permits the action taken). Second, what are the penalties if a violation is found? A complaining applicant or employee is usually "made whole" with orders of reinstatement and back pay, but additional remedies including compensatory and punitive damages and payment of the plaintiff's attorney and expert fees, can make the loss of even one case quite expensive. The stronger the defenses, and the milder the potential penalty, the more likely an employer will be to accept the legal risk and avoid possible practical problems.

2. Are there court or administrative cases suggesting that laws on related subjects may directly apply to the situation? For example, is a state law protecting the handicapped applicable to an applicant who announces in the interview that his roommate is dying of AIDS? If cases indicate that the applicant may be protected, again ask how valid are the defenses? And what are the penalties if a violation is found?

Suppose that neither a statute nor a judicial opinion clearly grants protection to homosexuals who are free of HIV but have a close relationship with a PWA. Once again, this is a point in favor of action adverse to the person with an AIDS condition.

3. If the HIV-positive applicant is hired or the employee with AIDS is left in his or her regular job, can it be reasonably anticipated that any of the following groups would take legal or other steps against the employer's interest: employees, customers, or patients? Specifically, would they sue for being exposed to the virus? Refuse to work with the PWA and perhaps encourage other employees to also withhold their services? Cease doing business with the employer? How effective or successsful would their efforts against the employer be? Is there any justification for these points in the law?

4. If the PWA is allowed to work in the job that he or she wants, what is the probability that others may be infected? The answer to this question should be based on an analysis of the specific job applied for or occupied by the PWA. Is it an office or clerical job, for example, or that of a nurse regularly treating patients with open wounds? Does the position involve sales, finance, or education, or the cleaning of teeth? Only exceptional jobs present reasonable opportunities for infecting others, and the employer bears the burden of proving the danger, relying upon a sincere, as opposed to an unrealistic, concern. Interviews with and documentation from medical doctors or dentists would be important in this area.

5. If the contemplated action against the person with AIDS is

not taken, what is the reasonably foreseeable impact on the "bottom line?" Specifically, will potential customers or patients really go to another hospital, causing substantial loss of business and profit, or are these fears speculative or unwarranted? How costly and otherwise burdensome would it be to hire the PWA applicant or retain the PWA employee in his or her current position?

A slight impact on cost permits no discrimination against the PWA. Any employer claiming substantial adverse impact should be prepared to prove it with objective evidence. Employers should realize, however, that judges do not extend much weight to such proof.

6. What is the impact of the contemplated action on the applicant or employee? Will he or she be deprived of needed insurance coverage? Will this be a devastating financial or emotional blow at a time when the PWA is already fragile and vulnerable? Or will he or she be grateful to take a leave of absence or accept a transfer to another position? There may not be a conflict between what the employer thinks is best for business and what is acceptable to the individual; there is no substitute for clear communcation, during which the employer's representative should noncoercively explain the options, solicit the PWA's views, and document the interview. People with AIDS conditions are legally classified as disabled and the Americans with Disabilities Act requires employers to engage in good faith discussions with disabled employees about accommodations that are reasonable.

Suppose that the employee with an AIDS condition strongly desires to continue working as long as he or she is physically and mentally able, and that the PWA's only financial resources are wages and insurance connected with the job. These facts, of course, support continuing his or her employment in some capacity.

7. What is the specific ability of the person with HIV, symptomatic HIV disease, or AIDS to perform the essential duties of the job in question, both presently and in the near future? Does he or she have symptomatic HIV disease, fully devleoped AIDS, or simply the virus? Is he or she physically or mentally impaired in any way that would interfere with job performance or reduce productivity or work quality? Can the PWA perform all of the essential duties of the job or only some of them? If the employer concludes that there already is or soon will be an impairment, what objetive, medically supported proof is available? If the employee cannot perform

the essential duties without accommodation, can he or she do them with accommodation? Have the possible accommodations been discussed with the employee? Has an analysis been conducted to determine whether each is reasonable or not? For those that are labeled unreasonable by the employer, has there been a determination of what type of hardship or burden, if any, each imposes on the owner? What is the financial cost to the employer of possible accommodations? Are there available jobs in other areas, perhaps somewhat isolated from the public or other employees, that the infected employee can perform? Can the employee be transferred to those jobs without loss of pay or benefits?

The burden will be on the employer to substantiate claims of impairment and lack of reasonable accommodation and undue burden with clear, direct, and objective testimony and exhibits. With respect to the first question—ability to both physically and mentally perform the essential duties of the job—the manager should list each of the duties connected with the job in question, ascertain which are essential and which are incidental, and then determine the physical and mental requirements for satisfactorily performing each of the essential duties. Many PWAs have long periods after an illness when they feel physically fit and believe they are able to perform the duties of their former positions. Typically, these AIDS patients inform their doctors that they are feeling much better, and the doctors are pleased to give them a letter stating that they are fit to return to their jobs. And, in most cases, they will be physically capable of performing the various duties of their jobs at that particular time, as verified by the doctors, but how long will that physical capability last? Moreover, what about their mental ability to perform the duties of their former positions? Though physically fit to work, a PWA may suffer mental deterioration that seriously impairs his or her ability to perform work duties, and that may even place fellow workers, customers, patients, or others in danger of harm.

One of the sad facts about AIDS is the devastation frequently visited in the victim's brain. A substantial percentage of AIDS patients show signs of brain disease or deterioration, including dementia. Specific symptoms include loss of memory, inability to make and carry out decisions, and a feeling of indifference. Some doctors have noted definite psychosis. How can an employer determine whether a particular PWA, reporting to work with a statement from the doctor that he or she is physically fit, has suffered mental deterioration that has severely impaired ability to work? The employer will need medical—including psychiatric—evaluations and documentation of those evaluations. Rather than relying upon the PWA's personal physician, it may be appropriate for the employer to retain its own doctor who has experience in treating AIDS conditions. The doctor should be given specific and detailed information concerning the duties of the job in question. For example, the possible consequences of mental deterioration in a PWA who works as a janitor in an office are far different from those of a computer operator, a surgeon, or a bank officer handling complex financial transactions. Tests can be administered to measure mental skills and abilities, and the results should be reported to the employer. Any oral information from the doctor concerning the results of examinations should be well documented. Whenever possible, a copy of written medical reports describing the evaluation, diagnosis, and conclusions of the doctor should be obtained and placed, along with other materials, in a secure file. The term "reasonable accommodation" means simply that the employer must make a reasonable attempt to accommodate the PWA. If the employer arranges and pays for medical evaluations and is informed that the PWA has suffered permanent mental or physical deterioration to the point of being incapable of performing the essential duties of his or her former job or any other job that is available, and no accomodations are reasonable, the employer has probably fulfilled its obligation.

It must be remembered that the employer retains the right to set and maintain standards of job performance. Any employee who can no longer meet those standards, regardless of past years of service and eligibility for handicapped status, may legally be removed from the job. Stated another way, any employee who can no longer perform the essential duties of his or her job due to the physical or mental deterioration caused by AIDS may be taken off the job, even if a law protecting the handicapped is applicable. This principle is especially critical to jobs requiring either sound, sharp exercise of judgment, such as doctors, lawyers, bankers, and computer operators, or constant vigorous exertion, such as operating heavy equipment or doing construction work.

The other question to pursue is just how long will the PWA be physically able to perform the essential duties of the job in question, with or without accommodation. Suppose special drugs or other medical treatment create a cycle in which the PWA has short periods of normal strength and activity (permitting work) followed by long periods of exhaustion. As time goes on the relapses become longer and the remissions shorter. Is the employer obligated to hold the job and accommodate the PWA again and again and again? If so initially, does the obligation terminate at some point? Once again the manager should carefully document all efforts at accommodation and the increasing burden of repeatedly reinstating the PWA for shorter periods followed by longer absences. The employer might eventually exhaust all obligations as the accommodations become unreasonable and the burdens undue.

8. Finally, carefully balance the risk and impact of being held in violation of the law and suffering the penalty if the action is taken, against the damage and disruption that are likely to occur if no action is taken and the person with an AIDS condition is hired or allowed to remain in his or her regular job. As I noted above, clearly applicable laws must be complied with, regardless of the possible damage and disruption. But genuine ambiguity and doubt will cloud most legal issues for years to come, and in these situations, this framework for analysis should be helpful.

Prevention of AIDS Claims

A major goal of any employee relations program is prevention of labor crises. Whether the potential problem involves the union, charges with the EEOC, or an OSHA investigation, sophisticated employers work hard to establish and administer personnel programs designed to prevent or at least minimize the damage and disruption often associated with legal claims. They realize that employers with effective, successful employee relations programs are more likely to have low employee turnover and absenteeism, high productivity, excellent quality, and few legal claims. Conversely, companies with poorly conceived and loosely administered programs have a higher probability of problems with turnover, quality, attendance, and unions, as well as more lawsuits and claims with governmental agencies.

A lawsuit involving AIDS has the potential to be particularly disruptive. The costs of lost time and attorneys' fees, and the possibility of monetary damages, are present in almost every legal case. With AIDS, however, would come the added dimension of extensive publicity, which could be especially detrimental to retail concerns, hotels, or health care facilities. Further possible ramifications include customer boycotts, employee refusals to work with the PWA, and continued coverage by the press. Normally, labor law matters are handled almost exclusively by the legal and human resources departments of a company, but an employer with an AIDS case may also require a public relations agent and a marketing manager to participate in an AIDS-related case.

An employer can protect itself from AIDS-related claims and lawsuits by acting intelligently to prevent their instigation. First, the employer should educate all personnel. Educate employees on the medical facts concerning AIDS now, *before* an issue involving HIV is experienced. Bring in a medical doctor, nurse, or other expert to your facility for the purpose of explaining, in basic language, facts and figures about AIDS and its transmission. Emphasis should be placed on the fact that it cannot be transmitted by casual contact. Be blunt in describing how it can and is transmitted. Make presentations pertinent to the particular type of facility and business in question. Use charts, graphs, and other visual aids, including films, to increase the effectiveness of the program. Allow ample time for questions and comments by employees. Consider meeting in small groups of ten to fifteen, which will facilitate discussion, as opposed to lecturing a large group of fifty or more employees. The educational effort should be ongoing—a one-time rush of information is not enough. Follow up these meetings with letters to employees' homes, notices on the bulletin board, and distribution of pamphlets summarizing the points and principles explained during the meeting.

The efforts at educating personnel should be particularly thorough and frequent at health care facilities. More detailed presentations, use of examples, and opportunities for discussion are appropriate here.

Second, all levels of management should receive special training, in addition to the education described above, on the handling of AIDS-related matters. If the company has a written policy, copies of that policy should be distributed to all managers, and its contents and the procedures for implementing it should be discussed in detail. Various hypothetical situations should be presented and managers tested on how they should respond. If a case-by-case approach is utilized, managers should be drilled on the need to coordinate all decisions and actions on the subject with the person or department designated to handle all AIDS-related problems (see below), as opposed to making unilateral decisions. They should be carefully instructed to immediately report all AIDS-related situations to the designated person or department, and to refrain from initiating any action on their own. Managers are agents of the employer; the employer is therefore legally responsible for all their actions on the job, including those that are ill-conceived or contrary to policy and past practice.

One of the most prevalent problems concerning AIDS in the workplace is rumors. Managers should be instructed to defuse instead of repeat rumors and to be sources of factual information among their employees.

Third, it is critical for all personnel—exempt and nonexempt, manager and staff employee—to keep communications (written and oral) with applicants and employees on this subject absolutely confidential. Access to personnel files or medical records with data on AIDS should be severely restricted to those managers and staff members with an absolute need to utilize the records. As part of their training, all managers should be instructed to refrain from discussing AIDS matters involving employees with other employees, family, friends, or any member of the public. Numerous state court claims could be filed, including slander, libel, defamation of character, negligent hiring, and negligent testing, if a manager breaches an employee's right to confidentiality. Rules should be drafted and publicized which classify breach of confidentiality of records as misconduct triggering discipline.

Fourth, a particular person or department should be selected to coordinate all matters involving AIDS in the workplace. While this usually would be the personnel office, any responsible manager could do the job. No decisions involving an applicant or employee with HIV, symptomatic HIV disease, or AIDS should be implemented without his or her input or review. This person should confer with legal counsel to ensure compliance with any applicable laws on the subject. It is highly important for the coordinator to always be up to date concerning local and state laws on this subject in each area where the employer does business. The coordinating person or department should plan the educational and training sessions described above for managers and employees in each facility.

It is critical to achieve consistency in the handling of these matters and to avoid situations whereby different managers apply different criteria to reach different results with basically the same set of facts. The only excuse for a lack of uniformity inside the company should be a facility's need to depart from past practice to comply with a local statute or ordinance.

Fifth, always follow policy or practice. While some employers want written policies disseminated to employees in handbooks and on bulletin boards, others are opting to resolve AIDS employment matters on a case-by-case basis. With the latter approach, it is especially important to follow uniformly the established practice or at least to avoid inconsistencies. To achieve consistency, the coordinator should maintain a file on the subject, document how each case is handled, and consult that file before implementing decisions in new cases.

The best approach for promoting consistency is to draft, implement, and administer a written policy. (See the recommendations in the next chapter and sample policies included in appendix D, documents 1–5. A sample provision for employee handbooks is included in appendix D, document 6.)

Sixth, establish procedures for internally resolving AIDS problems and complaints. Employees who file claims with governmental agencies or retain counsel to consider lawsuits against their employer often do so because they feel frustrated: they feel that no one in the company will listen to them or give proper consideration to their complaint. To avoid this undesirable result, establish and implement a definite procedure that employees can be taught to use to voice their complaints, problems, ideas, and suggestions. It should be a major goal to identify and resolve employee problems on an internal basis, as opposed to unwittingly pushing personnel to turn to the government or to a union for help. This concept is especially important in regard to employees and their concerns about AIDS: an employer ignores such concerns at its peril, for unresolved they can reappear in the form of a grievance, charge, or lawsuit.

The procedure must be somewhat specific and have teeth to it.

An employer is expecting too much merely to inform employees that the company has an "open door policy" and to rely upon them to utilize it. Such an approach will almost surely result in disappointment for both the employer and the employee. At the other extreme, a formal step-by-step grievance procedure can be forbidding, impersonal, and discouraging. What is appropriate is a definite procedure—set forth in the employee handbook, on the bulletin board, and communicated to employees from time to time during regular meetings—that encourages employees to consult their supervisor, but which also presents outlets for situations when the supervisor is not taking effective action. Hence, employees with AIDS-related concerns who are frustrated with the action—or inaction—of their supervisors should be encouraged to consult with the human resources director or other designated management representative. Supervisors must be trained to accept, instead of resent, employees going around them from time to time to voice a complaint or request an accommodation.

Defenses to AIDS Claims

At times, regardless of the sincerity of the commitment of an employer to prevent claims, lawsuits are filed and processed. Whenever a formal claim is lodged, the immediate and overall goal of the employer, now thrust into a defensive position, is to secure its dismissal. The applicant, employee, or former employee has formally accused the employer of illegal conduct and has requested a costly remedy, such as compensatory damages, attorney fees, and reinstatement. Depending on the particular law, other possible remedies include debarment from consideration for future contracts with the federal government and punitive damages. The employer is exposed to the risk of substantial liability. Moreover, resulting publicity could be harmful. While mediation and settlement efforts may occur, the bottom-line objective is to prevail. In these circumstances, the employer should exploit every conceivable defense that is legitimately available to it, procedural or substantive.

The following checklist of different employer defenses to claims involving AIDS in the workplace should be strongly considered for applicability:

1. No federal law expressly prohibits the discrimination that is alleged in the complaint or petition.
2. No state law expressly prohibits the discrimination that is alleged in the complaint or petition.
3. No local law expressly prohibits the discrimination that is alleged in the complaint or petition.
4. The court or administrative agency lacks jurisdiction over the claimant or plaintiff, who therefore has no standing to bring the claim.
5. The court or administrative agency has no jurisdiction over the subject matter described in the complaint or petition; the law or statute set forth in the complaint has no real application to what happened to the claimant.
6. Plaintiff only alleges discrimination because he or she is in a high-risk group for HIV infection. There are neither allegations nor evidence that he or she is infected with HIV. Hence, the laws listed in the complaint do not protect him or her.
7. Plaintiff is only allegedly infected with HIV. There is no claim that he or she is suffering the complications and impairments of symptomatic HIV disease or AIDS; therefore, he or she is not handicapped, and the Americans with Disabilities Act and Vocational Rehabilitation Act cannot be used by plaintiff.
8. Plaintiff's answers at the deposition show that he is not impaired in any way; thus he is not handicapped and the court is without jurisdiction.
9. Defendant has too few employees for the court to have jurisdiction under the Americans with Disabilities Act.
10. Defendant lacks the federal government contracts required for jurisdiction under the Vocational Rehabilitation Act.
11. The state laws relied upon in the complaint are preempted by federal handicap laws.
12. The plaintiff was physically unable to perform the essential duties or functions of his or her job, or the job for which he or she applied, with or without reasonable accommodation.
13. The plaintiff was mentally unable to perform the essential duties or functions of his or her job, or the job for which he or she applied, with or without reasonable accommodation.
14. The employer cannot reasonably accommodate the plaintiff.
15. The employer met with plaintiff, explained the duties of the

job in question, and solicited ideas for accommodation, but plaintiff had none.

16. The employer made reasonable attempts to accommodate the plaintiff but the plaintiff refused them and voluntarily quit.

17. The only accommodations that would be effective are unreasonable.

18. While the required accommodations are reasonable, they would unduly burden the employer.

19. There is a real and substantial risk of infecting other employees, customers, patients, or members of the public if the plaintiff were allowed to work in the position at issue, and the employer has a legal and moral obligation to protect the health and safety of employees in the workplace who would be jeopardized if the claimant were allowed to work in the position desired.

20. There is a serious potential loss of customers and revenue if the claimant were allowed to work in the position at issue.

21. The employer's health insurance costs would unreasonably and substantially increase if it did what the plaintiff wants.

22. The employer would be unreasonably subjecting itself to legal claims by patients or customers if it allowed the plaintiff to work in the position at issue.

23. The employer would be unreaonsably subjecting itself to legal claims by employees if it allowed the plaintiff to work in the position at issue.

24. The plaintiff has filed a grievance under the current collective bargaining agreement that his or her union is processing toward arbitration. The subject matter of the grievance is very similar to that of the legal claim, and the court or commission should dismiss the legal claim and defer to the arbitrator. Further, by first filing the grievance through the union, the plaintiff made a binding election of remedies. Finally, the legal claim is preempted by Section 301 of the Taft-Hartley Act.

25. The plaintiff made no attempt to use the employer's written procedure for resolving employee complaints and problems. This claim should be dismissed and the court or commission should defer to the internal procedures for filing and processing complaints.

26. A complaint raising the same AIDS-in-employment issue was previously filed by the plaintiff in state or city court. To avoid

duplication of effort and possibly inconsistent results, the present court should dismiss the lawsuit and defer to the other jurisdiction. Also, when the plaintiff filed first with the other court or commission, he or she made a binding election of remedies.

27. The employer decided to discharge plaintiff for violation of its rules before it learned that he or she was suffering from AIDS. At the time the decision to discharge was made, the employer lacked knowledge of the AIDS condition.

28. The employer acknowledges that the plaintiff was discharged, and that it had knowledge of his or her AIDS condition, but avers and explains that its decision was not motivated by plaintiff's infected status. Instead, the reason that the plaintiff was discharged was poor performance, for which he or she was counseled and reprimanded several times.

29. The plaintiff was not discharged: he or she clearly notified the relevant manager of the decision to quit. The employer then processed the termination as voluntary. The plaintiff was not pressured or coerced into leaving but simply decided to leave, voluntarily.

30. The lawsuit is barred by a settlement of these claims that was voluntarily negotiated by the plaintiff and the employer. After the plaintiff submitted medical confirmation of the AIDS condition to the personnel manager, there were a series of meetings during which various options were discussed. Eventually, the plaintiff and the personnel manager reached mutual agreement on these terms (for example, payment of vacation and severance pay to the plaintiff; a six-month unpaid leave of absence during which the plaintiff would continue to be covered under the group medical policy; and termination of all benefits, payments and employment status after expiration of the six-month leave). The employer thus fulfilled its obligations, and the plaintiff should be prevented from processing this suit when he or she has obtained past settlement and satisfaction. The plaintiff signed a release.

Employer Policies and Procedures

Relatively few employers have adopted written policies covering AIDS employment issues. Instead, the vast majority of public and private employers use a "hope and grope" method: they hope they are never confronted with the knowledge that an applicant or employee is HIV positive, and when the problem finally confronts them, they grope for ways to handle what they want to view as a single, unusual occurrence.

AIDS, however, cannot be ignored for a significant period of time. The virus, no longer largely confined to urban centers on the coasts (New York, San Francisco, and Los Angeles), is spreading to the Midwest, the South, and rural areas. As the thousands and thousands of people who were unknowingly infected in the 1980s develop symptomatic HIV disease and AIDS in the the 1990s, many who are denied employment or who believe that they have been abused in the workplace will seek counsel. Almost all employers of substantial size will then be forced to face AIDS issues in employment and be threatened with potential legal claims. Thus an employer would do well to heed the following reasons why a company should draft and implement a written policy concerning either infectious diseases in general or AIDS in particular *now*—prior to being presented with an actual problem that must be quickly addressed:

1. It is preferable to coolly and objectively anticipate problems that could occur in the future, and provide a framework for their

resolution, as opposed to subjectively and emotionally attempting, in a short period of time, to solve them on the spot.

2. The new Americans with Disabilities Act, which covers almost all employers, extends legal protections to applicants and employees with AIDS conditions.

3. The Achilles heel for employer defenses to claims of discrimination by rejected applicants or terminated employees is frequently lack of uniformity. When the plaintiff's attorney can point to inconsistencies in the manner in which his or her client was treated compared to the employer's past practice, the plaintiff scores major points. If, on the other hand, the employer has evidence establishing that the plaintiff's situation comes within the definition of a well-established and broadly communicated written policy that has been consistently applied in analogous past situations, the defense is clearly bolstered.

4. Supervisors, department heads, and other managers are less likely to "shoot from the hip" and make mistakes during conversations with an infected applicant or employee if they have been shown a written policy on the subject and trained to adhere to it.

5. Written policies on sensitive subjects administered by empathetic, educated managers improve the probability of avoiding costly litigation or—if claims are filed—of securing early dismissals or satisfactory settlements without the time and expense of a trial.

6. Medical progress requires human resources response. In the 1980s AIDS was an acute short-term illness with an average span of eighteen months between diagnosis and death. Most often employees reporting an AIDS diagnosis were incapable of working for extended durations due to declining physical and mental health. In those circumstances, significant numbers of PWAs accepted or even sought leaves of absences or terminations with severance payments. Currently, however, drugs and other forms of treatment are extending the time between diagnosis and death to five, seven, and perhaps even more years. This development means that many PWAs are capable of working longer periods of time than before. This also means that successful claimants can recover greater lifetime medical costs and larger potential compensatory damage awards. Employers with asymptomatic applicants and employees face more complex and costly situations.

7. The media may become informed of an employment matter

involving AIDS and do a story, with or without the employer's cooperation. The existence of a previously adopted, logically sound policy can be of assistance in drafting press releases and responding to questions.

Employers deciding to draft a written policy must first list its objectives. What is to be accomplished? Promoting the health and a safety of personnel and the public, preventing the spread of the disease, and achieving compliance with applicable laws are worthy goals. Others should be listed and analyzed.

The next step is to study past practice and determine if and how PWAs have been previously dealt with. If there has been no experience with PWAs, ask how applicants and employees with life-threatening illnesses such as hepatitis, tuberculosis, or cancer have been treated. Before the employer can provide for the future, it must learn what it has done in the past.

Appendix D includes five sample policies for consideration. The first two place AIDS in the general category of infectious or communicable diseases. The third is a policy that deals specifically with AIDS conditions. The fourth, entitled "Assisting Employees with Life-Threatening Illnesses," was created by Bank America. The fifth offers a sample policy for a food, beverage, restaurant, or hotel employer. Sample policies for health care facilities are included in appendix C.

Once a policy is adopted, employees must be notified about it. Document 6 in appendix D suggests various provisions for employee handbooks. Document 7 is a checklist for an employer faced with an employee having an AIDS condition. Finally, document 8 is a consent form for HIV testing to be executed by either an applicant or an employee.

Conclusion

AIDS is a subject employers would prefer to ignore. The increasingly likely prospect of being informed that an applicant is HIV positive or that an employee has been diagnosed as having AIDS, however, forces managers to face reality and requires them to answer a series of difficult questions with medical, legal, and personal overtones in short order. These sensitive situations place a premium on thoughtful anticipation of the possible problems, analysis of available options, and the drafting of a policy.

From the perspective of the individual with an AIDS condition, the syndrome is incurable, physically incapacitating, mentally debilitating, and finally lethal. In struggling through the final months of their lives, these PWAs—too often very young—require compassion and sensitivity. Discharge from employment and loss of insurance coverage should be avoided for humane, as well as legal reasons; instead, the employer should extend efforts to provide emotional support and financial assistance.

There are, however, limits to what can be expected of employers in these situations. Because of the infectious nature of HIV, certain employers have obligations to and concerns for customers, patients, fellow employees, and the general public. At times, the best interests of the infected employee are at odds with those of others. This is especially true in health care facilities. It must also be remembered that AIDS is an epidemic, and the number of people, including heterosexuals, infected with the HIV virus is greatly expanding each year. In these circumstances, the federal government should take steps to protect the public safety.

In its capacity of administering the Americans with Disabilities Act, the EEOC should solicit comments on the question of the risk of transmitting HIV to patients, customers, fellow employees, or the public while performing certain duties. Data collected in this manner would provide employers and their associations the opportunity to submit medical and other data to the commission in support of any contentions that they should be able to exclude HIV-positive personnel from particular positions. Assuming sufficient and valid documentation is submitted, the EEOC could then issue a rule that the risk is identifiable in jobs that are enumerated (for example: surgeon, emergency and operating room nurses, dental surgeon) and that employers may legally (1) test applicants for those positions for HIV antibodies and exclude those who are positive; (2) periodically test employees assigned to those classifications and transfer to "remote-risk" jobs any who test positive; and (3) require employees in the identified jobs to submit to antibody testing whenever there has been an exposure of their blood or body fluids to others in the employment context.

The federal government should enhance its efforts to educate the public about AIDS, reduce the risk of transmitting the virus, and improve treatment of those who are infected by (1) producing radio and television advertisements that explain basic *facts* about the virus and how it is and is not transmitted (the public could be urged to be voluntarily tested and counseled to eschew risky conduct); (2) subsidizing testing centers that would be easy and efficient for the public to voluntarily and anonymously use (trained counselors would be available for dispensing advice, needles, and condoms); and (3) gathering facts and figures on HIV tests, policies, and procedures utilized by employers across the country and making them available to the public (legislators, judges, and unions would be as interested in this clearinghouse data as employers).

U.S. Government Rules, Enforcement Procedures, Guidelines, and Other Information on AIDS

Document 1

U.S. Public Health Service: Summary of Recommendations

A. Recommendations to Prevent the Spread of AIDS
   1. Do not have sexual contact with persons known or suspected of having AIDS.
   2. Do not have sex with multiple partners, or with persons who have had multiple partners.
   3. Persons who are at increased risk for having AIDS should not donate blood.
   4. Physicians should order blood transfusions for patients only when medically necessary. Health workers should use extreme care when handling or disposing of hypodermic needles.
   5. Don't abuse intravenous drugs. If you use intravenous drugs, then don't share needles or syringes (boiling does not guarantee sterility).
   6. Don't have sex with people who abuse intravenous drugs.

B. Special recommendations for Persons Who Have Tested Positive for HIV for the Purpose of Preventing the Spread of AIDS
   1. A regular medical evaluation and follow-up is advised for persons with positive test results.
   2. Persons with positive blood test may pass the disease on to others and should not donate blood, plasma, body organs, other tissue, or sperm. They should take precautions against exchanging body fluids during sexual activity.
   3. There is a risk of infecting others by sexual intercourse, sharing of needles, and possibly exposure of others to saliva through oral genital contact or intimate kissing. The effectiveness of condoms in preventing infection with HIV is not proved, but their consistent use may reduce transmission, since exchange of body fluids is known to increase risk.
   4. Toothbrushes, razors, or other implements that could become contaminated with blood should not be shared.
   5. A woman whose sex partner is antibody-positive is at increased risk of acquiring AIDS. If she becomes pregnant, their children are also at increased risk of acquiring AIDS.

Document 2

OSHA: Worker Exposure to AIDS and Hepatitis B

Introduction

The Acquired Immune Deficiency Syndrome (AIDS) and hepatitis B (HBV) viruses merit serious concern for workers, especially those in the health care industry.

Workers at risk of blood, body fluid, or needle stick exposures are at the highest risk of infection. They include, but are not limited to, nurses, physicians, dentists and other dental workers, podiatrists, laboratory and blood bank technologists and technicians, phlebotomists, dialysis personnel, medical technicians, medical examiners, morticians, housekeepers, laundry workers, and others whose work involves contact with blood or other body fluids, or with corpses. Other personnel, such as paramedics, emergency medical technicians, law enforcement personnel, firefighters, lifeguards, and others whose jobs might require first-response medical care and potential contact with blood or body fluids are also at risk.

AIDS was first recognized in the United States in 1981. As of August 1987, the Centers for Disease Control (CDC) has received reports of more than 40,000 cases of AIDS, including 23,000 deaths. An additional 1.5 million people are estimated to be carriers of the virus that causes AIDS, but have no symptoms of the illness. Experts predict that by the end of 1991, there will have been a cumulative total of 270,000 AIDS cases in the U.S., including 179,000 deaths. Infection with the AIDS virus in the workplace represents a small but real hazard to health care workers. Only a few such cases have been reported to date.

According to CDC surveys, an estimated 300,000 new HBV infections occur each year in the U.S., and nearly 10 percent of those infected (1 out of every 300 persons in the U.S.) become long-term carriers. Of the 300,000, almost one-fourth become acutely ill or jaundiced, about 15,000 are hospitalized, and several thousand die from acute and chronic disease. HBV infections occur in about 8,000 to 12,000 health care workers per year and result in over 200 deaths per year due to acute and chronic effects.

AIDS and HBV infections have been reported from every state. The seriousness and immediacy of the problem have prompted the Occupational Safety and Health Administration (OSHA), in cooperation with the U.S. Public Health Service, to provide workers with information on the CDC recommended practices to protect against occupational exposure to AIDS and HBV. The recommended practices include precautions for the appropriate handling of blood and other body fluids, as well as items soiled with blood and other body fluids. Following these precautions should help prevent the spread of these viruses in the workplace.

AIDS

What is AIDS/ARC?

AIDS is a bloodborne and sexually transmitted disease in which a virus invades the body, damages the immune system, and allows other infectious agents to invade the body and cause disease. ARC, "AIDS Related Complex," refers to a variety of conditions caused by infection with the AIDS virus. These conditions range from mild symptoms to life-threatening ones.

What Causes AIDS/ARC?

AIDS/ARC is caused by the Human Immunodeficiency Virus (HIV), formerly called Human T-lymphotropic virus type III/lymphadenopathy-associated virus (HTLV-III/LAV).

How Is It Transmitted?

The AIDS virus is spread through body fluids, primarily blood and semen. Although other fluids have not been shown to transmit infection, all body fluids and tissues should be regarded as potentially infectious. AIDS is transmitted by sexual contact, by needle sharing, and through contaminated blood products. An infected woman can pass the virus to her fetus.

The AIDS virus is not transmitted by casual contact, touching or shaking hands, eating food prepared by an infected person, or from drinking fountains, telephones, toilets or other surfaces.

What Are the Symptoms?

Persons who are infected with the AIDS virus may have no symptoms, may have ARC, or may have AIDS. Individuals with ARC may have enlarged lymph nodes and a fungal infection of the mouth (thrush), which may be accompanied by fatigue, weight loss, and some problems with the immune system. AIDS is frequently diagnosed when the patient develops an opportunistic infection (an infectious disease that is only likely to occur when the immune system is depressed), such as *Pneumocystis carinii* pneumonia, or malignancies such as Kaposi's sarcoma (a rare form of skin cancer).

Is There a Vaccine for the Prevention of AIDS?

To date, no vaccine is available to prevent AIDS and no antiviral drugs are available to cure AIDS. Some drugs, however, have been found to inhibit the action of the virus and others are able to fight certain opportunistic infections. Research is currently underway to develop antiviral drugs and vaccines; however, prevention is currently the only approach to control the virus.

Hepatitis B

What Is Hepatitis?

Hepatitis is an inflammation of the liver. It can be caused by infectious agents, medications or toxins. There are several types of infectious hepatitis (A, B, non-A/non-B and delta), but hepatitis B presents the greatest risk to workers in the health care industry.

How Is HBV Transmitted?

Hepatitis B is transmitted by sexual contact, by needle sharing, and through contaminated blood or blood products. An infected mother can transmit the virus to her fetus.

HBV is not transmitted by casual contact, touching or shaking hands, eating food prepared by an infected person or from drinking fountains, telephones, toilets or other surfaces. Thus, the occupational risk of HBV infection directly relates to the extent of worker contact with infected blood or blood products. As with AIDS, all body fluids and tissues should be regarded as potentially infectious.

What Are the Symptoms?

Many people who are infected with the hepatitis B virus never have symptoms. The usual symptoms of acute infections are flu-like and include fatigue, mild fever, muscle and joint aches, nausea, vomiting, abdominal pain, diarrhea, and jaundice. Severe HBV infections may be fatal. Chronic carriers of HBV may develop a chronic hepatitis that may progress to cirrhosis, liver cancer, or death.

Is There a Vaccine for the Prevention of HBV?

A hepatitis B vaccine is available that is safe and effective in the prevention of HBV infection. This vaccine is recommended for persons at risk of HBV infection, including health care workers and emergency personnel.

Recommended Practices for Protection Against Occupational Exposure to AIDS and HBV

The Centers for Disease Control, with advice from health care professionals, has made recommendations to protect workers from AIDS and HBV infection. These precautions are prudent practices that apply to preventing the transmission of these viruses and other similar blood-borne-type infections and that should be used routinely.

Personal Protective Equipment

- Use gloves where blood, blood products, or body fluids will be handled.
- Use gowns, masks, and eye protectors for procedures that could involve more extensive splashing of blood or body fluids.
- Use pocket masks, resuscitation bags, or other ventilation devices to resuscitate a patient to minimize exposure that may occur during emergency mouth-to-mouth resuscitation. Employers should place these devices where the need for resuscitation is likely.

Workplace Practices

- Wash hands thoroughly after removing gloves, and immediately after contact with blood or body fluids.
- Use disposable needles and syringes whenever possible. Do not recap, bend, or cut needles. Place sharp instruments in a specially designated puncture-resistant container located as close as practical to the area where they are used. Handle and dispose of them with extraordinary care to prevent accidental injury.
- Follow general guidelines for sterilization, disinfection, housekeeping, and waste disposal. Use appropriate protective equipment. Place potentially infective waste in impervious bags and dispose of them as local regulations require.
- Clean up blood spills immediately with detergent and water. Use a solution of 5.25 percent sodium hypochlorite (household bleach) diluted between 1–10 and 1–100 parts water for disinfection.

Education

- Know the modes of transmission and prevention of these infections.

Other Recommendations for Prevention

- Treat all blood and body fluids as potentially infectious.
- Get an HBV vaccination if you are at substantial risk of acquiring HBV infection.

Enforcement

Various OSHA standards apply to exposure to the hazards of potential infection of both the AIDS and the HBV viruses. These standards cover personal protective equipment, sanitation, and waste disposal.

In addition, the General Duty Clause of the OSHA Act requires employers to provide "employment and a place of employment which are free from recognized hazards. . . ." Employers must comply with either the federal OSHA standards and the General Duty Clause or with state standards. States with approved plans to operate their own occupational safety and health program enforce standards comparable to the federal standards and are encouraged to enforce state counterparts to the General Duty Clause. State plan standards, unlike federal standards, apply to state, county, and municipal workers as well as to private employers.

Workers whose employers will not correct hazardous situations may complain to federal OSHA or to the appropriate state OSHA in states that operate their own OSHA program. Complainants' identities will not be revealed to employers. OSHA also investigates employee complaints of discriminatory actions by employers against employees who have exercised safety and health rights. For further information, call your local OSHA office listed at the end of this booklet.

For more information on AIDS, call the toll-free Public Health Service National AIDS Hotline (24 hours, 7 days a week): 1-800-342-2437 or 1-800-342-7514.

U.S. Department of Labor
Occupational Safety and Health Administration
Regional Offices

Region I
(CT,* MA, ME, NH, RI,
VT*)
16–18 North Street
1 Dock Square Building
4th Floor
Boston, MA 02109
Telephone: (617) 565-1161

Region II
(NJ, NY,* PR,*)
201 Varick Street
6th Floor
New York, NY 10014
Telephone: (212) 337-2325

Region III
(DC, DE, MD,* PA, VA,*
WV)
Gateway Building, Suite
2100
3535 Market Street
Philadelphia, PA 19104
Telephone: (212) 596-1201

Region IV
(AL, FL, GA, KY,* MS,
NC,* SC,* TN*)
1375 Peachtree Street, N.E.
Suite 587
Atlanta, GA 30367
Telephone: (404) 347-3573

Region V
(IL, IN,* MI,* MN,* OH,
WI)
230 South Dearborn Street
32nd Floor, Room 3244
Chicago, IL 60604
Telephone: (312) 353-2200

Region VI
(AR, LA, NM,* OK, TX)
525 Griffin Street
Room 602
Dallas, TX 75202
Telephone: (214) 767-3731

Region VII
(IA,* KS, MO, NE)
911 Walnut Street, Room
406
Kansas City, MO 64106
Telephone: (816) 374-5861

Region VIII
(CO, MT, ND, SD, UT,*
WY*)
Federal Building, Room
1576
1961 Stout Street
Denver, CO 80294
Telephone: (303) 844-3061

Region IX
(AZ,* CA,* HI,* NV,*)
71 Stevenson Street
4th Floor
San Francisco, CA 94105
Telephone: (415) 995-5672

Region X
(AK,* ID, OR,* WA*)
Federal Office Building
Room 6003
909 First Avenue
Seattle, WA 98174
Telephone: (206) 442-5930

*These states and territories operate their own OSHA-approved job safety and health programs (exept Connecticut and New York whose plans cover public employees only).

Document 3

OSHA: Proposed Rule on Hepatitis B and HIV (AIDS) Virus

1. Introduction

Many health-care workers are at risk of infection with the viruses that cause hepatitis B and acquired immune deficiency syndrome (AIDS) due to their exposure to contaminated blood and other body fluids. Occupational exposure, which can occur as the result of needlestick or cut injuries, occurs when contaminated blood or body fluids come in contact with mucous membranes or broken skin. Example of occupations with potential for exposure include physicians, nurses, dentists, phlebotomists, laboratory personnel, blood bank personnel, paramedics, morticians, and housekeepers and laundry workers in health-care facilities.

Although OSHA has no standard that was designed specifically to reduce occupational exposure to these viruses, there are a number of existing regulations that apply to this hazard. An example is 29 CFR 1910.132 (personal protective equipment) which requires employers to provide:

> Protective equipment, including presonal protective equipment for eyes, face, head and extremities, protective clothing, respiratory devices, and protective shields and barriers * * * wherever it is necessary by reason of hazards of processes or environment * * * encountered in a manner capable of causing injury or impairment in the function of any part of the body through absorption, inhalation or physical contact.

In addition, section 5(a) the General Duty Clause of the Act requires that each employer:

> * * * furnish to each of his employees employment and a place of employment which are free from recognized hazards that are causing or are likely to cause death or serious physical harm to his employees.

In 1983, OSHA issued a set of voluntary guidelines designed to reduce the risk of occupational exposure to hepatitis B (Docket H-370, Exhibit Number (Ex.) 4–25). The voluntary guidelines, which were sent to employers in the health-care industry, included a description of the disease, recommended work practices, and recommendations for use of immune globulins and the hepatitis B vaccine. Guidelines for vaccination and postexposure prophylaxis have been issued by the Centers for Disease Control (CDC)(Ex. 4–9). OSHA has not issued guidelines for reducing occupational exposure to HIV, but guidelines have been issued by the CDC (Ex. 6–153), the American Hospital Association (AHA) (Exs. 6–75; 6–76), and the American Occupational Medical Association (AOMA) (Ex. 6–112).

The Departments of Labor (DOL) and Health and Human Services (HHS) have formed a working group to develop an extensive and far reaching plan regarding blood-borne diseases in the workplace. Pursuant to this plan, and in order to provide immediate protection in the health-care workplace against HBV and HIV, the Department is taking the following steps:

• First, we are currently implementing a targeted inspection program under the

OSHA Act to examine actual work practices among health-care worker at risk from exposure to blood-borne diseases.

• Second, DOL and HHS have issued a Joint Advisory Notice (52 FR 41818, October 30, 1987) to insure that health-care and other affected employers are fully aware of the applicable guidelines regarding blood-borne disease.

• Third, DOL and HHS will jointly begin an extensive educational effort which targets health-care workers, involving as many interested employer and employee organizations and governmental agencies as possible, and emphasizing education, training and technical assistance.

OSHA will require adherence to existing regulations and will apply the General Duty clause in order to protect health-care workers from the risks of blood-borne diseases. In addition, a careful assessment of the extent to which actual work practices conform to the guidelines, as well as the reasons for any difference between practice and guidelines, is an essential starting point for the development of a proposed standard. OSHA intends to use information gathered in these targeted inspections as one part of a program to assess actual work practices.

The Department of Health and Human Services, which will continue to play a primary role in devloping consensus recommendations and guidelines for protecting against HBV and HIV infections in the workplace, will be reviewing the various guidelines already issued in this area to determine if the need exists for updating. OSHA will also work with HHS to develop additional materials intended for worker education that can be easily reproduced and distributed. There is agreement that education and training are important to assure optimum use of available protective measures.

OSHA will also be working with other Public Health Service agencies, local agencies, universities, hospitals, and state and local health-care departments in an effort to provide both health-care employers and workers with the latest information on blood-borne diseases. This will be useful in the country's overall response to address these infectious diseases.

2. Petitions for Emergency Temporary Standard

On September 19, 1986, the American Federation of State, County and Municipal Employees (AFSCME) petitioned OSHA to take action to reduce the risk to employees from exposure to certain infectious agents (Ex. 2A). They requested that OSHA issue an emergency temporary standard (ETS) under section 6(C) of the Act. The petitioners also requested that OSHA immediately initiate a section 6(b) rulemaking that would require employers to provide the HBV vaccine at no cost to emloyees at risk for HBV infection and would require employers to follow work practice guidelines such as those issued by the Centers for Disease Control. AFSCME also requested that OSHA amend the Hazard Communication Standard (48 FR 53280) to require a training program for employees exposed to infectious diseases, counseling for pregnant employees about diseases that have reproductive effects, and posting of isolation precautions in patient areas and in contaminated areas.

On September 22, 1986, the Service Employees International Union, the National Union of Hospital and Healthcare Employees, and RWDSU Local 1199—Drug, Hospital and Healthcare Union petitioned the Agency to promulgate a standard to protect health-care employees from the hazard posed by occupational exposure to hepatitis B (Ex. 3). They requested that, as a minimum, the standard should contain all of the provisions in OSHA's 1983 guideline with special emphasis on making workers aware of the benefits of vaccination. In addition, they wanted OSHA to immediately issue a directive stating that employers must provide the HBV vaccine free of charge to all high risk health-care workers.

After reviewing these petitions and the available data, OSHA determined that the appropriate course of action is to publish an ANPR to initiate rulemaking under section 6(b) of the Act and to collect further information. Concurrently with the collection of this information, the Agency will enforce existing regulations and section 5(a)(1) of the Act, and the Agency will undertake an educational program in coooperation with the Department of Health and Human Services. OSHA has determined that the available data do not meet the criteria for an ETS as set forth in section 6(c) of the Act. The petitions, therefore, have been denied.

How best to protect against blood-borne diseases in the health-care workplace is a question with broad public health implications in an area, control of biological hazards, where OSHA has not been traditionally involved. Before we proceed, we intend to have the benefit of a full airing of the issues through the public comment process. The Agency's objective is to assure both professional and support staff a safe working environment.

3. Health Effects

Hepatitis B

Hepatitis B, a liver disease, is caused by the hepatitis B virus. Many people who are infected with HBV never have symptoms. The usual symptoms of acute infection are flu-like and include fatigue, mild fever, muscle and joint aches, nausea, vomiting, loss of appetite, abdominal pain, diarrhea, and jaundice. Many pregnant women who are acutely or chronically infected in the months before and after delivery transmit the virus to their children. Although most infected individuals recover, severe HBV infections may be fatal. Chronic carriers of the hepatitis B virus may develop a chronic hepatitis which may progress to cirrhosis, liver cancer, or death.

The usual modes of transmission of HBV are contaminated blood or blood products, sexual contact, needle-sharing, and from infected mother to infant. HBV is not transmitted by casual contact, touching or shaking hands, eating food prepared by an infected person, or from drinking fountains, telephones, toilets or other surfaces.

The CDC estimates that 300,000 new hepatitis B infections occur each year with about 18,000 occurring in health-care workers. Of these, approximately two-thirds (12,000) are estimated to be the result of occupational exposure. Approximately 3,000 of these 12,000 cases are clinically recognizable infections, 600 are hospitalized, and more than 200 die from acute and chronic effects of the infection. Nearly 10 percent of all those infected become long-term carriers of HBV.

A hepatitis B vaccine is available which is safe and effective in the prevention of HBV infection. This vaccine has been recommended by the CDC for persons at substantial risk of HBV infection, including health-care workers and emergency personnel (Ex. 4–9).

Acquired Immune Deficiency Syndrome

AIDS is a disease in which the human immunodeficiency virus invades the body, destroys the immune system and allows other infectious agents to invade the body and cause disease. Persons who are infected with HIV may have no symptoms, may have AIDS-related complex (ARC), or may show symptoms diagnostic of AIDS. Individuals with ARC may have enlarged lymph nodes and a fungal infection of the mouth (thrush), which may be accompanied by fatigue, weight loss, and mild to moderate immunological abnormalities. AIDS is frequently diagnosed when the patient develops an opportunistic infection, (an infectious disease which is only likely to occur when the immune system is depressed), such as *Pneumocystis carinii* pneumonia or malignancies such as Kaposi's sarcoma.

The usual modes of transmission of HIV, as with HBV, are sexual contact, needle sharing, infected blood or blood products, and from infected mother to infant. HIV is not transmitted by casual contact, touching or shaking hands, eating food prepared by an infected person, or from drinking fountains, telephones, toilets or other surfaces.

AIDS was first recognized in 1981. More than 40,000 cases of AIDS have been reported. An additional 1.5 million people are estimated to be carriers of the virus that causes AIDS but have no symptoms of the illness. Experts predict that by the end of 1991, the United States will reach a cumulative total of 270,000 AIDS cases. Infection with HIV, the virus that causes AIDS, appears to represent a small but real occupational hazard to health-care workers. Only a few such cases of infection have been reported to date (Ex. 6–153).

To date, no antiviral drugs are available to cure AIDS. However, antiviral drugs and vaccines are being researched. Prevention of transmission is currently the only approach to controlling this disease.

Cytomegalovirus

The AFSCME petition also discussed occupational exposure to cytomegalovirus (CMV) and its potential threat to pregnant women. CMV, an ubiquitous virus that infects most people in the United States at some time in their lives, usually does not cause recognizable illness. However, the virus can cause serious illness in congenitally infected newborns and in immunocompromised individuals where the virus may be an opportunistic pathogen. Congenitally infected newborns may have cytomegalic inclusion disease, a serious infection that involves the liver, spleen, and the central nervous system. Many AIDS patients have CMV infections, and their body fluids may contain cytomegalovirus.

4. Occupational Exposure to HIV and HBV

Hepatitis B and acquired immune deficiency syndrome are caused by viruses, infectious agents that are capable of human to human transmission. This transmission from one individual to another may result in infection and disease. A link has been established between occupational exposure to blood and other body fluids and the transmission of both HIV and HBV. A common mode of occupational exposure has been a needlestick with a blood-contaminated needle. Cut injuries, caused by blood-contaminated sharp instruments, and splashes of contaminated blood onto non-intact skin or mucous membranes are other modes of occupational transmission.

Employees at risk of blood, body fluid, or needlestick exposures are at greater risk of infection with HBV or HIV. These include, but are not limited to nurses, physicians, dentists, and other dental workers, emergency room personnel, laboratory and blood bank technologists and technicians, phlebotomists, dialysis personnel, paramedics, emergency medical technicians, medical examiners, morticians, and others whose work involves close contact with patients or potential contact with their blood, with their body fluids, or with corpses. Other workers such as hospital housekeepers, hospital laundry workers, firefighters, and law enforcement officers may also be at risk when their duties result in exposure to contaminated blood.

5. State Plans

When a final federal standard is promulgated, the 25 states and territories with their own OSHA-approved occupational safety and health plans must adopt a comparable standard or amend their existing State standard, if not as effective as, the Federal standard, within 6 months. These states or territories are: Alaska, Arizona, California, Connecticut, Hawaii, Indiana, Iowa, Kentucky, Maryland, Michigan, Minnesota, Nevada, New Mexico, New York, North Carolina, Oregon, Puerto Rico, South Carolina, Tennessee, Utah, Vermont, Virginia, the Virgin Islands, Washington, and Wyoming. (In Connecticut and New York, the plan covers only State and local government employees.)

6. Request for Comments

Public comment is requested to assist OSHA in its evaluation of the risks and methods of reducing occupational exposure to HBV and HIV. OSHA also requests that interested parties submit any pertinent health data not discussed in this notice. Comment is requested on the following issues relating to health effects, technological and economic feasibility, and provisions which should be considered for inclusion in a comprehensive standard. Specifically, scientific and technical data and expert analysis and opinion are sought on the following issues:

(1) *Scope of coverage:* There is evidence that workers such as health-care employees exposed to blood and other body fluids are at increased risk of infection with HBV and HIV. Are there employees in occupations other than health-care who are at risk for HIV and HBV infections and who should be included in any rulemaking? What types of facilities should be included under health-care facilities? Should coverage be limited to health-care facilities or expanded to cover other facilities such as mortuaries or infectious wastes operations?

(2) *Public sector employees:* OSHA has no direct jurisdiction over state and local governments which may employ health-care workers, emergency medical technicians, fire fighters, and law enforcement officers. However, the 25 states with approved State Plans will be required to extend their coverage to public employees who are at occupational risk for HBV and HIV infection. What public sector employees are at increased risk for HBV and HIV infection? How many of these individuals are located in states with approved State Plans? Are there conditions unique to any of these occupations that are not seen in the private sector? What items of personal protective clothing and equipment can be used to reduce the risk of occupational exposure? When should they be used? What work practices will reduce their exposure? What training is needed? What are current practices?

(3) *Significance of risk:* How many employees are at risk for occupational exposure to HBV and HIV? What information should OSHA consider to assess potential health risks from exposure? Are there any data, such as medical records or unpublished studies not now in the record, that should be included in OSHA's decision-making process? Is there evidence that exposure to patients with cytomegalovirus presents an increased occupational risk for health-care workers, particularly pregnant health-care workers? If so, how should this risk be reduced?

(4) *Modes of transmission:* What is the risk of becoming infected as the result of a single or multiple exposure to blood or body fluids from individuals who are seropositive for HBV or HIV? What tasks in addition to those discussed place employees at risk of infection with HBV and/or HIV?

(5) Methods of controlling exposure: What current control technologies, work practices, or precautions are available or in use? How and when are they applied in specific work settings? How effective are they in preventing or reducing exposure? Are there situations when these work practices cannot or should not be employed? What is the extent of worker acceptance of these methods? What are their costs and what is the time necessary for their implementation? Should health-care facilities require that blood and body fluid precautions be followed for all patients? In addition to the guidelines published by OSHA, CDC, AHA, and AOMA, what other guidelines are available? To what extent are they followed? Are there specific medical instruments or other devices such as puncture resistant needle containers or self-sheathing needles available to reduce the potential for exposure? How can such devices reduce exposure? Where should these devices be located relative to their point of use? How much do they cost?

(6) Personal protective clothing and equipment: What barrier techniques are available to reduce the likelihood of infection? Under what conditions should gloves be used? When should eye protection and/or gowns be used? What additional clothing or equipment should be used? Should gowns or other clothing be fluid-proof or fluid-resistant? How often should gloves, gowns, eye protection or other equipment be changed? Should such equipment be cleaned and reused? Do adequate supplies of this clothing and equipment exist? What is the cost associated with this personal protective clothing and equipment?

(7) Vaccination programs: What are current practices for administering HBV vaccine to health-care employees? Should the employer be required to provide the hepatitis B vaccine to employees? If so, who should receive the vaccine? What possible risks are associated with the HBV vaccine? How many or what percentage of employees have already received the complete vaccine series? Are there circumstances where the vaccine is contraindicated? What are the elements of a successful vaccination program? What factors are associated with a high degree of employee compliance with such a program? What are the costs of a vaccine program? Are there any state or local governmental regulations that require vaccination against HBV?

(8) Management of needlestick/cut/splash injuries: These injuries are common occurrences in the health-care settings and are associated with the transmission of HBV and HIV. What is the appropriate management of such an injury when it results in exposure to blood from a patient known to be infected with HBV or with HIV? With blood from a patient of unknown status? Are these employees given the opportunity for voluntary antibody testing free of cost? How can the confidentiality of the employee's test results or other pertinent medical information be asssured?

(9) Medical surveillance: Is it necessary to establish medical surveillance programs for workers at risk of occupational exposure to HBV and HIV? Do employers currently provide specific procedures as part of medical surveillance for HBV and HIV? What is the basis for selecting these procedures? At what frequency are they performed? Is there evidence that risk is reduced due to implementation of medical surveillance programs? Should pregnant employees or women of childbearing age be subject to additional medical surveillance?

(10) Training and education: How are employees currently informed of the occupational hazards associated with HBV and HIV? How should employees be trained to ensure that they understand the nature of HIV and HBV infections and the ways to reduce the likelihood of occupational exposure to these viruses? How many employees currently received training? How often is or should this training be repeated? Are model training programs available? Should this training address

occupational exposures only or should it address personal behavior that increase risks as well?

(11) Generic standards: Are there diseases other than hepatitis B and AIDS whose modes of transmission and methods of control are sufficiently similar to warrant including them in a "generic standard" for bloodborne diseases? If such a generic standard would be more appropriate than a limited one encompassing only hepatitis B and AIDS, what diseases should be included? To what extent are health-care workers at risk of contracting these diseases in their workplaces?

(12) Advances in hazard control: How could OSHA structure a standard on bloodborne diseases so that the standard would reflect, on a continuing basis, technological advances and other improvements in methods of control which were developed after promulgation of the standard? Similarly, is there any way OSHA could use a source outside the agency, such as guidelines published by the Centers for Disease Control, which are updated frequently, as indicative of what regulatory protections employers must provide for their employees?

(13) Effectivness of alternative approaches: How can OSHA best accomplish its goal of ensuring that workers at significant risk are protected from occupational exposure to HIV and HBV? What additional protection would be afforded by a permanent standard, in light of the immediate on-going activities of DOL and HHS and existing regulations?

(14) Environmental effects: The National Environmental Policy Act (NEPA) of 1969 (42 U.S.C. 4321, *et seq.*) the Council of Environmental Quality (CEQ) regulations (40 CFR Part 1500; 43 FR 55978, November 29, 1978), and the Department of Labor (DOL) NEPA Compliance Regulations (29 CFR Part 11; 45 FR 51187 *et seq.*, August 1, 1980) require that Federal Agencies give appropriate consideration to environmental issues and impacts of proposed actions significantly affecting the quality of the human environment. OSHA is currently collecting written information and data on possible environmental impacts that may occur outside of the workplace as a direct or indirect result of promulgation of a standard for occupational exposure to the viruses that cause hepatitis B and AIDS. Possible environmental impacts include hazardous infectious wastes that are generated as the result of medical research or other related activities. Information submitted should include any negative or positive environmental effects that could result from the regulation. In particular, how would regulation of worker exposure to HBV and HIV alter ambient air quality, water quality, solid waste or land use?

7. Public Participation

Interested parties are invited to submit comments on any or all of these and other pertinent issues related to the development of a standard for HBV and HIV by January 26, 1988, in quadruplicate to the Docket Office, Docket No. H-370, Room N-3670, U.S. Department of Labor, 200 Constitution Ave., NW., Washington, DC 20210. All written comments submitted in response to this notice will be available for inspection and copying in the Docket Office at the above address between the hours of 8:15 am and 4:45 pm, Monday through Friday. All timely written submissions will be considered in determining the nature of any proposal.

List of Subjects in 29 CFR Part 1910

Occupational Safety and Health Administration, occupational safety and health; health; protective equipment, infectious diseases, AIDS, Acquired Immune Deficiency Syndrome, Hepatitis B.

Authority and Signature

This Advance Notice of Proposed Rulemaking was prepared under the direction of John A. Pendergrass, Assistant Secretary of Labor for Occupational Safety and Health, 200 Constitution Ave., NW., Washington, DC 20210. It is issued pursuant to section 6(b) of the Occupational Safety and Health Act (84 Stat. 1593; 29 U.S.C. 655).

Signed at Washington, DC this 24th day of November, 1987.
John A. Pendergrass,
Assistant Secretary.

Document 4

OSHA: Amended Proposed Rules

XII. The Proposed Standard

General Industry

Parts 1910 of Title 29 of the Code of Federal Regulations are proposed to be amended as follows:

Part 1910—[Amended]
Subpart Z—[Amended]

1. The general authority citation for Subpart Z of 29 CFR Part 1910 continues to read as follows and a new citation for § 1910.1030 is added:

Authority: Secs. 6 and 8, Occupational Safety and Health Act, 29 U.S.C. 655, 657, Secretary of Labor's Orders Nos. 12–71 (36 FR 8754), 8–76 (41 FR 25059), or 9–83 (48 FR 35736), as applicable; and 29 CFR Part 1911.

*   *   *   *   *

Section 1910.1030 also issued under 29 U.S.C. 653.

*   *   *   *   *

2. Section 1910.1030 is added to read as follows:

§ 1910.1030 Bloodborne pathogens.

(a) *Scope and application.* This section applies to all occupational exposure to blood or other potentially infectious materials as defined by paragraph (b) of this section.

(b) *Definitions.* For purposes of this section, the following shall apply:

"Assistant Secretary" means the Assistant Secretary of Labor for Occupational Safety and Health, or designated representative.

"Blood" means human blood, human blood components and products made from human blood.

"Bloodborne Pathogens" means pathogenic microorganisms that are present in human blood and can cause disease in humans. These pathogens include, but are not limited to, hepatitis B virus (HBV) and human immunodeficiency virus (HIV).

"Clinical Laboratory" means a workplace where diagnostic or other screening procedures are performed on blood or other potentially infectious materials.

"Director" means the Director of the National Institute for Occupational Safety and Health, U.S. Department of Health and Human Services, or designated representative.

"Disinfect" means to inactivate virtually all recognized pathogenic microorganisms but not necessarily all microbial forms (e.g., bacterial endospores) on inanimate objects.

"Engineering Controls" means controls that isolate or remove the hazard from the workplace.

"Exposure Incident" means a specific eye, mouth, other mucous membrane, non-intact skin, or parenteral contact with blood or other potentially infectious materials that results from the performance of an employee's duties.

"Infectious Waste" means blood and blood products, contaminated sharps, pathological wastes, and microbiological wastes.

"Occupational Exposure" means reasonably anticipated skin, eye, mucous membrane, or parenteral contact with blood or other potentially infectious materials that may result from the performance of an employee's duties. This definition excludes incidental exposures that may take place on the job, and that are neither reasonably nor routinely expected and that the worker is not required to incur in the normal course of employment.

"Other Potentially Infectious Materials" means

(1) The following body fluids: semen, vaginal secretions, cerebrospinal fluid, synovial fluid, pleural fluid, pericardial fluid, peritoneal fluid, amniotic fluid, saliva in dental procedures, and any body fluid that is visibly contaminated with blood.

(2) Any unfixed tissue or organ (other than intact skin) from a human (living or dead) and

(3) HIV- or HBV-containing cell or tissue cultures, organ cultures, and culture medium or other solutions; and blood, organs or other tissues from experimental animals infected with HIV or HBV.

"Parenteral" means exposure occurring as a result of piercing the skin barrier (e.g. subcutaneous, intramuscular, intravenous routes).

"Patient" means any individual, living or dead, whose blood, body fluids, tissues, or organs may be a source of exposure to the employee. Examples include, but are not limited to, hospital and clinic patients; clients in institutions for the mentally retarded; trauma victims; clients of drug and alcohol treatment facilities; residents of hospices and nursing homes; human remains prior to embalming; and individuals who donate or sell blood or blood components.

"Personal Protective Equipment" is specialized clothing or equipment worn by an employee to protect him/her from a hazard.

"Production Facility" means a facility engaged in industrial-scale, large-volume production of HIV or HBV or in high concentration production of HIV or HBV.

"Research Laboratory" means a laboratory producing research-laboratory-scale amounts of HIV or HBV.

"Sharps" means any object that can penetrate the skin including, but not limited to, needles, scalpels, and broken capillary tubes.

"Sterilize" means the use of a physical or chemical procedure to destroy all microbial life including highly resistant bacterial endospores.

"Universal precautions" is a method of infection control in which all human blood and certain human body fluids are treated as if known to be infectious for HIV, HBV and other bloodborne pathogens.

"Work Practice Controls" means controls that reduce the likelihood of exposure by altering the manner in which a task is performed.

(c) *Infection control*—(1) *Exposure Determination.* (i) Each employer who has employees with occupational exposure as defined by paragraph (b) of this section shall identify and document those tasks and procedures where occupational exposures may take place.

(ii) Each employer shall identify and document all positions with occupational exposure.

(iii) This exposure determination shall be made without regard to the use of personal protective equipment.

(2) *Infection Control Plan.* (i) Each employer having employees whose reasonably anticipated duties may result in occupational exposure shall establish a written infection control plan designed to minimize or eliminate employee exposure.

(ii) This infection control plan shall contain the following as a minimum:

(A) The exposure determination required by paragraph (c)(1) and

(B) The schedule and method of implementation for each of the applicable paragraphs of this standard.

(iii) This infection control plan shall be reviewed and updated as necessary to reflect significant changes in tasks or procedures.

(iv) The infection control plan shall be made available to the Assistant Secretary and the Director for examination and copying.

(d) *Methods of Compliance—*(1) *General.* Universal precautions shall be observed to prevent contact with blood and other potentially infectious materials, unless those precautions would interfere with the proper delivery of health care or public safety services in a particular circumstance, or would create a significant risk to the personal safety of the worker.

(2) *Engineering and work practice controls.* (i) Engineering controls shall be examined and maintained or replaced on a regular schedule to ensure their effectiveness.

(ii) Employees shall wash their hands immediately or as soon as possible after removal of gloves or other personal protective equipment and after hand contact with blood or other potentially infectious materials.

(iii) All personal protective equipment shall be removed immediately upon leaving the work area or as soon as possible if overtly contaminated and placed in an appropriately designated area or container for storage, washing, decontamination or disposal.

(iv) Used needles and other sharps shall not be sheared, bent, broken, recapped, or resheathed by hand. Used needles shall not be removed from disposable syringes.

(v) Eating, drinking, smoking, applying cosmetics or lip balm, and handling contact lenses are prohibited in work areas where there is a potential for occupational exposure.

(vi) Food and drink shall not be stored in refrigerators, freezers, or cabinets where blood or other potentially infectious materials are stored or in other areas of possible contamination.

(vii) All procedures involving blood or other potentially infectious materials shall be performed in such a manner as to minimize splashing, spraying, and aerosolization of these substances.

(viii) Mouth pipetting/suctioning is prohibited.

(3) *Personal protective equipment—*(i) *Provision and Use.* When there is a potential for occupational exposure, the employer shall provide and assure that the employee uses appropriate personal protective equipment such as, but not limited to, gloves; gowns, fluid-proof aprons, laboratory coats, and head and foot coverings; face shields or masks and eye protection; and mouthpieces, resuscitation bags, pocket masks, or other ventilation devices.

(ii) *Accessibility.* The employer shall assure that appropriate personal protective equipment in the appropriate sizes is readily accessible at the worksite or issued to employees. Hypoallergenic gloves shall be readily accessible to those employees who are allergic to the gloves normally provided.

(iii) *Cleaning.* The employer shall provide for the cleaning, laundering or disposal of personal protective equipment required by paragraphs (d) and (e) of this standard.

(iv) *Repair and replacement.* The employer shall repair or replace required personal protective equipment as needed to maintain its effectiveness.

(v) *Gloves.* Gloves shall be worn when the employee has the potential for the hands to have direct skin contact with blood, other potentially infectious materials, mucous membranes, non-intact skin, and when handling items or surfaces soiled with blood or other potentially infectious materials.

(A) Disposable (single use) gloves, such as surgical or examination gloves, shall be replaced as soon as possible when visibly soiled, torn, punctured, or when their abilty to function as a barrier is compromised. They shall not be washed or disinfected for re-use.

(B) Utility gloves may be disinfected for re-use if the integrity of the glove is not compromised, however they must be discarded if they are cracked, peeling, discolored, torn, punctured, or exhibit other signs of deterioration.

(vi) *Masks, Eye Protection, and Face Shields.* Masks and eye protection or chin-length face shields shall be worn whenever splashes, spray, spatter, droplets, or aerosols of blood or other potentially infectious materials may be generated and there is a potential for eye, nose, or mouth contamination.

(vii) *Gowns, Aprons, and Other Protective Body Clothing.* Appropriate protective clothing shall be worn when the employee has a potential for occupational exposure. The type and characteristics will depend upon the task and degree of exposure anticipated; however, the clothing selected shall form an effective barrier.

(A) Gowns, lab coats, aprons, or similar clothing shall be worn if there is a potential for soiling of clothes with blood or other potentially infectious materials.

(B) Fluid-resistant clothing shall be worn if there is a potential for splashing or spraying of blood or other potentially infectious materials.

(C) Surgical caps or hoods shall be worn if there is a potential for splashing or splattering of blood or other potentially infectious materials on the head.

(D) Fluid-proof clothing shall be worn if there is a potential for clothing becoming soaked with blood or other potentially infectious materials.

(E) Fluid-proof shoe covers shall be worn if there is a potential for shoes to become contaminated and/or soaked with blood or other potentially infectious materials.

(4) *Housekeeping*—(i) *General.* Employers shall assure that the worksite is maintained in a clean and sanitary condition. The employer shall determine and implement the appropriate written schedule for cleaning and method of disinfection based upon the location within the facility, type of surface to be cleaned, type of soil present, and tasks or procedures being performed.

(ii) *Cleaning and Disinfection.* All equipment and environmental and working surfaces shall be properly cleaned and disinfected after contact with blood or other potentially infectious materials.

(A) Work surfaces shall be decontaminated with an appropriate disinfectant after completion of procedures; when surfaces are overtly contaminated; immediately after any spill of blood or other potentially infectious materials; and at the end of the work shift.

(B) Protective coverings such as plastic wrap, aluminum foil, or imperviously-backed absorbent paper may be used to cover equipment and environmental surfaces. These coverings shall be removed and replaced at the end of the work shift or when they become overtly contaminated.

(C) Equipment which may become contaminated with blood or other potentially infectious materials shall be checked routinely and prior to servicing or shipping and shall be decontaminated as necessary.

(D) All bins, pails, cans, and similar receptacles intended for reuse which have a potential for becoming contaminated with blood or other potentially infectious materials shall be inspected, cleaned, and disinfected on a regularly scheduled basis and cleaned and disinfected immediately or as soon as possible upon visible contamination.

(E) Broken glassware which may be contaminated shall not be picked up directly with the hands. It shall be cleaned up using mechanical means, such as a brush and dust pan, a vacuum cleaner, tongs, cotton swabs or forceps.

(F) Specimens of blood or other potentially infectious materials shall be placed in a closable, leakproof container labeled or color-coded according to paragraph (g)(1)(ii) prior to being stored or transported. If outside contamination of the primary container is likely, then a second leakproof container that is labled or color-coded according to paragraph (g)(1)(ii) shall be placed over the outside of the first and closed to prevent leakage during handling, storage, or transport. If puncture of the primary container is likely, it shall be placed within a leakproof, puncture-resistant secondary container.

(G) Reusable items contaminated with blood or other potentially infectious materials shall be decontaminated prior to washing and/or reprocessing.

(iii) *Infectious Waste Disposal.* (A) All infectious waste destined for disposal shall be placed in closable, leakproof containers or bags that are color coded or labeled as required by paragraph (g)(1)(ii) of this standard.

(1) If outside contamination of the container or bag is likely to occur then a second leakproof container or bag which is closable and labeled or color-coded as described in paragraph (g)(1)(ii) shall be placed over the outside of the first and closed to prevent leakage during handling, storage, and transport.

(2) Disposal of all infectious waste shall be in accordance with applicable Federal, state, and local regulations.

(B) Immediately after use, sharps shall be disposed of in closable, puncture resistant, disposable containers which are leakproof on the sides and bottom and that are labeled or color-coded according to paragraph (g)(1)(ii).

(1) These containers shall be easily accessible to personnel and located in the immediate area of use.

(2) These containers shall be replaced routinely and not allowed to overfill.

(iv) *Laundry.* (A) Laundry from workplaces with employees covered under paragraph (a) of this section that is contaminated with blood or other potentially infectious materials or may contain contaminaed sharps shall be treated as if it were contaminated and shall be handled as little as possible and with a minimum of agitation.

(1) Contaminated laundry shall be bagged at the location where it was used and shall not be sorted or rinsed in patient-care areas.

(2) Contaminated laundry shall be placed and transported in bags that are labeled or color-coded as described in paragraph (g)(1)(ii). Whenever this laundry is wet and presents the potential for soak-through of or leakage from the bag, it shall be placed and transported in leakproof bags.

(B) The employer shall ensure that laundry workers wear protective gloves and other appropriate personal protective equipment to prevent occupational exposure during handling or sorting.

(e) *HIV and HBV Research Laboratories and Production Facilities.* (1) This paragraph applies to research laboratories and production facilities engaged in the culture, production, concentration, and manipulation of HIV and HBV. It does not apply to clinical diagnostic laboratories engaged solely in the analysis of blood, tissues, or organs. These requirements apply in addition to the other requirements of the standard.

(2) Research laboratories and production facilities shall meet the following criteria:

(i) *Standard microbiological practices.* All infectious liquid or solid waste shall be decontaminated before being disposed of.

(ii) *Special practices*. (A) Laboratory doors shall be kept closed when work involving HIV or HBV is in progress.

(B) Contaminated materials that are to be decontaminated at a site away from the work area shall be placed in a durable, leakproof container that is closed before being removed from the work area.

(C) Access to the work area shall be limited to authorized persons only. Policies and procedures shall be established whereby only persons who have been advised of the potential biohazard, who meet any specific entry requirements, and who comply with all entry and exit procedures shall be allowed to enter the work areas and animal rooms.

(D) When potentially infectious materials or infected animals are present in the work area or containment module, a hazard warning sign incorporating the universal biohazard symbol shall be posted on all access doors. The hazard warning sign shall comply with the provisions outlined in paragraph (g)(1)(i) of this standard.

(E) All activities involving potentially infectious materials shall be conducted in biological safety cabinets or other physical-containment devices within the containment module. No work shall be conducted in open vessels on the open bench.

(F) Laboratory coats, gowns, smocks, uniforms, or other appropriate protective clothing shall be used in the work area and animal rooms. Protective clothing shall not be worn outside of the work area and shall be decontaminated before being laundered.

(G) Special care shall be taken to avoid skin contamination with potentially infectious materials. Gloves shall be worn when handling infected animals and when making hand contact with potentially infectious materials is unavoidable.

(H) All waste from work areas including animal rooms shall be decontaminated before disposal.

(I) Vacuum lines shall be protected with high-efficiency particulate air (HEPA) filters and liquid disinfectant traps.

(J) Hypodermic needles and syringes shall be used only for parenteral injection and aspiration of fluids from laboratory animals and diaphragm bottles. Only needle-locking syringes or disposable syringe-needle units (i.e., the needle is integral to the syringe) shall be used for the injection or aspiration of potentially infectious fluids. Extreme caution shall be used when handling needles and syringes to avoid autoinoculation and the generation of aerosols during use and disposal. A needle shall not be bent, sheared, replaced in the sheath or guard, or removed from the syringe following use. The needle and syringe shall be promptly placed in a puncture-resistant container and decontaminated, preferably by autoclaving, before being discarded or reused.

(K) Spills and accidents that result in overt exposures of employees to potentially infectious materials shall be immediately reported to the laboratory director or other responsible person.

(L) A biosafety manual shall be prepared or adopted. Personnel shall be advised of potential hazards, shall be required to read instructions on practices and procedures, and shall be required to follow them.

(iii) *Containment equipment*. (A) Certified biological safety cabinets (Class I, II, or III) or other appropriate combinations of personal protection or physical containment devices, such as special protective clothing, respirators, centrifuge safety cups, sealed centrifuge rotors, and containment caging for animals, shall be used for all activities with potentially infectious materials that pose a threat of exposure to droplets, splashes, spills, or aerosols.

(B) Biological safety cabinets shall be certified when installed, whenever they are moved and at least annually.

(3) HIV and HBV research laboratories shall meet the following criteria:

(i) Each laboratory shall contain a sink for hand washing.

(ii) An autoclave for decontamination of infectious laboratory waste shall be available.

(4) HIV and HBV production facilities shall meet the following criteria:

(i) The work areas shall be separated from areas that are open to unrestricted traffic flow within the building. Passage through two sets of doors shall be the basic requirement for entry into the work area from access corridors or other contiguous areas. Physical separation of the high-containment work area from access corridors or other areas or activities may also be provided by a double-doored clothes-change room (showers may be included), airlock, or other access facility that requires passing through two sets of doors before entering the work area.

(ii) The interior surfaces of walls, floors and ceilings shall be water resistant so that they can be easily cleaned. Penetrations in these surfaces shall be sealed or capable of being sealed to facilitate decontamination of the work area.

(iii) Each work area shall contain a sink for washing hands. The sink shall be foot, elbow, or automatically operated and shall be located near the exit door of the work area.

(iv) Access doors to the work area or containment module shall be self-closing.

(v) An autoclave for decontamination of infectious waste shall be available within or as near as possible to the work area.

(vi) A ducted exhaust-air ventilation system shall be provided. This system shall create directional airflow that draws air into the work area through the entry area. The exhaust air shall not be recirculated to any other area of the building, shall be discharged to the outside, and shall be dispersed away from occupied areas and air intakes. The proper direction of the airflow shall be verified (i.e., into the work area).

(5) Training requirements. Additional training requirements for employees in HIV and HBV research laboratories and HIV and HBV production facilities are specified in paragraph (g)(2)(v).

(f) Hepatitis B Vaccination and Post Exposure Follow-up—(1) *General.* (i) The employer shall make available hepatitis B vaccination to all employees who have occupational exposure on average one or more times per month and post-exposure follow-up for all employees with an occupational exposure incident.

(ii) The employer shall assure that all medical evaluations and procedures are performed by or under the supervision of a licensed physician and that all laboratory tests are conducted by an accredited laboratory.

(iii) The employer shall assure that all evaluations, procedures, vaccinations, and post-exposure management are provided to the employee at a reasonable time and place, and according to standard recommendations for medical practice.

(2) *HBV Vaccination.* (i) HBV vaccination shall be offered to all employees occupationally exposed on an average of one or more times per month to blood or other potentially infectious materials, unless the employee has a previous HBV vaccination or unless antibody testing has revealed that the employee is immune. If the employee initially declines HBV vaccination but at a later date while still covered under the standard decides to accept the HBV vaccine, the employer shall provide the vaccine at that time. Should a booster dose(s) be recommended at a future date, such booster dose(s) shall be provided according to standard recommendations for medical practice.

(ii) HBV antibody testing shall be made available to an employee who desires such testing prior to deciding whether or not to receive HBV vaccination. If the employee is found to be immune to HBV by virtue of adequate antibody titer, then employer is not required to offer the HBV vaccine to that employee.

(3) *Post exposure evaluation and follow-up.* Following a report of an exposure incident, the employer shall make available to each employee covered by paragraph (a) a confidential medical evaluation and follow-up, including at least the following elements:

(i) Documentation of the route(s) of exposure, HBV and HIV antibody status of the source patient(s) (if known), and the circumstances under which the exposure occurred.

(ii) If the source patient can be determined and permission is obtained, collection of and testing of the source patient's blood to determine the presence of HIV or HBV infection.

(iii) Collection of blood from the exposed employee as soon as possible after the exposure incident for the determination of HIV and/or HBV status. Actual antibody or antigen testing of the blood or serum sample may be done at that time or at a later date if the employee so requests.

(iv) Follow-up of the exposed employee including antibody or antigen testing, counseling, illness reporting, and safe and effective post-exposure prophylaxis, according to standard recommendations for medical practice.

(4) *Information provided to the physician.* The employer shall provide the following information to the evaluating physician:

(i) A copy of this regulation and its appendices and

(ii) A description of the affected employee's duties as they relate to the employee's occupational exposure.

(5) *Physician's written opinion.* For each evaluation under this section, the employer shall obtain and provide the employee with a copy of the evaluating physician's written opinion within 15 working days of the completion of the evaluation. The written opinion shall be limited to the following information:

(i) The physician's recommended limitations upon the employee's ability to receive hepatitis B vaccination.

(ii) A statement that the employee has been informed of the results of the medical evaluation and that the employee has been told about any medical conditions resulting from exposure to blood or other potentially infectious materials which require further evaluation or treatment.

(iii) Specific findings or diagnoses, which are related to the employee's ability to receive HBV vaccination. Any other findings and diagnoses shall remain confidential.

(6) *Medical recordkeeping.* Medical records required by this standard shall be maintained in accordance with paragraph (h)(1) of this section.

(g) *Communication of Hazards to Employees—*(1) *Signs and Labels—*(i) *Signs.* The employer shall post signs at the entrance to work areas specified in paragraph (e) of this standard which shall bear the legend: Biohazard, with the symbol below and [Name of the Infectious Agent]
[Special requirements for entering the area]
[Name, telephone number of the laboratory director or other responsible person.]

(ii) *Labels.* (A) Warning labels shall be affixed to containers of infectious waste; refrigerators and freezers containing blood and other potentially infectious materials; and other containers used to store or transport blood or other potentially infectious materials except as provided in paragraph (g)(1)(ii)(E) and (F).

(B) Labels required by this section shall include the following legend:

BIOHAZARD

(C) These labels shall be fluorescent orange or orange-red or predominantly so, with lettering or symbols in a contrasting color.

(D) Labels required by paragraph (g)(1)(ii) shall either be an integral part of the container or shall be affixed as close as safely possible to the container by string, wire, adhesive, or other method that prevents their loss or unintentional removal.

(E) Red bags or red containers may be substituted for labels on containers of infectious waste.

(F) Containers of blood or blood components that are labeled as to their contents and have been released for distribution are exempted from the labeling requirements of paragraph (2).

(2) *Information and Training.* (i) Employers shall ensure that all employees with occupational exposure participate in a training program.

(ii) Training shall be provided at the time of initial employment or within 90 days after the effective date of this standard and at least annually thereafter.

(iii) Material appropriate in content and vocabulary to educational level, literacy, and language background of employees shall be used.

(iv) The training program shall contain the following elements:

(A) A copy of this standard and an explanation of its contents;

(B) A general explanation of the epidemiology and symptoms of bloodborne diseases;

(C) An explanation of the modes of transmission of bloodborne pathogens;

(D) An explanation of the employer's infection control program;

(E) An explanation of the appropriate methods for recognizing tasks and other activities that may involve exposure to blood and other potentially infectious materials;

(F) An explanation of the use and limitations of practices that will prevent or reduce exposure including appropriate engineering controls, work practices, and personal protective equipment;

(G) Information on the types, proper use, location, removal, handling, decontamination and/or disposal of personal protective equipment;

(H) An explanation of the basis for selection of personal protective equipment;

(I) Information on the hepatitis B vaccine, including information on its efficacy, safety, and the benefits of being vaccinated.

(J) Information on the appropriate actions to take and persons to contact in an emergency;

(K) An explanation of the procedure to follow if an exposure incident occurs, including the method of reporting the incident and the medical follow-up that will be made available. Also information on the medical counseling that the employer is providing for exposed individuals; and

(L) An explanation of the signs and labels and/or color coding required by paragraph (g)(1).

(v) *Additional training.* Employees in HIV or HBV research laboratories and HIV or HBV production facilities shall receive the following training in addition to the above training requirements:

(A) Employees shall be trained in and demonstrate proficiency in standard microbiological practices and techniques and in the practices and operations specific to the facility before being allowed to work with HIV or HBV.

(B) Employees shall be experienced in the handling of human pathogens or tissue cultures prior to working with HIV or HBV.

(C) A training program shall be provided to employees who have no prior experience in handling human pathogens. Initial work activities shall not include the handling of infectious agents. A progression of work activities shall be assigned as techniques are learned and proficiency is developed. The employee shall participate in work activities involving infectious agents only after proficiency has been demonstrated.

(b) *Recordkeeping*—(1) *Medical records.* (i) The employer shall establish and maintain an accurate record for each employee subject to paragraph (f) of this section, in accordance with 29 CFR 1910.20.

(ii) This record shall include:

(A) The name and social security number of the employee;

(B) A copy of the employee's hepatitis B vaccination records and medical records relative to the employee's ability to receive vaccination or the circumstances of an exposure incident;

(C) A copy of all results of physical examinations, medical testing, and follow-up procedures as they relate to the employee's ability to receive vaccination or to post exposure evaluation following an exposure incident;

(D) The employer's copy of the physician's written opinion; and

(E) A copy of the information provided to the physician as required by paragraphs (f)(4).

(iii) Confidentiality. The employer shall assure that employee medical records required by paragraph (f) are:

(A) Kept confidential; and

(B) Are not disclosed or reported to any person within or outside the workplace except as required by this section or as may be required by law.

(iv) The employer shall maintain this record for at least the duration of employment plus 30 years in accordance with 29 CFR 1910.20.

(2) *Training Records.* (i) Training records shall include the following information:

(A) The dates of the training sessions;

(B) The contents or a sumary of the training sessions;

(C) The names of persons conducting the training; and

(D) The names of all persons attending the training sessions.

(ii) These records shall be maintained for 5 years.

(3) *Availability.* (i) The employer shall assure that all records required to be maintained by this section shall be made available upon request to the Assistant Secretary and the Director for examination and copying.

(ii) Employee training records required by this paragraph shall be provided upon request for examination and copying to employees, employee representatives, and the Assistant Secretary in accordance with 29 CFR 1910.20.

(iii) Employee medical and training records required by this paragraph shall be provided upon request for examination and copying to the subject employee, to anyone having written consent of the subject employee, and to the Assistant Secretary in accordance with 29 CFR 1910.20.

(4) *Transfer of records.* (i) The employer shall comply with the requirements involving transfer of records set forth in 29 CFR 1910.20(h).

(ii) If the employer ceases to do business and there is no successor employer to receive and retain the records for the prescribed period, the employer shall notify the Director, at least three months prior to their disposal and transmit them to the Director if required by the Director to do so within that three month period.

(i) *Dates*—(1) Effective Date. The standard shall become effective on [Insert date 30 days after publication in the Federal Register].

(2) Exposure Determination. The exposure determination required by paragraph (c)(1) of this section shall be completed within 90 days of the effective date of this standard.

(3) Infection Control Plan. The Infection Control Plan required by paragraph (c)(2) of this section shall be completed within 120 days of the effective date of this standard.

(4) Paragraphs (d)(2) Engineering and Work Practice Controls, (d)(3) Personal Protective Equipment, (d)(4) Housekeeping, (e) HIV and HBV Research Laboratories and Production Facilities, (f) Hepatitis B Vaccination and Post-Exposure Follow-up, (g) Communication of Hazards to Employees, and (h) Recordkeeping shall take effect 150 days after the effective date of this standard. OSHA expects that the employer will have initiated, but perhaps not completed, the HBV vaccination series within this time period.

Document 5

CDC: Universal Precautions for Prevention of Transmission of HIV, Hepatitis B Virus, and Other Bloodborne Pathogens in Health-Care Settings

Introduction

The purpose of this report is to clarify and supplement the CDC publication entitled "Recommendations for Prevention of HIV Transmission in Health-Care Settings" (1).*

In 1983, CDC published a document entitled "Guideline for Isolation Precautions in Hospitals" (2) that contained a section entitled "Blood and Body Fluid Precautions." The recommendations in this section called for blood and body fluid precautions when a patient was known or suspected to be infected with bloodborne pathogens. In August 1987, CDC published a document entitled "Recommendations for Prevention of HIV Transmission in Health-Care Settings" (1). In contrast to the 1983 document, the 1987 document recommended that blood and body fluid precautions be consistently used for all patients regardless of their bloodborne infection status. This extension of blood and body fluid precautions to **all** patients is referred to as "Universal Blood and Body Fluid Precautions" or "Universal Precautions." Under universal precautions, blood and certain body fluids of all patients are considered potentially infectious for human immunodeficiency virus (HIV), hepatitis B virus (HBV), and other bloodborne pathogens.

Universal precautions are intended to prevent parenteral, mucous membrane, and nonintact skin exposures of health-care workers to bloodborne pathogens. In addition, immunization with HBV vaccine is recommended as an important adjunct to universal precautions for health-care workers who have exposures to blood (3,4).

Since the recommendations for universal precautions were published in August 1987, CDC and the Food and Drug Administration (FDA) have received requests for clarification of the following issues: 1) body fluids to which universal precautions apply, 2) use of protective barriers, 3) use of gloves for phlebotomy, 4) selection of gloves for use while observing universal precautions, and 5) need for making changes in waste management programs as a result of adopting universal precautions.

Body Fluids to Which Universal Precautions Apply

Universal precautions apply to blood and to other body fluids containing visible blood. Occupational transmission of HIV and HBV to health-care workers by blood is documented (4,5). Blood is the single most important source of HIV, HBV, and other bloodborne pathogens in the occupational setting. Infection control efforts for HIV, HBV, and other bloodborne pathogens must focus on preventing exposures to blood as well as on delivery of HBV immunization.

Universal precautions also apply to semen and vaginal secretions. Although both

---

*The August 1987 publication should be consulted for general information and specific recommendations not addressed in this update.

of these fluids have been implicated in the sexual transmission of HIV and HBV, they have not been implicated in occupational transmission from patient to health-care worker. This observation is not unexpected, since exposure to semen in the usual health-care setting is limited, and the routine practice of wearing gloves for performing vaginal examinations protects health-care workers from exposure to potentially infectious vaginal secretions.

Univeral precautions also apply to tissues and to the following fluids: cerebro-spinal fluid (CSF), synovial fluid, pleural fluid, peritoneal fluid, pericardial fluid, and amniotic fluid. The risk of transmission of HIV and HBV from these fluids is unknown; epidemiologic studies in the health-care and community setting are currently inadequate to assess the potential risk to health-care workers from oc-cupational exposures to them. However, HIV has been isolated from CSF, synovial, and amniotic fluid (6–8), and HBsAg has been detected in synovial fluid, amniotic fluid, and peritoneal fluid (9–11). One case of HIV transmission was reported after a percutaneous exposure to bloody pleural fluid obtained by needle aspiration (12). Whereas aseptic procedures used to obtain these fluids for diagnostic or therapeutic purposes protect health-care workers from skin exposures, they cannot prevent penetrating injuries due to contaminated needles or other sharp instruments.

Body Fluids to Which Universal Precautions Do Not Apply

Universal precautions do not apply to feces, nasal secretions, sputum, sweat, tears, urine, and vomitus unless they contain visible blood. The risk of transmission of HIV and HBV from these fluids and materials is extremely low or nonexistent. HIV has been isolated and HBsAg has been demonstrated in some of these fluids; however, epidemiological studies in the health-care and community setting have not implicated these fluids or materials in the transmission of HIV and HBV infections (13,14). Some of the above fluids and excretions represent a potential source for nosocomial and community-acquired infections with other pathogens, and recommendations for preventing the transmission of nonbloodborne pathogens have been published (2).

Precautions for Other Body Fluids in Special Settings

Human breast milk has been implicated in perinatal transmission of HIV, and HBsAg has been found in the milk of mothers infected with HBV (10,13). However, occupational exposure to human breast milk has not been implicated in the trans-mission of HIV nor HBV infection to health-care workers. Moreover, the health-care worker will not have the same type of intensive exposure to breast milk as the nursing neonate. Whereas universal precautions do not apply to human breast milk, gloves may be worn by health-care workers in situations where exposures to breast milk might be frequent, for example, in breast milk banking.

Saliva of some persons infected with HBV has been shown to contain HBV-DNA at concentrations 1/1,000 to 1/10,000 of that found in the infected person's serum (15). HBsAg-positive saliva has been shown to be infectious when injected into experimental animals and in human bite exposures (16–18). However, HBsAg-positive saliva has not been shown to be infectious when applied to oral mucous membranes in experimental primate studies (18) or through contamination of musical instruments or cardiopulmonary resuscitation dummies used by HBV car-riers (19,20). Epidemiologic studies of nonsexual household contacts of HIV-infected patients, including several small series in which HIV transmission failed to occur after bites or after percutaneous inoculation or contamination of cuts and open wounds with saliva from HIV-infected patients, suggest that the potential for salivary transmission of HIV is remote (5,13,14,21,22). One case report from Germany has suggested the possibility of transmission of HIV in a household setting from an infected child to a sibling through a human bite (23). The bite did not break the skin or result in bleeding. Since the date of seroconversion to HIV was not known for either child in this case, evidence for the role of saliva in the transmission of virus is unclear (23). Another case report suggested the possiblity of transmission of HIV from husband to wife by contact with saliva during kissing (24). However, follow-up studies did not confirm HIV infection in the wife (21).

Universal precautions do not apply to saliva. General infection control practices already in existence—including the use of gloves for digital examination of mucous membranes and endotracheal suctioning, and handwashing after exposure to saliva—should further minimize the minute risk, if any, for salivary transmission of HIV and HBV (1,25). Gloves need not be worn when feeding patients and when wiping saliva from skin.

Special precautions, however, are recommended for dentisty (1). Occupationally acquired infection with HBV in dental workers has been documented (4), and two possible cases of occupationally acquired HIV infection involving dentists have been reported (5,26). During dental procedures, contamination of saliva with blood is predictable, trauma to health-care workers' hands is common, and blood spattering may occur. Infection control precautions for dentistry minimize the potential for nonintact skin and mucous membrane contact of dental health-care workers to blood-contaminated saliva of patients. In addition, the use of gloves for oral examinations and treatment in the dental setting may also protect the patient's oral mucous membranes from exposures to blood, which may occur from breaks in the skin of dental workers' hands.

Use of Protective Barriers

Protective barriers reduce the risk of exposure of the health-care worker's skin or mucous membranes to potentially infective materials. For universal precautions, protective barriers reduce the risk of exposure to blood, body fluids containing visible blood, and other fluids to which universal precautions apply. Examples of protective barriers include gloves, gowns, masks, and protective eyewear. Gloves should reduce the incidence of contamination of hands, but they cannot prevent penetrating injuries due to needles or other sharp instruments. Masks and protective eyewear or face shields should reduce the incidence of contamination of mucous membranes of the mouth, nose, and eyes.

Universal precautions are intended to supplement rather than replace recommendations for routine infection control, such as handwashing and using gloves to prevent gross microbial contamination of hands (27). Because specifying the types of barriers needed for every possible clinical situation is impractical, some judgment must be exercised.

The risk of nosocomial transmission of HIV, HBV, and other bloodborne pathogens can be minimized if health-care workers use the following general guidelines:†

1. Take care to prevent injuries when using needles, scalpels, and other sharp instruments or devices; when handling sharp instruments after procedures;

†The August 1987 publication should be consulted for general information and specific recommendations not addressed in this update.

when cleaning used instruments; and when disposing of used needles. Do not recap used needles by hand; do not remove used needles from disposable syringes by hand; and do not bend, break, or otherwise manipulate used needles by hand. Place used disposable syringes and needles, scalpel blades, and other sharp items in puncture-resistant containers for disposal. Locate the puncture-resistant containers as close to the use areas as is practical.

2. Use protective barriers to prevent exposure to blood, body fluids containing visible blood, and other fluids to which universal precautions apply. The type of protective barrier(s) should be appropriate for the procedure being performed and the type of exposure anticipated.

3. Immediately and thoroughly wash hands and other skin surfaces that are contaminated with blood, body fluids containing visible blood, or other body fluids to which universal precautions apply.

Glove Use for Phlebotomy

Gloves should reduce the incidence of blood contamination of hands during phlebotomy (drawing blood samples), but they cannot prevent penetrating injuries caused by needles or other sharp instruments. The likelihood of hand contamination with blood containing HIV, HBV, or other bloodborne pathogens during phlebotomy depends on several factors: 1) the skill and technique of the health-care worker. 2) the frequency with which the health-care worker performs the procedure (other factors being equal, the cumulative risk of blood exposure is higher for a health-care worker who performs more procedures), 3) whether the procedure occurs in a routine or emergency situation (where blood contact may be more likely), and 4) the prevalence of infection with bloodborne pathogens in the patient population. The likelihood of infection after skin exposure to blood containing HIV or HBV will depend on the concentration of virus (viral concentration is much higher for hepatitis B than for HIV), the duration of contact, the presence of skin lesions on the hands of the health-care worker, and—for HBV—the immune status of the health-care worker. Although not accurately quantified, the risk of HIV infection following intact skin contact with infective blood is certainly much less than the 0.5% risk following percutaneous needlestick exposures (5). In universal precautions, *all* blood is assumed to be potentially infective for bloodborne pathogens, but in certain settings (e.g., volunteer blood-donation centers) the prevalence of infection with some bloodborne pathogens (e.g., HIV, HBV) is known to be very low. Some institutions have relaxed recommendations for using gloves for phlebotomy procedures by skilled phlebotomists in settings where the prevalence of bloodborne pathogens is known to be very low.

Institutions that judge that routine gloving for *all* phlebotomies is not necessary should periodically reevaluate their policy. Gloves should always be available to health-care workers who wish to use them for phlebotomy. In addition, the following general guidelines apply:

1. Use gloves for performing phlebotomy when the health-care worker has cuts, scratches, or other breaks in his/her skin.

2. Use gloves in situations where the health-care worker judges that hand contamination with blood may occur, for example, when performing phlebotomy on an uncooperative patient.

3. Use gloves for performing finger and/or heel sticks in infants and children.

4. Use gloves when persons are receiving training in phlebotomy.

Selection of Gloves

The Center for Devices and Radiological Health, FDA, has responsibility for regulating the medical glove industry. Medical gloves include those marketed as sterile surgical or nonsterile examination gloves made of vinyl or latex. General purpose utility ("rubber") gloves are also used in the health-care setting, but they are not regulated by FDA since they are not promoted for medical use. There are no reported differences in barrier effectiveness between intact latex and intact vinyl used to manufacture gloves. Thus, the type of gloves selected should be appropriate for the task being performed.

The following general guidelines are recommended:

1. Use sterile gloves for procedures involving contact with normally sterile areas of the body.
2. Use examination gloves for procedures involving contact with mucous membranes, unless otherwise indicated, and for other patient care or diagnostic procedures that do not require the use of sterile gloves.
3. Change gloves between patient contacts.
4. Do not wash or disinfect surgical or examination gloves for reuse. Washing with surfactants may cause "wicking," i.e., the enhanced penetration of liquids through undetected holes in the glove. Disinfecting agents may cause deterioration.
5. Use general-purpose utility gloves (e.g., rubber household gloves) for housekeeping chores involving potential blood contact and for instrument cleaning and decontamination procedures. Utility gloves may be decontaminated and reused but should be discarded if they are peeling, cracked, or discolored, or if they have punctures, tears, or other evidence of deterioration.

Waste Management

Universal precautions are not intended to change waste management programs previously recommended by CDC for health-care settings (1). Policies for defining, collecting, storing, decontaminating, and disposing of infective waste are generally determined by institutions in accordance with state and local regulations. Information regarding waste management regulations in health-care settings may be obtained from state or local health departments or agencies responsible for waste management.

Reported by: Center for Devices and Radiological Health, Food and Drug Administration, Hospital Infections Program, AIDS Program, and Hepatitis Br, Div of Viral Diseases, Center for Infectious Diseases. National Institute for Occupational Safety and Health, CDC.

Editorial Note: Implementation of universal precautions does not eliminate the need for other category- or disease-specific isolation precautions, such as enteric precautions for infectious diarrhea or isolation for pulmonary tuberculosis (1,2). In addition to universal precautions, detailed precautions have been developed for the following procedures and/or settings in which prolonged or intensive exposures to blood occur: invasive procedures, dentistry, autopsies or morticians' services, dialysis, and the clinical laboratory. These detailed precautions are found in the August 21, 1987, "Recommendations for Prevention of HIV Transmission in Health-Care Settings" (1). In addition, specific precautions have been developed for research laboratories (28).

Document 6

OSHA: Recommendations for Prevention of HIV Transmission in Health Care Settings

Introduction

Human immunodeficiency virus (HIV), the virus that causes acquired immuno-deficiency syndrome (AIDS), is transmitted through sexual contact and exposure to infected blood or blood components and perinatally from mother to neonate. HIV has been isolated from blood, semen, vaginal secretions, saliva, tears, breast milk, cerebrospinal fluid, amniotic fluid, and urine and is likely to be isolated from other body fluids, secretions, and excretions. However, epidemiologic evidence has implicated only blood, semen, vaginal secretions, and possibly breast milk in trans-mission.

The increasing prevalence of HIV increases the risk that health-care workers will be exposed to blood from patients infected with HIV, especially when blood and body-fluid precautions are not followed for all patients. Thus, this document emphasizes the need for health-care workers to consider all patients as potentially infected with HIV and/or other blood-borne pathogens and to adhere rigorously to infection-control precautions for minimizing the risk of exposure to blood and body fluids of all patients.

The recommendations contained in this document consolidate and update CDC recommendations published earlier for preventing HIV transmission in health-care settings: precautions for clinical and laboratory staffs (1) and precautions for health-care workers and allied professionals (2); recommendations for preventing HIV transmission in the workplace (3) and during invasive procedures (4); recommendations for preventing possible transmission of HIV from tears (5); and recommendations for providing dialysis treatment for HIV-infected patients (6). These recommendations also update portions of the "Guideline for Isolation Precautions in Hospitals" (7) and reemphasize some of the recommendations contained in "Infection Control Practices for Dentistry" (8). The recommendations contained in this document have been developed for use in health-care settings and emphasize the need to treat blood and other body fluids from all patients as potentially infective. These same prudent precautions also should be taken in other settings in which persons may be exposed to blood or other body fluids.

Definition of Health-Care Workers

Health-care workers are defined as persons, including students and trainees, whose activities involve contact with patients or with blood or other body fluids from patients in a health-care setting.

Health-Care Workers with AIDS

As of July 10, 1987, a total of 1,875 (5.8%) of 32,395 adults with AIDS, who had been reported to the CDC national surveillance system and for whom occu-pational information was available, reported being employed in a health-care or clinical laboratory setting. In comparison, 6.8 million persons—representing 5.6% of the U.S. labor force—were employed in health services. Of the health-care

246 · Appendix A

workers with AIDS, 95% have been reported to exhibit high-risk behavior; for the remaining 5%, the means of HIV acquisition was undetermined. Health-care workers with AIDS were significantly more likely than other workers to have an undetermined risk (5% versus 3%, respectively). For both health-care workers and non-health-care workers with AIDS, the proportion with an undetermined risk has not increased since 1982.

AIDS patients initially reported as not belonging to recognized risk groups are investigated by state and local health departments to determine whether possible risk factors exist. Of all health-care workers with AIDS reported to CDC who were initially characterized as not having an identified risk and for whom follow-up information was available, 66% have been reclassified because risk factors were identified or because the patient was found not to meet the surveillance case definition for AIDS. Of the 87 health-care workers currently categorized as having no identifiable risk, information is incomplete on 16 (18%) because of death or refusal to be interviewed; 38 (44%) are still being investigated. The remaining 33 (38%) health-care workers were interviewed or had other follow-up information available. The occupations of these 33 were as follows: five physicians (15%), three of whom were surgeons; one dentist (3%); three nurses (9%); nine nursing assistants (27%); seven housekeeping or maintenance workers (21%); three clinical laboratory technicians (9%); one therapist (3%); and four others who did not have contact with patients (12%). Although 15 of these 33 health-care workers reported parenteral and/or other non-needlestick exposure to blood or body fluids from patients in the 10 years preceding their diagnosis of AIDS, none of these exposures involved a patient with AIDS or known HIV infection.

Risk to Health-Care Workers of Acquiring HIV in Health-Care Settings

Health-care workers with documented percutaneous or mucous-membrane exposures to blood or body fluids of HIV-infected patients have been prospectively evaluated to determine the risk of infection after such exposures. As of June 30, 1987, 883 health-care workers have been tested for antibody to HIV in an ongoing surveillance project conducted by CDC (9). Of these, 708 (80%) had percutaneous exposures to blood, and 175 (20%) had a mucous membrane or an open wound contaminated by blood or body fluid. Of 396 health-care workers, each of whom had only a convalescent-phase serum sample obtained and tested ≥90 days post-exposure, one—for whom heterosexual transmission could not be ruled out—was seropositive for HIV antibody. For 425 additional health-care workers, both acute- and convalescent-phase serum samples were obtained and tested; none of 74 health-care workers with nonpercutaneous exposures seroconverted, and three (0.9%) of 351 with percutaneous exposures seroconverted. None of these three health-care workers had other documented risk factors for infection.

Two other prospective studies to assess the risk of nosocomial acquisition of HIV infection for health-care workers are ongoing in the United States. As of April 30, 1987, 332 health-care workers with a total of 453 needlestick or mucous-membrane exposures to the blood or other body fluids of HIV-infected patients were tested for HIV antibody at the National Institutes of Health (10). These exposed workers included 103 with needlestick injuries and 229 with mucous-membrane exposures; none had seroconverted. A similar study at the University of California of 129 health-care workers with documented needlestick injuries or mucous-membrane exposures to blood or other body fluids from patients with HIV infection has not identified any seroconversions (11). Results of a prospective study in the United Kingdom identified no evidence of transmission among 150 health-care workers with parenteral or mucous-membrane exposures to blood or other body fluids, secretions, or excretions from patients with HIV infection (12).

In addition to health-care workers enrolled in prospective studies, eight persons who provided care to infected patients and denied other risk factors have been reported to have acquired HIV infection. Three of these health-care workers had needlestick exposures to blood from infected patients (13–15). Two were persons who provided nursing care to infected persons; although neither sustained a needlestick, both had extensive contact with blood or other body fluids, and neither observed recommended barrier precautions (16,17). The other three were health-care workers with non-needlestick exposures to blood from infected patients (18). Although the exact route of transmission for these last three infections is not known, all three persons had direct contact of their skin with blood from infected patients, all had skin lesions that may have been contaminated by blood, and one also had a mucous-membrane exposure.

A total of 1,231 dentists and hygienists, many of whom practiced in areas with many AIDS cases, participated in a study to determine the prevalence of antibody to HIV; one dentist (0.1%) had HIV antibody. Although no exposure to a known HIV-infected person could be documented, epidemiologic investigation did not identify any other risk factor for infection. The infected dentist, who also had a history of sustaining needlestick injuries and trauma to his hands, did not routinely wear gloves when providing dental care (19).

Precautions to Prevent Transmission of HIV

Universal Precautions

Since medical history and examination cannot reliably identify all patients infected with HIV or other blood-borne pathogens, blood and body-fluid precautions should be consistently used for all patients. This approach, previously recommended by CDC (3,4) and referred to as "universal blood and body-fluid precautions" or "universal precautions," should be used in the care of all patients, especially including those in emergency-care settings in which the risk of blood exposure is increased and the infection status of the patient is usually unknown (20).

1. All health-care workers should routinely use appropriate barrier precautions to prevent skin and mucous-membrane exposure when contact with blood or other body fluids of any patient is anticipated. Gloves should be worn for touching blood and body fluids, mucous membranes, or non-intact skin of all patients, for handling items or surfaces soiled with blood or body fluids, and for performing venipuncture and other vascular access procedures. Gloves should be changed after contact with each patient. Masks and protective eyewear or face shields should be worn during procedures that are likely to generate droplets of blood or other body fluids to prevent exposure of mucous membranes of the mouth, nose, and eyes. Gowns or aprons should be worn during procedures that are likely to generate splashes of blood or other body fluids.
2. Hands and other skin surfaces should be washed immediately and thoroughly if contaminated with blood or other body fluids. Hands should be washed immediately after gloves are removed.
3. All health-care workers should take precautions to prevent injuries caused by needles, scalpels, and other sharp instruments or devices during procedures; when cleaning used instruments; during disposal of used needles; and when handling sharp instruments after procedures. To prevent needlestick injuries, needles should not be recapped, purposely bent or broken by hand, removed

from disposable syringes, or otherwise manipulated by hand. After they are used, disposable syringes and needles, scalpel blades, and other sharp items should be placed in puncture-resistant containers for disposal; the puncture-resistant containers should be located as close as practical to the use area. Large-bore reusable needles should be placed in a puncture-resistant container for transport to the reprocessing area.

4. Although saliva has not been implicated in HIV transmission, to minimize the need for emergency mouth-to-mouth resuscitation, mouthpieces, resuscitation bags, or other ventilation devices should be available for use in areas in which the need for resuscitation is predictable.

5. Health-care workers who have exudative lesions or weeping dermatitis should refrain from all direct patient care and from handling patient-care equipment until the condition resolves.

6. Pregnant health-care workers are not known to be at greater risk of contracting HIV infection than health-care workers who are not pregnant; however, if a health-care worker develops HIV infection during pregnancy, the infant is at risk of infection resulting from perinatal transmission. Because of this risk, pregnant health-care workers should be especially familiar with and strictly adhere to precautions to minimize the risk of HIV transmission.

Implementation of universal blood and body-fluid precautions for all patients eliminates the need for use of the isolation category of "Blood and Body Fluid Precautions" previously recommended by CDC (7) for patients known or suspected to be infected with blood-borne pathogens. Isolation precautions (e.g., enteric, "AFB" [7]) should be used as necessary if associated conditions, such as infectious diarrhea or tuberculosis, are diagnosed or suspected.

Precautions for Invasive Procedures

In this document, an invasive procedure is defined as surgical entry into tissues, cavities, or organs or repair of major traumatic injuries 1) in an operating or delivery room, emergency department, or outpatient setting, including both physicians' and dentists' offices; 2) cardiac catheterization and angiographic procedures; 3) a vaginal or cesarean delivery or other invasive obstetric procedure during which bleeding may occur; or 4) the manipulation, cutting, or removal of any oral or perioral tissues, including tooth structure, during which bleeding occurs or the potential for bleeding exists. The universal blood and body-fluid precautions listed above, combined with the precautions listed below, should be the minimum precautions for all such invasive procedures.

1. All health-care workers who participate in invasive procedures must routinely use appropriate barrier precautions to prevent skin and mucous-membrane contact with blood and other body fluids of all patients. Gloves and surgical masks must be worn for all invasive procedures. Protective eyewear or face shields should be worn for procedures that commonly result in the generation of droplets, splashing of blood or other body fluids, or the generation of bone chips. Gowns or aprons made of materials that provide an effective barrier should be worn during invasive procedures that are likely to result in the splashing of blood or other body fluids. All health-care workers who perform or assist in vaginal or cesarean deliveries should wear gloves and gowns when handling the placenta or the infant until blood and amniotic fluid have been removed

from the infant's skin and should wear gloves during post-delivery care of the umbilical cord.

2. If a glove is torn or a needlestick or other injury occurs, the glove should be removed and a new glove used as promptly as patient safety permits; the needle or instrument involved in the incident should also be removed from the sterile field.

Precautions for Dentistry*

Blood, saliva, and gingival fluid from <u>all</u> dental patients should be considered infective. Special emphasis should be placed on the following precautions for preventing transmission of blood-borne pathogens in dental practice in both institutional and non-institutional settings.

1. In addition to wearing gloves for contact with oral mucous membranes of all patients, all dental workers should wear surgical masks and protective eyewear or chin-length plastic face shields during dental procedures in which splashing or spattering of blood, saliva, or gingival fluids is likely. Rubber dams, high-speed evacuation, and proper patient positioning, when appropriate, should be utilized to minimize generation of droplets and spatter.
2. Handpieces should be sterilized after use with each patient, since blood, saliva, or gingival fluid of patients may be aspirated into the handpiece or waterline. Handpieces that cannot be sterilized should at least be flushed, the outside surface cleaned and wiped with a suitable chemical germicide, and then rinsed. Handpieces should be flushed at the beginning of the day and after use with each patient. Manufacturers' recommendations should be followed for use and maintenance of waterlines and check valves and for flushing of handpieces. The same precautions should be used for ultrasonic scalers and air/water syringes.
3. Blood and saliva should be thoroughly and carefully cleaned from material that has been used in the mouth (e.g., impression materials, bite registration), especially before polishing and grinding intra-oral devices. Contaminated materials, impressions, and intra-oral devices should also be cleaned and disinfected before being handled in the dental laboratory and before they are placed in the patient's mouth. Because of the increasing variety of dental materials used intra-orally, dental workers should consult with manufacturers as to the stability of specific materials when using disinfection procedures.
4. Dental equipment and surfaces that are difficult to disinfect (e.g., light handles or X-ray-unit heads) and that may become contaminated should be wrapped with impervious-backed paper, aluminum foil, or clear plastic wrap. The coverings should be removed and discarded, and clean coverings should be put in place after use with each patient.

Precautions for Autopsies or Morticians' Services

In addition to the universal blood and body-fluid precautions listed above, the following precautions should be used by persons performing postmortem procedures:

1. All persons performing or assisting in postmortem procedures should wear gloves, masks, protective eyewear, gowns, and waterproof aprons.
2. Instruments and surfaces contaminated during postmortem procedures should be decontaminated with an appropriate chemical germicide.

*General infection-control precautions are more specifically addressed in previous recommendations for infection-control practices for dentistry (8).

Precautions for Dialysis

Patients with end-stage renal disease who are undergoing maintenance dialysis and who have HIV infection can be dialyzed in hospital-based or free-standing dialysis units using conventional infection-control precautions (21). Universal blood and body-fluid precautions should be used when dialyzing all patients.

Strategies for disinfecting the dialysis fluid pathways of the hemodialysis machine are targeted to control bacterial contamination and generally consist of using 500–750 parts per million (ppm) of sodium hypochlorite (household bleach) for 30–40 minutes or 1.5%–2.0% formaldehyde overnight. In addition, several chemical germicides formulated to disinfect dialysis machines are commercially available. None of these protocols or procedures need to be changed for dialyzing patients infected with HIV.

Patients infected with HIV can be dialyzed by either hemodialysis or peritoneal dialysis and do not need to be isolated from other patients. The type of dialysis treatment (i.e., hemodialysis or peritoneal dialysis) should be based on the needs of the patient. The dialyzer may be discarded after each use. Alternatively, centers that reuse dialyzers—i.e., a specific single-use dialyzer is issued to a specific patient, removed, cleaned, disinfected, and reused several times on the same patient only—may include HIV-infected patients in the dialyzer-reuse program. An individual dialyzer must never be used on more than one patient.

*Precautions for Laboratories**

Blood and other body fluids from all patients should be considered infective. To supplement the universal blood and body-fluid precautions listed above, the following precautions are recommended for health-care workers in clinical laboratories.

1. All specimens of blood and body fluids should be put in a well-constructed container with a secure lid to prevent leaking during transport. Care should be taken when collecting each specimen to avoid contaminating the outside of the container and of the laboratory form accompanying the specimen.
2. All persons processing blood and body-fluid specimens (e.g., removing tops from vacuum tubes) shoud wear gloves. Masks and protective eyewear should be worn if mucous-membrane contact with blood or body fluids is anticipated. Gloves should be changed and hands washed after completion of specimen processing.
3. For routine procedures, such as histologic and pathologic studies or microbiologic culturing, a biological safety cabinet is not necessary. However, biologic safety cabinets (Class I or II) should be used whenever procedures are conducted that have a high potential for generating droplets. These include activities such as blending, sonicating, and vigorous mixing.
4. Mechanical pipetting devices should be used for manipulating all liquids in the laboratory. Mouth pipetting must not be done.
5. Use of needles and syringes should be limited to situations in which there is no alternative, and the recommendations for preventing injuries with needles outlined under universal precautions should be followed.
6. Laboratory work surfaces should be decontaminated with an appropriate chemical germicide after a spill of blood or other body fluids and when work activities are completed.

*Additional precautions for research and industrial laboratories are addressed elsewhere (22,23).

7. Contaminated materials used in laboratory tests should be decontaminated before reprocessing or be placed in bags and disposed of in accordance with institutional policies for disposal of infective waste (24).
8. Scientific equipment that has been contaminated with blood or other body fluids should be decontaminated and cleaned before being repaired in the laboratory or transported to the manufacturer.
9. All persons should wash their hands after completing laboratory activities and should remove protective clothing before leaving the laboratory.

Implementation of universal blood and body-fluid precautions for **all** patients eliminates the need for warning labels on specimens since blood and other body fluids from all patients should be considered infective.

Environmental Considerations for HIV Transmission

No environmentally mediated mode of HIV transmission has been documented. Nevertheless, the precautions described below should be taken routinely in the care of **all** patients.

Sterilization and Disinfection

Standard sterilization and disinfection procedures for patient-care equipment currently recommended for use (25,26) in a variety of health-care settings—including hospitals, medical and dental clinics and offices, hemodialysis centers, emergency-care facilities, and long-term nursing-care facilities—are adequate to sterilize or disinfect instruments, devices, or other items contaminated with blood or other body fluids from persons infected with blood-borne pathogens including HIV (21,23).

Instruments or devices that enter sterile tissue or the vascular system of any patient or through which blood flows should be sterilized before reuse. Devices or items that contact intact mucous membranes should be sterilized or receive high-level disinfection, a procedure that kills vegetative organisms and viruses but not necessarily large numbers of bacterial spores. Chemical germicides that are registered with the U.S. Environmental Protection Agency (EPA) as "sterilants" may be used either for sterilization or for high-level disinfection depending on contact time.

Contact lenses used in trial fittings should be disinfected after each fitting by using a hydrogen peroxide contact lens disinfecting system or, if compatible, with heat (78 C-80 C [172.4 F-176.0 F]) for 10 minutes.

Medical devices or instruments that require sterilization or disinfection should be thoroughly cleaned before being exposed to the germicide, and the manufacturer's instructions for the use of the germicide should be followed. Further, it is important that the manufacturer's specifications for compatibility of the medical device with chemical germicides be closely followed. Information on specific label claims of commercial germicides can be obtained by writing to the Disinfectants Branch, Office of Pesticides, Environmental Protection Agency, 401 M Street, SW, Washington, D.C. 20460.

Studies have shown that HIV is inactivated rapidly after being exposed to commonly used chemical germicides at concentrations that are much lower than used in practice (27–30). Embalming fluids are similar to the types of chemical germicides that have been tested and found to completely inactivate HIV. In addition to commercially available chemical germicides, a solution of sodium hypochlorite (household bleach) prepared daily is an inexpensive and effective germicide. Concentrations ranging from approximately 500 ppm (1:100 dilution of household bleach) sodium hypochlorite to 5,000 ppm (1:10 dilution of household bleach) are effective depending on the amount of organic material (e.g., blood, mucus) present on the surface to be cleaned and disinfected. Commercially available chemical germicides may be more compatible with certain medical devices that might be corroded by repeated exposure to sodium hypochorite, especially to the 1:10 dilution.

Survival of HIV in the Environment

The most extensive study on the survival of HIV after drying involved greatly concentrated HIV samples, i.e., 10 million tissue-culture infectious doses per milliliter (31). This concentration is at least 100,000 times greater than that typically found in the blood or serum of patients with HIV infection. HIV was detectable by tissue-culture techniques 1–3 days after drying, but the rate of inactivation was rapid. Studies performed at CDC have also shown that drying HIV causes a rapid (within several hours) 1–2 log (90%–99%) reduction in HIV concentration. In tissue-culture fluid, cell-free HIV could be detected up to 15 days at room temperature, up to 11 days at 37 C (98.6 F), and up to 1 day if the HIV was cell-associated.

When considered in the context of environmental conditions in health-care facilities, these results do not require any changes in currently recommended sterilization, disinfection, or housekeeping strategies. When medical devices are contaminated with blood or other body fluids, existing recommendations include the cleaning of these instruments, followed by disinfection or sterilization, depending on the type of medical device. These protocols assume "worst-case" conditions of extreme virologic and microbiologic contamination, and whether viruses have been inactivated after drying plays no role in formulating these strategies. Consequently, no changes in published procedures for cleaning, disinfecting, or sterilizing need to be made.

Housekeeping

Environmental surfaces such as walls, floors, and other surfaces are not associated with transmission of infections to patients or health-care workers. Therefore, extraordinary attempts to disinfect or sterilize these environmental surfaces are not necessary. However, cleaning and removal of soil should be done routinely.

Cleaning schedules and methods vary according to the area of the hospital or institution, type of surface to be cleaned, and the amount and type of soil present. Horizontal surfaces (e.g., bedside tables and hard-surfaced flooring) in patient-care areas are usually cleaned on a regular basis, when soiling or spills occur, and when a patient is discharged. Cleaning of walls, blinds, and curtains is recommended only if they are visibly soiled. Disinfectant fogging is an unsatisfactory method of decontaminating air and surfaces and is not recommended.

Disinfectant-detergent formulations registered by EPA can be used for cleaning environmental surfaces, but the actual physical removal of microorganisms by scrubbing is probably at least as important as any antimicrobial effect of the cleaning agent used. Therefore, cost, safety, and acceptability by housekeepers can be the main criteria for selecting any such registered agent. The manufacturers' instructions for appropriate use should be followed.

Cleaning and Decontaminating Spills of Blood or Other Body Fluids

Chemical germicides that are approved for use as "hospital disinfectants" and are tuberculoidal when used at recommended dilutions can be used to decontaminate spills of blood and other body fluids. Strategies for decontaminating spills of blood and other body fluids in a patient-care setting are different than for spills of cultures or other materials in clinical, public health, or research laboratories. In patient-care areas, visible material should first be removed and then the area should be decontaminated. With large spills of cultured or concentrated infectious agents in the laboratory, the contaminated area should be flooded with a liquid germicide before cleaning, then decontaminated with fresh germicidal chemical. In both settings, gloves should be worn during the cleaning and decontaminating procedures.

Laundry

Although soiled linen has been identified as a source of large numbers of certain pathogenic microorganisms, the risk of actual disease transmission is negligible. Rather than rigid procedures and specifications, hygienic and common-sense storage and processing of clean and soiled linen are recommended (26). Soiled linen should be handled as little as possible and with minimum agitation to prevent gross microbial contamination of the air and of persons handling the linen. All soiled linen should be bagged at the location where it was used; it should not be sorted or rinsed in patient-care areas. Linen soiled with blood or body fluids should be placed and transported in bags that prevent leakage. If hot water is used, linen should be washed with detergent in water at least 71 C (160 F) for 25 minutes. If low-temperature (≤70 C [158 F] laundry cycles are used, chemicals suitable for low-temperature washing at proper use concentration should be used.

Infective Waste

There is no epidemiologic evidence to suggest that most hospital waste is any more infective than residential waste. Moreover, there is no epidemiologic evidence that hospital waste has caused disease in the community as a result of improper disposal. Therefore, identifying wastes for which special precautions are indicated is largely a matter of judgment about the relative risk of disease transmission. The most practical approach to the management of infective waste is to identify those wastes with the potential for causing infection during handling and disposal and for which some special precautions appear prudent. Hospital wastes for which special precautions appear prudent include microbiology laboratory waste, pathology waste, and blood specimens or blood products. While any item that has had contact with blood, exudates, or secretions may be potentially infective, it is not usually considered practical or necessary to treat all such waste as infective (23,26). Infective waste, in general, should either be incinerated or should be autoclaved before disposal in a sanitary landfill. Bulk blood, suctioned fluids, excretions, and secretions may be carefully poured down a drain connected to a sanitary sewer. Sanitary sewers may also be used to dispose of other infectious wastes capable of being ground and flushed into the sewer.

Implementation of Recommended Precautions

Employers of health-care workers should ensure that policies exist for:

1. Initial orientation and continuing education and training of all health-care workers—including students and trainees—on the epidemiology, modes of transmission, and prevention of HIV and other blood-borne infections and the need for routine use of universal blood and body-fluid precautions for all patients.
2. Provision of equipment and supplies necessary to minimize the risk of infection with HIV and other blood-borne pathogens.

3. Monitoring adherence to recommended protective measures. When monitoring reveals a failure to follow recommended precautions, counseling, education, and/or re-training should be provided and, if necessary, appropriate disciplinary action should be considered.

Professional associations and labor organizations, through continuing education efforts, should emphasize the need for health-care workers to follow recommended precautions.

Serologic Testing for HIV Infection

Background

A person is identified as infected with HIV when a sequence of tests, starting with repeated enzyme immunoassays (EIA) and including a Western blot or similar, more specific assay, are repeatedly reactive. Persons infected with HIV usually develop antibody against the virus within 6–12 weeks after infection.

The sensitivity of the currently licensed EIA tests is at least 99% when they are performed under optimal laboratory conditions on serum specimens from persons infected for ≥12 weeks. Optimal laboratory conditions include the use of reliable reagents, provision of continuing education of personnel, quality control of procedures, and participation in performance-evaluation programs. Given this performance, the probability of a false-negative test is remote except during the first several weeks after infection, before detectable antibody is present. The proportion of infected persons with a false-negative test attributed to absence of antibody in the early stages of infection is dependent on both the incidence and prevalence of HIV infection in a population (Table 1).

The specificity of the currently licensed EIA tests is approximately 99% when repeatedly reactive tests are considered. Repeat testing of initially reactive specimens

TABLE 1

Estimated annual number of patients infected with HIV not detected by HIV-antibody testing in a hypothetical hospital with 10,000 admissions/year*

Beginning prevalence of HIV infection	Annual incidence of HIV infection	Approximate number of HIV-infected patients	Approximate number of HIV-infected patients not detected
5.0%	1.0%	550	17–18
5.0%	0.5%	525	11–12
1.0%	0.2%	110	3–4
1.0%	0.1%	105	2–3
0.1%	0.02%	11	0–1
0.1%	0.01%	11	0–1

*The estimates are based on the following assumptions: 1) the sensitivity of the screening test is 99% (i.e., 99% of HIV-infected persons with antibody will be detected); 2) persons infected with HIV will not develop detectable antibody (seroconvert) until 6 weeks (1.5 months) after infection; 3) new infections occur at an equal rate throughout the year; 4) calculations of the number of HIV-infected persons in the patient population are based on the mid-year prevalence, which is the beginning prevalence plus half the annual incidence of infections.

by EIA is required to reduce the likelihood of laboratory error. To increase further the specificity of serologic tests, laboratories must use a supplemental test, most often the Western blot, to validate repeatedly reactive EIA results. Under optimal laboratory conditions, the sensitivity of the Western blot test is comparable to or greater than that of a repeatedly reactive EIA, and the Western blot is highly specific when strict criteria are used to interpret the test results. The testing sequence of a repeatedly reactive EIA and a positive Western blot test is highly predictive of HIV infection, even in a population with a low prevalence of infection (Table 2). If the Western blot test result is indeterminant, the testing sequence is considered equivocal for HIV infection. When this occurs, the Western blot test should be repeated on the same serum sample, and, if still indeterminant, the testing sequence should be repeated on a sample collected 3–6 months later. Use of other supplemental tests may aid in interpreting of results on samples that are persistently indeterminant by Western blot.

Testing of Patients

Previous CDC recommendations have emphasized the value of HIV serologic testing of patients for: 1) management of parenteral or mucous-membrane exposures of health-care workers, 2) patient diagnosis and management, and 3) counseling and serologic testing to prevent and control HIV transmission in the community. In addition, more recent recommendations have stated that hospitals, in conjunction with state and local health departments, should periodically determine the prevalence of HIV infection among patients from age groups at highest risk of infection (32).

Adherence to universal blood and body-fluid precautions recommended for the care of all patients will minimize the risk of transmission of HIV and other blood-borne pathogens from patients to health-care workers. The utility of routine HIV serologic testing of patients as an adjunct to universal precautions is unknown. Results of such testing may not be available in emergency or outpatient settings. In addition, some recently infected patients will not have detectable antibody to HIV (Table 1).

Personnel in some hospitals have advocated serologic testing of patients in settings in which exposure of health-care workers to large amounts of patients' blood may

TABLE 2

Predictive value of positive HIV-antibody tests in hypothetical populations with different prevalences of infection

	Prevalence of infection	Predictive value of positive test*
Repeatedly reactive	0.2%	28.41%
enzyme immunoassay (EIA)†	2.0%	80.16%
	20.0%	98.02%
Repeatedly reactive EIA	0.2%	99.75%
followed by positive	2.0%	99.97%
Western blot (WB)‡	20.0%	99.99%

*Proportion of persons with positive test results who are actually infected with HIV.
†Assumes EIA sensitivity of 99.0% and specificity of 99.5%.
‡Assumes WB sensitivity of 99.0% and specificity of 99.9%.

be anticipated. Specific patients for whom serologic testing has been advocated include those undergoing major operative procedures and those undergoing treatment in critical-care units, especially if they have conditions involving uncontrolled bleeding. Decisions regarding the need to establish testing programs for patients should be made by physicians or individual institutions. In addition, when deemed appropriate, testing of individual patients may be performed on agreement between the patient and the physician providing care.

In addition to the universal precautions recommended for all patients, certain additional precautions for the care of HIV-infected patients undergoing major surgical operations have been proposed by personnel in some hospitals. For example, surgical procedures on an HIV-infected patient might be altered so that hand-to-hand passing of sharp instruments would be eliminated; stapling instruments rather than hand-suturing equipment might be used to perform tissue approximation; electrocautery devices rather than scalpels might be used as cutting instruments; and, even though uncomfortable, gowns that totally prevent seepage of blood onto the skin of members of the operative team might be worn. While such modifications might further minimize the risk of HIV infection for members of the operative team, some of these techniques could result in prolongation of operative time and could potentially have an adverse effect on the patient.

Testing programs, if developed, should include the following principles:

- Obtaining consent for testing.
- Informing patients of test results, and providing counseling for seropositive patients by properly trained persons.
- Assuring that confidentiality safeguards are in place to limit knowledge of test results to those directly involved in the care of infected patients or as required by law.
- Assuring that identification of infected patients will not result in denial of needed care or provision of suboptimal care.
- Evaluating prospectively 1) the efficacy of the program in reducing the incidence of parenteral, mucous-membrane, or significant cutaneous exposures of health-care workers to the blood or other body fluids of HIV-infected patients and 2) the effect of modified procedures on patients.

Testing of Health-Care Workers

Although transmission of HIV from infected health-care workers to patients has not been reported, transmission during invasive procedures remains a possibility. Transmission of hepatitis B virus (HBV)—a blood-borne agent with a considerably greater potential for nosocomial spread—from health-care workers to patients has been documented. Such transmission has occurred in situations (e.g., oral and gynecologic surgery) in which health-care workers, when tested, had very high concentrations of HBV in their blood (at least 100 million infectious virus particles per milliliter, a concentration much higher than occurs with HIV infection), and the health-care workers sustained a puncture wound while performing invasive procedures or had exudative or weeping lesions or microlacerations that allowed virus to contaminate instruments or open wounds of patients (33,34).

The hepatitis B experience indicates that only those health-care workers who perform certain types of invasive procedures have transmitted HBV to patients. Adherence to recommendations in this document will minimize the risk of transmission of HIV and other blood-borne pathogens from health-care workers to patients during invasive procedures. Since transmission of HIV from infected health-care workers performing invasive procedures to their patients had not been reported and would be expected to occur only very rarely, if at all, the utility of routine testing of such health-care workers to prevent transmission of HIV cannot be assessed. If consideration is given to developing a serologic testing program for health-care workers who perform invasive procedures, the frequency of testing, as well as the issues of consent, confidentiality, and consequences of test results—as previously outlined for testing programs for patients—must be addressed.

Management of Infected Health-Care Workers

Health-care workers with impaired immune systems resulting from HIV infection or other causes are at increased risk of acquiring or experiencing serious complications of infectious disease. Of particular concern is the risk of severe infection following exposure to patients with infectious diseases that are easily transmitted if appropriate precautions are not taken (e.g., measles, varicella). Any health-care worker with an impaired immune system should be counseled about the potential risk associated with taking care of patients with any transmissible infection and should continue to follow existing recommendations for infection control to minimize risk of exposure to other infectious agents (7,35). Recommendations of the Immunization Practices Advisory Committee (ACIP) and institutional policies concerning requirements for vaccinating health-care workers with live-virus vaccines (e.g., measles, rubella) should also be considered.

The question of whether workers infected with HIV—especially those who perform invasive procedures—can adequately and safely be allowed to perform patient-care duties or whether their work assignments should be changed must be determined on an individual basis. These decisions should be made by the health-care worker's personal physician(s) in conjunction with the medical directors and personnel health service staff of the employing institution or hospital.

Management of Exposures

If a health-care worker has a parenteral (e.g., needlestick or cut) or mucous-membrane (e.g., splash to the eye or mouth) exposure to blood or other body fluids or has a cutaneous exposure involving large amounts of blood or prolonged contact with blood—especially when the exposed skin is chapped, abraded, or afflicted with dermatitis—the source patient should be informed of the incident and tested for serologic evidence of HIV infection after consent is obtained. Policies should be developed for testing source patients in situations in which consent cannot be obtained (e.g., an unconscious patient).

If the source patient has AIDS, is positive for HIV antibody, or refuses the test, the health-care worker should be counseled regarding the risk of infection and evaluated clinically and serologically for evidence of HIV infection as soon as possible after the exposure. The health-care worker should be advised to report and seek medical evaluation for any acute febrile illness that occurs within 12 weeks after the exposure. Such an illness—particularly one characterized by fever, rash, or lymphadenopathy—may be indicative of recent HIV infection. Seronegative health-care workers should be retested 6 weeks post-exposure and on a periodic basis thereafter (e.g., 12 weeks and 6 months after exposure) to determine whether transmission has occurred. During this follow-up period—especially the first 6–12 weeks after exposure, when most infected persons are expected to seroconvert—exposed health-care workers should follow U.S. Public Health Service (PHS) recommendations for preventing transmission of HIV (36,37).

No further follow-up of a health-care worker exposed to infection as described above is necessary if the source patient is seronegative unless the source patient is at high risk of HIV infection. In the latter case, a subsequent specimen (e.g., 12 weeks following exposure) may be obtained from the health-care worker for antibody testing. If the source patient cannot be identified, decisions regarding appropriate follow-up should be individualized. Serologic testing should be available to all health-care workers who are concerned that they may have been infected with HIV.

If a patient has a parenteral or mucous-membrane exposure to blood or other body fluid of a health-care worker, the patient should be informed of the incident, and the same procedure outlined above for management of exposures should be followed for both the source health-care worker and the exposed patient.

Evaluation of Employer Training and Education Programs

Training programs must be evaluated through program review and discussion with management and employees.

1. Training programs shall normally include epidemiology, clinical presentation, modes of transmission and prevention of HBV and HIV as well protective measures to be taken to prevent exposure.
2. The following questions provided a general outline of training topics to be reviewed when conducting an inspection at a health care facility. Responses shall be documented in the case file. Areas of interest include, but are not limited to, direct patient care areas, emergency room, operating rooms, clinical laboratories, x-ray, housekeeping and laundry.
   a. Has a training and information program been established for employees actually or potentially exposed to blood and/or body fluids?
   b. How often is training provided and does it cover:
      (1) Universal precautions?
      (2) Personal protective equipment?
      (3) Workplace practices include blood drawing, room cleaning, laundry handling, cleanup of blood spills?
      (4) Needlestick exposure/management?
      (5) Hepatitis B Vaccination?
   c. Does new employee orientation cover infection disease control?
   d. Does the employer evaluate the effectiveness of the training program through monitoring of employee compliance with the guidelines?
   e. Have employees been informed of the precautionary measures outlined in the CDC guidelines?
   f. Is personal protective equipment provided to employees? In all appropriate locations? (Specifically, ask about gloves, mask, eye protection, gowns (as appropriate).)
   g. Is the necessary equipment (i.e., mouthpieces, resuscitation bags, or other ventilation devices) provided for administering mouth-to-mouth resuscitation on potentially infected patients?
   h. Does training identify the specific procedures implemented by the employer to provide protection, such as proper use of personal protective equipment?
   i. Are facilities available to comply with workplace practices, such as handwashing sinks, needle containers, detergents and disinfectants to clean up spills?
   j. Are employees aware of specific workplace practices to follow when appropriate? Specifically ask about:
      • Handwashing.
      • Handling sharp instruments.

- Routine examinations.
- Blood spills.
- Handling spills.
- Disposal of contaminated materials.
- Reusable equipment.

k. Are workers aware of procedures to follow after a needlestick or blood exposure? Have they had such experiences, and are the guidelines followed?

l. Are employees aware of the Hepatitis B vaccination program? Do they take advantage of it?

Document 7
CDC: Guidelines for Health Care Workers

This document has been developed by the Centers for Disease Control (CDC) to update recommendations for prevention of transmission of human immunodeficiency virus (HIV) and hepatitis B virus (HBV) in the health-care setting. Current data suggest that the risk for such transmission from a health-care worker (HCW) to a patient during an invasive procedure is small; a precise assessment of the risk is not yet available. This document contains recommendations to provide guidance for prevention of HIV and HBV transmission during those invasive procedures that are considered exposure-prone.

Introduction

Recommendations have been made by the Centers for Disease Control (CDC) for the prevention of transmission of the human immunodeficiency virus (HIV) and the hepatitis B virus (HBV) in health-care settings (1-6). These recommendations emphasize adherence to universal precautions that require that blood and other specified body fluids of all patients be handled as if they contain blood-borne pathogens (1,2).

Previous guidelines contained precautions to be used during invasive procedures (defined in Appendix) and recommendations for the management of HIV- and HBV-infected health-care workers (HCWs) (1). These guidelines did not include specific recommendations on testing HCWs for HIV or HBV infection, and they did not provide guidance on which invasive procedures may represent increased risk to the patient.

The recommendations outlined in this document are based on the following considerations:

- Infected HCWs who adhere to universal precautions and who do not perform invasive procedures pose no risk for transmitting HIV or HBV to patients.
- Infected HCWs who adhere to universal precautions and who perform certain exposure-prone procedures (see page 4) pose a small risk for transmitting HBV to patients.
- HIV is transmitted much less readily than HBV.

In the interim, until further data is available, additional precautions are prudent to prevent HIV and HBV transmission during procedures that have been linked to HCW-to-patient HBV transmission or that are considered exposure-prone.

Background

Infection-Control Practices

Previous recommendations have specified that infection-control programs should incorporate principles of universal precautions (i.e., appropriate use of hand washing, protective barriers, and care in the use and disposal of needles and other sharp instruments) and should maintain these precautions rigorously in all health-care settings (1,2,5). Proper application of these principles will assist in minimizing the risk of transmission of HIV or HBV from patient to HCW, HCW to patient, or patient to patient.

As part of standard infection-control practice, instruments and other reusable equipment used in performing invasive procedures should be appropriately disinfected and sterilized as follows (7):

- Equipment and devices that enter the patient's vascular system or other normally sterile areas of the body should be sterilized before being used for each patient.
- Equipment and devices that touch intact mucous membranes but do not penetrate the patient's body surfaces should be sterilized when possible or undergo high-level disinfection if they cannot be sterilized before being used for each patient.
- Equipment and devices that do not touch the patient or that only touch intact skin of the patient need only be cleaned with a detergent or as indicated by the manufacturer.

Compliance with universal precautions and recommendations for disinfection and sterilization of medical devices should be scrupulously monitored in all health-care settings (1,7,8). Training of HCWs in proper infection-control technique should begin in professional and vocational schools and continue as an ongoing process. Institutions should provide all HCWs with appropriate inservice education regarding infection control and safety and should establish procedures for monitoring compliance with infection-control policies.

All HCWs who might be exposed to blood in an occupational setting should receive hepatitis B vaccine, preferably during their period of professional training and before any occupational exposures could occur (8,9).

Transmission of HBV During Invasive Procedures

Since the introduction of serologic testing for HBV infection in the early 1970s, there have been published reports of 20 clusters in which a total of over 300 patients were infected with HBV in association with treatment by an HBV-infected HCW. In 12 of these clusters, the implicated HCW did not routinely wear gloves; several HCWs also had skin lesions that may have facilitated HBV transmission (10–22). These 12 clusters included nine linked to dentists or oral surgeons and one cluster each linked to a general practitioner, an inhalation therapist, and a cardiopulmonary-bypass-pump technician. The clusters associated with the inhalation therapist and the cardiopulmonary-bypass-pump technician—and some of the other 10 clusters—could possibly have been prevented if current recommendations on universal precautions, including glove use, had been in effect. In the remaining eight clusters, transmission occurred despite glove use by the HCWs; five clusters were linked to obstetricians or gynecologists, and three were linked to cardiovascular surgeons (6, 22–28). In addition, recent unpublished reports strongly suggest HBV transmission from three surgeons to patients in 1989 and 1990 during colorectal (CDC, unpublished data), abdominal, and cardiothoracic surgery (29).

Seven of the HCWs who were linked to published clusters in the United States were allowed to perform invasive procedures following modification of invasive techniques (e.g., double gloving and restriction of certain high-risk procedures) (6,11–13,15,16,24). For five HCWs, no further transmission to patients was observed in two instances involving an obstetrician-gynecologist and an oral surgeon, HBV was transmitted to patients after techniques were modified (6,12).

Review of the 20 published studies indicates that a combination of risk factors accounted for transmission of HBV from HCWs to patients. Of the HCWs whose hepatitis B e antigen (HBeAg) status was determined (17 of 20), all were HBeAg positive. The presence of HBeAg in serum is associated with higher levels of circulating virus and therefore with greater infectivity of hepatitis-B-surface-antigen (HBsAg)-positive individuals; the risk of HBV transmission to an HCW after a percutaneous exposure to HBeAg-positive blood is approximately 30% (30–32). In addition, each report indicated that the potential existed for contamination of surgical wounds or traumatized tissue, either from a major break in standard infection-control practices (e.g., not wearing gloves during invasive procedures) or from unintentional injury to the infected HCW during invasive procedures (e.g., needle sticks incurred while manipulating needles without being able to see them during suturing).

Most reported clusters in the United States occurred before awareness increased of the risks of transmission of blood-borne pathogens in health-care settings and before emphasis was placed on the use of universal precautions and hepatitis B vaccine among HCWs. The limited number of reports of HBV transmission from HCWs to patients in recent years may reflect the adoption of universal precautions and increased use of HBV vaccine. However, the limited number of recent reports does not preclude the occurence of undetected or unreported small clusters or individual instances of transmission; routine use of gloves does not prevent most injuries caused by sharp instruments and does not eliminate the potential for exposure of a patient to an HCW's blood and transmission of HBV (6, 22–29).

Transmission of HIV During Invasive Procedures

The risk of HIV transmission to an HCW after percutaneous exposure to HIV-infected blood is considerably lower than the risk of HBV transmission after percutaneous exposure to HBeAg-positive blood (0.3% versus approximately 30%) (33–35). Thus, the risk of transmission of HIV from an infected HCW to a patient during an invasive procedure is likely to be proportionately lower than the risk of HBV transmission from an HBeAg-positive HCW to a patient during the same procedure. As with HBV, the relative infectivity of HIV probably varies among individuals and over time for a single individual. Unlike HBV infection, however, there is currently no readily available laboratory test for increased HIV infectivity.

Investigation of a cluster of HIV infections among patients in the practice of one dentist with acquired immunodeficiency syndrome (AIDS) strongly suggested that HIV was transmitted to five of the approximately 850 patients evaluated through June 1991 (36–38). The investigation indicates that HIV transmission occurred during dental care, although the precise mechanisms of transmission have not been determined. In two other studies, when patients cared for by a general surgeon and a surgical resident who had AIDS were tested, all patients tested, 75 and 62, respectively, were negative for HIV infection (39, 40). In a fourth study, 143 patients who had been treated by a dental student with HIV infection and were later tested were all negative for HIV infection (41). In another investigation, HIV antibody testing was offered to all patients whose surgical procedures had been performed by a general surgeon within 7 years before the surgeon's diagnosis of AIDS; the date at which the surgeon became infected with HIV is unknown (42). Of 1,340 surgical patients contacted, 616 (46%) were tested for HIV. One patient, a known intravenous drug user, was HIV positive when tested but may already have been infected at the time of surgery. HIV test results for the 615 other surgical patients were negative (95% confidence interval for risk of transmission per operation = 0.0%–0.5%).

The limited number of participants and the differences in procedures associated with these five investigations limit the ability to generalize from them and to define precisely the risk of HIV transmission from HIV-infected HCWs to patients. A precise estimate of the risk of HIV transmission from infected HCWs to patients can be determined only after careful evaluation of a substantially larger number of patients whose exposure-prone procedures have been performed by HIV-infected HCWs.

Exposure-Prone Procedures

Despite adherence to the principles of universal precautions, certain invasive surgical and dental procedures have been implicated in the transmission of HBV from infected HCWs to patients, and should be considered exposure-prone. Reported examples include certain oral, cardiothoracic, colorectal (CDC, unpublished data), and obstetric/gynecologic procedures (6, 12, 22–29).

Certain other invasive procedures should also be considered exposure-prone. In a prospective study CDC conducted in four hospitals, one or more percutaneous injuries occurred among surgical personnel during 96 (6.9%) of 1,382 operative procedures on the general surgery, gynecology, orthopedic, cardiac, and trauma services (43). Percutaneous exposure of the patient to the HCW's blood may have occurred when the sharp object causing the injury recontacted the patient's open wound in 28 (32%) of the 88 observed injuries to surgeons (range among surgical specialities = 8%–57%; range among hospitals = 24%–42%).

> Characteristics of exposure-prone procedures include digital palpation of a needle tip in a body cavity or the simultaneous presence of the HCW's fingers and a needle or other sharp instrument or object in a poorly visualized or highly confined anatomic site. Performance of exposure-prone procedures presents a recognized risk of percutaneous injury to the HCW, and—if such an injury occurs—the HCW's blood is likely to contact the patient's body cavity, subcutaneous tissues, and/or mucous membranes.

Experience with HBV indicates that invasive procedures that do not have the above characteristics would be expected to pose substantially lower risk, if any, of transmission of HIV and other blood-borne pathogens from an infected HCW to patients.

Recommendations

Investigations of HIV and HBV transmission from HCWs to patients indicate that, when HCWs adhere to recommended infection-control procedures, the risk of transmitting HBV from an infected HCW to a patient is small, and the risk of transmitting HIV is likely to be even smaller. However, the likelihod of exposure of the patient to an HCW's blood is greater for certain procedures designated as exposure-prone. To minimize the risk of HIV or HBV transmission, the following measures are recommended:

- All HCWs should adhere to universal precautions, including the appropriate use of hand washing, protective barriers, and care in the use and disposal of needles and other sharp instruments. HCWs who have exudative lesions or weeping dermatitis should refrain from all direct patient care and from handling patient-care equipment and devices used in performing invasive procedures until the condition resolves. HCWs should also comply with current guidelines for disinfection and sterilization of reusable devices used in invasive procedures.
- Currently available data provide no basis for recommendations to restrict the practice of HCWs infected with HIV or HBV who perform invasive procedures not identified as exposure-prone, provided the infected HCWs practice rec-

ommended surgical or dental technique and comply with universal precautions and current recommendations for sterilization/disinfection.

- Exposure-prone procedures should be identified by medical/surgical/dental organizations and institutions at which the procedures are performed.
- HCWs who perform exposure-prone procedures should know their HIV antibody status. HCWs who perform exposure-prone procedures and who do not have serologic evidence of immunity to HBV from vaccination or from previous infection should know their HBsAg status and, if that is positive, should also know their HBeAg status.
- HCWs who are infected with HIV or HBV (and are HBeAg positive) should not perform exposure-prone procedures unless they have sought counsel from an expert review panel and been advised under what circumstances, if any, they may continue to perform these procedures.* Such circumstances would include notifying prospective patients of the HCW's seropositivity before they undergo exposure-prone invasive procedures.
- Mandatory testing of HCWs for HIV antibody, HBsAg, or HBeAg is not recommended. The current assessment of the risk that infected HCWs will transmit HIV or HBV to patients during exposure-prone procedures does not support the division of resources that would be required to implement mandatory testing programs. Compliance by HCWs with recommendations can be increased through education, training, and appropriate confidentiality safeguards.

HCWs Whose Practices are Modified Because of HIV or HBV Status

HCWs whose practices are modified because of their HIV or HBV infection status should, whenever possible, be provided opportunities to continue appropriate patient-care activities. Career counseling and job retraining should be encouraged to promote the continued use of the HCW's talents, knowledge, and skills. HCWs whose practices are modified because of HBV infection should be reevaluated periodically to determine whether their HBeAg status changes due to resolution of infection or as a result of treatment (44).

Notification of Patients and Follow-up Studies

The public health benefits of notification of patients who have had exposure-prone procedures performed by HCWs infected with HIV or positive for HBeAg should be considered on a case-by-case basis, taking into consideration an assessment of specific risks, confidentiality issues, and available resources. Carefully designed and implemented follow-up studies are necessary to determine more precisely the risk of transmission during such procedures. Decisions regarding notification and

*The review panel should include experts who represent a balanced perspective. Such experts might include all of the following: a) the HCW's personal physician(s), b) an infections disease specialist with expertise in the epidemiology of HIV and HBV transmission, c) a health professional with expertise in the procedures performed by the HCW, and d) state or local public health official(s). If the HCW's practice is institutionally based, the expert review panel might also include a member of the infection-control commitee, preferably a hospital epidemiologist. HCWs who perform exposure-prone procedures outside the hospital/institutional setting should seek advice from appropriate state and local public health officials regarding the review process. Panels must recognize the importance of confidentiality and the privacy rights of infected HCWs.

follow-up studies should be made in consultation with state and local public health officials.

Additional Needs

- Clearer definition of the nature, frequency, and circumstances of blood contact between patients and HCWs during invasive procedures.
- Development and evaluation of new devices, protective barriers, and techniques that may prevent such blood contact without adversely affecting the quality of patient care.
- More information on the potential for HIV or HBV transmission through contaminated instruments.
- Improvements in sterilization and disinfection techniques for certain reusable equipment and devices.
- Identification of factors that may influence the likelihood of HIV or HBV transmission after exposure to HIV- or HBV-infected blood.

Appendix

Definition of Invasive Procedure

An invasive procedure is defined as "surgical entry into tissues, cavities, or organs or repair of major traumatic injuries" associated with any of the following: "1) an operating or delivery room, emergency department, or outpatient setting, including both physicians' and dentists' offices; 2) cardiac catheterization and angiographic procedures; 3) a vaginal or cesarean delivery or other invasive obstetric procedure during which bleeding may occur; or 4) the manipulation, cutting, or removal of any oral or perioral tissues, including tooth structure, during which bleeding occurs or the potential for bleeding exists."

Reprinted from: Centers for Disease Control. Recommendation for prevention of HIV transmission in health-care settings. MMWR 1987;36 (suppl. no. 2S):6S–7S.

Document 8

American Hospital Association 1992 Review:
OSHA's Final Bloodborne Pathogens Standard

Checklist

Exposure Control Plan

• Does it identify in writing all employees who have a reasonable likelihood of occupational exposure during the performance of their assigned duties without regard to the use of personal protective equipment; the schedule and procedures for implementing *all* the provisions of the standards; and the method for evaluation of exposure incidents that allows appropriate corrective action to be taken?
• Has a mechanism been established for annual review of it?
• Is the Exposure Control Plan accessible to all employees?

Universal Precautions

• Do you have a written policy that adopts the use of universal precautions for the handling of blood and potentially infectious materials to reduce the risk of occupational exposure?
• Does your facility's definition of potentially infectious materials include at least those human body fluids that are included in OSHA's definition?

Handling and Disposal of Sharps

• Does the Exposure Control Plan identify the
  • engineering controls that will be used to reduce occupational exposure;
  • schedule for regular inspection and replacement of engineering controls;
  • the schedule and method for determining the need for replacement of sharps containers?
• Is there a mechanism to evaluate safe needle devices for their appropriateness and efficacy? After efficacy has been established, are these devices made available to employees?
• Does employee training include proper use of these devices?
• Are there written policies that
  • prohibit recapping of needles using a two-handed technique;
  • prohibit removal of needles from syringes by hand;
  • prohibit bending, shearing, or breaking of contaminaed needles;
  • specify the situations where recapping is allowed and the safe practices or devices that are required to reduce the risk of injury;
  • specify the safe practices to be used when handling or reprocessing reusable sharps;
  • require the use of mechanical means (such as a brush and a dust pan, or tongs) to clean up broken glassware?
• Are the containers used to store or transport contaminated reusable sharps
  • puncture-resistant and leakproof;
  • red in color or labeled with the biohazard symbol?

- Are containers used for disposal of contaminated sharps
  - closable, puncture-resistant, leakproof on sides and bottom;
  - red in color or labeled with the biohazard symbol;
  - located as close as feasible to the immediate area of use;
  - located in areas where sharps may not normally be used, but can be reasonably anticipated to be found, such as the laundry;
  - replaced routinely and not allowed to overfill;
  - maintained in an upright position during transport?

Safe Work Practices

- Are handwashing facilities reasonably accessible to employees? If handwashing facilities with soap and running water are not accessible, are appropriate alternatives provided, such as antiseptic hand cleansers or towelettes?
- Are employees instructed about not eating, drinking, smoking, applying cosmetics or lip balm, or handling contact lenses in contaminated work areas?
- Are food and drink prohibited from storage in refrigerators, freezers, shelves, cabinets, or counter tops where blood and other potentially infectious materials are present?
- Are employees who perform procedures that may create splashing or spraying of blood or other potentially infectious materials trained to perform such procedures in a manner that reduces risk of exposure?
- Are employees trained to recognize specimen containers as containing potentially infectious materials? Are they trained to use universal precautions when handling all specimens? If not, are the containers red or labeled with the biohazard symbol?
- Are containers that are used to transport specimen, such as phlebotomy trays, appropriated labeled?
- Are employees instructed to place all specimen containers that may be contaminated or leak in a secondary container that is leak-resistant or, if necessary, puncture-resistant?
- Is contaminated equipment decontaminated prior to servicing? If unable to be decontaminated, is it labeled and does it specify which portions of the equipment remain contaminated?

Personal Protective Barriers

- Have personal protective clothing and equipment been provided to your employees that are
  - appropriate for the task performed;
  - effective in preventing the penetration of blood and other potentially infectious materials;
  - free of charge;
  - accessible and conveniently located;
  - available in proper sizes;
- Is there a mechanism for repairing, replacing, reprocessing protective barriers and clothing;
- Are emergency ventilation devices provided for use in emergency resuscitation;
- Are employees trained in the proper selection, indications, mandated use, and proper procedures for disposal or reprocessing of personal protective equipment?

Protective Clothing

- Have employee job duties with occupational exposure been reviewed to determine what protective clothing must be provided?
- Is appropriate personal protective clothing provided to employees?
  - at no cost;
  - in appropriate sizes;
  - in accessible locations?
- Is a mechanism in place for cleaning, laundering, or disposing of employees' protective clothing?
- Is there a mechanism for replacement or washing of an employee-owned uniform or clothing if it becomes contaminated?
- Does employee training include
  - indications for selection, proper use, replacement, and disposal of protective clothing;
  - the need to remove protective clothing prior to leaving the work area and when it becomes penetrated by blood and other potentially infectious materials?

Gloves

- Are gloves made available to employees in accessible locations? Are they suitable for the tasks being performed?
- Are gloves required to be worn
  - when there is reasonable likelihood of contact with blood and other potentially infectious materials;
  - during all vascular access procedures;
  - when there is contact with mucous membranes and non-intact skin;
  - when contaminated items or surfaces are handled?
- Are alternatives provided for employees who are allergic to the gloves normally provided?
- Do hospital procedures
  - prohibit washing and decontamination for reuse of disposable gloves;
  - specify the methods for decontamination, indications for replacement, and length of use of utility gloves?

Masks, Eye Protection, and Face Shields

- Are face and eye protection provide when there is a potential for splashing, spraying, or splattering of blood or potentially infectious materials;
- If glasses are used as protective eyewear, do they have side shields?

Housekeeping

- Is there a written procedure for cleaning and decontamination of
  - environmental surfaces, e.g., floors;
  - work surfaces;
  - equipment?
- Does the written procedure specify that work surfaces must be cleaned and decontaminated
  - upon completion of procedure;
  - after overt contamination during a procedure;
  - at the end of the work shift?

- Has a written procedure been established for reusable trash receptacles used to hold contaminated items, including
  - a regular schedule for inspection and decontamination of containers;
  - procedures for cleaning and decontamination when visibly contaminated?

Laundry

- Are there written procedures for bagging, handling, and transporting of contaminated laundry that
  - prohibit the sorting or rinsing in patient care areas;
  - specify the types of bags or containers that will be used to prevent leakage;
  - specify the alternative labeling when universal precautions are used for handling all contaminated laundry?
- Does your employee training cover all procedures for identifying, bagging, handling, and transporting of contaminated laundry?
- Are laundry employees provided with appropriate protective clothing to prevent occupational exposure? Are these employees trained on the proper use of the protective clothing?

Regulated Waste

- Has the definition of regulated waste been reviewed and revised to be consistent with OSHA's definition?
- Are the containers for regulated waste
  - closable;
  - able to prevent leakage of fluids;
  - labeled with the biohazard symbol or colored red?
- Are secondary containers provided in situations where the outside of the primary container becomes contaminated?
  - Do these secondary containers meet the same requirements as the primary containers?
- Are employees instructed to close all regulated waste containers prior to removal to prevent spillage during handling, transporting, or shipping?

Compliance Monitoring

- Do policies and procedures identify the responsibility of department heads, managers, and staff in complying with recommended practices?
- Do these policies and procedures include
  - the responsibility of the employee;
  - recommended practices;
  - how compliance monitoring will be done;
  - how noncompliance will be reported and documented;
  - how follow-up will be conducted;
  - the action to be taken for noncompliance; e.g., disciplinary action, if necessary?

Postexposure Evaluation and Follow-up Procedures

- Have exposure incidents been defined?
- Has a mechanism been established to
  - document the route(s) of exposure and circumstances under which all
  - exposure incidents occur;
  - evaluate exposure incidents that allow corrective action to be taken?

- Is a confidential medical evaluation and follow-up provided immediately following exposure incidents, including
  - evaluation of the exposure incident;
  - collection and testing of the source individual's blood for HBV and HIVserological status, if not already known;
  - collection and testing of employee's blood for HIV and HBV status;
  - postexposure prophylaxis when medically indicated, as recommended by the USPHS at the time of the exposure;
  - counseling;
  - evaluation of any reported illnesses related to the exposure incident?
- Is information on the results of the source individual's blood testing provided to the employee?
- Are there procedures that specify what should be done if consent cannot be obtained from the source individual?
- Are baseline blood samples from exposed employees who initially decline HIV testing held for 90 days? Is there a policy that provides for testing these samples upon request of the employee?
- Is the evaluating health care professional provided with
  - a copy of the standard;
  - a description of the exposed employee's duties as they relate to the exposure incident;
  - documentation of the route(s) of exposure and circumstances under which the exposure occurred;
  - results of the source individual's blood testing, if available;
  - all medical records relevant to treatment of the employee including vaccination status?
- Is the employer provided with a copy of the evaluating health care professional's written opinion, which includes information that the employee has been informed about
  - the results of the medical evaluation;
  - any medical conditions that may arise from exposure that may require further treatment?
- Are needlestick injuries and other exposure incidents that result in medical treatment or seroconversion recorded on the OSHA 200 Log and Summary of Occupational Injuries or Illnesses? Is identifying information related to bloodborne pathogens removed prior to granting access to the records?
- Does employee training include information on the actions to be taken following an exposure incident, including the reporting method, and the availability of medical follow-up?

Hazard Communication

- When indicated, is the universal biohazard symbol always used in conjunction with the word "biohazard?"
- Are there written procedures that outline the specific labeling that is required for
  - specimens if universal precautions are not observed for handling all specimens;
  - laundry bags if universal precautions are not observed for handling all laundry;
  - refrigerators and freezers that contain blood or other potentially infectious materials;

- containers used to store, transport, or ship regulated waste, blood, or other potentially infectious materials;
- sharps disposal containers;
- contaminated equipment that is sent for servicing or repair;
- are employees trained to recognize the institution's method for identification of hazards and any alternative labeling or color-coding that is used?

Employee Training

- Is a mechanism in place to provide training
  - to all current employees by June 4, 1992;
  - to new employees at the time of initial employment?

- Is training provided to all employees with occupational exposure as defined in the exposure control plan
  - at no cost to the employee;
  - during working hours;
  - at a reasonable location;
  - by an individual that is knowledgeable in the subject matter?

- Does the training include
  - an accessible copy of the regulatory text of the standard;
  - a general explanation of the epidemiology and symptoms of bloodborne diseases;
  - an explanation of the modes of transmission of bloodborne pathogens;
  - an explanation of the employer's exposure control plan and the means by which the employee can obtain a copy of the written plan;
  - an explanation of the appropriate methods for recognizing tasks and other? activities that may involve exposure to blood and other potentially infectious materials;
  - an explanation of the use and limitations of methods that will prevent or reduce exposure including appropriate engineering controls, work practices, and personal protective equipment;
  - information on the types, proper use, location, removal, handling, decontamination, and disposal of personal protective equipment;
  - an explanation of the basis for selection of personal protective equipment;
  - information on the hepatitis B vaccine, including information on its efficacy, safety, method of administration, the benefits of being vaccinated, and that the vaccine and vaccination will be offered free of charge;
  - information on the appropriate actions to take and persons to contact in an emergency involving blood or other potentially infectious materials;
  - an explanation of the procedure to follow if an exposure incident occurs, including the method of reporting the incident and the medical follow-up that will be made available;
  - information on the postexposure evaluation and follow-up that the employer is required to provide for the employee following an exposure incident;
  - an explanation of the signs and labels and/or color coding used to identify hazards;
  - an opportunity for interactive questions and answers with the person conducting the training?

- Is the training appropriate in content, language, and vocabulary to the educational, literacy, and language background of the employee?
- Are written training records kept for three years that include

- the dates of the training sessions;
- the contents or a summary of the training;
- the names and qualifications of the persons conducting the training sessions;
- the names and job titles of all persons attending the training sessions?

Medical Records

- Has a mechanism been established for creating and maintaining confidential medical records for each employee with occupational exposure that contain
  - an evaluation of the indications and contraindications for hepatitis B vaccination;
  - a medical evaluation of exposure incidents;
  - the results of employee HIV and HBV serologic testing;
  - the counseling information provided;
  - the postexposure prophylaxis provided;
  - an evaluation of any reported illness related to exposure incidents?

- Does the employer's records for each employee with occupational exposure contain
  - the name and social security number of the employee;
  - indications for hepatitis B vaccination and date of vaccination, if received;
  - signed declination statements;
  - routes and circumstances of all exposure incidents;
  - results of sources individual's blood testing, if available;
  - documentation that the employee was informed of the evaluation of the results of postexposure medical evaluation and the need for follow-up?

- Are the employer's records kept separate from the confidential medical record?
- Is there a mechanism to ensure that medical records are kept confidential?
  - Do employees have access to their medical records?

Document 9

OSHA: Bloodborne Facts

(A) Protect Yourself When Handling Sharps

A needlestick or a cut from a contaminated scalpel can lead to infection from hepatitis B virus (HBV) or human immunodeficiency virus (HIV) which causes AIDS. Although few cases of AIDS have been documented from occupational exposure, approximately 8,700 health care workers each year contract hepatitis B. About 200 will die as a result. The new OSHA standard covering bloodborne pathogens specifies measures to reduce these risks of infection.

Prompt Disposal

The best way to prevent cuts and sticks is to minimize contact with sharps. That means disposing of them immediately after use. Puncture-resistant containers must be available nearby to hold contaminated sharps—either for disposal or, for reusable sharps, later decontamination for re-use. When reprocessing contaminated reusable sharps, employees must not reach by hand into the holding container. Contaminated sharps must never be sheared or broken.

Recapping, bending, or removing needles is permissible only if there is no feasible alternative or if required for a specific medical procedure such as blood gas analysis. If recapping, bending, or removal is necessary, workers must use either a mechanical device or a one-handed technique. If recapping is essential—for example, between multiple injections for the same patient—employees must avoid using both hands to recap. Employees might recap with a one-handed "scoop" technique, using the needle itself to pick up the cap, pushing cap and sharp together against a hard surface to ensure a tight fit. Or they might hold the cap with tongs or forceps to place it on the needle.

Sharps Containers

Containers for used sharps must be puncture resistant. The sides and the bottom must be leakproof. They must be labeled or color coded red to ensure that everyone knows the contents are hazardous. Containers for disposable sharps must have a lid, and they must be maintained upright to keep liquids and sharps inside.

Employees must never reach by hand into containers of contaminated sharps. Containers for reusable sharps could be equipped with wire basket liners for easy removal during reprocessing, or employees could use tongs or forceps to withdraw the contents. Reusable sharps disposal containers may not be opened, emptied, or cleaned manually.

Containers need to be located as near to as feasible the area of use. In some cases, they may be placed on carts to prevent access to mentally disturbed or pediatric patients. Containers also should be available wherever sharps may be found, such as in laundries. The containers must be replaced routinely and not be overfilled, which can increase the risk of needlesticks or cuts.

Handling Containers

When employees are ready to discard containers, they should first close the lids. If there is a chance of leakage from the primary container, the employees should use a secondary container that is closable, labeled, or color coded and leak resistant.

Careful handling of sharps can prevent injury and reduce the risk of infection. By following these work practices, employees can decrease their chances of contracting bloodborne illness.

(B) Personal Protective Equipment Cuts Risk

Wearing gloves, gowns, masks, and eye protection can significantly reduce health risks for workers exposed to blood and other potentially infectious materials. The new OSHA standard covering bloodborne disease requires employers to provide appropriate personal protective equipment (PPE) and clothing free of charge to employees.

Workers who have direct exposure to blood and other potentially infectious materials on their jobs run the risk of contracting bloodborne infections from hepatitis B virus (HBV), human immunodeficiency virus (HIV) which causes AIDS, and other pathogens. About 8,700 health care workers each year are infected with HBV, and some 200 die from the infection. Although the risk of contracting AIDS through occupational exposure is much lower, wearing proper personal protective equipment can greatly reduce potential exposure to all bloodborne infections.

Selecting PPE

Personal protective clothing and equipment must be suitable. This means the level of protection must fit the expected exposure. For example, gloves would be sufficient for a laboratory technician who is drawing blood, whereas a pathologist conducting an autopsy would need considerably more protective clothing.

PPE may include gloves, gowns, laboratory coats, face shields or masks, eye protection, pocket masks, and other protective gear. The gear must be readily accessible to employees and available in appropriate sizes.

If an employee is expected to have hand contact with blood or other potentially infectious materials or contaminated surfaces, he or she must wear gloves. Single use gloves cannot be washed or decontaminated for reuse. Utility gloves may be decontaminated if they are not compromised. They should be replaced with they show signs of cracking, peeling, tearing, puncturing, or deteriorating. If employees are allergic to standard gloves, the employer must provide hypoallergenic gloves or similar alternatives.

Routine gloving is not required for phlebotomy in voluntary blood donation centers, though it is necessary for all other phlebotomies. In any case, gloves must be available in voluntary blood donation centers for employees who want to use them. Workers in voluntary blood donation centers must use gloves (1) when they have cuts, scratches or other breaks in their skin; (2) while they are in training; and (3) when they believe contamination might occur.

Employees should wear eye and mouth protection such as goggles and masks, glasses with solid side shields, and masks or chin-length face shields when splashes, sprays, splatters, or droplets of potentially infectious materials pose a hazard through the eyes, nose or mouth. More extensive coverings such as gowns, aprons, surgical caps and hoods, and shoe covers or boots are needed when gross contamination is expected. This often occurs, for example, during orthopedicc surgery or autopsies.

Avoiding Contamination

The key is that blood or other infectious materials must not reach an employee's work clothes, street clothes, undergarments, skin, eyes, mouth, or other mucous membranes under normal conditions for the duration of exposure.

Employers must provide the PPE and ensure that their workers wear it. This means that if a lab coat is considered PPE, it must be supplied by the employer rather than the employee. The employer also must clean or launder clothing and equipment and repair or replace it as necessary.

Additional protective measures such as using PPE in animal rooms and decontaminating PPE before laundering are essential in facilities that conduct research on HIV or HBV.

Exception

There is one exception to the requirement for protective gear. An employee may choose, temporarily and briefly, under rare and extraordinary circumstances, to forego the equipment. It must be the employee's professional judgment that using the protective equipment would prevent the delivery of health care or public safety services or would pose an increased hazard to the safety of the worker or co-worker. When one of these excepted situations occurs, employers are to investigate and document the circumstances to determine if there are ways to avoid it in the future. For example, if a firefighter's resuscitation device is damaged, perhaps another type of device should be used or the device should be carried in a different manner. Exceptions must be limited—this is not a blanket exemption.

Decontaminating and Disposing of PPE

Employees must remove personal protective cothing and equipment before leaving the work area or when the PPE becomes contaminated. If a garment is penetrated, workers must remove it immediately or as soon as feasible. Used protective clothing and equipment must be placed in designated containers for storage, decontamination, or disposal.

Other Protective Practices

If an employee's skin or mucous membranes come into contact with blood, he or she is to wash with soap and water and flush eyes with water as soon as feasible. In addition, workers must wash their hands immediately or as soon as feasible after removing protective equipment. If soap and water are not immediately available, employers may provide other handwashing measures such as moist towelettes. Employees still must wash with soap and water as soon as possible.

Employees must refrain from eating, drinking, smoking, applying cosmetics or lip balm, and handling contact lenses in areas where they may be exposed to blood or other potentially infectious materials.

(C) Holding the line on Contamination

Keeping work areas in a clean and sanitary condition reduces employees' risk of exposure to bloodborne pathogens. Each year about 8,700 health care workers are infected with hepatitis B virus, and 200 die from contracting hepatitis B through their work. The chance of contracting human immunodeficiency virus (HIV), the bloodborne pathogen which causes AIDS, from occupational exposure is small, yet a good housekeeping program can minimize this risk as well.

Decontamination

Every employer whose employees are exposed to blood or other potentially infectious materials must develop a written schedule for cleaning each area where exposures occur. The methods of decontaminating different surfaces must be specified, determined by the type of surface to be cleaned, the soil present and the tasks or procedures that occur in that area.

For example, different cleaning and decontamination measures would be used for a surgical operatory and a patient room. Similarly, hard surfaced flooring and carpeting require separate cleaning methods. More extensive efforts will be necessary for gross contamination than for minor spattering. Likewise, such varied tasks as laboratory analyses and normal patient care would require different techniques for clean-up.

Employees must decontaminate working surfaces and equipment with an appropriate disinfectant after completing procedures involving exposure to blood. Many laboratory procedures are performed on a continual basis throughout a shift. Except as discussed below, it is not necessary to clean and decontaminate between procedures. However, if the employee leaves the area for a period of time, for a break or lunch, then contaminated work surfaces must be cleaned.

Employees also must clean (1) when surfaces become obviously contaminated; (2) after any spill of blood or other potentially infectious materials; and (3) at the end of the work shift if contamination might have occurred. Thus, employees need not decontaminate the work area after each patient care procedure, but only after those that actually result in contamination.

If surfaces or equipment are draped with protective coverings such as plastic wrap or aluminum foil, these coverings should be removed or replaced if they become obviously contaminated. Reusable receptacles such as bins, pails and cans that are likely to become contaminated must be inspected and decontaminated on a regular basis. If contamination is visible, workers must clean and decontaminate the item immediately, or as soon as feasible.

Should glassware that may be potentially contaminated break, workers need to use mechanical means such as a brush and dustpan or tongs or forceps to pick up the broken glass—never by hand, even when wearing gloves.

Before any equipment is serviced or shipped for repairing or cleaning, it must be decontaminated to the extent possible. The equipment must be labeled, indicating which portions are still contaminated. This enables employees and those who service the equipment to take appropriate precautions to prevent exposure.

Regulated Waste

In addition to effective decontamination of work areas, proper handling of regulated waste is essential to prevent unnecessary exposure to blood and other potentially infectious materials. Regulare waste must be handled with great care—i.e., liquid or semi-liquid blood and other potentially infectious materials, items caked with these materials, items that would release blood or other potentially infected materials if compressed, pathological or microbiological wastes containing them and contaminated sharps.

Containers used to store regulated waste must be closable and suitable to contain the contents and prevent leakage of fluids. Containers designed for sharps also must be puncture resistant. They must be labeled or color-coded to ensure that employees are aware of the potential hazards. Such containers must be closed before removal to prevent the contents from spilling. If the outside of a container becomes contaminated, it must be placed within a second suitable container.

Regulated waste must be disposed of in accordance with applicable state and local laws.

Laundry

Laundry workers must wear gloves and handle contaminated laundry as little as possible, with a minimum of agitation. Contaminated laundry should be bagged or placed in containers at the location where it is used, but not sorted or rinsed there.

Laundry must be transported within the establishment or to outside laundries in labeled or red color-coded bags. If the facility uses Universal Precautions for handling all soiled laundry, then alternate labeling or color coding that can be recognized by the employees may be used. If laundry is wet and it might soak through laundry bags, then workers must use bags that prevent leakage to transport it.

Research Facilities

More stringent decontamination requirements apply to research laboratories and production facilities that work with concentrated strains of HIV and HBV.

(D) Reporting Exposure Incidents

OSHA's new bloodborne pathogens standard includes provisions for medical follow-up for workers who have an exposure incident. The most obvious exposure incident is a needlestick. But any specific eye, mouth, other mucous membrane, non-intact skin, or parenteral contact with blood or other potentially infectious materials is considered an exposure incident and should be reported to the employer.

Exposure incidents can lead to infection from hepatitis B virus (HBV) or human immunodeficiency virus (HIV) which causes AIDS. Although few cases of AIDS are directly traceable to workplace exposure, every year about 8,700 health care workers contract hepatitis B from occupational exposures. Approximately 200 will die from this bloodborne infection. Some will become carriers, passing the infection on to others.

Why Report?

Reporting an exposure incident right away permits immediate medical follow-up. Early action is crucial. Immediate intervention can forestall the development of hepatitis B or enable the affected worker to track potential HIV infection. Prompt reporting also can help the worker avoid spreading bloodborne infection to others.

Further, it enables the employer to evaluate the circumstances surrounding the exposure incident to try to find ways to prevent such a situation from occurring again.

Reporting is also important because part of the follow-up includes testing the blood of the source individual to determine HBV and HIV infectivity if this is unknown and if permission for testing can be obtained. The exposed employee must be informed of the results of these tests.

Emloyers must tell the employee what to do if an exposure incident occurs.

Medical Evaluation and Follow-up

Employers must provide free medical evaluation and treatment to employees who experience an exposure incident. They are to refer exposed employees to a licensed health care provider who will counsel the individual about what happened and how to prevent further spread of any potential infection. He or she will prescribe appropriate treatment in line with current U.S. Public Health Service recommendations. The licensed health care provider also will evaluate any reported illness to determine if the symptoms may be related to HIV or HBV development.

The first step is to test the blood of the exposed employee. Any employee who wants to participate in the medical evaluation program must agree to have blood drawn. However, the employee has the option to give the blood sample but refuse permission for HIV testing at that time. The employer must maintain the employee's blood sample for 90 days in case the employee changes his or her mind about testing—should symptoms develop that might relate to HIV or HBV infection.

The health care provider will counsel the employee based on the test results. If the source individual was HBV positive or in a high risk category, the exposed employee may be given hepatitis B immune globulin and vaccination, as necessary. If there is no information on the source individual or the test is negative, and the employee has not been vaccinated or does not have immunity based on his or her test, he or she may receive the vaccine. Further, the health care provider will discuss any other findings from the tests.

The standard requires that the employer make the hepatitis B vaccine available, at no cost to the employee, to all employees who have occupational exposure to blood and other potentially infectious materials. This requirement is in addition to post-exposure testing and treatment responsibilties.

Written Opinion

In addition to counseling the employee, the health care provider will provide a written report to the employer. This report simply identifies whether hepatitis B vaccination was recommended for the exposed employer and whether or not the employee received vaccination. The health care provider also must note that the employee has been informed of the results of the evaluation and told of any medical conditions resulting from exposure to blood which require further evaluation or treatment. Any added findings must be kept confidential.

Confidentiality

Medical records must remain confidential. They are not available to the employer. The employee must give specific written consent for anyone to see the records. Records must be maintained for the duration of employment plus 30 years in accordance with OSHA's standard on access to employee exposure and medical records.

Legal Documents Pertaining to AIDS

Document 1

Americans with Disabilities Act: Title I—Employment

SEC. 101. Definitions.

As used in this title:

(1) COMMISSION.—The term "Commission" means the Equal Employment Opportunity Commission established by section 705 of the Civil Rights Act of 1964 (42 U.S.C. 2000e–4).

(2) COVERED ENTITY.—The term "covered entity" means an employer, employment agency, labor organization, or joint labor-management committee.

(3) DIRECT THREAT.—The term "direct threat" means a significant risk to the health or safety of others that cannot be eliminated by reasonable accommodation.

(4) EMPLOYEE.—The term "employee" means an individual employed by an employer.

(5) EMPLOYER.—

    (A) IN GENERAL.—The term "employer" means a person engaged in an industry affecting commerce who has 15 or more employees for each working day in each of 20 or more calendar weeks in the current or preceding calendar year, and any agent of such person, except that, for two years following the effective date of this title, an employee means a person engaged in an industry affecting commerce who has 25 or more employees for each working day in each of 20 or more calendar weeks in the current or preceding year, and any agent of such person.

    (B) EXCEPTIONS.—The term "employer" does not include—

        (i) the United States, a corporation wholly owned by the government of the United States, or an Indian tribe; or

        (ii) a bona fide private membership club (other than a labor organization) that is excempt from taxation under section 501(c) of the Internal Revenue Code of 1986.

(6) ILLEGAL USE OF DRUGS.—

    (A) IN GENERAL.—The term "illegal use of drugs" means the use of drugs, the possession or distribution of which is unlawful under the Controlled Substances Act (21 U.S.C. 812). Such term does not include the use of a drug taken under supervision by a licensed health care professional, or other uses authorized by the Controlled Substances Act or other provisions of Federal law.

    (B) DRUGS.—The term "drug" means a controlled substance, as defined in schedules I through V of section 202 of the Controlled Substances Act.

(7) PERSON, ETC.—The terms "person", "labor organization", "employment agency", "commerce", and "industry affecting commerce", shall have the same meaning given such terms in section 701 of the Civil Rights Act of 1964 (42 U.S.C. 2000e).

(8) QUALIFIED INDIVIDUAL WITH A DISABILITY.—The term "qualified individual with a disability" means an individual with a disability who, with or without reasonable accommodation, can perform the essential functions of

the employment position that such individual holds or desires. For the purposes of this title, consideration shall be given to the employer's judgment as to what functions of a job are essential, and if an employer has prepared a written description before advertising or interviewing applicants for the job, this description shall be considered evidence of the essential functions of the job.

(9) REASONABLE ACCOMMODATION.—The term "reasonable accommodation" may include—

   (A) making existing facilities used by employees readily accessible to and usable by individuals with disabilities; and

   (B) job restructuring, part-time or modified work schedules, reassignment to a vacant position, acquisition or modification of equipment or devices, appropriate adjustment or modifications of examinations, training materials or policies, the provision of qualified readers or interpreters, and other similar accommodations for individuals with disabilities.

(10) UNDUE HARDSHIP.—

   (A) IN GENERAL.—The term "undue hardship" means an action requiring significant difficulty or expense, when considered in light of the factors set forth in subparagraph (B).

   (B) FACTORS TO BE CONSIDERED.—In determining whether an accommodation would impose an undue hardship on a covered entity, factors to be considered include—

      (i) the nature and cost of the accommodation needed under this Act;

      (ii) the overall financial resources of the facility or facilities involved in the provision of the reasonable accommodation; the number of persons employed at such facility; the effect on expenses and resources, or the impact otherwise of such accommodation upon the operation of the facility;

      (iii) the overall financial resources of the covered entity; the overall size of the business of a covered entity with respect to the number of its employees; the number, type, and location of its facilities; and

      (iv) the type of operation or operations of the covered entity, including the composition, structure, and functions of the workforce of such entity; the geographic separateness, administrative, or fiscal relationship of the facility or facilities in question to the covered entity.

SEC. 102. Discrimination.

(a) GENERAL RULE.—No covered entity shall discriminate against a qualified individual with a disability because of the disability of such individual in regard to job application procedures, the hiring, advancement, or discharge of employees, employee compensation, job training, and other terms, conditions, and privileges of employment.

(b) CONSTRUCTION.—As used in subsection (a), the term "discriminate" includes—

   (1) limiting, segregating, or classifying a job applicant or employee in a way that adversely affects the opportunities or status of such applicant or employee because of the disability of such applicant or employee;

   (2) participating in a contractual or other arrangement or relationship that has the effect of subjecting a covered entity's qualified applicant or employee with a disability to the discrimination prohibited by this title (such relationship includes a relationship with an employment or referral

agency, labor union, an organization providing fringe benefits to an employee of the covered entity, or an organization providing training and apprenticeship programs);

(3) utilizing standards, criteria, or methods of administration—

    (A) that have the effect of discrimination on the basis of disability; or

    (B) that perpetuate the discrimination of others who are subject to common administrative control;

(4) excluding or otherwise denying equal jobs or benefits to a qualified individual because of the known disability of an individual with whom the qualified individual is known to have a relationship or association;

(5) (A) not making reasonable accommodations to the known physical or mental limitations of an otherwise qualified individual with a disability who is an applicant or employee, unless such covered entity can demonstrate that the accommodation would impose an undue hardship on the operation of the business of such covered entity; or

    (B) denying employment opportunities to a job applicant or employee who is an otherwise qualified individual with a disability, if such denial is based on the need of such covered entity to make reasonable accommodation to the physical or mental impairments of the employee or applicant;

(6) using qualification standards, employment tests or other selection criteria that screen out or tend to screen out an individual with a disability or a class of individuals with disabilities unless the standard, test or other selection criteria, as used by the coverd entity, is shown to be job-related for the position in question and is consistent with business necessity; and

(7) failing to select and administer tests concerning employment in the most effective manner to ensure that, when such test is administered to a job applicant or employee who has a disability that impairs sensory, manual, or speaking skills, such test results accurately reflect the skills, aptitude, or whatever other factor of such applicant or employee that such test purports to measure, rather than reflecting the impaired sensory, manual, or speaking skills of such employee or applicant (except where such skills are the factors that the test purports to measure).

(c) MEDICAL EXAMINATIONS AND INQUIRIES.—

    (1) IN GENERAL.—The prohibition against discrimination as referred to in subsection (a) shall include medical examinations and inquiries.

    (2) PREEMPLOYMENT.—

        (A) PROHIBITED EXAMINATION OR INQUIRY.—Except as provided in paragraph (3), a covered entity shall not conduct a medical examination or make inquiries of a job applicant as to whether such applicant is an individual with a disability or as to the nature or severity of such disability.

        (B) ACCEPTABLE INQUIRY.—A covered entity may make preemployment inquiries into the ability of an applicant to perform job-related functions.

    (3) EMPLOYMENT ENTRANCE EXAMINATION.—A covered entity may require a medical examination after an offer of employment has been made to a job applicant and prior to the commencement of the employment duties of such applicant, and may condition an offer of employment on the results of such examination, if—

        (A) all entering employees are subjected to such an examination regardless of disability;

(B) information obtained regarding the medical condition or history of the applicant is collected and maintained on separate forms and in separate medical files and is treated as a confidential medical record, except that—

   (i) supervisors and managers may be informed regarding necessary restrictions on the work or duties of the employee and necessary accommodations;

   (ii) first aid and safety personnel may be informed, when appropriate, if the disability might require emergency treatment; and

   (iii) government officials investigating compliance with this Act shall be provided relevant information on request; and

(C) the results of such examination are used only in accordance with this title.

  (4) EXAMINATION AND INQUIRY.—

   (A) PROHIBITED EXAMINATIONS AND INQUIRIES.—A covered entity shall not require a medical examination and shall not make inquiries of an employee as to whether such employee is an individual with a disabilty or as to the nature or severity of the disability, unless such examination or inquiry is shown to be job-related and consistent with business necessity.

   (B) ACCEPTABLE EXAMINATIONS AND INQUIRIES.—A covered entity may conduct voluntary medical examinations, including voluntary medical histories, which are part of an employee health program available to employees at that work site. A covered entity may make inquiries into the ability of an employee to perform job-related functions.

   (C) REQUIREMENT.—Information obtained under subparagraph (B) regarding the medical condition or history of any employee are subject to the requirements of subparagraphs (B) and (C) of paragraph (3).

SEC. 103. Defenses.

(a) IN GENERAL.—It may be a defense to a charge of discrimination under this Act that an alleged application of qualification standards, tests, or selection criteria that screen out or tend to screen out or otherwise deny a job or benefit to an individual with a disability has been shown to be job-related and consistent with business necessity, and such performance cannot be accomplished by reasonable accommodation, as required under this title.

(b) QUALIFICATION STANDARDS.—The term "qualification standards" may include a requirement that an individual shall not pose a direct threat to the health or safety of other individuals in the workplace.

(c) RELIGIOUS ENTITIES.—

  (1) IN GENERAL.—This title shall not prohibit a religious corporation, association, educational institution, or society from giving preference in employment to individuals of a particular religion to perform work connected with the carrying on by such corporation, association, educational institution, or society of its activities.

  (2) RELIGIOUS TENETS REQUIREMENT.—Under this title, a religious organization may require that all applicants and employees conform to the religious tenets of such organization.

(d) LIST OF INFECTIOUS AND COMMUNICABLE DISEASES.—

  (1) IN GENERAL.—The Secretary of Health and Human Services, not later than 6 months after the date of enactment of this Act, shall—

(A) review all infectious and communicable diseases which may be transmitted through handling the food supply;
(B) publish a list of infectious and communicable diseases which are
transmitted through handling the food supply;
(C) publish the methods by which such diseases are transmitted; and
(D) widely disseminate such information regarding the list of diseases and
their modes of transmissability to the general public.

Such list shall be updated annually.

(2) APPLICATIONS.—In any case in which an individual has an infectious or
communicable disease that is transmitted to others through the handling
of food, that is included on the list developed by the Secretary of Health
and Human Services under paragraph (1), and which cannot be eliminated
by reasonable accommodation, a covered entity may refuse to assign or
continue to assign such individual to a job involving food handling.

(3) CONSTRUCTION.—Nothing in this Act shall be construed to preempt,
modify, or amend any State, county, or local law, ordinance, or regulation
applicable to food handling which is designed to protect the public health
from individuals who pose a significant risk to the health or safety of
others, which cannot be eliminated by reasonable accommodation, pursuant to the list of infectious or communicable diseases and the modes
of transmissability published by the Secretary of Health and Human
Services.

SEC. 104. Illegal Use of Drugs and Alcohol.

(a) QUALIFIED INDIVIDUAL WITH A DISABILITY.—For purposes of this title, the
term "qualified individual with a disability" shall not include any employee
or applicant who is currently engaging in the illegal use of drugs, when the
covered entity acts on the basis of such use.

(b) RULES OF CONSTRUCTION.—Nothing in subsection (a) shall be construed
to exclude as a qualified individual with a disability an individual who—
(1) has successfully completed a supervised drug rehabilitation program and
is no longer engaging in the illegal use of drugs, or has otherwise been
rehabilitated successfully and is no longer engaging in such use;
(2) is participating in a supervised rehabilitation program and is no longer
engaging in such use; or
(3) is erroneously regarded as engaging in such use, but is not engaging in
such use;

except that it shall not be a violation of this Act for a covered entity to adopt
or administer reasonable policies or procedures, including but not limited to
drug testing, designed to ensure that an individual described in paragraph (1)
or (2) is no longer engaged in the illegal use of drugs.

(c) AUTHORITY OF COVERED ENTITY.—A covered entity—
(1) may prohibit the illegal use of drugs and the use of alcohol at the workplace by all employees;
(2) may require that employes shall not be under the influence of alcohol or
be engaging in the illegal use of drugs at the workplace;
(3) may require that employees behave in conformance with the requirements
established under the Drug-Free Workplace Act of 1988 (41 U.S.C. 701
et seq.);
(4) may hold an employee who engages in the illegal use of drugs or who is
an alcoholic to the same qualification standards for employment or job

286 · Appendix B

performance and behavior that such entity holds other employees, even if any unsatisfactory performance or behavior is related to the drug use or alcoholism of such employee; and

(5) may, with respect to Federal regulations regarding alcohol and the illegal use of drugs, require that—

(A) employees comply with the standards established in such regulations of the Department of Defense, if the employees of the covered entity are employed in an industry subject to such regulations, including complying with regulations (if any) that apply to employment in sensitive positions in such an industry, in the case of employees of the covered entity who are employed in such positions (as defined in the regulations of the Department of Defense);

(B) employees comply with the standards established in such regulations of the Nuclear Regulatory Commission, if the employees of the covered entity are employed in an industry subject to such regulations, including complying with regulations (if any) that apply to employment in sensitive positions in such an industry, in the case of employees of the covered entity who are employed in such positions (as defined in the regulations of the Nuclear Regulatory Commission); and

(C) employees comply with the standards established in such regulations of the Department of Transportation, if the employees of the covered entity are employed in a transportation industry subject to such regulations, including complying with such regulations (if any) that apply to employment in sensitive positions in such an industry, in the case of employees of the covered entity who are employed in such positions (as defined in the regulations of the Department of Transportation).

(d) DRUG TESTING.—

(1) IN GENERAL.—For purposes of this title, a test to determine the illegal use of drugs shall not be considered a medical examination.

(2) CONSTRUCTION.—Nothing in this title shall be construed to encourage, prohibit, or authorize the conducting of drug testing for the illegal use of drugs by job applicants or employees or making employment decisions based on such test results.

(e) TRANSPORTATION EMPLOYEES.—Nothing in this title shall be construed to encourage, prohibit, restrict, or authorize the otherwise lawful exercise by entities subject to the jurisdiction of the Department of Transportation of authority to—

(1) test employees of such entities in, and applicants for, positions involving safety-sensitive duties for the illegal use of drugs and for on-duty impairment by alcohol; and

(2) remove such persons who test positive for illegal use of drugs and on-duty impairment by alcohol pursuant to paragraph (1) from safety-sensitive duties in implementing subsection (c).

SEC. 105. Posting Notices.

Every employer, employment agency, labor organization, or joint labor-management committee covered under this title shall post notices in an accessible format to applicants, employees, and members describing the applicable provisions of this Act, in the manner prescribed by section 711 of the Civil Rights Act of 1964 (42 U.S.C. 2000e–10).

SEC. 106. Regulations.

Not later than 1 year after the date of enactment of this Act, the Commission shall issue regulations in an accessible format to carry out this title in accordance with subchapter II of chapter 5 of title 5, United States Code.

SEC. 107. Enforcement.

(a) POWERS, REMEDIES, AND PROCEDURES.—The powers, remedies, and procedures set forth in sections 705, 706, 707, 709, and 710 of the Civil Rights Act of 1964 (42 U.S.C. 2000e–4, 2000e–5, 2000e–6, 2000e–8, and 2000e–9) shall be the powers, remedies, and procedures this title provides to the Commission, to the Attorney General, or to any person alleging discrimination on the basis of disability in violation of any provision of this Act, or regulations promulgated under section 106, concerning employment.

(b) COORDINATION.—The agencies with enforcement authority for actions which allege employment discrimination under this title and under the Rehabilitation Act of 1973 shall develop procedures to ensure that administrative complaints filed under this title and under the Rehabilitation Act of 1973 are dealt with in a manner that avoids duplication of effort and prevents imposition of inconsistent or conflicting standards for the same requirements under this title and the Rehabilitation Act of 1973. The Commission, the Attorney General, and the Office of Federal Contract Compliance Programs shall establish such coordinating mechanisms (similar to provisions contained in the joint regulations promulgated by the Commission and the Attorney General at part 42 of title 28 and part 1691 of title 29, Code of Federal Regulations, and the Memorandum of Understanding between the Commission and the Office of Federal Contract Compliance Programs dated January 16, 1981 (46 Fed. Reg. 7435, January 23, 1981-) in regulations implementing this title and Rehabilitation Act of 1973 not later than 18 months after the date of enactment of this Act.

SEC. 108. Effective Date.

This title shall become effective 24 months after the date of enactment.

Document 2

Equal Opportunity Employment Commission: Regulations to Implement the Equal Employment Provisions of the Americans with Disabilities Act

1630.1 Purpose, applicability, and construction.

(a) *Purpose.* The purpose of this part is to implement title I of the Americans with Disabilities Act (ADA), requiring equal employment opportunities for qualified individuals with disabilities, and sections 3(2), 3(3), 501, 503, 508, 510, and 511 of the ADA as those sections pertain to the employment of qualified individuals with disabilities.

(b) *Applicability.* This part applies to "covered entities" as defined at § 1630.2(b).

(c) *Construction.*—(1) *In general.* Except as otherwise provided in this part, this part does not apply a lesser standard than the standards applied under title V of the Rehabilitation Act of 1973 (29 U.S.C. 780–794a), or the regulations issued by Federal agencies pursuant to that title.

(2) *Relationship to other laws.* This part does not invalidate or limit the remedies, rights, and procedures of any Federal law or law of any State or political subdivision of any State or jurisdiction that provides greater or equal protection for the rights of individuals with disabilities than are afforded by this part.

1630.2 Definitions.

(a) *Commission* means the Equal Employment Opportunity Commission established by section 705 of the Civil Rights Act of 1964 (42 U.S.C. 2000e–4).

(b) *Covered Entity* means an employer, employment agency, labor organization, or joint labor management committee.

(c) *Person, labor organization, employment agency, commerce and industry affecting commerce* shall have the same meaning given those terms in section 701 of the Civil Rights Act of 1964 (42 U.S.C. 2000e).

(d) *State* means each of the several States, the District of Columbia, the Commonwealth of Puerto Rico, Guam, American Samoa, the Virgin Islands, the Trust Territory of the Pacific Islands and the Commonwealth of the Northern Mariana Islands.

(e) *Employer.*—(1) *In general.* The term "employer" means a person engaged in an industry affecting commerce who has 15 or more employees for each working day in each of 20 or more calendar weeks in the current or preceding calendar year, and any agent of such person, except that, from July 26, 1992 through July 25, 1994, an employer means a person engaged in an industry affecting commerce who has 25 or more employees for each working day in each of 20 or more calendar weeks in the current or preceding year and any agent of such person.

(2) *Exceptions.* The term employer does not include—

(i) The United States, a corporation wholly owned by the government of the United States, or an Indian tribe; or

(ii) A bona fide private membership club (other than a labor organization) that is exempt from taxation under section 501(c) of the Internal Revenue Code of 1986.

(f) *Employee* means an individual employed by an employer.

(g) *Disability* means, with respect to an individual—

(1) A physical or mental impairment that substantially limits one or more of the major life activities of such individual;

(2) A record of such an impairment; or

(3) Being regarded as having such an impairment.

(See § 1630.3 for exceptions to this definition.)

(h) *Physical or mental impairment* means:

(1) Any physiological disorder, or condition, cosmetic disfigurement, or anatomical loss affecting one or more of the following body systems: neurological, musculoskeletal, special sense organs, respiratory (including speech organs), cardiovascular, reproductive, digestive, genitourinary, hemic and lymphatic, skin, and endocrine; or

(2) Any mental or psychological disorder, such as mental retardation, organic brain syndrome, emotional or mental illness, and specific learning disabilities.

(i) *Major Life Activities* means functions such as caring for oneself, performing manual tasks, walking, seeing, hearing, speaking, breathing, learning, and working.

(j) *Substantially limits.*—(1) The term "substantially limits" means:

(i) Unable to perform a major life activity that the average person in the general population can perform; or

(ii) Significantly restricted as to the condition, manner or duration under which an individual can perform a particular major life activity as compared to the condition, manner, or duration under which the average person in the general population can perform that same major life activity.

(2) The following factors should be considered in determining whether an individual is substantially limited in a major life activity:

(i) The nature and severity of the impairment;

(ii) The duration or expected duration of the impairment; and

(iii) The permanent or long term impact, or the expected permanent or long term impact of or resulting from the impairment.

(3) With respect to the major life activity of "working"—

(i) The term "substantially limits" means significantly restricted in the ability to perform either a class of jobs or a broad range of jobs in various classes as compared to the average person having comparable training, skills and abilities. The inability to perform a single, particular job does not constitute a substantial limitation in the major life activity of working.

(ii) In addition to the factors listed in paragraph (j)(2) of this section, the following factors should be considered in determining whether an individual is substantially limited in the major life activity of "working":

(A) The geographical area to which the individual has reasonable access;

(B) The job from which the individual has been disqualified because of an impairment, and the number and types of jobs utilizing similar training, knowledge, skills or abilities, within that geographical area, from which the individual is also disqualified because of the impairment (class of jobs); and/or

(C) The job from which the individual has been disqualified because of an impairment, and the number and types of other jobs not utilizing similar training, knowledge, skills or abilities, within that geographical area, from which the individual is also disqualified because of the impairment (broad range of jobs in various classes).

(k) *Has a record of such impairment* means has a history of, or has been misclassified as having, a mental or physical impairment that substantially limits one or more major life activities.

(l) *Is regarded as having such an impairment* means:

(1) Has a physical or mental impairment that does not substantially limit major life activities but is treated by a covered entity as constituting such limitation;

(2) Has a physical or mental impairment that substantially limits major life activities only as a result of the attitudes of others toward such impairment; or

(3) Has none of the impairments defined in paragraphs (h)(1) or (2) of this section but is treated by a covered entity as having such an impairment.

(m) *Qualified individual with a disabilty* means an individual with a disability who satisfies the requisite skill, experience and education requirements of the employment position such individual holds or desires, and who, with or without reasonable accommodation, can perform the essential functions of such position. (See § 1630.3 for exceptions to this definition).

(n) *Essential functions.*—(1) *In general.* The term "essential functions" means primary job duties that are intrinsic to the employment position the individual holds or desires. The term "essential functions" does not include the marginal or peripheral functions of the position that are incidental to the performance of primary job functions.

(2) A job function may be considered essential for any of several reasons, including but not limited to the following:

(i) The function may be essential because the reason the position exists is to perform that function;

(ii) The function may be essential because of the limited number of employees available among whom the performance of that job function can be distributed; and/or

(iii) The function may be highly specialized so that the incumbent in the position is hired for his or her expertise or ability to perform the particular function.

(3) Evidence that may be considered in determining whether a particular function is essential includes but is not limited to:

(i) The employer's judgment as to which functions are essential;

(ii) Written job descriptions prepared before advertising or interviewing applicants for the job;

(iii) The amount of time spent on the job performing the function;

(iv) The consequences of not requiring the incumbent to perform the function;

(v) The work experience of past incumbents in the job; and/or

(vi) The current work experience of incumbents in similar jobs.

(o) *Reasonable accommodation.*—(1) The term *reasonable accommodation* means:

(i) Any modification or adjustment to a job application process that enables a qualified individual with a disability to be considered for the position such qualified individual desires, and which will not impose an undue hardship on the covered entity's business; or

(ii) Any modification or adjustment to the work environment, or to the manner or circumstances under which the position held or desired is customarily performed, that enables a qualified individual with a disability to perform the essential functions of that position, and which will impose an undue hardship on the operation of the covered entity's business; or

(iii) Any modification or adjustment that enables a covered entity's employee with a disability to enjoy the same benefits and privileges of employment as are enjoyed by its other similarly situated employees without disabilities, and which will not impose an undue hardship on the operation of the covered entity's business.

(2) *Reasonable accommodation* may include but is not limited to:

(i) Making existing facilities used by employees readily accessible to and usable by individuals with disabilities; and

(ii) Job restructuring; part-time or modified work schedules; reassignment to a vacant position; acquisition or modifications of equipment or devices; appropriate adjustment or modifications of examinations, training materials, or policies; the provision of qualified readers or interpreters; and other similar accommodations for individuals with disabilities.

(3) To determine the appropriate reasonable accommodation it may be necesssary for the covered entity to initiate an informal, interactive process with the qualified individual with a disability in need of the accommodation. This process should identify the precise limitations resulting from the disability and potential reasonable accommodations that could overcome those limitations.

(p) *Undue hardship.*—(1) *In general. Undue hardship* means, with respect to the provision of an accommodation, significant difficulty or expense incurred by a covered entity, when considered in light of the factors set forth in paragraph (p)(2) of this section.

(2) *Factors to be considered.* In determining whether an accommodation would impose an undue hardship on a covered entity, factors to be considered include:

(i) The nature and cost of the accommodation needed under this part;

(ii) The overall financial resources of the site or sites involved in the provision of the reasonable accommodation, the number of persons employed at such site, and the effect on expenses and resources;

(iii) The overall financial resources of the covered entity, the overall size of the business of the covered entity with respect to the number of its employees, and the number, type and location of its facilities;

(iv) The type of operation or operations of the covered entity, including the composition, structure and functions of the workforce of such entity, and the geographic separateness and administrative or fiscal relationship of the site or sites in question to the covered entity; and

(v) The impact of the accommodation upon the operation of the site, including the impact on the ability of other employees to perform their duties and the impact on the site's ability to conduct business.

(3) *Site* means a geographically separate subpart of a covered entity.

(q) *Qualification standards* means the personal and professional attributes including the skill, experience, education, physical, medical, safety and other requirements established by a covered entity as requirements which an individual must meet in order to be eligible for the position held or desired. Qualification standards may include a requirement that an individual not pose a direct threat to the health or safety of the individual or others. (See §1630.10 Qualification standards, tests and other selection critera).

(r) *Direct Threat* means a significant risk of substantial harm to the health or safety of the individual or others that cannot be eliminated by reasonable accommodation. The determination that an individual with a disability poses a "direct threat" should be based on a reasonable medical judgment that relies on the most current medical knowledge and/or on the best available objective evidence. In determining whether an individual would pose a direct threat, the factors to be considered include:

(1) The duration of the risk;

(2) The nature and severity of the potential harm; and

(3) The likelihood that the potential harm will occur.

1630.3 Exceptions to the definitions of "Disability" and "Qualified Individual with a Disability."

(a) The terms *disability* and *qualified individual with a disability* do not include individuals currently engaging in the illegal use of drugs, when the covered entity acts on the basis of such use.

(1) *Drug* means a controlled substance, as defined in schedules I through V of section 202 of the Controlled Substances Act (21 U.S.C. 812).

(2) *Illegal use of drugs* means the use of drugs the possession or distribution of which is unlawful under the Controlled Substances Act, as periodically updated by the Food and Drug Administration. This term does not include the use of a drug taken under the supervision of a licensed health care professional, or other uses authorized by the Controlled Substances Act or other provisions of Federal law.

(b) However, the terms *disability* and *qualified individual with a disability* may not exclude an individual who:

(1) Has successfully completed a supervised drug rehabilitation program and is no longer engaging in the illegal use of drugs, or has otherwise been rehabilitated successfully and is no longer engaging in the illegal use of drugs; or

(2) Is participating in a supervised rehabilitation program and is no longer engaging in such use; or

(3) Is erroneously regarded as engaging in such use, but is not engaging in such use.

(c) It shall not be a violation of this part for a covered entity to adopt or administer reasonable policies or procedures, including but not limited to drug testing, designed to ensure that an individual described in paragraph (b) (1) or (2) of this section is no longer engaging in the illegal use of drugs. (See § 1630.16(c) Drug testing).

(d) *Disability* does not include:

(1) Transvestism, transsexualism, pedophilia, exhibitionism, voyeurism, gender identity disorders not resulting from physical impairments, or other sexual behavior disorders;

(2) Compulsive gambling, kleptomania, or pyromania; or

(3) Psychoactive substance use disorders resulting from current illegal use of drugs.

(e) *Homosexuality and bisexuality* are not impairments and so are not disabilities as defined in this part.

1630.4 Discrimination prohibited.

It is unlawful for a covered entity to discriminate on the basis of disability against a qualified individual with a disability in regard to:

(a) Recruitment, advertising, and job application procedures;

(b) Hiring, upgrading, promotion, award of tenure, demotion, transfer, layoff, termination, right of return from layoff, and rehiring;

(c) Rates of pay or any other form of compensation and changes in compensation;

(d) Job assignments, job classifications, organizational structures, position descriptions, lines of progression, and seniority lists;

(e) Leaves of absence, sick leave, or any other leave;

(f) Fringe benefits available by virtue of employment, whether or not administered by the covered entity;

(g) Selection and financial support for training, including, apprenticeships, professional meetings, conferences and other related activities, and selection for leaves of absence to pursue training;

(h) Activities sponsored by a covered entity including social and recreational programs; and

(i) Any other term, condition, or privilege of employment.

The term *discrimination* includes but is not limited to the acts in §§ 1630.5 through 1630.13 of this part.

1630.5 Limiting, segregating, and classifying.

It is unlawful for a covered entity to limit, segregate, or classify a job applicant or employee in a way that adversely affects his or her employment opportunities or status on the basis of disability.

1630.6 Contractual or other arrangements.

(a) *In general.* It is unlawful for a covered entity to participate in a contractual or other arrangement or relationship that has the effect of subjecting the covered entity's own qualified applicant or employee with a disability to the discrimination prohibited by this part.

(b) *Contractual or other arrangement defined.* The phrase "contractual or other arrangement or relationship" includes, but is not limited to, a relationship with an employment or referral agency; labor union, including collective bargaining agreements; an organization providing fringe benefits to an employee of the covered entity; or an organization providing training and apprenticeship programs.

(c) *Application.* This section applies to a covered entity, with respect to its own applicants or employees, whether the entity offered the contract or initiated the relationship, or whether the entity accepted the contract or acceded to the relationship. A covered entity is not liable for the actions of the other party or parties to the contract which only affect that other party's employees or applicants.

1630.7 Standards, criteria, or methods of administration.

It is unlawful for a covered entity to use standards, criteria, or methods of administration, which are not job-related and consistent with business necessity, and:

(a) That have the effect of discriminating on the basis of disability; or

(b) That perpetuate the discrimination of others who are subject to common administrative control.

1630.8 Relationship or association with an individual with a disability.

It is unlawful for a covered entity to exclude or otherwise deny equal jobs or benefits to a qualified individual because of the known disability of an individual with whom the qualified individual is known to have a family, business, social or other relationship or association.

1630.9 Not making reasonable accommodation.

(a) It is unlawful for a covered entity not to make reasonable accommodation to the known physical or mental limitations of an otherwise qualified applicant or employee with a disability, unless such covered entity can demonstrate that the accommodation would impose an undue hardship on the operation of its business.

(b) It is unlawful for a covered entity to deny employment opportunities to an otherwise qualified job applicant or employee with a disability based on the need of such covered entity to make reasonable accommodation to such individual's physical or mental impairments.

(c) A covered entity shall not be excused from the requirements of this part because of any failure to receive technical assistance, including any failiure in the development or dissemination of any technical assistance manual authorized by the ADA.

(d) A qualified individual with a disability is not required to accept an accommodation, aid, service, opportunity or benefit which such qualified individual chooses not to accept. However, if such individual rejects a reasonable accommodation, aid, service, opportunity or benefit that is necessary to enable the individual to perform the essential functions of the position held or desired, and cannot, as a result of that rejection, perform the essential functions of the position, the individual will not be considered a qualified individual with a disability.

1630.10 Qualification standards, tests, and other selection criteria.

(a) *In general.* It is unlawful for a covered entity to use qualification standards, employment tests or other selection criteria that screen out or tend to screen out an individual with a disability or a class of individuals with disabilities unless the standard, test or other selection criteria, as used by the covered entity, is shown to be job-related for the position in question and is consistent with business necessity.

(b) *Direct threat as a qualification standard.* Notwithstanding paragraph (a) of this section, a covered entity may use as a qualification standard the requirement that an individual be able to perform the essential functions of the position held or desired without posing a direct threat to the health or safety of the individual or others. (See § 1630.2(r) defining "direct threat").

1630.11 Administration of tests.

It is unlawful for a covered entity to fail to select and administer tests concerning employment in the most effective maner to ensure that, when a test is administered to a job applicant or employee who has a disability that impairs sensory, manual or speaking skills, the test results accurately reflect the skills, aptitude, or whatever other factor of the applicant or employee that the test purports to measure, rather than reflecting the impaired sensory, manual, or speaking skills of such employee or applicant (except where such skills are the factors that the test purports to measure).

1620.12 Retaliation and coercion.

(a) *Retaliation.* It is unlawful to discriminate against any individual because that individual has opposed any act or practice made unlawful by this part or because that individual made a charge, testified, assisted, or participated in any manner in an investigation, proceeding, or hearing to enforce any provision contained in this part.

(b) *Coercion, interference or intimidation.* It is unlawful to coerce, intimidate, threaten, or interfere with any individual in the exercise or enjoyment of, or because that individual aided or encouraged any other individual in the exercise of, any right granted or protected by this part.

1630.13 Prohibited medical examinations and injuries.

(a) *Pre-employment examination or inquiry.* Except as permitted by § 1630.14, it is unlawful for a covered entity to conduct a medical examination of an applicant or to make inquiries as to whether an applicant is an individual with a disability or as to the nature or severity of such disability.

(b) *Examination or inquiry of employees.* Except as permitted by § 1630.14, it is unlawful for a covered entity to require a medical examination of an employee or to make inquiries as to whether an employee is an individual with a disability or as to the nature or severity of such disability, unless the examination or inquiry is shown to be job-related and consistent with business necessity.

1630.14 Medical examinations and inquiries specifically permitted.

(a) *Acceptable pre-employment inquiry.* A covered entity may make pre-employment inquiries into the abilty of an applicant to perform job-related functions.

(b) *Employment entrance examination.* A covered entity may require a medical examination after making an offer of employment to a job applicant and before the applicant begins his or her employment duties, and may condition an offer of employment on the results of such examination, if all entering employees in the same job category are subjected to such an examination regardless of disability.

(1) Information obtained regarding the medical condition or history of the applicant shall be collected and maintained on separate forms and in separate medical files and be treated as a confidential medical record, except that:

(i) Supervisors and managers may be informed regarding necessary restrictions on the work or duties of the employee and necessary accommodations;

(ii) First aid and safety personnel may be informed, when appropriate, if the disability might require emergency treatment; and

(iii) Government officials investigating compliance with this part shall be provided relevant information on request.

(2) The results of such examination may be used only in accordance with this part.

(3) Medical examinations conducted in accordance with this Section do not have to be job-related and consistent with business necessity. However, if certain criteria are used to screen out an employee or employees with disabilities as a result of such an examination or inquiry, the exclusionary criteria must be job-related and consistent with business necessity, and performance of the essential job functions cannot be accomplished with reasonable accommodation as required in this part. (See § 1630.15(b) Defenses to charges of discriminatory application of selection criteria).

(c) *Other acceptable examinations and inquiries.* A covered entity may conduct voluntary medical examinations and activities, including voluntary medical histories, which are part of an employee health program available to employees at the work site. A covered entity may make inquiries into the ability of an employee to perform job-related functions.

(1) Information obtained under paragraph (c) of this section regarding the medical condition or history of any employee shall be collected and maintained on separate forms and in separate medical files and be treated as a confidential medical record, except that:

(i) Supervisors and managers may be informed regarding necessary restrictions on the work or duties of the employee and necessary accommodations;

(ii) First aid and safety personnel may be informed, when appropriate, if the disability might require emergency treatment; and

(iii) Government officials investigating compliance with this Part shall be provided relevant information on request.

(2) Information obtained under paragraph (c) of this section regarding the medical condition or history of any employee shall not be used for any purpose inconsistent with this part.

1630.15 Defenses.

Defenses to an allegation of discrimination under this part may include, but are not limited to, the following:

(a) *Disparate treatment charges.* It may be a defense to a charge of disparate treatment brought under §§ 1630.4–1630.8 and 1630.11–1630.12 that the challenged action is justified by a legitimate, nondiscriminatory reason.

(b) *Charges of discriminatory application of selection criteria.* It may be a defense to a charge of discrimination, as described in § 1630.10, that an alleged application of qualification standards, tests, or selection criteria that screens out or tends to screen out or otherwise denies a job or benefit to an individual with a disability has been shown to be job-related and consistent with business necessity, and such performance cannot be accomplished with reasonable accommodation, as required in this part.

(c) *Other disparate impact charges.* It may be a defense to a charge of discrimination brought under this part that a uniformly applied standard, criteria, or policy has a disparate impact on an individual or class of individuals with disabilities that the challenged standard, criteria or policy has been shown to be job-related and consistent with business necessity and such performance cannot be accomplished with reasonable accommodation, as required in this part.

(d) *Charges of not making reasonable accommodation.* It may be a defense to a charge of discrimination, as described in § 1630.9, that a requested or necessary accommodation would impose an undue hardship on the operation of the covered entity's business.

(e) *Conflict with other Federal laws.* It may be a defense to a charge of discrimination under this part that a challenged action is required or necessitated by another Federal law or regulation, or that another Federal law or regulation prohibits an action (including the provision of a particular reasonable accommodation) that would otherwise be required by this part.

(f) *Additional defenses.* It may be a defense to a charge of discrimination under this part that the alleged discriminatory action is specifically permitted by §§ 1630.14 or 1630.16.

1630.16 Specific activities permitted.

(a) *Religious entities.* A religious corporation, association, educational institution, or society is permitted to give preference in employment to individuals of a partiuclar religion to perform work connected with the carrying on by that corporation, association, educational institution, or society of its activities. A religious entity may require that all applicants and employees conform to the religious tenets of such organization. However, a religious entity may not discriminate against a qualified individual, who satisfies the permitted religious criteria, because of his or her disability.

(b) *Regulation of alcohol and drugs.* A covered entity:

(1) May prohibit the illegal use of drugs and the use of alcohol at the workplace by all employees;

(2) May require that employees not be under the influence of alcohol or be engaging in the illegal use of drugs at the workplace;

(3) May require that all employees behave in conformance with the requirements established under the Drug-Free Workplace Act of 1988 (41 U.S.C. 701 et. seq.);

(4) May hold an employee who engages in the illegal use of drugs or who is an alcoholic to the same qualification standards for employment or job performance and behavior to which the entity holds its other employees, even if any unsatisfactory performance or behavior is related to the employee's drug use or alcoholism;

(5) May require that its employees employed in an industry subject to such regulations comply with the standards established in the regulations of the Departments of Defense and Transportation, and of the Nuclear Regulatory Commission, regarding alcohol and the illegal use of drugs; and

(6) May require that employees employed in sensitive positions comply with the regulations (if any) of the Departments of Defense and Transportation and of the Nuclear Regulatory Commission that apply to employment in sensitive positions subject to such regulations.

(c) *Drug testing.*—(1) *General policy.* For purposes of this part, a test to determine the illegal use of drugs is not considered a medical examination. Thus, the administration of drug tests by a covered entity to its job applicants or employees is not a violation of § 1630.13 of this part. However, this part does not encourage, prohibit, or authorize a covered entity from conducting drug testing of job applicants or employees for the illegal use of drugs or from making employment decisions based on such test results.

(2) *Transporation Employees.* This part does not encourage, prohibit, or authorize the otherwise lawful exercise by entities subject to the jurisdiction of the Department of Transportation of authority to:

(i) Test employees of entities in, and applicants for positions involving safety, sensitive duties for the illegal use of drugs or for on-duty impairment by alcohol; and

(ii) Remove from safety-sensitive positions persons who test positive for illegal use of drugs or on-duty impairment by alcohol pursuant to paragraph (c)(2)(i) of this section.

(3) Any information regarding the medical condition or history of any employee or applicant obtained from a drug test, except information regarding the illegal use of drugs, is subject to the requirements of § 1630.14(b)(2) and (3) of this part.

(d) *Regulation of smoking.* A covered entity may prohibit or impose restrictions on smoking in places of employment. Such restrictions do not violate any provision of this part.

(e) *Infectious and communicable diseases; food handling jobs.*—(1) *In general.* Under title I of the ADA, section 103(d)(1), the Secretary of Health and Human Services is to prepare a list, to be updated annually, of infectious and communicable diseases which can be transmitted through the handling of food. If an individual with a disability is disabled by one of the infectious or communicable diseases included on this list, and if the risk of transmitting the disease associated with the handling of food cannot be eliminated by reasonable accommodation, a covered entity may refuse to assign or continue to assign such individual to a job involving food handling. However, if the individual with a disability is a current employee, the employer must consider whether he or she can be accommodated by reassignment to a vacant position not involving food handling.

(2) *Effect on State or other laws.* This part does not preempt, modify, or amend

any State, county, or local law, ordinance or regulation applicable to food handling which:

(i) Is in accordance with the list, referred to in paragraph (e)(1) of this section, of infectious or communicable diseases and the modes of transmissibility published by the Secretary of Health and Human services; and

(ii) Is designed to protect the public health from individuals who pose a significant risk to the health or safety of others, where that risk cannot be eliminated by reasonable accommodation.

(f) *Health insurance, life insurance, and other benefit plans.*—(1) An insurer, hospital, or medical service company, health maintenance organization, or any agent or entity that administers benefit plans or similar organizations may underwrite risks, classify risks, or administer such risks that are based on or not inconsistent with State law regulating insurance.

(2) A covered entity may establish, sponsor, observe or administer the terms of a bona fide benefit plan that are based on underwriting risks, classifying risks, or administering such risks that are based on or not inconsistent with State law regulating insurance.

(3) A covered entity may establish, sponsor, observe, or administer the terms of a bona fide benefit plan that is not subject to State laws that regulate insurance.

(4) The activities described in paragraphs (f)(1), (2), and (3) of this section are permitted unless these activities are being used as a subterfuge to evade the purposes of this part.

Appendix to Part 1630—Interpretive Guidance on Title I of the Americans with Disabilities Act

Introduction

The Equal Employment Opportunity Commission (the Commission or EEOC) is responsible for enforcement of title I of the Americans with Disabilties Act (ADA), 42 U.S.C. 12101 (1990), which prohibits employment discrimination on the basis of disability. The Commission believes that it is essential to issue interpretive guidance concurrently with the issuance of these regulations in order to ensure that qualified individuals with disabilities understand their rights under these regulations and to facilitate and encourage compliance by covered entities. This appendix represents the Commission's interpretation of the issues discussed, and the Commission will be guided by it when resolving charges of employment discrimination. The appendix addresses the major provisions of the regulations and explains the major concepts of disability rights.

The terms "employer" or "employer or other covered entity" are used interchangeably throughout this document to refer to all covered entities subject to the employment provisions of the ADA.

Section 1630.1 Purpose, Applicability and Construction
Section1630.1(a) Purpose

The Americans with Disabilities Act was signed into law on July 26, 1990. It is an antidiscrimination statute which requires that individuals with disabilities be given the same consideration for employment that individuals without disabilities are given. An individual who is qualified for an employment opportunity cannot be denied that opportunity because of the fact that the individual is disabled. The purpose of title I and these regulations is to ensure that qualified individuals with disabilities are protected from discrimination on the basis of disability.

The ADA uses the term "disabilities" rather than the term "handicaps" used in the Rehabilitation Act of 1973, 29 U.S.C. 701–796. Substantively, these are equivalent. As noted by the House Committee on the Judiciary, "[t]he use of the term 'disabilities' instead of the term 'handicaps' reflects the desire of the Committee to use the most current terminology. It reflects the preference of persons with disabilities to use that term rather than 'handicapped' as used in previous laws, such as the Rehabilitation Act of 1973 . . . " H.R. Rep. No. 485 part 3, 101st Cong., 2d Sess. 26–27 (1990) (hereinafter House Judiciary Report); see also S. Rep. No. 116, 101st Cong., 1st Sess. 21 (1989) [hereinafter Senate Report]; H.R. Rep. No. 485 part 2, 101st Cong., 2d Sess. 50–51 (1990) [hereinafter House Labor Report].

The use of the term "Americans" in the title of the ADA is not intended to imply that the Act only applies to United States citizens. Rather, the ADA protects all qualified individuals with disabilities, regardless of their citizenship status or nationality.

Section 1630.1(b) and (c) Applicability and Construction

Unless expressly stated otherwise, the standards applied in the ADA are not intended to be lesser than the standards applied under the Rehabilitation Act of 1973.

The ADA does not preempt any Federal law, or any state or local law, that grants to individuals with disabilities protection greater than or equivalent to that provided by the ADA. This means that the existence of a lesser standard of protection to individuals with disabilities under the ADA will not provide a defense for failing to meet a higher standard under another law. Thus, for example, title I of the ADA would not be a defense to failing to collect information required to satisfy the affirmative action requirements of Section 503 of the Rehabilitation Act. On the other hand, the existence of a lesser standard under another law will not provide a defense for failing to meet a higher standard under the ADA. See House Labor Report at 135; House Judiciary Report at 69–70.

The ADA does not preempt medical standards or safety requirements established by Federal law or regulations. It does not preempt State, county, or local laws, ordinances or regulations that are consistent with this Part, and are designed to protect the public health from individuals who pose a direct threat which cannot be eliminated by reasonable accommodation to the health or safety of others. However, the ADA does preempt inconsistent requirements established by state or local law for safety or security sensitive positions. See Senate Report at 27; House Labor Report at 57.

An employer allegedly in violation of this part cannot successfully defend its actions by relying on the obligation to comply with the requirements of any state or local law that imposes prohibitions or limitations on the eligibility of qualified individuals with disabilities to practice any occupation or profession. For example, suppose a municipality has an ordinance that prohibits individuals with tuberculosis from teaching school children. If an individual with dormant tuberculosis challenges a private school's refusal to hire him or her because of the tuberculosis, the private school would not be able to rely on the city ordinance as a defense under the ADA.

Sections 1630.2(a)–(f) Commission, Covered Entity, etc.

The definitions section of the regulations includes several terms that are identical, or almost identical, to the terms found in title VII of the Civil Rights Act of 1964. Among these terms are "Commission," "Person," "State," "Employer" and "Employee." These terms are to be given the same meaning under the ADA that they are given under title VII. The term "covered entity" is not found in title VII. However, the title VII definitions of the entities included in the term "covered entity" (*e.g.*, employer, employment agency, *etc.*) are applicable to the ADA.

Section 1630.2(g) Disability

In addition to the term "covered entity," there are several other terms that are unique to the ADA. The first of these is the term "disability." Congress adopted the definition of this term from the Rehabilitation Act definition of the term "Individual with handicaps." By so doing, Congress intended that the relevant caselaw developed under the Rehabilitation Act be generally applicable to the term "disability" as used in the ADA. Senate Report at 21; House Labor Report at 58; House Judiciary Report at 27.

The definition of the term "disability" is divided into three parts. An individual must satisfy at least one of these parts in order to be considered an individual with a disability for purposes of this regulation. An individual is considered to have a "disability" if that individual either (1) has a physical or mental impairment which substantially limits one of more of that person's major life activities, (2) has a record of such an impairment, or (3) is regarded by the covered entity as having such an impairment.

To understand the meaning of the term "disability," it is necessary to understand, a preliminary matter, what is meant by the terms "physical or mental impairment," "major life activity," and "substantially limits." Each of these terms is discussed below.

Section 1630.2(h) Physical or Mental Impairment

This term adopts the definition of the term "physical or mental impairment" found in the regulations implementing section 504 of the Rehabilitation Act at 34 CFR part 104. It defines physical or mental impairment as any physiological disorder or condition, cosmetic disfigurement, or anatomical loss affecting one or more of several body systems, or any mental or psychological disorder.

The existence of an impairment is to be determined without regard to mitigating measures such as medicines or prosthetic devices. *See* Senate Report at 23, House Labor Report at 52, House Judiciary Report at 28. For example, an individual with epilepsy would be considered to have an impairment even if the symptoms of the disorder were completely controlled by medicine. Similarly, an individual with hearing loss would be considered to have an impairment even if the condition were correctable through the use of a hearing aid.

It is important to distinguish between conditions that are impairments and physical, psychological, environmental, cultural and economic characteristics that are not impairments. The definition of the term "impairment" does not include physical characteristics such as eye color, hair color, left-handedness, or height, weight or muscle tone that are within "normal" range and are not the result of a physiological disorder. Nor does the definition include common personality traits such as poor judgment or a quick temper where these are not symptoms of a mental or psychological disorder. Environmental, cultural, or economic disadvantages such as poverty, lack of education or a prison record are not impairments. Advanced age, in and of itself, is also not an impairment. However, various medical conditions commonly associated with age, such as hearing loss, osteoporosis, or arthritis would constitute impairments within the meaning of these regulations. See Senate Report at 22–23; House Labor Report at 51–52; House Judiciary Report at 28–29.

Section 1630.2(i). Major Life Activities

This term adopts the definition of the term "major life activities" found in the regulations implementing section 504 of the Rehabilitation Act at 34 CFR part 104: "Major life activities" are those basic activities that the average person in the general population can perform with little or no difficulty. Major life activities include caring for oneself, performing manual tasks, walking, seeing, breathing, learning, working. This list is not exhaustive. For example, other major life activities include but are not limited to, sitting, standing, lifting, and reaching. See Senate Report at 22; House Labor Report at 52; House Judiciary Report at 28.

Section 1630.2(j) Substantially Limits

Determining whether a physical or mental impairment exists is only the first step in determining whether or not an individual is disabled. Many impairments do not impact an individual's life to the degree that they constitute disabling impairments. An impairment rises to the level of disability if the impairment substantially limits one or more of the individual's major life activities. Multiple impairments that combine to substantially limit one or more of an individual's major life activities also constitute a disabilty.

An impairment that prevents an individual from performing a major life activity substantially limits that major life activity. For example, so individual whose legs are paralyzed is substantially limited in the major life activity of walking because he or she is unable, due to the impairment, to perform that major life activity.

Alternatively, an impairment is subtantially limiting if it significantly restricts the condition, manner or duration under which an individual can perform a particular major life activity as compared to the average person in the general population. For example, an individual who uses artificial legs is substantially limited in the major life activity of walking because the individual can only perform that major life activity in a significantly restricted manner, *i.e.*, only with the use of prosthetic devices. An individual is also substantially limited in the major life activity of walking if the individual can only walk for very brief periods of time. Similarly, a diabetic who without insulin would lapse into a coma would be substantially limited because the individual can only perform major life activities with the aid of medication. See Senate Report at 23; House Labor Report at 52. It should be noted that the term "average person" is not intended to imply a precise mathematical "average."

The regulation notes several factors that should be considered in making the determination of whether an impairment is substantially limiting. These factors are (1) the nature and severity of the impairment, (2) the duration or expected duration of the impairment, and (3) the permanent or long term impact, or the expected permanent or long term impact of, or resulting from, the impairment. The term "duration," as used in this context, refers to the length of time an impairment persists, while the term "impact" refers to the residual effects of an impairment. Thus, for example, a broken leg that takes eight weeks to heal is an impairment of fairly brief duration. However, if the broken leg heals improperly that "impact" of the impairment would be the resulting permanent limp.

The determination of whether an individual is substantially limited in a major life activity must be made on a case by case basis. An individual is not substantially limited in a major life activity if the limitation, when viewed in light of the factors noted above, does not amount to a significant restriction when compared with the abilities of the average person. For example, an individual who has once been able to walk at an extraordinary speed would not be substantially limited in the major life activity of walking if, as a result of a physical impairment, he or she were only able to walk at an average speed, or even at moderately below average speed.

It is important to remember that the restriction on the performance of the major life activity must be the result of a condition that is an impairment. As noted earlier, advanced age, physical or personality characteristics, and environmental, cultural, and economic disadvantages are not impairments. Consequently, even if such factors substantially limit an individual's ability to perform a major life activity, this limitation will not constitute a disability. For example, an individual who is unable to read because he or she was never taught to read would not be an individual with a disability because lack of education is not an impairment. However, an individual with a disability because lack of education is not an impairment. However, an individual who is unable to read because of dyslexia would be an individual with a disability because dyslexia, a learning disability, is an impairment.

An individual who is not substantially limited with respect to any other major life activity may be substantially limited with respect to the major life activity of working. The determination of whether an individual is substantially limited in working must also be made on a case by case basis. If an individual is substantially limited in another major life activity, it is not necessary to consider whether he or she is substantially limited in working.

The regulation lists specific factors that should be used in making the determination of whether the limitation in working is "substantial." These factors are:

(1) The geographical areas to which the individual has reasonable access;

(2) The job from which the individual has been disqualified because of an impairment, and the number and types of jobs utilizing similar training, knowledge, skills or abilities, within that geographical area, from which the individual is also disqualified because of the impairment (class of jobs); and/or

(3) The job from which the individual has been disqualified because of an impairment, and the number and types of other jobs not utilizing similar training, knowledge, skills or abilities, within that geographical area, from which the individual is also disqualified because of the impairment (broad range of jobs in various classes).

Thus, an individual is not substantially limited in working just because he or she is unable to perform a particular job for one employer, or because he or she is unable to perform a specialized job or profession requiring extraordinary skill, prowess or talent. For example, a surgeon who is no longer able to perform surgery because of an impairment that results in a slightly shaky hand would not be substantially limited in working merely because of the inability to perform this chosen specialty. This is so because the surgeon would only be excluded from a narrow range of jobs, and would still be able to perform various other positions, in the same class, utilizing his or her training as a physician. For instance, the surgeon could continue to examine patients and advise on the need for surgery, or teach medicine or surgical techniques within the same geographical area. Nor would a professional baseball pitcher who develops a bad elbow and can no longer throw a baseball be considered substantially limited in the major life activity of working. In both examples, the individuals are not substantially limited in the ability to perform any other major life activity and, with regard to the major life activity of working, are only unable to perform a particular specialized job. See *Forrisi* v. *Bowen*, 794 F.2d 931 (4th Cir. 1986); *Jasany* v. *U.S. Postal Service*, 755 F.2d 1244 (6th Cir. 1985); *E.E. Black, Ltd.* v. *Marshall*, 497 F. Supp. 1088 (D. Hawaii 1980).

On the other hand, an individual does not have to be totally unable to work in order to be considered substantially limited in the major life activity of working. An individual is substantially limited in working if the individual is significantly restricted in the ability to perform a class of jobs or a broad range of jobs in various classes, when compared with the ability of the average person with comparable qualifications to perform those same jobs. For example, an individual who has a back condition that prevents the individual from performing any heavy labor job would be substantially limited in the major life activity of working because the individual's impairment eliminates his or her ability to perform a class of jobs. This would be so even if the individual were able to perform jobs in another class, *e.g.,* the class of semi-skilled jobs. Similarly, suppose an individual has an allergy to a substance found in most high rise office buildings, but seldom found elsewhere, that makes breathing extremely difficult. Since this individual would be substantially limited in the ability to perform the broad range of jobs in various classes that are conducted in high rise office buildings within the geographical area to which he or she has reasonable access, he or she would be substantially limited in working.

If an individual has a "mental or physical impairment" that "substantially limits" his or her ability to perform one or more "major life activities," that individual will satisfy the first part of the regulatory definition of "disability" and will be considered an individual with a disability. An individual who satisfies this first part of the definition of the term "disability" is not required to demonstrate that he or she satisfies either of the other parts of the definition. However, if an individual is unable to satisfy this part of the definition, he or she may be able to satisfy one of the other parts of the definition.

Section 1630.2(k) Record of a Substantially Limiting Condition

The second part of the definition provides that an individual with a record of an impairment that substantially limits a major life activity is an individual with a disability. The intent of this provision, in part, is to ensure that people are not discriminated against because of a history of disability. For example, this provision protects former cancer patients from discrimination based on their prior medical history. This provision also ensures that individuals are not discriminated against because they have been misclassified as disabled. For example, individuals misclassified as learning disabled are protected from discrimination on the basis of that erroneous classification. Senate Report at 23; House Labor Report at 52–53; House Judiciary Report at 29.

This part of the definition is satisfied if a record relied on by an employer indicates that the individual has or has had a substantially limiting impairment. The impairment indicated in the record must be an impairment that would substantially limit one or more of the individual's major life activities. There are many types of records that could potentially contain this information, including but not limited to, education, medical, employment or other records.

The fact that an individual has a record of being a disabled veteran, or of disability retirement, or is classified as disabled for other purposes does not guarantee that the individual will satisfy the definition of "disability" under these regulations. Other statutes, regulations and programs may have a definition of "disability" that is not the same as the definition set forth in the ADA and contained in these regulations. Accordingly, in order for an individual who has been classified in a record as "disabled" for some other purpose to be considered disabled for purposes of these regulations, the impairment indicated in the record must be a physical or mental impairment that substantially limits one or more of the individual's major life activities.

Section 1630.2(I) Regarded as Substantially Limited in a Major Life Activity

If an individual cannot satisfy either the first part of the definition of "disability" or the second "record of" part of the definition, he or she may be able to satisfy the third part of the definition. The third part of the definition provides that an individual who is regarded by an employer or other covered entity as having an impairment that substantially limits a major life activity is an individual with a disability.

There are three different ways in which an individual may satisfy the definition of "being regarded as having a disability":

(1) The individual may have an impairment which is not substantially limiting but is perceived by the employer or other covered entity as constituting a substantially limiting impairment;

(2) The individual may have an impairment which is only substantially limiting because of the attitude of others toward the impairment; or

(3) The individual may have no impairment at all but is regarded by the employer or other covered entity as having a substantially limiting impairment. Senate Report at 23; House Labor Report at 53; House Judiciary Report at 29.

An individual satisfies the first part of this definition if the individual has an impairment that is not substantially limiting, but the covered entity perceives the impairment as being substantially limiting. For example, an employee with controlled high blood pressure that is not, in fact, substantially limiting who is reassigned to less strenuous work because of the employer's unsubstantiated fears that the individual will suffer a heart attack if he or she continues to perform strenuous work would be "regarded as" disabled.

An individual satisfies the second part of the "regarded as" definition if the individual has an impairment that is only substantially limiting because of the attitude of others toward the condition. For example, an individual may have a prominent facial scar or disfigurement, or may have a condition that periodically causes an involuntary jerk of the head but does not limit the individual's major life activities. If an employer discriminates against such an individual because of the negative reactions of customers, the employer would be regarding the individual as disabled and acting on the basis of that perceived disability. *See* Senate Report at 24; House Labor Report at 53; House Judiciary Report at 30–31.

An individual satisfies the third part of the "regarded as" definition of "disability" if the employer or other covered entity erroneously believes the individual has a substantially limiting impairment that the individual actually does not have. This situation could occur, for example, if an employer discharged an employee in response to a rumor that the employee is infected with Human Immunodeficiency Virus (HIV). Even though the rumor is totally unfounded and the individual has no impairment at all, the individual is considered an individual with a disability because the employer perceived of this individual as being disabled. Thus, in this example, the employer, by discharging this employee, is discriminating on the basis of disability.

In determining whether or not an individual is regarded as substantially limited in the major life activity of working, it should be assumed that all similar employers would apply the same exclusionary qualification standard that the employer charged with discrimination has used. The determination of whether there is a substantial limitation in working is contingent upon the number and types of jobs from which the individual is excluded because of an impairment. An assessment of the number and types of jobs from which an individual "regarded as" disabled in working would be excluded can only be achieved if the qualification standard of the employer charged with discrimination is attributed to all similar employers. Were it otherwise, an employer would be able to use a discriminatory qualification standard as long as the standard was not widely followed.

For example, suppose an individual has a heart murmur that has gone undetected and has not caused any limitations on the individual's activities. In the course of a routine medical examination given to all newly employed heavy machine operators, the murmur is discovered. The employer then withdraws the offer of employment because it believes the heart murmur disqualifies the individual from operating the heavy machinery. Assuming all employers hiring heavy machine operators use this standard, the individual would be excluded from the broad range of jobs requiring the use of heavy machinery. Therefore, the employer is regarding the impairment as a substantial limitation of the major life activity of working and has acted on the basis of that perception.

Frequently Disabling Impairments

The ADA, like the Rehabilitation Act of 1973, does not attempt a "laundry list" of impairments that are "disabilities." The determination of whether an individual has a disability is not based on the name or diagnosis of the impairment the person has, but rather on the effect of that impairment on the life of the individual. Some impairments may be disabling for particular individuals but not for others, depending on the stage of the disease or disorder, the presence of other impairments that combine to make the impairment disabling or any number of other factors.

There are, however, a number of impairments that far more often than not result in disability. The following list is provided to indicate the types of impairments that usually are disabling. However, an individual should not automatically be considered an individual with a disability merely because he or she has one of the impairments indicated on this list. Rather, such an individual is an individual with a disability only if the impairment impacts on the individual to such a degree that it substantially limits a major life activity. Commonly disabling impairments include substantial orthopedic, visual, speech, and hearing impairments, tuberculosis, HIV infection, AIDS, cerebral palsy, epilepsy, muscular dystrophies, multiple sclerosis, cancers, heart disease, diabetes, mental retardation, and emotional or mental illness.

By contrast, temporary, non-chronic impairments of short duration, with little or no long term or permanent impact are usually not disabilities. Such impairments may include, but are not limited to, broken limbs, sprained joints, concussions, appendicitis, and influenza. Similarly, except in rare and limiting circumstances, obesity is not considered a disabling impairment.

Section 1630.2(m) Qualified Individual with a Disability

The ADA prohibits discrimination on the basis of disability against qualified individuals with disabilities. The determination of whether an individual with a disability is "qualified" should be made in two steps. The first step is to determine if the individual satisfies the prerequisites for the position, such as possessing the appropriate educational background, employment experience, skills, licenses, etc. For example, the first step in determining whether an accountant who is paraplegic is qualified for a certified public accountant (CPA) position is to examine the individual's credentials to determine whether the individual is a licensed CPA. This is sometimes referred to in the Rehabilitation Act caselaw as determining whether the individual is "otherwise qualified" for the position. See Senate Report at 33;

House Labor Report at 64–65. (See Section 1630.9 Not Making Reasonable Accommodation.)

The second step is to determine whether or not the individual can perform the essential functions of the position held or desired, with or without reasonable accommodation. The purpose of this second step is to ensure that individuals with disabilities who can perform the essential functions of the position held or desired are not denied employment opportunities because they are not able to perform marginal or peripheral functions of the position. House Labor Report at 55.

Section 1630.2(n) Essential Functions

The determination of which functions are essential may be critical to the determination of whether or not the individual with a disability is qualified. The essential functions are those functions that the individual who holds the position must be able to perform unaided or with the assistance of a reasonable accommodation.

The inquiry into whether a particular function is essential initially focuses on whether the employer actually requires employees in the position to perform the functions that the employer asserts are essential. For example, an employer may state that typing is an essential function of a position. If, in fact, the employer has never required any employee in that particular position to type, this will be evidence that typing is not actually an essential function of the position.

If the individual who holds the position is actually required to perform the function the employer asserts is an essential function, the inquiry will then center around whether removing the function would fundamentally alter the position. This determination of whether or not a particular function is essential will generally include one or more of the following factors listed in the regulation.

The first factor is whether the reason the position exists is to perform that function. For example, an individual may be hired to proofread documents. The ability to proofread the documents would then be an essential function, since this is the only reason the position exists.

The second factor in determining whether a function is essential is the number of other employees available to perform that job function or among whom the performance of that job function can be distributed. This may be a factor either because the total number of employees is low, or because of the fluctuating demands of the business operations. For example, if an employer has a relatively small number of employees for the volume of work to be performed, it may be necessary that each employee perform a multitude of different functions. Therefore, the performance of those functions by each employee becomes more critical and the options for reorganizing the work become more limited. In such a situation, functions that might not be essential if there were a larger staff may become essential because the staff size is small compared to the volume of work that has to be done. *See Treadwell v. Alexander*, 707 F.2d 473 (11th Cir. 1983).

A similar situation might occur in a larger work force if the workflow follows a cycle of heavy demand for labor intensive work followed by low demand periods. This type of workflow might also make the performance of each function during the peak periods more critical and might limit the employer's flexibility in reorganizing operating procedures. *See Dexler v. Tisch*, 660 F. Supp. 1418 (D. Conn. 1987).

The third factor is the degree of expertise or skill required to perform the function. In certain professions and highly skilled positions the employee is hired for his or her expertise or ability to perform the particular function. In such a situation, the performance of that specialized task would be an essential function.

Whether a particular function is essential is a factual determination that must be made on a case by case basis. In determining whether or not a particular function is essential, all relevant evidence should be considered. The regulation lists various types of evidence, such as an established job description, that may be considered in determining whether a particular function is essential. Since the list is not exhaustive, other relevant evidence may also be presented. Greater weight will not be granted to the types of evidence included on the list than to the types of evidence not listed.

The employer's judgment as to what functions are essential and written job descriptions prepared before advertising or interviewing applicants for the job are among the relevant evidence to be considered in determining whether a particular function is essential. The work experience of past employees in the job or of current employees in similar jobs is also relevant to the determination of whether a particular function is essential. *See* H.R. Conf. Rep. No. 101–596, 101st Cong., 2d Sess. 58 (1990) [hereinafter Conference Report]: House Judiciary Report at 33–34. See also *Hall* v. *U.S. Postal Service*, 857 F.2d 1073 (6th Cir. 1988).

The time spent performing the particular function may be an indicator of whether that function is essential. For example, if an employee spends the vast majority of his or her time working at a cash register, this would be evidence that operating the cash register is an essential function. The consequence of failing to require the employee to perform the function may be another indicator of whether a particular function is essential. For example, although a firefighter may not regularly have to carry an unconscious adult out of a burning building, the consequence of failing to require the firefighter to be able to perform this function would be serious.

It is important to note that the inquiry into essential functions is not intended to second guess an employer's business judgment with regard to production standards, whether qualitative or quantitative, nor to require employers to lower such standards. (See section 1630.10 Qualification Standards, Tests and Other Selection Criteria.) If an employer requires its typists to be able to type 75 words per minute, it will not be called upon to explain why a typing speed of 65 words per minute would not be adequate. Similarly, if a hotel requires its service workers to clean 16 rooms a day, it will not have to explain why it chose a 16 room requirement rather than a 10 room requirement. However, if an employer does not require 75 words per minute typing or the cleaning of 16 rooms, it will have to show that it actually imposes such requirements on its employees in fact, and not simply on paper. It should also be noted that, if it is alleged that the employer intentionally selected the particular level of production to exclude individuals with disabilities, the employer may have to offer a legitimate, nondiscriminatory reason for its selection.

Section 1630.2(o) Reasonable Accommodation

An individual is considered a "qualified individual with a disability" if the individual can perform the essential functions of the position held or desired with or without reasonable accommodation. In general, an accommodation is any change in the work environment or in the way things are customarily done that enables an individual with a disability to enjoy equal employment opportunities. There are three categories of reasonable accommodations. These are (1) accommodations that are required to ensure equal opportunity in the application process; (2) accommodations that enable the employer's employees with disabilities to perform the essential functions of the position held or desired; and (3) accommodations that enable the employer's employees with disabilities to enjoy the same benefits and privileges of employment as are enjoyed by employees without disabilities. It should be noted that nothing in these regulations prohibits employers or other covered entities from providing accommodations beyond those required by these regulations.

The regulations list the examples, specified in title I of the ADA, of the most common types of accommodation that an employer or other covered entity may be required to provide. There are any number of other specific accommodations that may be appropriate for particular situations but are not specifically mentioned in this listing. This listing is not intended to be exhaustive of accommodation possibilities. For example, other accommodations could include permitting the use of accrued paid leave or providing additional unpaid leave for necessary treatment, making employer provided transportation accessible, providing personal assistants—such as a page turner or travel attendant, and providing reserved parking spaces. Senate Report at 31; House Labor Report at 62; House Judiciary Report at 39.

The accommodations included on the list of reasonable accommodations are generally self explanatory. However, there are a few that require further explanation. One of these is the accommodation of making existing facilities used by employees readily accessible to, and usable by, individuals with disabilities. This accommodation includes both those areas that must be accessible for the employee to perform essential job functions, as well as non-work areas used by the employer's employees for other purposes. For example, accessible break rooms, lunch rooms, training rooms, etc. may be required as reasonable accommodations.

Another of the potential accommodations listed is "job restructuring." An employer or other covered entity may restructure a job by reallocating or redistributing nonessential, marginal job functions. For example, an employer may have two jobs, each of which entails the performance of a number of marginal functions. The employer hires a qualified individual with a disability who is able to perform some of the marginal functions of each job but not all of the marginal functions of either job. As an accommodation, the employer may redistribute the marginal functions so that all of the marginal functions that the qualified individual with a disability can perform are made a part of the position to be filled by the qualified individual with a disability. The remaining marginal functions that the individual with a disability cannot perform would then be transferred to the other position. See Senate Report at 31; House Labor Report at 62.

An employer or other covered entity is not required to reallocate essential functions. The essential functions are by definition those that the individual who holds the job would have to perform, with or without reasonable accommodation, in order to be considered qualified for the position. For example, suppose a security guard position requires the individual who holds the job to inspect identification cards. An employer would not have to provide an individual who is legally blind with an assistant to look at the identification cards for the legally blind employee. In this situation the assistant would be performing the job for the individual with a disability rather than assisting the individual to perform the job. See *Coleman v. Darden*, 595 F.2d 533 (10th Cir. 1979).

Reassignment to another vacant position is also listed as a potential reasonable accommodation. In general, reassignment should be considered only when accommodation within the individual's current position would pose an undue hardship. Reassignment is not available to applicants. An applicant for a position must be qualified for, and be able to perform the essential functions of, the position sought with or without reasonable accommodation.

Reassignment may not be used to limit, segregate, or otherwise discriminate against employees with disabilities by forcing reassignments to undesirable positions or to designated offices or facilities. Employers should reassign the individual to an equivalent position, in terms of pay, status, etc., if the individual is qualified and if the position is vacant. An employer may reassign an individual to a lower graded position if there are no accommodations that would enable the employee to remain in the current position and there are no vacant equivalent positions for which the individual is qualified with or without reasonable accommodation. An employer is not required to promote an individual with a disability as an accommodation. See Senate Report at 31–32; House Labor Report at 63.

The determination of which accommodation is appropriate in a particular situation involves a process in which the employer and employee identify the precise limitations imposed by the disability and explore potential accommodations that would overcome those limitations. This process is discussed more fully in § 1630.9 Not Making Reasonable Accommodation.

Section 1630.2(p) Undue Hardship

An employer or other covered entity is not required to provide an accommodation that will impose an undue hardship on the operation of the employer's or other covered entity's business. The term "undue hardship" means significant difficulty or expense in, or resulting from, the provision of the accommodation. The "undue hardship" provision is sensitive to the financial realities of the particular employer or other covered entity. However, the concept of undue hardship is not limited to financial difficulty. "Undue hardship" refers to any accommodation that would be unduly costly, extensive, substantial, or disruptive, or that would fundamentally alter the nature or operation of the business. See Senate Report at 35; House Labor Report at 67.

For example, suppose an individual with a disabling visual impairment that makes it extremely difficult to see in dim lighting applies for a position as a waiter in a nightclub and requests that the club be brightly lit as a reasonable accommodation. Although the individual may be able to perform the job in bright lighting, the nightclub will probably be able to demonstrate that that particular accommodation, though inexpensive, would impose an undue hardship if the bright lighting would destroy the ambience of the nightclub and/or make it difficult for the customers to see the stage show. The fact that that particular accommodation poses an undue hardship, however, only means that the employer is not required to provide that accommodation. If there is another accommodation that will not create an undue hardship, the employer would be required to provide the alternative accommodation.

An employer's claim that the cost of a particular accommodation will impose an undue hardship will be analyzed in light of the factors outlined in the regulations. In part, this analysis requires a determination of whose financial resources should be considered in deciding whether the accommodation is unduly costly. In many cases the financial resources of the employer or other covered entity in its entirety should be considered in determining whether the cost of an accommodation poses an undue hardship. In other cases, consideration of the financial resources of the employer or other covered entity as a whole may be inappropriate because it may not give an accurate picture of the financial resources available to the particular site that will actually be required to provide the accommodation. See House Labor Report at 68–69; House Judiciary Report at 40–41; see also Conference Report at 56–57.

If the employer or other covered entity asserts that only the financial resources of the site where the individual will be employed should be considered, the regulations require a factual determination of the relationship between the employer or other covered entity and the site that will provide the accommodation. As an example, suppose that an independently owned fast food franchise that receives no money from the franchisor refuses to hire an individual with a hearing impairment because it asserts that it would be an undue hardship to provide an interpreter to enable the individual to participate in monthly staff meetings. Since the financial relationship between the franchisor and the franchise is limited to payment of an annual franchise fee, only the financial resources of the franchise would be considered in determining whether or not providing the accommodation would be an undue hardship. See House Labor Report at 68; House Judiciary Report at 40.

If the employer or other covered entity can show that the cost of the accommodation would impose an undue hardship, it will still be required to provide the accommodation if the funding is available from another source, *e.g.*, a State vocational rehabilitation agency, or if Federal, State or local tax deductions or tax credits are available to offset the cost of the accommodation. If the employer or other covered entity receives or is eligible to receive monies from an external source that would pay the entire cost of the accommodation, it cannot claim cost as an undue hardship. To the extent that such monies pay or would pay for only part of the cost of the accommodation, only that portion of the cost of the accommodation that could be recovered—the final net cost to the entity—may be considered in determining undue hardship.

The individual with a disability requesting the accommodation must also be given the option of providing the accommodation or of paying that portion of the cost which constitutes the undue hardship on the operation of the business. As with outside funding available to enable the employer or other covered entity to provide the reasonable accommodation, only the net cost of the accommodation to the employer or other covered entity is to be included in the calculation of undue hardship. (See § 1630.9 Not Making a Reasonable Accommodation.) See Senate Report at 36; House Labor Report at 69.

Section 1630.2(r) Direct Threat

An employer may require, as a qualification standard, that an individual not pose a direct threat to the health or safety of himself/herself or others. Like any other qualification standard, such a standard must apply to all applicants or employees and not just to individuals with disabilities. If, however, an individual poses a direct threat as a result of a disability, the employer must determine whether a reasonable accommodation would either eliminate the risk or reduce it to an acceptable level. If no accommodation exists that would either eliminate or reduce the risk, the employer may refuse to hire an applicant or may discharge an employee who poses a direct threat.

An employer, however, is not permitted to deny an employment opportunity to an individual with a disability merely because of a slightly increased risk. The risk can only be considered when it poses a significant risk, *i.e.*, high probability, of substantial harm; a speculative or remote risk is insufficient. See Senate Report at 27; House Report Labor Report at 56–57; House Judiciary Report at 45.

Determining whether an individual poses a significant risk of substantial harm to others must be made on a case by case basis. The employer should identify the specific risk posed by the individual. For individuals with mental or emotional disabilities, the employer must identify the specific behavior on the part of the individual that would pose the direct threat. For individuals with physical disabilities, the employer must identify the aspect of the disability that would pose the direct threat. The employer should then consider the three factors listed in the regulations:

(1) The duration of the risk;

(2) The nature and severity of the potential harm; and

(3) The likelihood that the potential harm will occur.

Such consideration must rely on objective, factual evidence—not on subjective perceptions, irrational fears, patronizing attitudes, or stereotypes—about the nature or effect of a particular disability, or of disability generally. See Senate Report at 27; House Labor Report at 56–57; House Judiciary Report at 45–46. See also *Strathie* v. *Department of Transportation*, 716 F.2d 227 (3d Cir. 1983).

An employer is also permitted to require that an individual with a disability not pose a direct threat of harm to his or her own safety or health. If performing the particular functions of a job would result in a high probability of substantial harm to the individual, the employer would reject or discharge the individual unless a reasonable accommodation that would not cause an undue hardship would avert the harm. For example, an employer would not be required to hire an individual, disabled by narcolepsy, who frequently and unexpectedly loses consciousness for a carpentry job the essential functions of which require the use of power saws and other dangerous equipment, where no accommodation exists that will reduce or eliminate the risk.

The assessment that there exists a high probability of substantial harm to the individual with a disability must be strictly based on valid medical analyses or on other objective evidence. This determination must be based on individualized factual data rather than on stereotypic or patronizing assumptions and must consider potential reasonable accommodations. Generalized fears about risks from the employment environment, such as exacerbation of the disability caused by stress, cannot be used by an employer to disqualify an individual with a disability. Nor can generalized fears about risks to individuals with disabilities in the event of an evacuation or other emergency be used by an employer to disqualify an individual with a disability. See Senate Report at 56; House Labor at 73–74; House Judiciary Report at 45. See also *Mantolete* v. *Bolger*, 767 F.2d 1416 (9th Cir. 1985); *Bentivegna* v. *U.S. Department of Labor*, 694 F.2d 619 (9th Cir. 1982).

Section 1630.3 Exceptions to the Definitions of "Disability" and "Qualified Individual with a Disability"

Section 1630.3(a)–(c) Illegal Use of Drugs

The regulations provide that an individual currently engaging in the illegal use of drugs is not an individual with a disability for purposes of this part when the employer or other covered entity acts on the basis of such use. Illegal use of drugs refers both to the use of unlawful drugs such as cocaine and to the unlawful use of prescription drugs.

Employers, for example, may discharge or deny employment to persons who illegally use drugs, on the basis of such use, without fear or being held liable for discrimination. The term "currently engaging" is not intended to be limited to the use of drugs on the day of, or within a matter of days or weeks before, the employment action in question. Rather, the provision is intended to apply to the illegal use of drugs that has occurred recently enough to indicate that the individual is actively engaged in such conduct. See Conference Report at 64.

Individuals who are erroneously perceived as engaging in the illegal use of drugs, but are not in fact illegally using drugs are not excluded from the definitions of the terms "disability" and "qualified individual with a disability." Individuals who are no longer illegally using drugs and who have either been rehabilitated successfully or are in the process of completing a rehabilitation program are, likewise, not excluded from the definitions of those terms. The term "rehabilitation program" refers to both in-patient and out-patient programs, as well as to appropriate employee assistance or other programs that provide professional (not necessarily medical) assistance and counseling for individuals who illegally use drugs. See Conference Report at 64; see also House Labor Report at 77; House Judiciary Report at 47.

An individual cannot demonstrate that he or she is no longer engaging in the illegal use of drugs by simply showing participation in a drug treatment program. It is essential that the individual offer evidence, such as drug test results, to prove that he or she is not currently engaging in the illegal use of drugs. Employers are entitled to seek reasonable assurances that no illegal use of drugs is occurring or has occurred recently enough so that continuing use is a real and ongoing problem. An employer, such as a law enforcement agency, may also be able to impose a qualification standard that excludes individuals with a history of illegal use of drugs if it can show that the standard is job-related and consistent with business necessity. (See § 1630.10 Qualification Standards, Tests and Other Selection Criteria) See Conference Report at 64.

Section 1630.4 Discrimination Prohibited

This provision prohibits discrimination against a qualified individual with a disability in all aspects of the employment relationship. The range of employment decisions covered by this nondiscrimination mandate is to be construed in a manner consistent with the regulations implementing section 504 of the Rehabilitation Act of 1973.

These regulations are not intended to limit the ability of covered entities to choose and maintain a qualified workforce. Employers can continue to use job-related criteria to select qualified employees, and can continue to hire employees who can perform the essential functions of the job.

Section 1630.5 Limiting, Segregating and Classifying

This provision and the several provisions that follow describe various specific forms of discrimination that are included within the general prohibition of § 1630.4 Covered entities are prohibited from restricting the employment opportunities of qualified individuals with disabilities on the basis of stereotypes and myths about the individual's disability. Rather, the capabilities qualified individuals with disabilities must be determined on an individualized, case by case basis. Covered entities are also prohibited from segregating qualified employees with disabilities into separate work areas or into separate lines of advancement.

Thus, for example, it would be a violation of these regulations for an employer to limit the duties of an employee with a disability based on a presumption of what is best for an individual with such a disability, or on a presumption about the abilities of an individual with such a disability. It would be a violation of these regulations for an employer to adopt a separate track of job promotion or progression for employees with disabilities based on a presumption that employees with disabilities are uninterested in, or incapable of, performing particular jobs. Similarly, it would be a violation for an employer to assign or reassign (as a reasonable accommodation) employees with disabilities to one particular office or installation, or to require that employees with disabilities use only particular employer provided non-work facilities such as segregated break-rooms, lunch rooms, or lounges. It would also be a violation of these regulations to deny employment to an applicant or employee with a disability based on generalized fears about the safety of an individual with such a disability, or based on generalized assumptions about the absenteeism rate of an individual with such a disability.

In addition, it should also be noted that these regulations are intended to require that employees with disabilities be accorded equal access to whatever health insurance coverage the employer provides to other employees. These regulations do not, however, affect pre-existing condition clauses included in health insurance policies offered by employers. Consequently, employers may continue to offer policies that contain such clauses, even if they adversely affect individuals with disabilities, so long as the clauses are not used as a subterfuge to evade the purposes of these regulations.

So, for example, it would be permissible for an employer to offer an insurance policy that limits coverage for certain procedures or treatments to a specified number per year. Thus, if a health insurance plan provided coverage for five blood transfusions a year to all covered employees, it would not be discriminatory to offer this plan simply because a hemophiliac employee may require more than five blood transfusions annually. However, it would not be permissible to limit or deny the hemophiliac employee coverage for other procedures, such as heart surgery or the setting of a broken leg, even though the plan would not have to provide coverage for the additional blood transfusions that may be involved in these procedures. Likewise, limits may be placed on reimbursements for certain procedures or on the types of drugs or procedures covered (e.g. limits on the number of permitted X-rays or non-coverage of experimental drugs or procedures), but that limitation must be applied equally to individuals with and without disabilities. See Senate Report at 28–29; House Labor Report at 58–59; House Judiciary Report at 36.

Leave policies or benefit plans that are uniformly applied do not violate these regulations simply because they do not address the special needs of every individual with a disability. Thus, for example, an employer that reduces the number of paid sick leave days that it will provide to all employees, or reduces the amount of medical insurance coverage that it will provide to all employees, is not in violation of these regulations, even if the benefits reduction has an impact on employees with disabilities in need of greater sick leave and medical coverage. Benefits reductions adopted for discriminatory reasons are in violation of these regulations. See *Alexander* v. *Choate*, 469 U.S. 287 (1985). See Senate Report at 85; House Labor Report at 137. (See also, the discussion at Section 1630.16(f) Health Insurance, Life Insurance, and Other Benefit Plans.)

Section 1630.6 Contractual or Other Arrangements

An employer or other covered entity may not do through a contractual or other relationship what it is prohibited from doing directly. This provision only applies to situations where an employer or other covered entity has entered into a contractual relationship that has the effect of discriminating against its own employees or applicants with disabilities. Accordingly, it would be a violation for an employer to participate in a contractual relationship that results in discrimination against the employer's employees with disabilities in hiring, training, promotion, or in any other aspect of the employment relationship. This provision applies whether or not the employer or other covered entity intended for the contractual relationship to have the discriminatory effect.

The regulation notes that this provision applies to parties on either side of the contractual or other relationship. This is intended to highlight that an employer whose employees provide services to others, like an employer whose employees receive services, must ensure that those employees are not discriminated against on the basis of disability. Thus a copier company would be required to ensure the provision of any reasonable accommodation necessary to enable its copier service representative with a disability to service a client's machine.

The existence of the contractual relationship adds no new obligations, beyond those already imposed by these regulations. The employer, therefore, is not liable through the contractual arrangement for any discrimination by the contractor against the contractor's own employees or applicants, although the contractor, as an employer, may be liable for such discrimination.

An employer or other covered entity, on the other hand, cannot evade the obligations imposed by these regulations by engaging in a contractual or other relationship. For example, an employer cannot avoid its responsibility to make reasonable accommodation subject to the undue hardship limitation through a contractual arrangement. See Conference Report at 59; House Labor Report at 59–61; House Judiciary Report at 36–37.

To illustrate, assume that an employer is seeking to contract with a company to provide training for its employees. Any responsibilities of reasonable accommodation applicable to the employer in providing the training remain with that employer even if it contracts with another company for this service. Thus, if the training company were planning to conduct the training at an inaccessible location, thereby making it impossible for an employee who uses a wheelchair to attend, the employer would have a duty to make reasonable accommodation unless to do so would impose an undue hardship. Under these circumstances, appropriate accommodations might include (1) having the training company identify accessible training sites and relocate the training program; (2) having the training company make the training site accessible; (3) directly making the training site accessible or providing the training company with the means by which to make the site accessible; (4) identifying and contracting with another training company that uses accessible sites; or (5) any other accommodation that would result in making the training available to the employee.

As another illustration, assume that instead of contracting with a training company, the employer contracts with a hotel to host a conference for its employees. The employer will have a duty to ascertain and ensure the accessibility of the hotel and its conference facilities. To fulfill this obligation the employer could, for example, inspect the hotel first-hand or ask a local disability group to inspect the hotel. Alternatively, the employer could ensure that the contract with the hotel specifies it will provide accessible guest rooms for those who need them and that all rooms to be used for the conference, including exhibit and meeting rooms, are accessible. If the hotel breeches this accessibility provision, the hotel may be liable to the employer, under a non-ADA breach of contract theory, for the cost of any accommodation needed to provide access to the hotel and conference, and for any other costs accrued by the employer. (In addition, the hotel may also be independently liable under Title III of the ADA.) However, this would not relieve the employer of its responsibility under these regulations nor shield it from charges of discrimination by its own employees. See House Labor Report at 40; House Judiciary Report at 37.

Section 1630.8 Relationship or Association with an Individual with a Disability

This provision is intended to protect any qualified individual, whether or not that individual has a disability, from discrimination because that person is known to have an association or relationship with an individual who has a disability. This protection is not limited to those who have a familial relationship with an individual with a disability.

To illustrate the scope of this provision, assume that a qualified applicant without a disability applies for a job and discloses to the employer that his or her spouse has a disability. The employer thereupon declines to hire the applicant because the employer believes that the applicant would have to miss work or frequently leave work early in order to care for the spouse. Such a refusal to hire would be prohibited by this provision. Similarly, this provision would prohibit an employer from discharging an employee because the employee does volunteer work with AIDS patients, and the employer fears that the employee may contract the disease.

It should be noted, however, that an employer need not provide the applicant or employee without a disability with a reasonable accommodation because that duty only applies to qualified applicants or employees with a disability. Thus, for example, an employee would not be entitled to a modified work schedule as an accommodation to enable the employee to care for a spouse with a disability. See Senate Report at 30; House Labor Report at 61–62; House Judiciary Report at 38–39.

Section 1630.9 Not Making Reasonable Accommodation

The obligation to make reasonable accommodation is a form of nondiscrimination. It applies to all employment decisions and to the job application process. This obligation does not extend to the provision of adjustments or modifications that are primarily for the personal benefit of the individual with a disability. Thus, if an adjustment or modification is job-related, *e.g.*, specifically assists the individual in performing the duties of a particular job, it will be considered a type of reasonable accommodation. On the other hand, if an adjustment or modification assists the individual throughout his or her daily activities, on and off the job, it will be considered a personal item that the employer is not required to provide. Accordingly, an employer would not be required to provide an employee with a disability with a prosthetic limb, wheelchair, or eyeglasses. Nor would an employer have to provide as an accommodation any amenity or convenience that is not job-related, such as a private hot plate, hot pot or refrigerator that is not provided to employees without disabilities. See Senate Report at 31; House Labor Report at 62.

The term "supported employment," which has been applied to a wide variety of programs to assist individuals with severe disabilities in both competitive and non-competitive employment, is not synonymous with reasonable accommodation. Examples of supported employment include modified training materials, restructuring essential functions to enable an individual to perform a job, or hiring an outside professional ("job-coach") to assist in job training. Whether a particular form of assistance would be required as a reasonable accommodation must be determined on an individualized, case by case basis without regard to whether that assistance is referred to as "supported employment." For example, an employer, under certain circumstances, may be required to provide modified training materials or a temporary "job coach" to assist in the training of a qualified individual with a disability as a reasonable accommodation. However, an employer would not be required to restructure the essential functions of a position to fit the skills of an individual with a disability who is not otherwise qualified to perform the position, such as is done in certain supported employment programs. See 34 CFR part 383. It should be noted that it would not be a violation of this Part for an employer to provide any of these personal modifications or adjustments, or to engage in supported employment or similar rehabilitative programs.

The obligation to make reasonable accommodation applies to all services and programs provided in connection with employment, and to all non-work facilities provided or maintained by an employer for use by its employees. Accordingly, the obligation to accommodate is applicable to employer sponsored placement or counseling services, and to employer provided cafeterias, lounges, gymnasiums, auditoriums, transportation and the like.

The reasonable accommodation requirement is best understood as a means by which barriers to the equal employment opportunity of an individual with a disability are removed or alleviated. These barriers may, for example, be physical or structural obstacles that inhibit or prevent the access of an individual with a disability to job sites, facilities or equipment. Or they may be rigid work schedules that permit no flexibility as to when work is performed or when breaks may be taken, or inflexible job procedures that unduly limit the modes of communication that are used on the job, or the way in which particular tasks are accomplished.

The term "otherwise qualified" is intended to make clear that the obligation to make reasonable accommodation is owed only to an individual with a disability who is qualified within the meaning of § 1630.2(m) in that he or she satisfies all the skill, experience, education and other job-related selection criteria. An individual with a disability is "otherwise qualified," in other words, if he or she is qualified for a job, except that he or she needs a reasonable accommodation to be able to perform the job's essential functions.

For example, if a law firm requires that all incoming lawyers have graduated from an accredited law school and have passed the bar examination, the law firm need not provide an accommodation to an individual with a visual impairment who has not met these selection criteria. That individual is not entitled to a reasonable accommodation because the individual is not "otherwise qualified" for the position.

On the other hand, if the individual has graduated from an accredited law school and passed the bar examination, the individual would be "otherwise qualified." The law firm would thus be required to provide a reasonable accommodation, such as a reader, to enable the individual to perform the essential functions of the attorney position, unless the necessary accommodation would impose an undue hardship on the law firm. See Senate Report at 33–34; House Labor Report at 64–65.

The reasonable accommodation that is required by this regulation should provide the qualified individual with a disability with an equal employment opportunity. Equal employment opportunity means an opportunity to attain the same level of performance, or to enjoy the same level of benefits and privileges of employment as are available to the average similarly situated employee without a disability. Thus, for example, an accommodation made to assist an employee with a disability in the performance of his or her job must be adequate to enable the individual to perform the essential functions of the relevant position. The accommodation, however, does not have to be the "best" accommodation possible, so long as it is sufficient to meet the job-related needs of the individual being accommodated. Accordingly, an employer would not have to provide an employee disabled by a back impairment with a state-of-the-art mechanical lifting device if it provided the employee with a less expensive or more readily available device that enabled the employee to perform the essential functions of the job. See Senate Report at 35; House Labor Report at 66; see also Carter v. Bennett, 840 F.2d 63 (D.C. Cir. 1988).

Employers are obligated to make reasonable accommodation only to the physical or mental limitations of a qualified individual with a disability that are known to the employer. Thus, an employer would not be expected to accommodate disabilities of which it is unaware. If an employee with a known disability is having difficulty performing his or her job, an employer may inquire whether the employee is in need of a reasonable accommodation. In general, however, it is the responsibility of the individual with a disability to inform the employer that an accommodation is needed. See Senate Report at 34; House Labor Report at 65.

Process of Determining the Appropriate Reasonable Accommodation

Once a qualified individual with a disability has requested provision of a reasonable accommodation, the employer must make a reasonable effort to determine the appropriate accommodation. The process of determining the appropriate reasonable accommodation is an informal, interactive, problem solving technique involving both the employer and the qualified individual with a disability. Although this process is described below in terms of accommodation that enable the individual with a disability to perform the essential functions of the position held or desired, it is equally applicable to accommodations involving the job application process, and to accommodations that enable the individual with a disability to enjoy equal benefits and privileges of employment. See Senate Report at 34–35; House Labor Report at 65–67.

When a qualified individual with a disability has requested a reasonable accommodation to assist in the performance of a job, the employer, using a problem solving approach, should:

(1) Analyze the particular job involved and determine its purpose and essential functions;

(2) Consult with the individual with a disability to ascertain the precise job-related limitations imposed by the individual's disability and how those limitations could be overcome with a reasonable accommodation;

(3) In consultation with the individual to be accommodated, identify potential accommodations and assess the effectiveness each would have in enabling the individual to perform the essential functions of the position; and

(4) Consider the preference of the individual to be accommodated and select and implement the accommodation that is most appropriate for both the employee and the employer.

In many instances, the appropriate reasonable accommodation may be so obvious to either or both the employer and the qualified individual with a disability that it may not be necessary to proceed in this step-by-step fashion. For example, if an employee who uses a wheelchair requests that his or her desk be placed on blocks to elevate the desktop above the arms of the wheelchair and the employer complies, an appropriate accommodation has been requested, identified, and provided without either the employee or employer being aware of having engaged in any sort of "reasonable accommodation process."

However, in some instances neither the individual requesting the accommodation nor the employer can readily identify the appropriate accommodation. For example, the individual needing the accommodation may not know enough about the equipment used by the employer or the exact nature of the work site to suggest an appropriate accommodation. Likewise, the employer may not know enough about the individual's disability or the limitations that disability would impose on the performance of the job to suggest an appropriate accommodation. Under such circumstances, it may be necessary for the employer to initiate a more defined problem solving process, such as the step-by-step process described above, as part of its reasonable effort to identify the appropriate reasonable accommodation.

This process requires the individual assessment of both the particular job at issue, and of the specific physical or mental limitations of the particular individual

318 · Appendix B

in need of reasonable accommodation. With regard to assessment of the job, "individual assessment" means analyzing the actual job duties and determining the true purpose or object of the job. Such an assessment is necessary to ascertain which job functions are the essential functions that an accommodation must enable an individual with a disability to perform.

After assessing the relevant job, the employer, in consultation with the individual requesting the accommodation, should make an assessment of the specific limitations imposed by the disability on the individual's performance of the job's essential functions. This assessment will make it possible to ascertain the precise barrier to the employment opportunity which, in turn, will make it possible to determine the accommodation(s) that could alleviate or remove that barrier.

If consultation with the individual in need of the accommodation still does not reveal potential appropriate accommodations, then the employer, as part of this process, may find that technical assistance is helpful in determining how to accommodate the particular individual in the specific situation. Such assistance could be sought from the Commission, from state or local rehabilitation agencies, or from disability constituent organizations. It should be noted, however, that the failure to obtain or receive technical assistance will not excuse the employer from its reasonable accommodation obligation.

Once potential accommodations have been identified, the employer should assess the effectiveness of each potential accommodation in assisting the individual in need of the accommodation in the performance of the essential functions of the position. If more than one of these accommodations will enable the individual to perform the essential functions, the preference of the individual with a disability should be given primary consideration. However, the employer providing the accommodation has the ultimate discretion to choose between effective accommodations, and may choose the less expensive accommodation or the accommodation that is easier to provide.

Reasonable Accommodation Process Illustrated

The following example illustrates the informal reasonable accommodation process. Suppose a sack handler position requires that the employee pick up fifty pound sacks and carry them from the company loading dock to the storage room, and that a sack handler who is disabled by a back impairment requests a reasonable accommodation. Upon receiving the request, the employer analyzes the sack handler job and determines that the essential function and purpose of the job is not the requirement that the job holder physically lift and carry the sacks, but the requirement that the job holder cause the sack to move from the loading dock to the storage room.

The employer then meets with the sack handler to ascertain precisely the barrier posed by the individual's specific disability to the performance of the job's essential function of relocating the sacks. At this meeting the employer learns that the individual can, in fact, lift the sacks to waist level, but is prevented by his or her disability from carrying the sacks from the loading dock to the storage room. The employer and the individual agree that any of a number of potential accommodations, such as the provision of a dolly, hand truck, or cart, could enable the individual to transport the sacks that he or she has lifted.

Upon further consideration, however, it is determined that the provision of a cart is not a feasible effective option. No carts are currently available at the company, and those that can be purchased by the company are the wrong shape to hold many of the bulky and irregularly shaped sacks that must be moved. Both the dolly and the hand truck, on the other hand, appear to be effective options. Both are readily available to the company, and either will enable the individual to relocate the sacks that he or she has lifted. The sack handler indicates his or her preference for the dolly. In consideration of this expressed preference, and because the employer feels that the dolly will allow the individual to move more sacks at a time and so be more efficient than would a hand truck, the employer ultimately provides the sack handler with a dolly in fulfillment of the obligation to make reasonable accommodation.

Section 1630.9(b)

This provision states that an employer or other covered entity cannot prefer or select a qualified individual without a disability over an equally qualified individual with a disability merely because the individual with a disability will require a reasonable accommodation. In other words, an individual's need for an accommodation cannot enter into the employer's or other covered entity's decision regarding hiring, discharge, promotion, or other similar employment decisions, unless the accommodation would impose an undue hardship on the employer. See House Labor Report at 70.

Section 1630.9(d)

The purpose of this provision is to clarify that an employer or other covered entity may not compel a qualified individual with a disability to accept an accommodation, where that accommodation is neither requested nor needed by the individual. However, if a necessary reasonable accommodation is refused, the individual may not be considered qualified. For example, an individual with a visual impairment that restricts his or her field of vision but who is able to read unaided would not be required to accept a reader as an accommodation. However, if the individual were not able to read unaided and reading was an essential function of the job, the individual would not be qualified for the job if he or she refused a reasonable accommodation that would enable him or her to read. *See* Senate Report at 34; House Labor Report at 65; House Judiciary Report at 71–72.

Section 1630.10 Qualification Standards, Tests, and Other Selection Criteria

The purpose of this provision is to ensure that individuals with disabilities are not excluded from job opportunities unless they are actually unable to do the job. It is to ensure that there is a fit between job criteria and an applicant's (or employee's) actual ability to do the job. Accordingly, job criteria that even unintentionally screen out, or tend to screen out, an individual with disabilities or a class of individuals with disabilities may not be used unless the employer demonstrates that that criteria, as used by the employer, are job-related to the position to which they are being applied and are consistent with business necessity. The concept of "business necessity" has the same meaning as the concept of "business necessity" under section 504 of the Rehabilitation Act of 1973.

Selection criteria that exclude, or tend to exclude, an individual with a disability or a class of individuals with disabilities but do not concern an essential function of the job would not be consistent with business necessity.

It is possible for the use of selection criteria that concern an essential function to be consistent with business necessity. However, selection criteria that concern an essential function may not be used to exclude an individual with a disability if that individual could satisfy the criteria with the provision of a reasonable accommodation, including the adoption of an alternative, less discriminatory criterion. Experience under a similar provision of the regulations implementing section

504 of the Rehabilitation Act indicates that challenges to selection criteria are, in fact, most often resolved by reasonable accommodation. It is therefore anticipated that challenges to selection criteria brought under these regulations will generally be resolved in a like manner.

This provision is applicable to all types of selection criteria, including requirements that an employee not pose a direct threat to self or others, vision or hearing requirements, walking requirements, lifting requirements, and employment tests. See Senate Report at 37–39; House Labor Report at 70–72; House Judiciary Report at 42. As previously noted, however, it is not the intent of these regulations to second guess an employer's business judgment with regard to production standards. (See § 1630.2(n) Essential Functions). Consequently, production standards will generally not be subject to a challenge under this provision.

The Uniform Guidelines on Employee Selection Procedures (UGESP) 29 CFR part 1607 do not apply to the Rehabilitation Act and are similarly inapplicable to these regulations.

Section 1630.11 Administration of Tests

The intent of this provision is to further emphasize that individuals with disabilities are not to be excluded from jobs that they can actually perform merely because a disability prevents them from taking a test, or negatively influences the results of a test, that is prerequisite to the job. Read together with the reasonable accommodation requirement of §1630.9, this provision requires that employment tests be administered to eligible applicants or employees with disabilities that impair sensory, manual, or speaking skills in formats that do not require the use of the impaired skill.

The employer or other covered entity is only required to provide such reasonable accommodation if it knows that the individual is disabled and that the disability impairs sensory, manual or speaking skills. Thus, for example, it would be unlawful to administer a written employment test to an individual that the employer knows is disabled with dyslexia and unable to read. In such a case, as a reasonable accommodation and in accordance with this provision, an alternative oral test should be administered to that individual. By the same token, a written test may need to be substituted for an oral test if the applicant taking the test is an individual with a disability that impairs speaking skills or impairs the processing of auditory information.

Other alternative or accessible test modes or formats include the administration of tests in large print or braille, or via a reader or sign interpreter. An employer may also be required, as a reasonable accommodation, to allow more time to complete the test. In addition, the employer's obligation to make reasonable accommodation extends to ensuring that the test site is accessible. See Senate Report at 37–38; House Labor Report at 70–72; House Judiciary Report at 42; *see also Stutts* v. *Freeman,* 694 F.2d 886 (11th Cir. 1983); *Crane* v. *Dole,* 617 F. Supp. 158 (D.D.C. 1985).

The provision does not require that an employer offer every applicant his or her choice of test format. Rather, this provision only requires that an employer provide, upon request, alternative, accessible tests to individuals with disabilities that impair sensory, manual, or speaking skills needed to take the test.

This provision does not apply to employment tests that require the use of sensory, manual, or speaking skills where the tests are intended to measure those skills. Thus, an employer could require that an applicant with dyslexia take a written test for a particular position if the ability to read is essential to the effective performance of the job. However, the results of such a test could not be used to exclude an individual with a disability unless the skill was necessary to perform an essential function of the position and no reasonable accommodation was available to enable the individual to perform that function, or the necessary accommodation would impose an undue hardship.

Section 1630.13 Prohibited Medical Examinations and Inquiries

Section 1630.13(a) Pre-employment Examination or Inquiry

This provision makes clear that an employer cannot inquire as to whether an individual has a disability at the pre-offer stage of the selection process. Employers may ask questions that relate to the applicant's ability to perform job-related functions. However, these questions should not be phrased in terms of disability. An employer, for example, may ask whether the applicant has a driver's license, if driving is a job function, but may not ask whether the applicant has a visual disability. Employers may ask about an applicant's ability to perform both essential and marginal job functions. Employer's, though, may not refuse to hire an applicant with a disability because the applicant's disability prevents him or her from performing marginal functions. See Senate Report at 39; House Labor Report at 72–73; House Judiciary Report at 42–43.

Section 1630.13(b) Examination or Inquiry of Employees

The purpose of this provision is to prevent the administration to employees of medical tests or inquiries that do not serve a legitimate business purpose. For example, if an employee suddenly starts to use increased amounts of sick leave or starts to appear sickly, an employer could not require that employee to be tested for AIDS, HIV infection, or cancer unless the employer can demonstrate that each testing is job-related and consistent with business necessity. See Senate Report at 39; House Labor Report at 75; House Judiciary Report at 44.

This provision does not prohibit employers from making inquiries or requiring medical examinations (fitness for duty exams) when there is a need to determine whether an employee is still able to perform the essential functions of his or her job. Nor does this provision prohibit periodic physicals to determine fitness for duty if such physicals are required by medical standards or requirements established by Federal, state, or local law that are consistent with the ADA (or in the case of a federal standard, with section 504 of the Rehabilitation Act) in that they are job-related and consistent with business necessity. Such standards may include federal safety regulations that regulate bus and truck driver qualifications, as well as laws establishing medical requirements for pilots or other air transportation personnel. These standards also include health standards promulgated pursuant to the Occupational Safety and Health Act of 1970, the Federal Coal Mine Health and Safety Act of 1969, or other similar statutes that require that employees exposed to certain toxic and hazardous substances be medically monitored at specific intervals. See House Labor Report at 74–75.

Section 1630.14 Medical Examinations and Inquiries Specifically Permitted

Section 1630.14(a) Pre-employment Inquiry

Employers are permitted to make pre-employment inquiries into the ability of an applicant to perform job-related functions. This inquiry must be narrowly tailored. The employer may describe or demonstrate that job function and inquire whether or not the applicant can perform that function with or without accommodation.

For example, an employer may explain that the job requires assembling small parts and ask if the individual will be able to perform that function. See Senate Report at 39; House Labor Report at 73; House Judiciary Report at 43.

On the other hand, however, an employer may not use an application form that lists a number of potentially disabling impairments and ask the applicant to check any of the impairments he or she may have. Nor may an employer ask how a particular individual became disabled or the prognosis of the individual's disability. The employer is also prohibited from asking how often the individual will require leave for treatment or use leave as a result of incapacitation because of the disability. However, the employer may state the attendance requirements of the job and inquire whether the applicant can meet them.

Section 1630.14(b) Employment Entrance Examination

An employer is permitted to require post-offer medical examinations before the employee actually starts working. The employer may condition the offer of employment on the results of the examination, provided that all entering employees in the same job category are subjected to such an examination, regardless of disability, and that the confidentiality requirements specified in the regulations are met.

This provision recognizes that in many industries, such as air transportation or construction, applicants for certain positions are chosen on the basis of many factors including relevant physical and psychological criteria, some of which may be identified as a result of post-offer medical examinations given prior to entry on duty. Only those employees who meet the employer's relevant physical and psychological criteria for the job will be qualified to receive confirmed offers of employment and begin working.

Medical examinations permitted by this section are not required to be job-related and consistent with business necessity. However, if an employer withdraws an offer of employment because the medical examination reveals that the employee does not satisfy certain employment criteria, either the exclusionary criteria must not screen out or tend to screen out an individual with disabilities or a class of individuals with disabilities, or they must be job-related and consistent with business necessity. As part of the showing that an exclusionary criteria is job-related and consistent with business necessity, the employer must also demonstrate that there is no reasonable accommodation that will enable the individual with a disability to perform the essential functions of the job. See Conference Report at 59–60; Senate Report at 39; House Labor Report at 73–74; House Judiciary Report at 43.

As an example, suppose an employer makes a conditional offer of employment to an applicant, and it is an essential function of the job that the incumbent be available to work every day for the next three months. An employment entrance examination then reveals that the applicant has a disabling impairment that, according to reasonable medical judgment that relies on the most current medical knowledge, will require treatment that will render the applicant unable to work for a portion of the three month period. Under these circumstances, the employer would be able to withdraw the employment offer without violating these regulations.

The information obtained in the course of a permitted entrance examination is to be treated as a confidential medical record and may only be used for the limited purposes specified in the regulation at § 1630.14(b) (2) and (3).

Section 1630.14(c) Other Acceptable Examinations and Inquiries

The regulations permit voluntary medical examinations, including voluntary medical histories, as part of the employee health programs. These programs often include, for example, medical screening for high blood pressure, weight control counseling, and cancer detection. Voluntary activities, such as blood pressure monitoring and the administering of prescription drugs, such as insulin, are also permitted. It should be noted, however, that the medical records developed in the course of such activities must be maintained in the confidential manner required by this regulation and must not be used for any purpose in violation of these regulations, such as limiting health insurance eligibility. House Labor Report at 75; House Judiciary Report at 43–44.

Section 1630.15 Defenses

The section on defenses in the regulation is not intended to be exhaustive. However, it is intended to inform employers of some of the potential defenses available to a charge of discrimination under the ADA.

Section 1630.15(a) Disparate Treatment Defenses

The "traditional" defense to a charge of disparate treatment under Title VII, as expressed in *McDonnell Douglas Corp.* v. *Green*, 411 U.S. 792 (1973), *Texas Department of Community Affairs* v. *Burdine*, 450 U.S. 248 (1981), and their progeny, is applicable to charges of disparate treatment brought under the ADA. See *Prewitt* v. *U.S. Postal Service*, 662 F.2d 292 (5th Cir. 1981). Disparate treatment means, with respect to Title I of the ADA, that an individual was treated differently on the basis of his or her disability. For example, disparate treatment has occurred where an employer excludes an employee with a severe facial disfigurement from staff meetings because the employer does not like to look at the employee. The individual is being treated differently because of the employer's attitude towards his or her perceived disability.

Disparate treatment has also occurred where an employer has a policy of not hiring individuals with AIDS regardless of the individuals' qualifications. The crux of the defense to this type of charge is that the individual was treated differently not because of his or her disability but for a legitimate nondiscriminatory reason such as poor performance unrelated to the individual's disability. The defense is rebutted if the alleged legitimate nondiscriminatory reason is shown to be pretextual.

Section 1630.15(b) and (c) Disparate Impact Defenses

Disparate impact means, with respect to title I of the ADA, that uniformly applied criteria have an adverse impact on an individual with a disability or a disproportionately negative impact on a class of individuals with disabilities. Section 1630.15(b) clarifies that an employer may use selection criteria that have such a disparate impact, *i.e.*, that screen out or tend to screen out an individual with a disability or a class of individuals with disabilities only when they are job related and consistent with business necessity.

For example, an employer interviews two candidates for a position, one of whom is blind. Both are equally qualified. The employer decides that while it is not essential to the job it would be convenient to have an employee who has a driver's license and so could occasionally be asked to run errands by car. The employer hires the individual who is sighted because this individual has a driver's license. This is an example of a uniformly applied criterion, having a driver's license, that screens out an individual who has a disability that makes it impossible to obtain a driver's permit. The employer would, thus, have to show that this criterion is job-related and consistent with business necessity. See House Labor Report at 55.

However, even if the criterion is job-related and consistent with business necessity, an employer could not exclude an individual with a disability if there is a less discriminatory alternative criterion that meets the legitimate needs of the business, or if the criterion could be met or job performance accomplished with a reasonable accommodation. For example, suppose an employer requires as part of its application process an interview that is job-related and consistent with business necessity. The employer would not be able to refuse to hire a hearing impaired applicant because he or she could not be interviewed. This is so because an interpreter could be provided as a reasonable accommodation that would allow the individual to be interviewed, and thus satisfy the selection criteria.

Section 1630.15(c) clarifies that there may be uniformly applied standards, criteria and policies not relating to selection that may also screen out or tend to screen out an individual with a disability or a class of individuals with disabilities. Like selection criteria that have a disparate impact, non-selection criteria having such an impact may also have to be job-related and consistent with business necessity, subject to consideration of reasonable accommodation.

It should be noted, however, that some uniformly applied employment policies or practices, such as leave policies, are not subject to challenge under the adverse impact theory. "No-leave" policies (e.g., no leave during the first six months of employment) are likewise not subject to challenge under the adverse impact theory. However, an employer, in spite of its "no-leave" policy, may, in appropriate circumstances, have to consider the provision of leave to an employee with a disability as a reasonable accommodation, unless the provision of leave would impose an undue hardship. See discussion at § 1630.5 Limiting, Segregating and Classifying, and § 1630.10 Qualification Standards, Tests, and Other Selection Criteria.

Section 1630.15(d) Defense to Not Making Reasonable Accommodation

An employer or other covered entity alleged to have discriminated because it did not make reasonable accommodation, as required by this regulation, may offer as a defense that it would have been an undue hardship to make the required accommodation.

It should be noted, however, that an employer cannot simply assert that a needed accommodation will cause it undue hardship, as defined in §1630.2(p), and thereupon be relieved of the duty to provide accommodation. Rather, an employer will have to present evidence and demonstrate that the accommodation will, in fact, cause it undue hardship. Whether a particular accommodation will impose an undue hardship for a particular employer is determined on a case-by-case basis. Consequently, an accommodation that poses an undue hardship for one employer at a particular time may not pose an undue hardship for another employer, or even for the same employer at another time. See House Judiciary Report at 42.

The concept of undue hardship that has evolved under section 504 of the Rehabilitation Act and is embodied in these regulations is unlike the "undue hardship" defense associated with the provision of religious accommodation under title VII of the Civil Rights Act of 1964. To demonstrate undue hardship pursuant to the ADA, an employer must show substantially more difficulty or expense than would be needed to satisfy the "de minimis" title VII standard of undue hardship. For example, to demonstrate that the cost of an accommodation poses an undue hardship, an employer would have to show that the cost is undue as compared to the employer's budget. Simply comparing the cost of the accommodation to the salary of the individual with a disability in need of the accommodation will not suffice. Moreover, even if it is determined that the cost of an accommodation would unduly burden an employer, the employer cannot avoid making the accommodation if the individual with a disability can arrange to cover that portion of the cost that rises to the undue hardship level, or can otherwise arrange to provide the accommodation. Under such circumstances, the necessary accommodation would no longer pose an undue hardship. See Senate Report at 36; House Labor Report at 68–69; House Judiciary Report at 40–41.

Excessive cost is only one of several possible bases upon which an employer might be able to demonstrate undue hardship. Alternatively, for example, an employer could demonstrate that the provision of a particular accommodation would be unduly disruptive to its other employees or to the functioning of its business. Accordingly, by way of illustration, an employer would likely be able to show undue hardship if the employer could show that the requested accommodation of the upward adjustment of the business' thermostat would result in it becoming unduly hot for its other employees, or for its patrons or customers. The employer would thus not have to provide this accommodation. However, if there were an alternate accommodation that would not result in undue hardship, the employer would have to provide that accommodation. It should be noted, moreover, that the employer would not be able to show undue hardship if the disruption to its employees was the result of those employees' fears or prejudices toward the individual's disability and not the result of the provision of the accommodation.

Section 1630.15(e) Defense—Conflicting Federal Laws and Regulations

There are several Federal laws and regulations that address medical standards and safety requirements. If the alleged discriminatory action was taken in compliance with another Federal law or regulation, the employer may offer its obligation to comply with the conflicting standard as a defense. The employer's defense of a conflicting Federal requirement of regulation may be rebutted by a showing of pretext, or by showing that the Federal standard did not require the discriminatory action, or that there was a less discriminatory means to comply with the statute that would not conflict with these regulations. See House Labor Report at 74.

Section 1630.16 Specific Activities Permitted

Section 1630.16(a) Religious Entities

Religious organizations are not exempt from Title I of the ADA. A religious corporation, association, educational institution, or society may give a preference in employment to individuals of the particular religion, and may require that applicants and employees conform to the religious tenets of the organization. However, a religious organization may not discriminate against an individual who satisfies the permitted religious criteria because that individual is disabled. The religious entity, in other words, is required to consider qualified individuals with disabilities who satisfy the permitted religious criteria on an equal basis with qualified individuals without disabilities who similarly satisfy the religious criteria. See Senate Report at 42; House Labor Report at 76–77; House Judiciary Report at 46.

Section 1630.16(b) Regulation of Alcohol and Drugs

This provision permits employers to establish or comply with certain standards regulating the use of drugs and alcohol in the workplace. It also allows employers to hold alcoholics and persons who engage in the illegal use of drugs to the same performance and conduct standards to which it holds other employees. Individuals disabled by alcoholism are otherwise entitled to the same protections accorded other individuals with disabilities under these regulations. As noted above, individuals currently engaging in the illegal use of drugs are not individuals with disabilities for purposes of these regulations when the employer acts on the basis of such use.

Section 1630.16(c) Drug Testing

This provision reflects Title I's neutrality toward drug testing. Drug tests are neither encouraged nor prohibited. The results of drug tests may be used as a basis for disciplinary action. Drug tests are not considered medical examinations for purposes of these regulations. If the results reveal information about an individual's medical condition beyond whether the individual is currently engaging in the illegal use of drugs, this additional information is to be treated as a confidential medical record. For example, if a test for the illegal use of drugs reveals the presence of a controlled substance that has been lawfully prescribed for a particular medical condition, this information is to be treated as a confidential medical record. See House Labor Report at 79; House Judiciary Report at 47.

Section 1630.16(e) Infectious and Communicable Diseases; Food Handling Jobs

This provision addressing food handling jobs applies the "direct threat" analysis to the particular situation of accommodating individuals with infectious or communicable diseases that are transmitted through the handling of food. The Department of Health and Human Services is to prepare a list of infectious and communicable diseases that are transmitted through the handling of food. If an individual with a disability has one of the listed diseases and works in or applies for a position in food handling, the employer must determine whether there is a reasonable accommodation that will eliminate the risk of transmitting the disease through the handling of food. If there is an accommodation that will not pose an undue hardship, and that will prevent the transmission of the disease through the handling of food, the employer must provide the accommodation to the individual. The employer, under these circumstances, would not be permitted to discriminate against the individual because of the need to provide the reasonable accommodation and would be required to maintain the individual in the food handling job.

If no such reasonable accommodation is possible, the employer may refuse to assign, or to continue to assign the individual to a position involving food handling. This means that if such an individual is an applicant for a food handling position the employer is not required to hire the individual. However, if the individual is a current employee, the employer would be required to consider the accommodation of reassignment to a vacant position not involving food handling for which the individual is qualified. Conference Report at 61–63. (See § 1630.2(r) Direct Threat.)

Section 1630.16(f) Health Insurance, Life Insurance, and Other Benefit Plans

This provision is a limited exemption that is only applicable to those who establish, sponsor, observe or administer benefit plans, such as health and life insurance plans. It does not apply to those who establish, sponsor, observe or administer plans not involving benefits, such as liability insurance plans.

The purpose of this provision is to permit the development and administration of benefit plans in accordance with accepted principles of risk assessment. This provision is not intended to disrupt the current regulatory structure for self-insured employers. These employers may establish, sponsor, observe, or administer the terms of a bona fide benefit plan not subject to state laws that regulate insurance.

This provision is also not intended to disrupt the current nature of insurance underwriting, or current insurance industry practices in sales, underwriting, pricing, administrative and other services, claims and similar insurance related activities based on classification of risks as regulated by the States.

The activities permitted by this provision do not violate these regulations even if they result in limitations on individuals with disabilities, provided that these activities are not used as a subterfuge to evade the purposes of these regulations. Whether or not these activities are being used as a subterfuge is to be determined without regard to the date the insurance plan or employee benefit plan was adopted.

However, an employer or other covered entity cannot deny a qualified individual with a disability equal access to insurance or subject a qualified individual with a disability to different terms or conditions of insurance based on disability alone, if the disability does not pose increased risks. This regulation requires that decisions not based on risk classification be made in conformity with non-discrimination requirements. See Senate Report at 84–86; House Labor Report at 136–138; House Judiciary Report at 70–71. See the discussion of § 1630.5 Limiting, Segregating and Classifying.

[FR Doc. 91–4638 Filed 2–27–91; 8:45 am]

Document 3

Checklist for Determining Whether an Employer Is a Federal Government Contractor

1. The company has 50 or more employees; *and*
   a. has a contract of $50,000 or more; *or*
   b. has government bills of lading which in any twelve-month period total or can reasonably be expected to total $50,000 or more; *or*
   c. the company serves as a depository of government funds in any amount; *or*
   d. the company is a financial institution which is an issuing and paying agent for U.S. Savings Bonds and Savings Notes in any amount.

2. The foregoing requirements are also applicable to *subcontractors* of covered companies.

3. The regulations define government contract as:
   . . . any agreement or modification thereof between any contracting agency and any person for the furnishing of supplies or service or for the use of real or personal property, *including lease arrangements*. The term "services" as used in this section includes, but is not limited to the following services: utility, construction, transportation, research, insurance, and fund depository. (Emphasis supplied.)

4. The $50,000/50 employee standard would apply to any of the foregoing agreements.

Document 4

Section 503 of the Vocational Rehabilitation Act of 1973

EMPLOYMENT UNDER FEDERAL CONTRACTS

Sec. 503. (a) Any contract in excess of $2,500 entered into by any Federal department or agency for the procurement of personal property and nonpersonal services (including construction) for the United States shall contain a provision requiring that, in employing persons to carry out such contract the party contracting with the United States shall take affirmative action to employ and advance in employment qualified handicapped individuals as defined in section 7(8) of this title. The provisions of this section shall apply to any subcontract in excess of $2,500 entered into by a prime contractor in carrying out any contract for the procurement of personal property and nonpersonal services (including construction) for the United States. The President shall implement the provisions of this section by promulgating regulations within ninety days after September 26, 1973. [As last amended by P.L. 99–506, effective October 21, 1986.]

(b) If any handicapped individual believes any contractor has failed or refuses to comply with the provisions of his contract with the United States, relating to employment of handicapped individuals, such individual may file a complaint with the Department of Labor. The Department shall promptly investigate such complaint and shall take such action thereon as the facts and circumstances warrant, consistent with the terms of such contract and the laws and regulations applicable thereto.

(c) The requirements of this section may be waived, in whole in part, by the President with respect to a particular contract or subcontract, in accordance with guidelines set forth in regulations which he shall prescribe, when he determines that special circumstances in the national interest so require and states in writing his reasons for such determination. (29 U.S.C. §793)

Document 5

Section 504 of the Vocational Rehabilitation Act of 1973

NONDISCRIMINATION UNDER FEDERAL GRANTS AND PROGRAMS
Sec.504. No otherwise qualified handicapped individual in the United States as defined in section 7(8), shall solely by reason of his handicap, be excluded from the participation in, be denied the benefits of, or be subjected to discrimination under any program or activity conducted by any Executive agency or by the United States Postal Service. The head of each such agency shall promulgate such regulations as may be necessary to carry out the amendments to this section made by the Rehabilitation, Comprehensive Services, and Developmental Disabilities Act of 1978. Copies of any proposed regulation shall be submitted to appropriate authorizing committees of the Congress, and such regulation may take effect no earlier than the thirtieth day after the date on which such regulation is so submitted to such committiees. (29 U.S.C. §794) [As last amended by P.L. 99–506, effective Oct. 21, 1986]

Document 6
OFCCP: Directive On AIDS

1. *SUBJECT*: Acquired Immune Deficiency Syndrome (AIDS) and Related Conditions as Protected Handicaps Under Section 503 of the Rehabilitation Act of 1973, as amended

2. *PURPOSE*: To issue Appendix 6D to Chapter 6 (Complaint Investigations) of the Federal Contract Compliance Manual

3. *BACKGROUND*: Since the beginning of the AIDS epidemic it has been unclear whether AIDS and related conditions may be considered protected handicaps under Section 503 of the Rehabilitation Act of 1973, as amended. With the issuance of Appendix 6D to FCCM Chapter 6, the Office of Federal Contract Compliance Programs (OFCCP) established its policy on the issue. In addition, Appendix 6D sets out guidelines for processing and investigating complaints filed by or on behalf of persons with AIDS and related conditions, and provides accurate information on which EOSs may rely in processing such complaints.

As time permits, amendments to the FCCM chapters will be made to provide appropriate cross references to Appendix 6D.

4. *POLICY*: It is the policy of OFCCP that all conditions related to human immunodeficiency virus (HIV or the AIDS virus) infection—AIDS, ARC, and asymptomatic HIV infection—are covered handicapping conditions under Section 503 of the Rehabilitation Act of 1973, provided that the individual's condition does not pose a direct threat to the health or safety of others or prevent successful job performance. The attached Appendix 6D contains detailed guidelines and instructions on processing complaints filed by or on behalf of persons with AIDS or related conditions.

5. *INSTRUCTIONS*: File Appendix 6D after Appendix 6C and before the Index to Chapter 6 (Complaint Investigations) of the FCCM.

6. *DISTRIBUTION*: A, B, C

7. *EXPIRATION DATE*: This Notice expires after filing the Appendix in the chapter and may be discarded.

/s/Fred W. Alvarez
Assistant Secretary for Employment Standards
Date: 12-23-88

Appendix D

1. ACQUIRED IMMUNE DEFICIENCY SYNDROME (AIDS) AND RELATED CONDITIONS AS PROTECTED HANDICAPS UNDER SECTION 503 OF THE REHABILITATION ACT OF 1973, AS AMENDED.

2. This appendix establishes policies under Section 503 of the Rehabilitation Act of 1973 concerning AIDS and related conditions and guidelines for processing and investigating complaints filed by or on behalf of persons with AIDS and related conditions, and provides accurate information on which compliance personnel may rely in processing such complaints.

3. BACKGROUND:

A. *Medical.*[1] AIDS is primarily a disease of the body's immune system, which causes the system's collapse, and consequently, renders the afflicted individual vulnerable to many infections and cancers. AIDS results from infection by the human immunodeficiency virus (HIV or the AIDS virus). The virus cannot be transmitted through casual interpersonal contact, but only through sexual contact with infected persons, the introduction of infected blood into the bloodstream (e.g., by the sharing of syringes and needles), or from an infected mother to her infant during the birth process (or possibly by breast-feeding). Currently no cure for AIDS is known.

AIDS is the most severe form of a progressive immunologic compromise caused by HIV. The spectrum of health effects associated with HIV infection is divided generally into three categories for purposes of monitoring the progression of disease: AIDS itself, AIDS-related complex (ARC), and "asymptomatic" infection.[2] ARC refers to a specific set of clinical signs and symptoms related to HIV infection but which do not fully meet the diagnostic criteria for AIDS. "Asymptomatic" HIV infection refers to infection which is currently unaccompanied by overt signs or symptoms of related disease. All three will be collectively referred to herein as "HIV-related conditions."

B. *The Rehabilitation Act.*[3]

1. *Statutory Requirements.* Section 503 of the Rehabilitation Act (29 U.S.C. §793) together with its implementing regulations (41 CFR Part 60–741) requires Government contractors and subcontractors to take affirmative action to employ, and to refrain from discriminating against, qualified handicapped persons. The Act protects "individuals with handicaps," defined as "any person who (i) has a physical or mental impairment which substantially limits one or more of such person's major life activities, (ii) has a record of such an impairment, or (iii) is regarded as having such an impairment." 29 U.S.C. §706(8)(B).[4]

In 1988, the Rehabilitation Act was amended by the Civil Rights Restoration Act to clarify the application of the definition of "individual with handicaps" with respect to contagious diseases and infection. The amendment (which will be referred to herein as the "contagious disease" amendment) provides (at 29 U.S.C. §706(8)(C) that the term "individual with handicaps" does not include an individual who has a currently contagious disease of infection and who, by reason of such disease or infection, would constitute a direct threat to the health or safety of other individuals or who, by reason of the currently contagious disease or infection, is unable to perform the duties of the job.

2. *The Supreme Court Decision in Arline.* Prior to the passage of the contagious disease amendment discussed above, the Supreme Court held in *School Board of Nassau County* v. *Arline*, 107 S. Ct. 1123 (1987), that a person with a contagious disease may be deemed a protected handicapped person under Section 504 of the Rehabilitation Act. The Court also held that in order to determine whether a person handicapped by a contagious disease is qualified to perform a particular job, an individualized inquiry must generally be made concerning the specific risk of contagion at issue. However, the Court declined to decide the questions whether an asymptomatic carrier of a contagious disease such as AIDS could be considered physically impaired, or whether he/she could be considered handicapped by virtue of his/her contagiousness. The contagious disease amendment does not attempt to answer the question either; rather, it simply adopts the "qualified" standard set out in *Arline*.

3. *The Department of Justice Opinion Regarding HIV Infection.* On October 6, 1988, the United States Department of Justice (DOJ), Office of Legal

Counsel, issued an Opinion regarding the application of Section 504 of the Rehabilitation Act to HIV-infected individuals. Briefly stated, the Opinion concluded that persons with symptomatic or asymptomatic HIV-infection are substantially limited in their major life activities, and may be deemed protected "individuals with handicaps," provided that (consistent with both *Arline* and the contagious disease amendment) their HIV infection neither prevents them from performing the duties of the job nor poses a direct threat to the health and safety of others.

4. POLICY:
   A. OFCCP finds that all HIV-related conditions—AIDS, ARC and asymptomatic HIV infection—are substantially limiting impairments, and should be treated as covered handicapping conditions under Section 503 of the Rehabilitation Act, provided that the individual's condition does not pose a direct threat to the health or safety of others or prevent successful job performance.
   B. OFCCP will accept, process and investigate complaints alleging handicap discrimination based on all HIV-related conditions.
   C. In resolving Section 503 issues involving discrimination based on HIV-related conditions, OFCCP will follow the 1988 Rehabilitation Act amendment relating to the coverage of contagious diseases, the *Arline* decision and other appropriate Rehabilitation Act case law, and the 1988 Department of Justice Opinion regarding HIV infection.
   D. Recognizing the potentially urgent circumstances facing complainants who allege discrimination based on HIV-related conditions, until further notice; all offices are to expedite the processing of these complaints by assigning them for investigation before all other pending complaints on which investigations have not yet been initiated.
   E. All offices shall promptly notify the National Office of all complaints alleging a violation based on an HIV-related condition.

5. INVESTIGATIVE GUIDELINES:[5]
   In order to establish that a person complaining of handicap discrimination based on an HIV-related condition is an individual with handicaps (and thus covered by Section 503), it is necessary to show (1) that the person had a substantially limiting impairment, and (2) that the person's condition did not pose a direct health or safety threat or prevent successful job performance. The following subsections address each of these elements and detail specific factual material which should be sought during the course of the investigation.
   A. *Substantially Limiting Impairment.* As is set forth in Section 4.A. above, OFCCP's policy is that all HIV-related conditions are substantially limiting impairments. Therefore, under the policy this element normally would be satisfied by facts showing that the alleged discriminatee had (or had a record of, or was regarded as having) an HIV-related condition.
   However, in order to develop a complete factual record (which may be needed for litigation or other future activity), it is important for the EOS to gather all factual and medical information relating to the degree of the individual's impairment and the extent to which the impairment limited major life activities. A complete factual record may be particularly important with respect to asymptomatic HIV infection, inasmuch as only a small number of court decisions have considered whether asymptomatic infection is a substantially limiting impairment.
   In this regard, the third clause of the definition of "individual with handicaps" (the "regarded as" clause) might be particularly significant in establishing that the impairment (i.e., HIV-realted condition) was substantially limiting. For instance,

a substantial limitation might be established by showing that the adverse decision was based on the contractor's belief (whether accurate or not) that the individual posed a risk of infection to others. In such a case, the contractor, in essence, "regarded" the individual's impairment, HIV infection, as preventing safe interaction with coworkers, customers and/or the public. Stated alternatively, the contractor's perception or attitude was that the individual's impairment restricted his major life activities of "employment" and "socialization."

Moreover, protection for persons with asymptomatic infection might be established under the "regarded as" clause by showing that the contractor's adverse action was based on the perception that the individual had AIDS (or ARC). Such a misunderstanding might occur because of, for instance, a lack of sophistication regarding HIV-related pathology. In equating asymptomatic HIV infection with AIDS (or ARC), the contractor "regarded" the individual as having a substantially limiting impairment.

Alternatively, it might be shown that the contractor viewed the individual as an "AIDS risk," and denied him/her an employment opportunity based on concern regarding future debilitation. In this regard, the EOS should be mindful that the Federal Centers for Disease Control (CDC) has stated that certain groups bear an increased risk of HIV infection. These include homosexual and bisexual men, past and present intravenous drug abusers, and the sexual partners of persons in these groups. Because of the risk status these groups bear, they may be prime targets for being regarded as handicapped by HIV infection (irrespective of whether they are actually infected).

Thus, when investigating the existence of a substantially limiting impairment the EOS should attempt to establish facts relating to the following:

1. The individual's medical condition (at the time the alleged discrimination occurred), including:

    a. the results of any tests for HIV infection;

    b. medical diagnoses, and related medical reports;

    c. any medical restrictions placed on the individual or recommended by his/her physician or other health authority;

    d. any debilitation or other symptoms (such as skin lesions associated with Kaposi's sarcoma, swollen lymph glands, fatigue or weight loss) being experienced by the individual.

2. Employer reactions to the individual's condition, including:

    a. whether the individual has been (allegedly due to an HIV-related condition) denied employment or promotion opportunities other than the one now complained of, and if so, all pertinent facts:

    b. information (including employer and third party statements) indicating that the employer regarding the individual as physically unable to perform the job, as having a condition more severe than the condition the individual actually had, as posing a risk of contagion, or as posing a risk of future infection and/or debilitation.

B. *Health and Safety/Successful Job Performance*. Under the contagious disease amendment to the Rehabilitation Act (see Section 3.B.1. and Attachment B, part II), persons with HIV-related conditions will be deemed not to be individuals with handicaps if their condition—not withstanding the contractor's reasonable accommodation efforts—poses a health or safety threat to others or prevents successful job performance. As discussed below, *Arline* (and other Rehabilitation Act case law) generally requires individual determinations based on reasonable medical judgments. Accordingly, a contractor may not use an HIV antibody test (see Attachment A) or other job qualification requirement which tends to screen out qualified persons who are handicapped with HIV-related conditions, unless the contractor can demonstrate that the requirement is related to the particular job at issue and is consistent with business necessity and safe performance of the job. See 41 CFR 60–741.6(c)(2).

An individual who would pose a health or safety threat or who would be unable to successfully perform the job because of factors involving HIV-related debilitation, would not be entitled to protection. One key factor is the precise nature and severity of the debilitation from which the individual suffered, if any. A third key factor is the contractor's ability (and actual efforts) to make reasonable accommodations to assist the individual in successfully performing the job in issue. Appropriate accommodations might include restructuring job duties, modifying work schedules and permitting advance sick leave. Depending on the nature of the job and the contractor's operations, and the extent of the individual's debilitation, accommodation might pose an undue hardship, and therefore, would not be required. However, the contractor must demonstrate that accommodation would be an undue hardship. 41 CFR 60–741.6(d).

With respect to issues regarding HIV-related contagion, the EOS should be aware that few, if any, exclusionary employment decisions can be justified on this basis. For example, the CDC has found, based on medical and epidemiologic evidence indicating that the AIDS virus is not transmitted through casual physical contact, that there is no risk of HIV transmission to co-workers, clients or consumers in ordinary employment settings, including, for example, offices, factories, schools, construction sites, and food service establishments.[6] In this regard, a contractor which seeks to justify a particular adverse employment decision on a risk of HIV transmission, should be required to show that, based on reasonable medical judgments, the particular risk of HIV contagion posed a significant threat to the health and safety of others.

Relatedly, the EOS should be aware that the vast majority of the secondary opportunistic infections which result from HIV infection are not transmissible in ordinary work or social settings to persons with normal immune systems. A few of these infections, such as tuberculosis, may be communicable in some settings, however. Accordingly, the contractor is obligated to assess persons who develop such communicable infections under *Arline* on an individualized basis to determine whether they are qualified for the position in issue. With regard to either HIV or a related secondary infection, the contractor must demonstrate that it could not satisfactorily reduce the risk of contagion through some method of reasonable accommodation.

In this connection, it may be appropriate (where medically indicated) for a contractor to obtain periodic physician's reports for the purpose of monitoring an individual's condition and the risk of contagion. Also, it is not uncommon in some workplaces for supervisors and co-workers of persons suspected or known to be HIV-infected to be concerned about a risk of contagion.[7] In such situations (and preferably before a problem situation arises), contractors should consider providing both ongoing training for supervisors and managers regarding medical and personnel issues related to AIDS in the workplace, and general educational and counseling programs to allay employee concerns.

Thus, when investigating the health and safety/successful job performance element of the definition, the EOS should attempt to establish facts relating to the following:

1. he duties of the job, both as the job is formally defined and as the job is actually performed.

2. The extent of the individual's debilitation, if any, and any job duties the individual was unable to perform as a result of the debilitation.

3. The contractor's efforts to accommodate the individual, including any accommodations actually implemented and accommodations considered but rejected.

4. If the contractor's failure to provide accommodation is based upon assertions of undue hardship, the particulars regarding the asserted hardship (e.g., cost to the contractor in relation to the contractor's revenues, degree to which the job would have to be altered to accommodate the individual).

5. If the contractor asserts that the adverse employment decision was based on a risk of HIV transmission:

    a. the medical opinions and other information (including all sources thereof) relied upon by the contractor in reaching that conclusion;

    b. the basis for any conclusion reached by the contractor that reasonable accommodation could not satisfactorily reduce the risk of contagion.

6. Any contractor policies, formal or informal, relating to employment of individuals with HIV-related conditions.

7. Whether, and to what extent, the adverse employment decision was based upon a blanket policy or upon individualized assessment of the person involved.

Once those and other relevant facts have been established, the EOS must determine, applying the principles discussed above, whether the person's condition posed a direct health or safety threat or prevented successful job performance (e.g., was there an unacceptable risk of HIV contagion, and was no accommodation reasonably possible).

Document 7

Letter from Plaintiff Attorney to an Employer, Threatening to File Suit in an AIDS Situation

R. JAMES KELLOGG
——————————— ATTORNEY AT LAW ———————————
840 GOVERNOR NICHOLLS
NEW ORLEANS, LOUISIANA 70116
TELEPHONE (504) 524-2487

CERTIFIED RETURN RECEIPT REQUESTED

Mr. —————
Director of Human Services
————— Medical Center
————— Louisiana

Re:

Dear Mr. ————— :

I represent ————— concerning the termination of his employment with the ————— Medical Center. Please be advised, in accordance with the Louisiana Civil Rights for Handicapped Persons Act, R.S. 40:2251, et seq., that —————

intends to pursue court action against you in thirty days if we are unable to resolve this dispute. The details of the discrimination are as follows:

Mr. ————— was employed as a staff Licensed Practical Nurse with ————— Medical Center from June, 1978 to April, 1986. In late March, 1986, Mr. ————— 's friend and roommate was admitted to the ————— Medical Center. Before he was transferred to a hospital in New Orleans as his condition worsened, Mr. ————— 's friend was diagnosed as having Acquired Immune Deficiency Syndrome (AIDS).

On April 10, Mr. ————— met with ————— , Infection Control Nurse for the Medical Center, at her request. Ms. ————— spoke with him about AIDS and her knowledge that he and his friend were roommates. She instructed him to take a blood test designed to determine if a person has been exposed to the virus which is thought to cause AIDS and give her the results.

On April 11, Ms. ————— called Mr. ————— for the results of his test and, after conferring with ————— , the Director of Nursing, told Mr. ————— he could not return to work without the test results.

On each occasion he was scheduled to work between April 10 and April 30, Mr. ————— , on the advice of counsel, telephoned the Medical Center and was on each occasion informed he could not return to work without the test results.

On April 30, Mr. ————— was terminated from employment. He has looked for comparable employment in the ————— and New Orleans area but has not been able to secure such employment.

It is our position that the termination of Mr. ————— is a violation of the Louisiana Civil Rights for Handicapped Persons Act, R.S. 46:2251 et seq., the Federal Rehabilitation Act of 1973, as amended 29 U.S.C. 794 and the Federal Employee Retirement Income Security Act, 29 U.S.C. 1000 et seq. It is our intention to file suit against you and other possible defendants in the United States District

Court for the Eastern District of Louisiana at the expiration of thirty days from your receipt of this letter unless the matter is resolved amicably. The suit will include, but not be limited to, claims for compensatory damages, attorney's fees, costs and any other relief deemed appropriate, including reinstatement.

I call upon you to make a good faith effort, in accordance with R.S. 46:2256, to resolve this dispute before court action is commenced.

I would appreciate hearing from your attorney at the earliest opportunity.

Sincerely,

R. James Kellog

cc:
    Ruth Colker, Louisiana ACLU
    Nan Hunter, Staff Attorney, National ACLU
    Abby Rubenfeld, Lambda Legal Defense and Education Fund, Inc.

Document 8

Federal Court Complaint Alleging Illegal Discrimination Against an Employee in an AIDS Situation

UNITED STATES DISTRICT COURT
EASTERN DISTRICT OF LOUISIANA
Plaintiff _____

—against—
BOARD OF COMMISSIONERS OF HOSPITAL _____

Defendants
COMPLAINT
I. JURISDICTION AND VENUE

1. This Court has jurisdiction of this matter pursuant to 29 U.S.C. 794 (the Rehabilitation Act of 1973 as amended, Section 504), 28 U.S.C. 1331, 28 U.S.C. 1343(3) and the Fourteenth Amendment to the Constitution of the United States for violations under color of state law of rights, privileges and immunities protected under the United States Constitution and federal law (including the above-mentioned statutes and 42 U.S.C. 1983).

2. Pendent jurisdiction is alleged for those matters cognizable under the laws of the state of Louisiana, including R.S. 46:2251 et seq. (Civil Rights for Handicapped Persons), and the Declaration of Rights of the Louisiana Constitution, including, among others, the rights to due process and equal protection of the laws, the right to individual dignity (including the right against discrimination because of physical condition), and the right to privacy.

3. Venue is proper pursuant to 28 U.S.C. 1391(b) and 29 U.S.C. 1132. The cause of action arose in _____ Parish, Louisiana, located in the Eastern District of Louisiana.

II. PARTIES

4. Plaintiff _____ is a resident and citizen of the United States and the State of Louisiana.

5. Defendent BOARD OF COMMISSIONERS OF HOSPITAL SERVICE DISTRICT _____ (the Commissioners) is a governmental entity created under the Louisiana Hospital Service District Law of 1950, as amended. The Commissioners are appointed by the _____ Parish Police Jury pursuant to LSA R.S. 46:1052 and are charged with the governance of the _____ Medical Center, as well as the making, altering and promulgating of rules and regulations governing the conduct of the Medical Center.

6. Defendants are the incumbent members of the Board of Commissioners, and were so at all pertinent times. They are sued in their official capacities.

7. Defendant _____ is the executive director of the _____ Medical Center, appointed by the Board of Commissioners. He is charged with administering the Medical Center and carrying out the policies of the Board. He is sued in his individual and official capacity.

8. Defendants _____ and _____ are, respectively, the Director of

Nursing and the Infection Control Nurse of the _____ Medical Center. They are sued individually and in their official capacity.

9. Defendant _____ is the Director of Human Resources for the Hospital. He is sued in his individual and official capacity.

III. FACTS

10. Plaintiff _____ was employed by the defendant _____ MEDICAL CENTER as a staff Licensed Practical Nurse from June, 1978 to April, 1986.

11. In the latter part of March, 1986, plaintiff's friend and roommate was admitted to _____ Medical Center for what was later diagnosed as a complication of Acquired Immune Deficiency Syndrome (AIDS). The friend remained at that facility until April 10, 1986, when he was transferred to a private hospital in New Orleans because of a rapid deterioration in his health. He died on April 21, 1986 of a secondary infection incident to AIDS.

12. On April 10, 1986, the day his friend was transferred, plaintiff _____ was telephoned at home and asked to come in to meet with Defendant _____ , the Infection Control Nurse for the defendant MEDICAL CENTER.

13. At their meeting, held the same day, defendant _____ spoke with plaintiff about AIDS and her knowledge that plaintiff and his friend were roommates. She asked plaintiff to take blood tests which would determine whether plaintiff had been exposed to the virus believed to cause AIDS.

14. On information and belief, there were at that time two separate tests designed to test exposure to the virus believed to cause AIDS. Those tests are (1) the enzyme-linked immunosorbent assay ("ELISA") and (2) the Western blot assay.

15. Defendant _____ wanted _____ to take both tests mentioned in paragraph 14 above.

16. On the following day, defendant _____ telephoned plaintiff and asked him for the results of his tests. Plaintiff stated that he did not have the results and that, even if he had them, he would not submit them to her.

17. On information and belief, Defendant _____ spoke with Defendant _____ , Director of Nursing, and related to her the substance of her conversation with plaintiff.

18. After speaking with Defendant _____ , Defendant _____ again telephoned plaintiff and instructed him that he would not be allowed to return to work unless he submitted the results of the tests.

19. On April 11, 12 and 13, plaintiff did not work for medical reasons unrelated to AIDS (an infectious cyst). He informed the hospital of his medical problem and was released by his doctor to return to work on April 14.

20. Plaintiff was next scheduled to work April 16. Shortly prior to his scheduled work period, plaintiff was contacted by defendant _____ and again instructed not to return to work until he submitted results of the tests.

21. Plaintiff confirmed with the evening house supervisor that he would not report for work on April 16 and 17. Plaintiff was scheduled off for April 18, 19 and 20.

22. On April 21, plaintiff spoke with the nursing staff coordinator and was again told he would not be allowed to report for work until he submitted the results of the tests. He replied he would not submit the results and was told not to report on April 21 or 22.

23. Plaintiff was scheduled off for April 23 and 24.

24. On April 25, plaintiff was again told by the nursing staff coordinator he would not be allowed to work until he submitted the results of his tests. He was not allowed to work as scheduled April 25, 26 and 27.

25. Plaintiff was scheduled off for April 28 and 29, but was requested to meet with Defendant _____ , Director of Human Resources.

26. Plaintiff met with Defendant _____ on April 29 and was told he was being terminated for failure to report for work April 25, 26 and 27.

27. On information and belief, had plaintiff submitted test results which showed that he had been exposed to the virus believed to cause AIDS, he would have been terminated by the defendants.

28. Plaintiff, since his termination on April 29, has actively pursued employment in _____ and _____ and has attempted to minimize damages.

29. Plaintiff, in his employment with the defendants, because of a previous exposure to hepatitis, employed barrier precautions in all his work-related duties for at least the last five years and continues to do so. The defendants were aware that the plaintiff was employing such precautions.

30. Plaintiff, in his employment with the defendants, performed no invasive procedures.

31. Plaintiff was and remains physically and mentally capable to perform the duties of his job and did not and does not evidence any signs or symptoms of AIDS or AIDS-related illnesses. He offered to continue to perform the duties of his job on a number of occasions, but was not allowed to do so.

32. Plaintiff is in all respects fully qualified for his position with the defendants.

33. On information and belief, the reasons for the termination of plaintiff by defendant _____ were one or more of the following:

(A) A fear that plaintiff had or would develop AIDS or AIDS-related complex (ARC, a less severe form of AIDS).

(B) A perception that plaintiff had been exposed to or infected with the virus that is believed to cause AIDS.

(C) A perception that because of plaintiff's exposure as set forth in (B) above, he was contagious.

(D) Plaintiff's refusal to submit the results of tests to determine whether or not he had been exposed to the virus believed to cause AIDS.

34. On information and belief, plaintiff was regarded by the defendants as having an impairment under 45 C.F.R. 84.3(j)(2)(iv) and 45 C.F.R. Pt. 84, App. A at 311.

35. The MEDICAL CENTER is a recipient of federal financial assistance as defined in the Rehabilitation Act of 1973, as amended and is an employer as defined in the Louisiana Civil Rights for Handicapped Persons Act.

36. The actions of the employees of the Medical Center in refusing to allow plaintiff to return to work and in terminating him were under color of state law and in compliance with the official policies or customs of the Board of Commissioners, executive director _____ and/or other persons with policy-making authority.

37. Plaintiff gave written notice to the defendants of the fact he intended to bring this action at least thirty days prior to the filing of this litigation, but has been unable to resolve this matter with the defendants.

38. The actions of the defendants set forth above were taken in reckless and callous indifference to the plaintiff's federally protected rights.

IV. CAUSES OF ACTION

39. The termination of plaintiff is a violation of the Rehabilitation Act of 1973, as amended, Section 504, 29 U.S.C. 794, because it constituted discrimination against a handicapped person or a person regarded as having a handicap who is otherwise qualified to perform the essential functions of his job as a staff licensed practical nurse.

40. The termination of plaintiff is a violation of the Louisiana Civil Rights for Handicapped Persons Act, R.S. 46:2251, et seq., because it constituted discrimination against a handicapped person or a person regarded as having a handicap who is otherwise qualified to perform the essential functions of his job as a staff licensed practical nurse.

41. The termination of plaintiff by the defendants is a violation of his federal constitutional and statutory rights under color of state law under 42 U.S.C. 1983.

42. The termination of plaintiff by the defendants acting under color of state law is a violation of his rights to due process of law and equal protection of the law under the Fourteenth Amendment to the United States Constitution.

43. The termination of plaintiff by the defendants is a violation of his rights under the Declaration of Rights of the Louisiana Constitution.

V. PRAYER

WHEREFORE, plaintiff prays for the following relief:

1. Compensatory damages dating from April 10, 1986, jointly, severally and *in solido* against the defendants;

2. Punitive damages in an amount to be determined by the court after full hearing on the merits;

3. Declaratory and injunctive relief declaring the actions of the defendants to be illegal and reinstating him in his job with all the rights, privileges and seniority to which he would have been entitled had his service not been illegally interrupted by the defendants;

4. Hospitalization, disability, death and retirement benefits and any other fringe benefits to which plaintiff would have been entitled;

5. Attorney's fees and costs;

6. Interest from the date of judicial demand; and

7. Such other relief as may appear necessary and proper.

Dated: September 29, 1986

Respectfully submitted,

AMERICAN CIVIL LIBERTIES
UNION OF LOUISIANA

LAMBDA LEGAL DEFENSE AND
EDUCATION FUND

THE ADVOCACY CENTER FOR
THE ELDERLY AND DISABLED

BY: _____

, Trial Attorney
for Plaintiffs

Please Serve:

(1) Board of Commissioners of
Medical Center
(2) _____, Executive Director
(3) _____, R.N., Infections Control
(4) _____, R.N., Director of Nursing
(5) _____, Director of Human Services
At:

_____ Medical Center

_____

Louisiana

Document 9

State Court Lawsuit Requesting Damages for Discharge after the Plaintiff was Diagnosed as Having AIDS

CIVIL DISTRICT COURT FOR THE PARISH OF ORLEANS
STATE OF LOUISIANA
DIVISION " " DOCKET NO.
WILLIAM _____
VERSUS
_____ HOTEL

FILED: _____ DEPUTY CLERK: _____
PETITION

The petition of William _____, domiciled in the Parish of Orleans, State of Louisiana, respectfully represents that:

1.

Defendent, _____ Hotel, is a Delaware corporation domiciled and doing business in the Parish of Orleans, State of Louisiana, which has fifteen or more employees.

2.

Defendant is indebted to plaintiff for monetary and equitable relief pursuant to the Louisiana Civil Rights for Handicapped Persons Act, LSA-R.S. 46:2251 et seq., and under Louisiana tort law, LSA-C.C. Article 2315 for the following reasons.

3.

Plaintiff was hired by defendant as a room service waiter on March 26, 1985.

4.

Plaintiff successfully completed his probationary period with defendant.

5.

During the course of his employment with defendant, plaintiff was promoted from the day shift to the night shift, to be effective August 29, 1985.

6.

Room service waiters employed by defendant on the night shift earn, on average, more than room service waiters on the day shift.

7.

At defendant's request, as a condition of continued employment, plaintiff had a medical examination at his expense on or about August 25, 1985 to determine whether he was in good health, and specifically whether he suffered from Acquired Immune Deficiency Syndrome ("A.I.D.S.").

8.

Plaintiff furnished defendant a copy of the results of his medical examination on or about August 27, 1985 which indicated that he was in good health, and had no symptoms of Acquired Immune Deficiency Syndrome ("A.I.D.S.") or A.I.D.S.-related complex.

9.

When plaintiff arrived at work with the defendant on August 29, 1985, the cashiers who were employed by the defendant were wearing white gloves.

10.

On August 29, 1985 when plaintiff asked the cashiers, referred to in paragraph 9, why they were white wearing gloves, they responded "to avoid the plague".

11.

The cashiers referred to in paragraphs 9 and 10 were regular employees of defendant on August 29, 1985.

12.

Plaintiff was terminated from his position by defendant on August 29, 1985.

13.

The reason provided in writing by defendant to the plaintiff for plaintiff's termination was that plaintiff was "unable to function in department under present conditions."

14.

The real reason for plaintiff's termination was that defendant was aware that plaintiff was regarded by defendant's employees as having an impairment which substantially limits his life activities, solely because a friend of plaintiff's had been diagnosed as having Acquired Immune Deficiency Syndrome ("A.I.D.S.").

15.

At the time of his termination, plaintiff was in good medical condition and did not suffer from any physical and physiological disorder or condition which would have impaired his ability to perform any functions of his former job. He did not have A.I.D.S., nor A.I.D.S.-related complex, nor any secondary infections which are indications of A.I.D.S.

16.

Plaintiff was and is qualified to perform all functions of his former job with defendant.

17.

The actions of defendant in tolerating harassment of plaintiff by employees of the defendant due to a perceived handicapping condition and in terminating plaintiff because of his perceived handicap, despite his continued ability to perform the functions of his former job, constitute a violation of the Louisiana Civil Rights for Handicapped Persons Act, LSA-R.S. 46:2251 et seq.

18.

The actions of defendant in knowingly terminating plaintiff and tolerating harrassment of plaintiff by employees of the defendant in violation of his civil rights constitute intentional or reckless infliction of emotional distress in violation of LSA-C.C. Article 2315 and LSA-R.S. 46:2251 et seq. These actions have caused and continue to cause plaintiff psychological injury, embarrassment and humiliation.

19.

Plaintiff itemizes the damages that he has sustained due to defendant's action as follows:

a) Back pay $12,000.00
b) Compensatory damages....................................$ 2,000.00
c) Psychological injury, embarrassment
      and humiliation.......................................$ 5,000.00
d) Punitive damages $38,000.00
TOTAL $57,000.00

20.

Plaintiff has given defendant timely written notice of the discrimination alleged herein, and has made a good faith effort to resolve this dispute, to no avail.

WHEREFORE, plaintiff prays that after due proceedings there be judgment in his favor and against defendant as follows:

a) Declaring that the actions of defendant complained of herein violate plaintiff's rights as secured by the Louisiana Civil Rights for Handicapped Persons Act, LSA-R.S. 46:2251 et seq. and by Louisiana tort law, LSA-C.C. Article 2315;

b) Awarding plaintiff reinstatement with full back pay and benefits, remedial seniority, compensatory damages, damages for psychological injury, embarrassment and humiliation, and punitive damages, totalling $57,000.00 plus compounded interest from date of demand;

c) Awarding plaintiff attorney's fees and costs of litigation;

d) Awarding plaintiff any/and all such further relief as may be necessary and proper.

Respectfully submitted,

Document 10

State Court Complaint by ACLU against Employer for Firing Employee with AIDS

CIVIL DISTRICT COURT FOR THE PARISH OF ORLEANS
STATE OF LOUISIANA
DIVISION " "
BOB _____

versus

CHANNEL _____, INC.

COMPLAINT
I. JURISDICTION

1. This Court has jurisdiction over this matter pursuant to R.S. 46:2256, which provides that a person who is aggrieved under the Civil Rights Act for Handicapped Persons may file a complaint in the appropriate civil district court within one hundred eighty days from the date of discovery of a discriminatory act.

2. Plaintiff_____ was terminated from his employment with Defendant Channel _____, Inc, on July 7, 19___ in Orleans Parish in violation of LSA. R.S. 46:2251 et seq.

II. PARTIES

3. Plaintiff Bob _____ is a citizen of the State of Louisiana of the full age of majority, residing in Orleans Parish. He formerly was employed by the defendants, Channel _____, Inc.

4. Plaintiff_____ has been diagnosed to have Acquired Immune Deficiency Syndrome (A.I.D.S.), which is an impairment which substantially limits his major life activities.

5. Alternatively, plaintiff _____ is regarded by the defendant as having such an impairment.

6. Plaintiff _____ is an otherwise qualified handicapped person who can perform the essential functions of his former employment with the defendant.

7. Defendant Channel _____, Inc. (Defendant Channel) is a Louisiana corporation employing fifteen or more employees.

III. FACTS

8. Plaintiff _____ was hired by defendant Channel _____ in December, 1984 for the position of Accounts Payable clerk.

9. On February 1, 19___, plaintiff _____ was promoted on the basis of merit to the position of Credit Manager.

10. During the month of February, 19___, plaintiff _____ was diagnosed as having A.I.D.S.-related complex (ARC). ARC is a set of symptoms which sometimes is a precursor to A.I.D.S. In other people, ARC apparently does not progress to a full case of A.I.D.S. as defined by the Centers for Disease Control.

11. A.I.D.S. is a medical syndrome which is an acquired immune deficiency. The syndrome is usually defined as the occurrence of secondary infections which are otherwise relatively rare. The two major secondary infections which are indications

of A.I.D.S. are a certain form of pneumonia and Karposi's Sarcoma, a cancer.

12. Over 13,000 cases of A.I.D.S. have been reported by the Centers for Disease Control as of September 1, 19___, using its strict definition. Of these, almost 150 have been reported in Louisiana.

13. Of these reported cases, approximately fifty percent are dead. The longest that a person with A.I.D.S. has survived to date is approximately three years.

14. A.I.D.S. is not transmitted by casual non-intimate contact. Transmission requires sexual contact or the sharing of needles with an infected person. The virus which is believed to cause A.I.D.S., HTLV-III, is extremely labile (fragile) and can be killed with a weak bleach solution. There is not a single known case of transmission of A.I.D.S. by casual contact.

15. In early May, plaintiff _____ approached his supervisor and told him that he had ARC. With _____'s permission, the management approached his doctor concerning the details of the illness.

16. In early June, plaintiff _____ developed pneumocystis pneumonia and was hospitalized. Because of the pneumonia, plaintiff _____ was diagnosed as having A.I.D.S.

17. Plaintiff _____ had a good attendance record at work prior to his development of pneumocystis pneumonia.

18. Upon his hospitalization, plaintiff _____ told the management of Channel _____ that he had been diagnosed as having A.I.D.S. On information and belief, the management discussed plaintiff _____'s condition with personal physician, Dr._____.

19. After his discharge from the hospital, plaintiff _____ was terminated from his position by the defendant on July 7, 19___. Although the reason given for his termination by the management was the handling of four particular accounts, plaintiff _____ had not been assigned two of the accounts and had turned the other two over to a collection agency prior to his hospitalization.

20. On information and belief, the real reason for the termination was plaintiff _____'s handicapping condition, Acquired Immune Deficiency Syndrome.

21. Counsel for plaintiff addressed a letter to the management of defendant on August 2, 19___. _____, Vice President of defendant in a telephone conversation with plaintiff's counsel refused to meet to discuss the situation.

22. Plaintiff has, through counsel, made a good faith effort to resolve the dispute prior to instituting this action.

23. Plaintiff _____ remains willing and able to work at the current time. He can perform the essential functions of his former job in its entirety with no accommodation.

IV. CAUSE OF ACTION

24. The actions of the defendant in terminating the plaintiff because of his handicap despite his continued ability to perform the essential functions of his former job is a violation of the Civil Rights Act for Handicapped Persons, R.S. 46:2251 et seq.

V. EQUITY

25. There is an actual controversy between parties having adverse legal interests. Plaintiff has no adequate remedy at law.

VI. PRAYER

WHEREFORE, plaintiff prays as follows:

1. For judgment in his favor and against the defendant for compensatory damages, attorney's fees and costs, as provided in R.S. 46:2256,

2. For declaratory and injunctive relief to make him whole,

3. For such other relief as may be necessary and proper.

Dated: December 20, 19___.

Respectfully submitted,

American Civil Liberties Union
of Louisiana
840 Gov. Nicholls
New Orleans, LA 70116
(504) 524-2487
Attorney for Plaintiff

PLEASE SERVE:

CHANNEL _____, INC.
through their registered agent
for the service of process:

New Orleans, Louisiana 70112

Document 11

Sample Complaint to be Filed in Federal Court by an Employee with an AIDS Condition Against Union and Employer

IN THE UNITED STATES DISTRICT COURT FOR THE
MIDDLE DISTRICT OF (State)

_____DIVISION

JOHN DOE,
Plaintiff,

vs.

CIVIL ACTION NO. _____

CMS CORPORATION AND RETAIL
AND OFFICE WORKERS UNION
AND ITS LOCAL NO. 14,
Defendants.

COMPLAINT

I.
Jurisdiction

Jurisdiction is based upon the existence of a federal question, Section 301 of the Labor Management Relations Act, 29 U.S.C. §185, and various decisions of the United States Supreme Court setting forth the statutory duty of the Labor Union to represent its members fairly and the opportunity of employees to file suit against their employers and unions for certain violations.

II.
Parties

The plaintiff is a citizen of the State of _____ and resides in _____

_____. He was a member of the Defendant Union for five years prior to his discharge. He was also employed by Defendant Company for five years prior to his termination. Further, he was a member of the bargaining unit covered under a collective bargaining agreement between the Defendant CMS Corporation and the Defendant Union.

The Defendant, CMS Corporation, is a corporation organized and existing in the State of _____, with a place of business located in _____, _____, where it operates a manufacturing facility.

The Defendant Union, with headquarters in Washington, D.C., has a local with an office in _____, _____. It is organized and functioning as a labor union under federal labor laws.

Count I.

(1) Plaintiff, for a period of five years prior to the date this Complaint was filed, was employed by the Defendant Company and a member of the Defendant Union.

(2) In January, 1986, Plaintiff felt ill, was forced to miss work, and sought medical treatment. As a result of a medical examination and various tests, Plaintiff was informed that he was in an early stage of AIDS.

(3) In late January, 1986, Plaintiff returned to work with a letter from his doctor stating that while he was suffering from AIDS, he was physically and mentally able to perform all of the duties of his job, and he was released to return to work. Plaintiff presented this letter to the personnel director, who immediately sent him home. The next day a letter from the personnel manager was hand-delivered to Plaintiff's house, which informed Plaintiff that he was being involuntarily placed on a thirty-day leave of absence. At the expiration of the thirty-day period, he received another letter from the personnel director, certified mail, return receipt requested, stating that he was being terminated because of the risk of infecting other employees.

(4) The day after receiving his letter of termination, Plaintiff went to the office of his local union, where he explained to the receptionist what had happened, showed her the letter of termination, and asked to see the business agent. Despite waiting at the office of the local union for three hours, he was never given the opportunity to speak with either the business agent or any other official of the union. Instead, he was handed a grievance form by the receptionist.

(5) Plaintiff completed the grievance form, as best he could, without any assistance from union officials. The next day he returned to the office of the local union and once again asked to speak to the business agent. Again, the business agent failed to confer with Plaintiff despite Plaintiff waiting for over an hour.

(6) Approximately two weeks later, Plaintiff received another letter from the Company stating that his grievance was being denied because it was incomplete, not in compliance with procedural requirements, and lacking in merit.

(7) Plaintiff made repeated attempts to call the local union office for the purpose of discussing the grievance. His call was not returned until the next day. The union business agent gave an unsatisfactory explanation for the Union's failure to successfully process the grievance.

(8) Plaintiff was terminated by the Company for reasons other than "just cause" as required by the collective bargaining agreement. More specifically, Plaintiff was terminated because he has AIDS, a medical condition over which he has no control. Plaintiff compiled an excellent work record and never violated any rule or policy. The Company is in violation of the collective bargaining agreement in deciding to terminate Plaintiff.

(9) The Union is in breach of its duty to fairly and vigorouly represent Plaintiff and protect his interests. Specifically, Defendant Union and its representatives failed to meet with Plaintiff, failed to properly represent him, failed to assist him in drafting and processing his grievance, and failed to secure his reinstatement with back pay. Instead, through negligence and collusion with the Company, the Union arranged or condoned his termination.

(10) As a proximate result of the improper and illegal actions of both Defendant Company and Defendant Union in violating provisions of the collective bargaining agreement and in failing and refusing to render proper representation to Plaintiff, Plaintiff has suffered irreparable damages, including lost income in the form of wages; lost benefits, including holiday pay; vacation pay; insurance; and pension

contributions; and suffered mental anguish, loss of reputation, and emotional trauma.

Count II.

(1) Plaintiff hereby incorporates by reference all factual allegations contained in all paragraphs contained in Count I of this Complaint.

WHEREFORE, Plaintiff demands judgment against Defendant Company in the amount of $500,000, plus interest, costs, and attorney's fees. Further, Plaintiff requests an Order directing Defendant Company to immediately reinstate Plaintiff to his former position and to instruct all employees to work and cooperate with plaintiff without harassment or ridicule.

Count III.

(1) Plaintiff hereby incorporates by reference all factual allegations contained in all paragraphs contained in Count I of this Complaint.

WHEREFORE, Plaintiff demands judgment against Defendant Union, both the International and its Local No. 14, in the sum of $250,000, plus interest, costs, and attorney's fees. Further, Plaintiff requests an Order compelling Defendant Union to properly, thoroughly, and vigorously represent Plaintiff in any further grievances that may be filed that elate, directly or indirectly, to his AIDS condition.

Respectfully submitted this _____day of March, 19___.

_____

(Name, Address, and Telephone
Number of Attorney for
Plaintiff)

Document 12

Sample Unfair Labor Practice Charge to Be Filed with the NLRB by an Employee with AIDS against His Union

FORM N, RB 508 (8-53)	UNITED STATES OF AMERICA NATIONAL LABOR RELATIONS BOARD **CHARGE AGAINST LABOR ORGANIZATION OR ITS AGENTS**	FORM EXEMPT UNDER 44 U S C 3512

DO NOT WRITE IN THIS SPACE

Case	Date Filed

INSTRUCTIONS: File an original and 3 copies of this charge and an additional copy for each organization, each local, and each individual named in Item 1 with the NLRB Regional Director of the region in which the alleged unfair labor practice occurred or is occurring.

1. LABOR ORGANIZATION OR ITS AGENTS AGAINST WHICH CHARGE IS BROUGHT

a. Name RETAIL AND OFFICE WORKERS UNION, LOCAL NO. 14	b Union Representative to contact John Smith

c Telephone No 123-1000	d Address (street, city, state and ZIP code) 456 A Street, Indianapolis, Indiana

e. The above-named organization(s) or its agents has (have) engaged in and is (are) engaging in unfair labor practices within the meaning of section 8(b), subsection(s) (list subsections) _____ of the National Labor Relations Act. and these unfair labor practices are unfair practices affecting commerce within the meaning of the Act

2 Basis of the Charge (be specific as to facts, names, addresses, plants involved, dates, places, etc.)

The union has arbitrarily and unreasonably failed to process my grievance involving the company's decision to terminate me because I have AIDS. This action and inaction on the part of the union constitutes an unfair labor practice within the meaning of the National Labor Relations Act.

3. Name of Employer John Doe Corporation	4. Telephone No. 789-2000
5. Location of plant involved (street, city, state and ZIP code) #1 Highway, Indianapolis, Indiana	6. Employer representative to contact Jack Jones

7. Type of establishment (factory, mine, wholesaler, etc.) factory	8. Identify principal product or service	9. Number of workers employed

10 Full name of party filing charge

John Johnson

11. Address of party filing charge (street, city, state and ZIP code) 1986 7th Street, Indianapolis, Indiana	12. Telephone No. 444-5555

13. DECLARATION

I declare that I have read the above charge and that the statements therein are true to the best of my knowledge and belief.

By _____
(signature of representative or person making charge)

_____
(title or office, if any)

Address _____

(Telephone No.)   (date)

WILLFUL FALSE STATEMENTS ON THIS CHARGE CAN BE PUNISHED BY FINE AND IMPRISONMENT (U. S. CODE, TITLE 18, SECTION 1001)

Health Care Materials: Policies, Forms, Guidelines, and Checklists

Document 1

Sample Policy: HIV, Patients, and Personnel

ABC HOSPITAL
PATIENT AND PERSONNEL POLICIES
SUBJECT: HIV

A. Purposes:
   1. To protect the health and safety of both patients and employees.
   2. To reduce the exposures of both groups to the HIV virus.
   3. To implement specific rules and procedures to achieve these objectives.

B. Rules and Procedures Regarding Patients:
   1. Inform patients, at the time of admission, that they are required to report any infectious disease they know or suspect they have, including HIV, and to supply informed, written consent to disclosure of any positive condition to the Director for Infection Control and health care personnel who will be directly treating them, as well as their physicians.
   2. Inform patients that they are required to execute a form consenting to various tests, including one for the HIV antibodies (option: for hospitals which desire voluntary as opposed to mandatory testing of patients, use "encouraged" in lieu of "required").
   3. Inform all patients being admitted for invasive procedures that they must, as a condition of their admission, supply informed written consent to test for the HIV virus and to disseminate that test result, if positive, to the Director for Infection Control for the hospital and health care personnel directly involved in their treatment, as well as their physicians.
   4. Inform patients that they are required, as a condition of their admission, to execute a form consenting to testing for HIV antibodies in the event of an employee exposure to their blood or body fluids through an accidental stick, splash, or other means.
   5. If an HIV-positive employee of the hospital directly involved in treatment exposes his or her blood or other body fluids to a particular patient, the patient will be informed of the exposure if the risk of transmission is *identifiable.*
   6. Patients infected with the HIV virus will not be refused treatment because of that status.

C. Rules and Procedures Regarding Employees
   1. All employees are required to report all exposures to the HIV virus to the hospital's Director for Infection Control. Said notice must be in writing, providing date and description, regardless of whether said exposure occurred on or off the job and must be filed within 48 hours of the exposure. Employees who observe an accidental exposure or otherwise become aware that a fellow employee has been exposed are required to report that knowledge to the Director for Infection Control.
   2. All personnel are required to agree to a mandatory testing program for the HIV virus following exposure to HIV, whether said exposure to HIV, whether said exposure occurs on or off the job. The hospital will absorb

all costs for these tests, which normally will be conducted throughout the year following the exposure. All employees in these circumstances must execute a consent form and cooperate with the testing program.

3. Personnel in a position which has an identifiable risk of exposure to the blood and other body fluids of patients during the performance of their duties must submit, as a condition of their employment, to periodic, mandatory testing for the HIV virus. The infection control department, in consultation with medical staff members, will prepare and maintain a list of jobs with an identifiable risk of exposure. These jobs will include all which involve exposure-prone or invasive procedures. (Options: for hospitals which desire voluntary as opposed to mandatory testing, use "are encouraged to submit to voluntary, periodic testing.")

4. Personnel infected with HIV are usually neither restricted in their job duties nor required to disclose their status to patients. However, the hospital will make the decisions concerning practice restriction, duty to disclose, and related issues following an analysis which will include a medical evaluation of the risk of transmission to patients or fellow employees. If said risk is identifiable, then practice restriction, reasonable accommodations, and a transfer to another position will be considered along with other options.

5. Personnel assigned to positions where the risk of exposure to the HIV virus is present must comply with universal precautions and wear all protective gear provided them. Personnel engaged in patient procedures where the risk of transmission is identifiable must take special precautions and wear special gear.

6. Employees are required to treat all reports of patients and fellow employees being HIV positive as confidential.

7. Information on patients being HIV positive will be reported to all personnel directly involved in their treatment with notation on medical records and coded sign on the door; employees privy to this sensitive data must maintain it on a confidential basis and understand that access to the patient's records will be restricted. Breaches of confidentiality and unauthorized releases of medical record data are strictly prohibited.

8. Personnel, including staff physicians, who refuse to treat HIV-positive patients are subject to disciplinary action, including discharge and suspension of privileges.

D. Discipline:
Employees who ignore or violate any of the above rules and procedures are subject to various types of disciplinary penalties, including counseling, reprimand, written warning, suspension, and discharge.

Document 2

Sample Policy: Hospital Personnel Infected with HIV

I. POLICY

Hospital personnel diagnosed with HIV, ARC, or AIDS shall adhere to the protocols established in this policy. The health of the employee and patients is of foremost concern. Individuals infected with HIV are at risk from opportunistic infection, and it may be necessary to restrict contact with patients known to have a communicable disease. Patient contact may be restricted for certain duties or occupations due to risk of transmission to the patient.

II. DEPARTMENTS AFFECTED:

All

III. GUIDELINES:

1. Personnel who are aware they have been diagnosed with HIV, ARC, or AIDS shall report this to the Employee Health Department. This information must be reported as soon as the employee becomes knowledgeable of his or her positive HIV status. Failure to report or delay in reporting violates this policy and subjects the employee to disciplinary action.

2. ALL RECORDS IN EMPLOYEE HEALTH ARE KEPT IN STRICTEST CONFIDENCE AND ARE ONLY AVAILABLE ON A NEED-TO-KNOW BASIS.

3. The medical director of Employee Health will meet with the employee and in joint consultation with the attending physician evaluate the current health status of the employee. At that time, the medical director will also assess the duties of the employee in relation to risk of transmission to patients or co-workers and will counsel the employee concerning precautions which are applicable to the area where employed.

    Personnel known to be infected with HIV present a difficult issue that requires special consideration on an individual basis. Additional precautions or restrictions of duties, when invasive procedures are performed, may be in order. The employee will also be advised of the need for avoiding contact with patients known to be infected with easily communicated diseases. It may be necessary to contact the employee's department director to facilitate reassignment of duties, which may include a nonpatient contact role. Every reasonable effort will be made to accommodate the employee who wishes to continue working in the same job. However, in some situations it may be medically necessary to transfer the infected employee to another position.

    A record of meetings, detailing precautions and other pertinent topics discussed, will be made by the medical director of Employee Health. The documentation shall include acknowledgment of the discussion by the employee and authorization to permit the employee's private physician to communicate with the medical director of Employee Health regarding the employee's health status.

    The document will be reviewed by the Administrator and a sealed copy of it will be placed in the employee's file in Employee Health.

The work duties of the employee will continue to be evaluated as part of an ongoing medical evaluation by the employee's private physician in conjunction with Employee Health.

4. The Infection Control coordinator and the employee's department director shall be notified of the employee's diagnosis by the Employee Health supervisor.

5. It shall be the responsibility of the individual department director to reassign (if possible) the employee to nonpatient contact or otherwise modify the employee's duties if indicated by the medical director of Employee Health.

6. On a semiannual basis the employee must obtain documentation, from his/her personal physician, indicating current health status as well as the employee's ability to continue working. Examination by the medical director of Employee Health may be required at this time. Precautionary procedures applicable to his/her work assignment will again be addressed at this time and will be documented. As before, all documents will be reviewed by the Administrator and a sealed copy will be placed in the employee's employee health record.

7. AIDS is a reportable disease by state law, requiring confidential notification to the State Public Health Department, AIDS Surveillance Unit. The Infection Control Department will be responsible for completion of reportable disease notification related to diagnosed cases of AIDS, in consultation with the employee's personal physician.

IV. This policy represents the most current available information relative to AIDS in the workplace. As new data becomes available, this policy is subject to revision, modification, or change.

Approved by Administrator, Medical Director,
and Infection Control Committee

Document 3

Sample Policy: Dealing with Applicants and Employees Having HIV, ARC, and AIDS

XYZ HOSPITAL
PERSONNEL POLICY ON AIDS

(Date)

I. Objectives

Objectives of this policy are to prevent the transmission of HIV in our facilities, protect hospital employees and patients from contracting the virus, and treat employees with HIV, ARC, or AIDS in a dignified, humane manner that recognizes, to the extent practicable, their individual concerns for privacy and confidentiality.

II. HIV Virus

A. Applicants

(1) The infection control manager and personnel director shall work with medical experts in developing a listing of "AIDS High Risk" positions which shall include surgeons, operating and emergency room nurses, and other personnel directly and regularly involved with exposure-prone and other invasive procedures and handling blood.

(2) All applicants for AIDS High Risk positions who are otherwise qualified and being seriously considered for a job shall be given the ELISA test that screens for antibodies to HIV before being hired or ordered to begin work. Any who test positive shall be given the same test a second time. Any who test positive again shall be administered the Western Blot Test. Any who are positive for all three tests shall not be placed in a job on the list but may be considered for openings in other areas. If there are no openings for which the applicant is qualified, he or she shall not be hired.

(3) Applicants for positions not on the list of AIDS High Risk positions shall not be tested.

(4) Before being tested, applicants shall sign a form giving their authorization for HIV antibody tests and waiving any claim they may have connected to the tests. Both the executed, dated, and witnessed form and documents relating to the tests must be retained in secure files.

(5) Any applicant for a job on the list who refuses either to submit to the tests or sign the form shall not be considered for employment.

(6) The result of any HIV antibody test shall be communicated to both the applicant and the personnel department, but otherwise maintained on a strictly confidential basis.

B. Employees

(1) During new employee orientation, employees shall be told it is a condition of their employment that they agree to submit to HIV antibody tests when requested.

(2) The Hospital reserves the right to mandatorily test employees in the High Risk jobs on a periodic basis. This applies to any employee in

one of those jobs at any time, regardless of full-time or part-time or temporary, or a transfer as opposed to being hired into the position. Employees not in "AIDS High Risk" shall not be subject to periodic testing.

(3) A Rule shall be published which requires all employees to report to the infection control office and their department head any accident or incident which could possibly involve their being exposed to the HIV virus. Examples of exposure include needle sticks; splashes of contaminated fluids—mucous membranes—to eyes, mouth, or other openings; and spills of infected blood. A written report shall be compiled, signed by the employee, and a copy sent to the personnel department. Failure of an employee to make the report shall result in disciplinary action.

(4) Whenever the Hospital becomes aware of any employee becoming exposed to HIV (see above paragraph)—whether through a report or other means—that employee will be required to submit to a series of tests for the AIDS virus. The tests shall be performed immediately after the exposure and again at 1, 3, 6, 9, and 12 months following the exposure.

(5) If an employee tests positive on ELISA, the same test shall be administered again. If positive both times, the Western Blot shall be used. If all three tests are positive, and if applicable, the employee shall be removed from a job on the High Risk list. He or she could be transferred to another position without loss of pay, placed on leave of absence (with or without pay), or discharged, depending on availability of jobs and his physical and mental ability to perform work. Every reasonable effort will be made to place the infected employee in a non-high-risk job without loss of pay or benefits.

(6) Any employee who refuses to be tested shall be discharged for failing to cooperate with previously announced and communicated policy.

(7) The result of all HIV antibody tests shall be communicated to the employee and the infection control and personnel departments. However, the result shall be sealed when placed in the employee's personnel file to which there must be limited access. All records containing results of these tests shall be maintained on a confidential basis.

III. ARC and AIDS

A. When the Hospital is informed that employees have ARC or AIDS, the personnel director shall (a) review documentation of their medical condition, arranging for a physical or mental examination if appropriate; (b) determine if they are in a High Risk job and, regardless, whether they have been performing all the duties of the job in a satisfactory manner; (c) confer with the employees, soliciting their feelings about continuing to work (bear in mind that the risk of a hospital employee with AIDS contracting a fatal disease while continuing to work is far greater than fellow employees being infected with HIV by him or her); (d) review the availability of other jobs that they may be qualified for and capable of performing; and (e) recommend to the Administrator whether to leave them in their regular job, transfer them to another position, assign them work to perform at home or some other location, place them on leave of absence, or discharge them. The decision shall be based upon analysis of factors, including whether the job is classified as High Risk and continued mental and physical ability of the employees to perform the work in question and the availability of jobs for which they are both qualified and capable. Reasonable efforts to accommodate the employee will be made.

B. Employees with ARC or AIDS who continue working must submit to medical examinations by Hospital physicians as often as required. The physicians shall be informed of the duties of the jobs in question and asked whether the employee is fully capable of effectively and safely discharging all of those duties.

C. Employees with ARC or AIDS who are suffering some physical or mental impairments due to their condition shall be allowed to continue on the payroll as long as they can be reasonably accommodated.

D. Counseling shall be provided at Hospital expense for all employees suffering from ARC or AIDS. The counseling shall include advice and instruction on procedures to take to avoid spreading the infection both inside and outside the hospital. Specifically, instructions on wearing gloves and adhering carefully to all safety procedures must be given.

IV. Confidentiality

All tests for HIV and medical or personnel records concerning an applicant or employee must be maintained in secure, sealed files, with limited access. The tests results or medical condition cannot be discussed with other employees or the public.

V. The Law

Legal counsel shall be consulted about every AIDS or HIV situation before a decision is implemented to ensure compliance with any applicable federal, state, or local laws.

VI. Education

A. Doctors and nursing personnel heavily experienced in communicable diseases shall conduct educational sessions with all Hospital employees on a periodic basis. Factual information on transmission and prevention of HIV shall be presented.

B. The personnel department shall remind employees of Hospital rules and policies regarding AIDS during employee meetings.

C. All managers and supervisors shall attend special training sessions on administration of this policy.

Document 4

Sample Policy: Assisting Employees with Life-Threatening Illness

HOSPITAL PERSONNEL POLICY GUIDELINES

Subject   :   Assisting Employees with Life-Threatening Illness
Applies to: All Departments and Jobs

I. Policy
_____ Hospital recognizes that employees with life-threatening illnesses may wish to continue working as long as possible. If they are able to meet acceptable performance and attendance standards, and medical evidence indicates that their conditions are not a threat to themselves or others, managers should be sensitive to their conditions. Life-threatening illnesses include but are not limited to cancer, heart disease, chronic pulmonary disease, and AIDS (including HIV, ARC, and AIDS).

_____ Hospital also recognizes that employees with these conditions may be handicapped within the meaning of state and federal laws. In these cases, an evaluation will be performed of the physical and mental abilities to perform without accommodation, and the burden of any needed accommodation to the Hospital.

While concerned about ill employees, _____ Hospital also seeks to provide a safe environment for all employees, visitors, and patients. Therefore, precautions should be taken to ensure that an employee's condition does not present a health or safety threat to others.

Consistent with these concerns, the following guidelines will be used to address the handling of employees with life-threatening illnesses.

_____ Hospital considers the medical records and conditions of its employees to be strictly confidential and prohibits the discussion or mishandling of such information.

II. Guidelines
A. Special Procedures for HIV and HBV
   1. The Hospital is concerned about the transmission of HIV and HBV from patient to employee and from employee to patient.
   2. To minimize the risk of transmission:

      a) All employees must adhere to universal precautions, including the appropriate use of handwashing, protective barriers, and care in the use and disposal of needles and other sharp instruments. Employees who have exudative lesions or weeping dermatitis should refrain from all direct patient care and from handling patient care equipment and devices used in performing invasive procedures until the condition resolves. Employees should also comply with current guidelines for disinfection and sterilization of reusable devices used in invasive procedures.

b) Exposure-prone procedures have been identified by _____ Hospital. A current list of these procedures is available for review at (give location here).

c) Employees who perform exposure-prone procedures are strongly encouraged to learn their HIV antibody status. To that end, _____ Hospital will provide testing for HIV antibody for all employees, without fee or cost. Employees who perform exposure-prone procedures and who do not have serological evidence of immunity to HBV from vaccination or from previous infection should know their HBsAG status and, if positive, should also know their HBeAG status.

d) Regardless of whether they perform exposure-prone procedures, employees who are exposed to HIV through a splash, stick, or other type of accident, must report that incident and be tested for HIV antibodies. The Hospital will assume all costs associated with the tests.

e) Employees who test positive for HIV or HBV antibodies or who are, in other ways, diagnosed as infected with HIV or HBV must not perform exposure-prone procedures unless they have been specifically approved, in writing, for doing so, by the Hospital, which will rely upon recommendations submitted by an expert review panel appointed for such situations. Normally, the recommendation of the panel and the decision of the Hospital will be that employees performing exposure-prone procedures who are infected with HIV or HBV will be transferred to positions where exposure-prone procedures are not performed or prospective patients expected to come into direct contact with the infected employee will be notified of his or her seropositivity prior to undergoing exposure-prone procedures.

B. Notification requirements for Employees Diagnosed as Having a Life-Threatening Illness
   1. Employees who are diagnosed as having any type of life-threatening illness must immediately inform the Employee Health Department Manager.
   2. When such notification is given, the Employee Health Department Manager will consult with the Medical Director of Infection Control and the Vice President of Human Resources. Together they will assess all circumstances, including the ability of the employee to perform his/her duties and the potential harm to employees, visitors, and patients, and then recommend the proper course of action.

C. Procedure for Handling Employees Diagnosed of Life-Threatening Illnesses
   1. A thorough and complete assessment will be made on a case-by-case basis. In making this assessment, _____ will use all resources available, including, but not limited to, Medical Staff, Employee Relations Staff, and Legal Staff. The assessment will be done in a strictly confidential manner to ensure protection for the employee involved.
   2. Whenever practical, the employee shall be accommodated with assignment to his regular job or another position without loss of pay or benefits. All employees diagnosed with a life-threatening illness will be required to make periodic health monitoring visits to the Employee Health Department and submit to required medical tests. The frequency of these

364 · *Appendix C*

visits and the type of tests will be determined by the Employee Health Physician.

3. In cases where assignment to regular or alternative jobs at _____ is not appropriate, the employee will be either given work to perform at home or a location other than the Hospital or placed on leave of absence.

D. Guidelines for Managers of Employees Diagnosed of Life-Threatening Illnesses

1. Remember that an employee's health condition is personal and confidential, and reasonable precautions should be taken to protect information regarding an employee's health condition.

2. Contact the Director of Personnel if you believe that you or other employees need information about terminal illness, or if you need further guidance in managing a situation that involves an employee with a life-threatening illness.

3. Contact the Employee Health Department Manager if you have any concern about the possible contagious nature of an employee's illness.

4. If warranted, make reasonable accommodation for employees with life-threatening illnesses consistent with the business needs of the department.

5. Be sensitive and responsive to co-workers' concerns, and emphasize employee education available through the Employee Health Department.

6. Do not give special consideration beyond normal transfer requests for employees who feel threatened by a co-worker's life-threatening illness.

7. In the event that co-workers refuse to work with or around an employee with a life-threatening illness, contact the Director of Personnel immediately. Normally, education of those employees concerning the facts about the illness and how to prevent its transmission, will be accomplished. _____ medical personnel should be used to communicate facts to these employees and answer their questions.

Document 5

Sample Policy: AIDS Conditions

ABC HOSPITAL
PERSONNEL POLICIES
SUBJECT: AIDS CONDITIONS

Policy:

A. Health Care Workers Infected with HIV

1. Health Care Workers (HCWs) known to be infected with HIV who do not perform exposure-prone or invasive procedures need not be restricted from work unless they have evidence of other infection or illness for which any HCW should be restricted. HCWs infected with HIV must be medically evaluated prior to being allowed to perform exposure-prone or invasive procedures.
2. Each HCW infected with HIV who performs exposure-prone or invasive procedures shall be permitted to work once it is determined in consultation with the Hospital's physicians and the HCW's private physician that:
   a. The employee is free from any other infection or illness for which restriction is indicated.
   b. The employee is not a threat to the safety or health of the patients or fellow employees.
   c. The employee is not unduly at risk for contracting diseases.
3. Continuation of work duties shall be evaluated according to an ongoing clinical evaluation of the infected HCW's medical condition and the risks to the employee on the one hand and patients and fellow employees on the other. In case of conflict with the HCW's private physician, the Hospital's physician shall prevail.

B. HCWs working with HIV-Infected Patients or Employees

1. Pregnant employees shall not engage in the direct care of patients infected with HIV.
2. HCWs refusing to perform their work duties involving the care of an HIV-infected patient shall be disciplined.
3. HCWs refusing to work with another employee with HIV infection shall be disciplined.
4. Food service workers known to be infected with HIV need not be restricted from work unless they have evidence of other infection or illness for which any food service worker should also be restricted.

C. Serologic Testing of Employees

1. Routine serologic testing of HCWs is not provided.
2. Serologic testing is available at the County Local Health District to HCWs who wish to know their HIV status.
3. HCWs who have sustained a parenteral or mucous membrane exposure to blood or body fluids shall follow the protocol established for parenteral and mucous membrane exposures of HCWs.

Document 6

Personnel Post-Exposure Policy and Procedures

AIDS FOLLOW-UP, POST-EXPOSURE POLICY AND PROCEDURES

DISTRIBUTION:	All Departments
FORMULATED BY:	Infection Control
PURPOSE:	Appropriately render serological and clinical follow-up when exposed to a known AIDS or HIV-positive source via parenteral or mucous membrane exposure.
APPLIES TO:	All Personnel
POLICY:	All personnel involved in a needle puncture or mucous membrane exposure with a known AIDS or positive HIV source must adhere to these rules and procedures and be given serologic and clinical follow-up.
RESPONSIBILITY:	Human Resources/Risk Management/ Infection Control/Emergency Care Unit/Lab
PROCEDURE:	Define: Exposure to a known HIV, ARC, or AIDS patient shall include parenteral (e.g., needlestick or cut) and/or mucous membrane exposure (e.g., splash to eye or mouth) or significant contact with blood or other body fluids. Patients with no prior HIV antibody testing, but who are considered at high risk for AIDS or suspected cases should be referred to Infection Control/Risk Management for discussion with source's (patient's) attending physician.

1. The exposed health care worker must complete an employee incident report form and report to the Emergency Care Unit.

2. The exposed health care worker
   should be evaluated by:
   A. Routine Hepatitis protocol
   B. HIV antibody testing
3. The HIV blood samples drawn
   from the health care worker will be
   stored for future use and/or testing.
   The Blood Bank protocol for freez-
   ing should be followed. The sample
   should remain frozen indefinitely.
4. The source patient with the diagnosis of AIDS should be evaluated,
   utilizing the Hepatitis protocol.
5. The incident report should be for-
   warded to Risk Management immediately. The Infection Control
   Officer should be notified of the incident by calling _____.
   A message may be left with the
   Nursing Service Office.
6. The exposed health care worker's
   history shall be taken by an RN
   (Risk Manager or Infection Control
   Officer or their designate) as soon
   as possible after the exposure, with
   special attention to the attached criteria. Clinical evaluation will be
   done via the contacted Employee
   Health Physician. The Risk Management Department Secretary will
   arrange an appointment time. The
   evaluating physician is requested to
   note both positive and negative
   findings in relation to each of the
   criteria.
7. If the health care worker is seronegative, he should be retested at 6
   weeks and thereafter at 3, 6, and 12
   months following exposure. If
   health care worker sero-converts, he
   will be referred to a physician. The
   physician will be requested to evaluate, counsel, and follow-up at the
   physician's discretion.
8. The Infection Control Office will be
   available to answer questions posed
   by the health care worker.
9. The exposed health care worker has
   the option of refusing the above
   protocol; however, such refusal
   shall be in totality and no partial
   protocol will be offered/received.

Document 7

Checklist of Items To Be Communicated to Employees Occupationally Exposed to the HIV Virus

Because of your potential exposure to the HIV virus on the job (examples: by needle stick, splash from mucus membranes to the eyes or mouth, or exposure to blood or other body fluids), you should know these facts and procedures and instructions:

1. A test for HIV antbodies will be immediately performed on you, the employee. This test will tell whether your body has developed antibodies to the HIV virus— not whether you have AIDS. You must consent to the taking of a blood sample for this test.
2. The test will be done on you again at six weeks, three, six, nine and twelve months. If all of these are negative, the probability is you did not contract HIV from the exposure.
3. Until the twelve-month study is done, you are cautioned to avoid pregnancy, since it is known that the HIV virus can pass to the unborn baby.
4. You are to avoid donation of plasma, blood, body organs, and sperm.
5. You are cautioned to avoid exchanging body fluids during sexual activity, deep "French kissing," oral-genital contact, and use of IV drugs.
6. You must know that the vast majority of health care employees exposed to the HIV virus never develop it.
7. You must know that there is often a long incubation period (time between exposure and development of the disease), possibly as long as three years.
8. You are advised to inform any sexual or needle partners of your potential exposure and its ramifications.

I have read the above information, had it explained to me, and had the opportunity to ask questions.

Signed _____

Witness _____ Date _____

Document 8

Counseling Guidelines for Employees with HIV

Guidelines for persons in the workplace exhibiting any of the following:

A. Hepatitis B Antigenemia
B. Reactive HIV antibody
C. Inconclusive diagnostic testing for the above (A or B).

Care should be taken to avoid exposing your blood and/or body secretions with other people as long as any of the above conditions persist or as instructed by Infection Control/Employee Health.

The following guidelines are statements which are the expected standards you must adhere to as long as dictated.

Your Department Head, Employee Health Services, Infection Control and Human Resources are aware of your expected adherence, and these standards will be used to evaluate your continued employment status.

1. Avoid sustaining puncture wounds, abrasions or other nicks/scrapes to your skin surfaces, especially the hand surfaces. If this occurs, immediately notify your Supervisor and attempt to control bleeding yourself. Follow the standard Incident Report procedure and report to the Emergency Care Unit.

2. Wash your hands well before and after performing or assisting with invasive procedures or those procedures which require mucus membrane contact or contact with non-intact skin of patients. Gloves are not necessary unless the policy/procedure dictates the use of gloves.

3. Report any exudative lesions on your skin surfaces (especially the hands). Exudative lesions include, but are not limited to, fresh open wounds, exudative dermatitis, puncture wounds or cuts which may exude blood or other serous/sero-sanguineous/or purulent material. Report any lesion to your immediate Supervisor and to Employee Health or Infection Control immediately. If in doubt, call.

4. If exudative lesions are present, appropriate instructions will be given to you by Employee Health/Infection Control.

5. If while rendering patient care your blood or other body fluids should enter or come in contact with the patient's mucus membranes or non-intact skin, (i.e. patient bites you, perform mouth to mouth resuscitation, etc.) notify your Supervisor or Employee Health or Infection Control immediately.

The above guidelines have been explained in language appropriate to the employee's level of understanding. _____ has verbalized understanding and is able to answer questions regarding the expected employee behavior.

Signature of Counsellors: _____

Date

I have read the above guidelines and I understand the behavior expected of me. I have been given the opportunity to ask questions and have had my questions answered to my satisfaction.

I understand that any information regarding my health status will be held in confidence by my employer.

I have been given a copy of the above guidelines.

_____

Employee

_____

Date
Interim Policy Initiated

Document 9

Health Care Worker's Exposure to HIV Follow-Up Forms

Follow-Up Form #1

Employee Name: _____

Department: _____

Recent Medical History   Date: ⌐/ _ _

In the past six months, have any of these signs or symptoms been present as a chronic or persistent problem for at least 1 month? (Please specify all positive and negative info.)

Yes   No
____ ____ Fever
____ ____ Night Sweats
____ ____ Malaise/fatigue
____ ____ Chronic Lymphadenopathy,—Sites Noted: _____
____ ____ Arthralgias/myalgias
____ ____ Weight loss, unexpected, 15 pounds or 10% normal body
          weight
____ ____ Chronic diarrhea—No pathogenic/cause identified
                          —Specific pathogenic/cause identified
____ ____ Persistent bone marrow dysfunction _ Leukopenia
                                             _ Lymphopenia
                                             _ Thrombocytopenia
____ ____ Cough/Shortness of Breath
____ ____ Other (specify) _____
____ ____ None of above

Follow-Up Form #2
Physical Examination   Date: _/ _/ _

Weight in pounds _____

Lymphadenopathy ___ Yes ___ No
                        ___ Cervical   ___ Axillary   ___ Inguinal
                        ___ Supraclavicular___ Epitrochlear ___ Other
Oral Thrush   ___ Yes ___ No
Hepatomegaly___ Yes ___ No
Splenomegaly ___ Yes ___ No
Other mucocutaneous ulceration
       Location: ___ Oral Cavity ___ Pharynx ___ Genitals
Skin Lesions   ___ Yes ___ No
       Location: _____
       Description: _____
Other Abnormalities: ___ Yes ___ No
       Description:_____
Laboratory Examination
HIV Antibody ___ Baseline results
                 ___ Date
*See attached lab reports for periodic screening.
*Other diagnostic testing may be ordered at the discretion of the examining physician.
Comments:
_____
_____
_____
_____

_____   _____
Examining Physician   *Date*
Retain copy for physician's files

Follow-Up Form #3

DATE:
TO:
FROM: Risk Management Office
RE: Exposure/Needlestick of _____

In connection with your exposure/needlestick on _____, the following is a timetable of the HIV antibody testing follow-ups which *MUST* be followed:

6 Week	_____
3 Month	_____
6 Month	_____
12 Month	_____

IT IS IMPERATIVE THAT ALL TESTING BE COMPLETED ON OR BEFORE THE ABOVE LISTED DATES.

It is of primary importance to your health state that you follow the recommended protocol. Failure to do so may be detrimental to your health.
A memorandum for each testing date will be available in the Risk Management Office. Please contact Risk Management (prior to each date to make arrangements for you to pick up the appropriate memorandum.
No testing will be performed by the Lab unless the memorandum is presented to the Lab personnel.
Should you have any questions, please contact the Risk Management Office.

cc: Department Head—_____ ept/Unit

Follow-Up Form #4

NAME	HISTORY	PHYSICAL	6 WEEK HIV D. Due/D. Done	3 MONTH HIV D. Due/D. Done	6 MONTH HIV D. Due/D. Done	12 MONTH HIV D. Due/D. Done

Document 10

Sample Policy: Caring for the AIDS Patient

I. POLICY:

AIDS (Acquired Immunodeficiency Syndrome) is a serious disease caused by HIV, the Human Immunodeficiency Virus. The disease is characterized by damage to the immune system which renders the patient susceptible to opportunistic infection.

AIDS is not a casually spread disease. It is transmitted by sexual contact or blood to blood exposure. Personnel working at_____General Hospital may, in the course of their duties, render care to AIDS patients. AIDS patients will be rendered the same high quality care as is given to all patients. All hospital services shall be available to patients diagnosed or suspected of having AIDS.

It will be the responsibility of the attending physician to notify appropriate nursing personnel and the Infection Control Department when there is serious consideration of AIDS, ARC (AIDS Related Complex) or HIV virus infection as a diagnosis, so that proper precautions may be initiated.

II. DEPARTMENTS AFFECTED:

All

III. PROCEDURE:

1. Patients diagnosed with AIDS, ARC or a positive HIV antibody test will be assigned to a private room.
2. Patients with known or suspect AIDS/ARC or positive HIV serologic test shall be placed on Blood/Body Fluid Precautions. If the patient is admitted with such a diagnosis and appropriate isolation orders are not written, the nurse caring for the patient shall contact the attending physician and obtain the order for isolation. Blood/Body Fluid Precautions should be initiated immediately and maintained throughout the patient's hospitalization unless AIDS, ARC or HIV infection is excluded as a possible diagnosis.

   The nurse taking the order for isolation shall notify the Infection Control Department when she has completed initiation of the isolation protocol or if she does not receive the requested order.

   Unless exposure to blood/body fluids is anticipated, gowns, gloves, etc., need not be worn to enter the room for such procedures as obtaining vital signs. Visitors to the patient need not wear isolation garb unless there is concern for exposure to blood/body fluids, i.e., patient is vomiting, bleeding, etc.

   The use of gloves, gowns, etc., is recommended only if contact with blood/body fluids or secretions is anticipated in rendering care to the patient (i.e., starting an invasive line, insertion of a catheter or dressing change, emptying bedpans/urinals).

Wash hands following contact with the patient.

For additional information relating to isolation precautions, refer to the Hospital Isolation Manual.

3. Pulmonary resuscitation equipment, e.g., an ambu-bag and oral airway, should be immediately available for use with the patient should the need arise.

4. When requesting services from ancillary departments (i.e., Lab, X-Ray, Respiratory Care, etc.), indicate on the requisition that the patient is on Blood/Body Fluid Precautions. It is important for other departments to be aware there is a need for proper precautions when rendering care to the patient.

5. All non-disposable materials/supplies/equipment which are contaminated with blood or body fluids shall be red bagged and labeled with Blood/Body Fluid Precautions tag prior to being sent to Central Services for disinfection or sterilization. Disposable items contaminated with blood or body fluids will be placed in red bags and disposed as infectious waste.

6. A needle disposal box will be placed in the patient room. Needles are NOT to be recapped, purposely bent/broken or removed from syringe prior to placing in the needle box. Needle injuries most frequently occur during these activities. The foam filled needle protector will be utilized to prevent recapping.

7. The patient need not be restricted to his/her room and may walk about the unit, if physically capable of doing so. Blood/Body Fluids Precautions do not require a patient to remain in the room at all times.

8. The use of protective eye wear, such as goggles in connection with masks, is recommended in situations in which splatter of blood/body fluids or body secretions is possible. This is particularly recommended in the performance of procedures such as endotracheal intubation, bronchoscopy or GI endoscopy. The need for eye cover precautions during other procedures should be judged on an individual basis.

9. Soiled linens and other laundry shall be placed in the isolation linen bags.

10. Blood/body fluid spills should be cleaned up promptly with a solution of diluted bleach which is prepared daily. A fresh container of this solution should be obtained from Environmental Services each day as long as the patient is on the nursing unit.

11. Pregnant personnel are at no increased risk of acquiring AIDS while rendering care to the AIDS patient. Many AIDS patients do, however, excrete CMV (Cytomegalovirus). CMV may pose a risk to the unborn fetus, if the mother should become infected. For this reason, nursing personnel who are pregnant will not be assigned to care for the AIDS patient. If under emergency circumstances, reassignment cannot be arranged, pregnant personnel caring for the AIDS patient should scrupulously adhere to Blood/Body Fluid Precautions. This is especially important in respect to urine, where the CMV virus is concentrated.

12. Any personnel sustaining either needle injury or exposure to blood/body fluids should report this to Employee Health as soon as possible.

13. UNDER NO CIRCUMSTANCES SHOULD THE PATIENT'S DIAGNOSIS OR SUSPECTED DIAGNOSIS BE DISCUSSED WITH VISITORS OR THOSE NOT DIRECTLY INVOLVED IN THE CARE OF THE PATIENT. ANCILLARY DEPARTMENT PERSONNEL NEED ONLY BE INFORMED THAT THE PATIENT IS ON BLOOD/BODY

FLUID PRECAUTIONS.

THE TERM "AIDS" IS NOT TO BE PLACED ON THE PATIENT'S DOOR, ISOLATION SIGN, CHART COVER, NOR ENTERED ON REQUESTS TO ANCILLARY DEPARTMENTS.

MAINTAINING PATIENT CONFIDENTIALITY IS OF CRITICAL IMPORTANCE!

Document 11

Sample Patient Consent Form for HIV Testing

ABC Hospital, Clinic, or Nursing Home

Name or Number: _____

Date: _____

I hereby voluntarily authorize and permit a sample of blood to be taken from me and tested in order to detect whether I have antibodies to the HIV virus (human immunodeficiency virus) or any other identified causative agent of AIDS in my blood. I understand that the test results will be utilized for the purposes of my medical care and treatment.

I understand that the test is performed by withdrawing a sample of my blood and conducting laboratory tests to determine the presence of antibodies to HIV. I understand that the results of the blood tests considered to be positive will be reported to me, any physician or family member designated in writing by me, and (public health agency).

I further understand that a positive result does not mean I have AIDS, but that my blood has been exposed to the HIV virus and antibodies so that viruses are present in my blood. I understand that counseling concerning AIDS will be offered to me if my test results are found to be positive.

I have been informed and understand that test results, in a percentage of cases, may indicate that a person has antibodies to the virus when the person does not have the antibodies (a false positive result) or that the test may fail to detect that a person has antibodies to the virus when the person does in fact have these antibodies (a false negative result).

I understand that my test results will be released to my physicians and other health care providers providing my care.

My physician has advised me about the purpose, potential uses, limitations and meaning of the test results; the voluntary nature of the test; the right to withdraw at any time, prior to the completion of laboratory tests; the right to anonymity; and the confidentiality protections. With the information presented above having been completely and clearly explained to me and all of my questions having been answered, I hereby authorize a physician and/or hospital or health care facility to test my blood for HIV infection.

_____
(Signature or Notation of the
Test Subject or Signature of
a Legally Authorized
Representative)

_____
(Signature of Physician)

_____
Date Signed

Document 12

Sample Patient Consent Form for HIV Testing

I am a patient at _____Hospital. The subject of drawing a blood sample from me and testing it for the AIDS virus has been thoroughly discussed with me and I've been given opportunities to ask questions.

I understand that by signing this consent form, I acknowledge that the Hospital is authorized to draw my blood and obtain the test results and that any agent or employee of the Hospital may receive the results if that employee or agent provides patient care or handles specimens of body fluids or tissue and has a need to know the information. I further understand that committees of the Hospital may receive this information for the purposes of conducting program monitoring, program evaluation or service reviews. In addition, I authorize the release of the test results should they be required by any private or public third-party payor or insurance company as a condition of reimbursement for medical and/or hospital services rendered.

In recognition of the above, I agree to assume all risks and responsibilities of the test to detect antibodies to the HIV virus or AIDS and agree to release and hold harmless any Hospital employee, _____ Hospital, its agents, any physicians, representatives and assigns. I further covenant that I will never initiate legal action against any of the parties specified above and that this understanding may serve as a bar and defense to any action brought by me, my heirs, executors and/or assigns against any of the parties specified above.

I am aware of the test's limitations and the potential consequences of positive and negative test results. My signature indicates that I give my informed consent to have the HIV screening test performed on a sample of my blood.

_____

Patient/Legally Authorized Representative

_____

Witness

_____

Date

Document 13

Sample Patient Consent Form for HIV Testing

CONSENT TO ADMINISTER COMMUNICABLE DISEASE BLOOD TESTS

I, _____, am a patient of Dr. _____("Physician"), at _____. Physician has informed me that he recommends that I receive blood tests for the following communicable diseases in order to facilitate my treatment and protect hospital personnel and other patients: _____

I understand that the blood tests for the virus which is the probable cause of Acquired Immune Deficiency Syndrome ("AIDS") are not 100% accurate, and that these blood tests sometimes produce false positive or false negative test results. I further understand that the presence of antibodies means that a person probably has been infected with the AIDS virus, but does not necessarily mean that a person will develop AIDS.

I have been informed about the nature of the blood tests, their expected benefits and risks, and have been given the opportunity to ask questions about the blood tests.

I understand that Physician will notify me of the results of the blood tests and that the results will be explained to me.
(check one)

☐   I authorize _____ to furnish my insurance companies and other third party payors with any and all information it has or may have, either written or oral, pertaining to or in any manner connected with the tests authorized herein, that may aid in payment of any account presented to me or us, jointly or severally, and I further agree that no person, firm or corporation shall be held liable in any manner for furnishing or having furnished such information.

☐   I do not consent to the release of the nature of the test(s) to my insurance company or medical assistance program. I will pay the bill for the test myself.

Subject to the foregoing, _____ to the best of its ability, will not disclose the results of these tests to others except to the extent required by law or except to the extent such disclosure is required in order to safeguard the well-being of patients and employees at the Hospital or other persons at risk.

On this basis, I authorize _____, Physician and anyone authorized by them to perform the blood tests for the above described communicable diseases.

_____
DATE

_____
SIGNATURE OF PATIENT

_____
WITNESS

_____
WITNESS

_____
SIGNATURE OF PHYSICIAN

Document 14

Patient HIV Test Consent Form—Employee Exposure

I am a patient at _____ Hospital and have been advised that a Hospital employee (or other person) may have been unintentionally exposed to my blood or other bodily fluid during the course of my treatment.

I understand that as a precaution and in accordance with standard hospital procedures, I am being asked to consent to the drawing of a small amount of my blood. This blood will be tested for the following:

HBsAG—	a screening test for Hepatitis B
SGPT—	a liver enzyme test to screen for non-A, non-B hepatitis.
HIV antibody—	Human immunodeficiency virus antibody test is a screening test to determine if someone has been exposed to the causative agent of Acquired Immune Deficiency Syndrome, AIDS.

I understand that because this testing profile is being performed for the benefit of another, there will be no charge to me or my insurer; however, I will receive the benefit of the results of this free testing, as they will be reported both to me and to my physician. This testing will only be done with the concurrence and upon the order of my physician.

I certify that I have read and understand the above information and have been given the opportunity to ask questions. I hereby freely and voluntarily consent to the drawing of my blood for these purposes.

_____   _____

Date/Time   Patient

_____

Witness

Document 15

Employee HIV Test Consent Form

As a newly hired employee of _____ Hospital, I understand that during the course of my employment, I may come in contact with or be assigned to patients with communicable diseases. I have been supplied with and have reviewed the Hospital's policies on body substance precautions, employee injuries from patient use items and protection from and exposure to communicable diseases including HIV. I agree to adhere to the guidelines outlined in the Policies as a condition of employment.

I understand that during the course of my employment, blood tests may be requested by the Employee Health Physician in accordance with Hospital Policy. Such requests may be made if I am exposed to communicable diseases, including HIV—either on or off the job. I agree to report such exposures as required by Hospital policy and to consent to any HIV antibody or other tests that may be required post exposure. The tests may be also required if I am placed in a job that involves regular contact with HIV-infected patients. I understand that failure to cooperate in the administration of these policies or tests may result in disciplinary action up to termination.

I have read and have had the opportunity to discuss the above information. I agree to abide by the policies set forth as a condition of my employment.

Signature	Date	Signature	Date

Document 16

Patient Authorization for Disclosure of the Results of the HIV Antibody Blood Test

Patient: _____

A. EXPLANATION

This authorization for use or disclosure of the results of a blood test to detect antibodies to the Human Immunodeficiency Syndrome (HIV), the probable causative agent of Acquired Immune Deficiency Syndrome (AIDS), is being requested of you to comply with the terms of state law.

B. AUTHORIZATION

I hereby authorize

_____

(Name of Physician, Hospital or Health Care Provider)

to furnish to

_____

(Name or Title of Person Who is to Receive Results)

the results of the blood test for antibodies to the HIV.

C. USES

The requester may use the information for any purpose, subject only to the following limitations: _____

_____

D. DURATION

This authorization shall become effective immediately and shall remain in effect indefinitely, or until _____, 19___ whichever is shorter.

E. RESTRICTIONS

I understand that the requestory may not further use or disclose the medical information unless another authorization is obtained from me or unless such use or disclosure is specifically required or permitted by law.

F. ADDITIONAL COPY

I further understand that I have a right to receive a copy of this authorization upon my request.
Copy requested and received: _____ Yes _____ No   Initial _____

Date: _____, 19___ _____
                                              Signature
Time: _____ If signed by other than patient, give relationship:*
Witness: _____ _____
                                              Legal Relationship to Patient

_____

*This authorization may be signed by a person other than the patient only under the following circumstances

1. The patient is under twelve (12) years of age or, as a result of his/her physical condition, is incompetent to consent to the HIV antibody blood test or the release of the test results; and
2. The person authorizing the release of the test results is lawfully authorized to make health care decisions for the patient—e.g., an attorney-in-fact appointed under the Durable Power of Attorney for Health Care; the parent or guardian of a minor; an appropriately authorized conservator; or, under appropriate circumstances, the patient's closest available relative.

Document 17

American Hospital Association: Recommendations of the Advisory Committee on Infections within Hospitals

Development of an AIDS Program in Hospitals

In some hospitals, the admission of an AIDS patient has been disruptive to normal hospital routine and has significantly impaired the ability of the hospital to function effectively. This has occurred primarily because of widespread anxiety and misunderstanding about management, with maintaining patient census, with physician willingness to use the hospital, and with public relations. The advisory committee believes that a hospital that anticipates these problems and plans for them can avoid most of them.

Every hospital should address the policy and management issues raised by treatment of patients with AIDS. This is particularly important for hospitals that thus far have had little or no experience with AIDS patients, since most hospitals that have treated large numbers of AIDS patients have already developed policies and procedures to deal with the numerous issues that AIDS brings to the hospital.

A Prospective AIDS Education Program

The hospital should recognize that the admission of an AIDS patient may cause substantial anxiety among some staff members and patients who are concerned about their personal safety. Moreover, a victim of AIDS is also anxious and is having to cope with a serious disease. AIDS victims have sometimes been shunned or abandoned by family or close friends, and they may feel similarly neglected or abused by hospital personnel unless special supportive steps are taken by hospital staff members. These nonmedical needs of both patients and staff may become so pressing that medical care of AIDS and other patients may be compromised.

Hospitals that have developed aggressive education and intervention programs for their staff, including the medical staff, have been successful in minimizing anxiety and disruption. Intensive efforts at education and crisis intervention by skilled, knowledgeable, and respected hospital personnel are perhaps the most useful activities to ensure that a hospital continues to function adequately when an AIDS patient is present. Several hospitals have developed special teams of personnel who are readily available to answer medical questions about AIDS, advise about appropriate practices, and provide support to personnel and patients. These teams usually include persons such as an infection control nurse, a psychiatric social worker, a psychiatrist, a nursing administrator, and a patient advocate.

Widespread and open discussion of the issues raised by treating patients with AIDS appears to be beneficial, especially when that discussion occurs before a patient with AIDS is actually admitted. Some hospitals have made special efforts to involve persons from support services, such as housekeeping, dietary, laboratory, and radiology departments, in these discussions. Some hospitals have also found it useful to add hospital labor union representatives to these study groups. When a broadly based group of hospital employees participates in discussions of what is known and what is not known, they are likely to respond appropriately when given the opportunity to care for a patient with AIDS.

The advisory committee recommends, therefore, that hospitals consider the formation of special AIDS coordinating group, which would have broad educational and supportive responsibilities within the hospital setting. The group should be broadly representative of the hospital community, and should not be limited to "experts," or to ranking administrative personnel. The group must have visible and aggressive support from both administration and experts. In small hospitals, the group might consist of only one or two individuals. The coordinating group should develop education programs directed toward all levels of hospital personnel, and the program should, if possible, be implemented before an AIDS patient is admitted. Representatives from the employee or staff groups to be educated should be involved in determining the content of the educational program. Occasionally, physicians caring for patients with AIDS may wish to employ extraordinary or overly stringent precautions. Such instances have been demoralizing, both to the patient and to hospital personnel, and disruptive to patient care. It is particularly harmful when a physician uses extraordinary precautions since that unnecessarily raises anxiety on the part of patients and other hospital personnel. The AIDS coordinating group is encouraged to work with the medical staff organization to ensure uniform and consistent application throughout the hospital of recommended AIDS precautions.

Public Relations

Public relations issues present both problems and opportunities. Some hospitals have found that the treatment of patients with AIDS has had adverse public relations consequences. On occasion, members of the press have placed disruptive and time-consuming demands upon hospital staff. On other occasions, patients or members of the medical staff have placed inappropriate demands on the hospital, such as by asking that AIDS patients not be treated in the institution. The hospital must not allow these disruptions to interfere with patient care. The use of an AIDS coordinating team, as previously recomended, is especially useful in dealing with disruptions by staff members and patients, since education will often allay inappropriate concerns. In many communities, contact with news media will present unique opportunities for hospitals to assume leadership roles in public education about AIDS.

In dealing with the press, careful and honest sharing of information will usually diminish adverse publicity, and promote public education. The hospital should establish several principles for dealing with the press. First, patient confidentiality and dignity must be preserved. Second, a knowledgeable and authoritative representative of the hospital must be the designated representative to the press, and other hospital staff members should be required to coordinate all press communications through the representative.

Personnel Management

Some health care personnel, including physicians, have been reluctant to provide hands-on care to AIDS patients. However, at this time there is no evidence that the risks in doing so are any greater than the risks associated with caring for any other sick persons. The advisory committee recommends that otherwise healthy health care personnel should not be excused on their own request from providing care to patients with AIDS; there is no scientific or ethical reason to do so. If an employee simply refuses to perform his or her duties in relation to caring for AIDS patients, the issue becomes a legal and administrative problem to be resolved on an individual basis. Hospitals are urged to solicit the advice of their legal counsel in such situations.

Health care personnel who believe they may be at increased risk because they are immunosuppressed or have other clinical conditions that may confer an increased risk of acquiring an infection should discuss their work responsibilities with the employee health service or with their own personal physician. If the physician determines that that person is indeed at any increased risk, or that there are certain work assignments that the employee should not accept in relation to the care of AIDS patients, a written recommendation should be provided to the employing department for appropriate action in accordance with that institution's personnel policies and procedures.

Pregnant Personnel

There is no increased risk to pregnant personnel from caring for uninfected AIDS patients. However, many patients with AIDS excrete large amounts of cytomegalovirus; hence, it is recommended that hospitals follow existing policies with regard to possible cytomegalovirus exposure to pregnant personnel, or the CDC *Guidelines for Infection Control in Hospital Personnel.*

Personnel with AIDS or Suspect AIDS

As previously indicated, a small number of cases of AIDS have been reported among health care personnel, although most of these have occurred in personnel belonging to the high-risk groups previously defined. These infrequent occurrences have, nevertheless, required hospitals to make some decisions with regard to direct patient care responsibilities for employees with AIDS. This is a difficult issue that requires special consideration on an individual basis. Factors to be considered include not only the health status of the employee with AIDS, but also the nature of the employee's patient care responsibilities. Employees with AIDS who carry out intimate or invasive patient care procedures may be of special concern.

Two approaches are possible.

A hospital might reassign asymptomatic employees with AIDS to non-patient care positions in order to protect patient from exposure to the putative AIDS agent or from opportunistic pathogens that might be carried by the sympatomatic employee with AIDS and conversely, to protect the employee from nosocomial pathogens.

A hospital might arrange for a continuing evaluation of the employee with AIDS on an individual basis by the employee health service or the employee's personal physician. Patient care responsibilities might then be assigned, or not assigned, depending on such a continuing clinical evaluation of the individual employee's health status.

Similar considerations apply to physicians with AIDS. The hospital medical staff structure must be prepared to monitor and to deal with the possibility of excluding physicians from the hospital should it become apparent that there may be significant risks to either the physician or to patients. Hospitals who have employees or physicians with AIDS are urged to solicit advice from their legal counsel and the CDC.

Patient Care Precautions

1. A private room is not necessary unless the patient's hygiene is poor, or as may be mandated by the presence of other infections requiring a private room. A

patient sharing a room with an AIDS patient should not be immunosuppressed or infected with potentially transmissible pathogens. It will frequently be necessary to care for AIDS patients, particularly those with *Pneumocystis carinii* pneumonia or other serious opportunistic infections, in intensive care units. Hospitals must use particular care not to deny AIDS patients the potential benefits of intensive care facilities, if medically indicated. If ICU care is required, an isolation room in the ICU is desirable; a bed in an open ICU may also be used, however, as long as the additional requirements of blood and body fluid precautions can be observed.

2. To obviate concerns about mouth-to-mouth respiration, portable cardio-pulmonary resuscitation equipment, e.g., a disposable ambubag and oral airway, should be immediately available for use on AIDS patients.

3. Masks are not routinely necessary for the care of AIDS patients. The use of masks is recommended for health care personnel who have direct, sustained contact with a patient who is coughing extensively or a patient who is intubated and being suctioned.

4. The use of gowns is recommended only if soiling of clothing with blood or body fluids is anticipated.

5. The use of nonsterile gloves is recommended if contact with blood or body fluids, secretions, or excretions is anticipated. This recommendation is particularly important for personnel who have cuts or abrasions on their hands.

6. Hands must be washed routinely when caring for AIDS patients, especially if they are contaminated with blood, body fluids, secretions, or excretions. This precaution should be observed regardless of the use of gloves.

7. The use of protective eyewear, such as goggles, is recommended in situations in which splatter with blood, bloody secretions, or body fluids is possible. This is particularly recommended in the performance of procedures such as endotracheal intubation, bronchoscopy, or GI endoscopy. Precautions during other surgical procedures should be judged on an individual basis.

8. Needles and syringes should be disposable and should be disposed of in rigid, puncture-resistant containers. Needles should not be recapped and should not be purposely bent or broken by hand, since accidental needle puncture may occur. The use of needle-cutting devices is not recommended.

9. Extraordinary care should be taken to avoid accidental wounds from needles or other sharp instruments. Parenteral injections and blood drawing should be planned to keep these procedures at a minimum; they should be carried out by experienced personnel.

10. Blood and other specimens should be labeled prominently with a warning such as "Blood/Body Fluid Precautions." The label should accompany the specimen through all phases of processing until ultimate disposal. If the outside of the specimen container is visibly contaminated with blood, it should be cleaned with a disinfectant, such as a freshly prepared (once daily) 1:10 dilution of 5.25 percent sodium hypochlorite (household bleach) with water. All blood specimens should be placed in a second container, such as an impervious bag, for transport. The container or bag should be examined carefully for leaks or cracks.

11. Soiled linens and other laundry should be bagged, appropriately labeled or color-coded, and processed according to the hospital's existing policy regarding linens from patients on isolation precautions.

12. Nondisposable articles contaminated with blood or body fluids should be bagged and labeled before being sent for decontamination and reprocessing.

Disposable items should be incinerated or disposed of in accordance with the hospital's policies for disposal of infectious waste.

13. No special precautions for dishes are necessary; either reusable or disposable dishes may be used.

14. Patients with AIDS who are being transported require no special precautions other than blood/body fluid precautions. AIDS patients with infections requiring isolation precautions should be managed according to existing policy or the CDC *Guideline for Isolation Precautions in Hospitals*. Personnel in the area to which the patient is to be taken should be notified of precautions to be used.

15. Decontamination of surgical equipment, endoscopes, and so forth, should be accomplished by the same sterilization procedures (for such equipment used on patients with AIDS) as those currently recommended for equipment used for patients with hepatitis B. If possible, surgical procedures on AIDS patients should be scheduled at the end of a day, to allow sterilization of endoscopes overnight (shorter-term procedures result in high level disinfection, rather than sterilization). Invasive patient care equipment should be disposable or should be sterilized. Lensed instruments should be sterilized with ethylene oxide. Ventilator tubing should be either disposable or sterilized before reuse. Instruments that come into contact with blood, secretions, excretions, or tissues, including laryngoscopes and endotracheal tubes, should be sterilized before reuse.

16. Blood spills should be cleaned up promptly with a solution of 5.25 percent sodium hypochlorite, diluted 1:10 water (prepared daily).

17. Patients with AIDS who may require hemodialysis or peritoneal dialysis should be managed in a manner comparable to patients who are known to be carriers of hepatitis B surface antigen (HBsAg). Disposable components in dialysis equipment must not be reused.

18. Patients with AIDS who must undergo dental procedures should be managed just as patients known to be carriers of HbsAg. The use of protective eyewear, masks, and nonsterile gloves is recommended. Dental instruments must, of course, be sterilized after such procedures.

Document 18

Sample Posters for Educating Employees

To order call The Johns Hopkins Office of Public Affairs (301) 955-6680.
$5 for a set of four. Two-color posters, original size: 10" x 13 - 1/2".
©Johns Hopkins Health System 1991

Employer Policies, Procedures, and Checklists

Document 1

Sample Policy: Rule and Policy Pertaining to Infectious or Communicable Diseases

January, 1992

1. RULE

   Employees must notify (name of appropriate high-level manager) if either they or members of their immediate family contract an infectious disease. All such communications shall be confidential. Examples of infectious diseases include hepatitis A and B, HIV, ARC, AIDS, tuberculosis, German measles (Rubella) and chicken pox. Employees who fail to notify the company, in violation of this rule, are subject to disciplinary action.

2. POLICY AND PROCEDURES FOR HANDLING INFECTIOUS OR COMMUNICABLE DISEASES

   A. The Employer recognizes its duty to protect and promote the health and safety of its employees at all work locations.

   B. The health of the work force is threatened when either a fellow employee or a member of his immediate family contracts an infectious or communicable disease. Either fellow employees could potentially contract the disease from the infected employee, or—in the case of AIDS—the infected employee could contract debilitating and fatal medical conditions from other personnel.

   C. Employees are periodically informed and reminded of the Rule that they must notify the appropriate company representative if either they or members of their immediate family contract an infectious or communicable disease.

   The communication of this Rule shall be by bulletin board announcement, employee handbook, and during employee meetings when employment rules and policies are reviewed. All such communications must be documented and maintained in a secure file (for example, note shall be made of the date and place of employee meetings when the subject is discussed, and copies of bulletin board announcements shall be placed in the appropriate file).

   D. The Employer has the right to require medical data be provided it on the risk incurred, if any, of the infected employee continuing to work and his or her physical and mental capability to perform the duties of the job in question. The Employer also has the right to have a doctor of its choice examine the infected employee and review medical data. All medical information will be maintained on a confidential basis.

   E. A central manager shall be designated to receive all reports from employees, confer with appropriate doctors, obtain pertinent medical documentation, and recommend whether any action should be taken by the Employer. The manager is responsible for working with the affected employee to review all options and implement the decision of the Employer. The decision shall be based upon an analysis of all pertinent factors, including the ability (physical and mental) of the employee to perform all of the essential duties of the position and the availability of other jobs for which he is qualified and capable. Normally, attempts shall be made to reasonably accommodate employees with infectious diseases to the extent practicable. However, all considerations of possible accommodation shall include an analysis of their burden, if any, on the Employer. Any which are unduly burdensome will be rejected.

F. If legally required, information on the infectious disease shall be communicated to the state or city health department. However, neither the manager coordinating the matter nor any supervisor or manager with knowledge of it shall communicate this information to rank-and-file employees, their families, or members of the public.

Document 2

Sample Policy: Infectious or Communicable Diseases

January, 1992

A. Whenever an employee reports to a supervisor or other manager that he or she is suffering from an infectious, communicable disease, that information shall be immediately relayed to the human resource office.

B. Infectious or communicable disease are defined as tuberculosis, German measles, chicken pox, hepatitis, and all AIDS conditions (HIV virus, ARC, and AIDS).

C. The Employer recognizes its duty to protect and promote the health and safety of its employees at all work locations. The Employer also recognizes its duty to refrain from improperly discriminating against any employee who may be handicapped and to achieve continuous complicance with federal and state laws protecting the handicapped from discrimination.

D. The human resource office is designated to receive all reports of communicable diseases from employees, confer with appropriate doctors, obtain pertinent medical documentation, and recommend whether any action should be taken by the Employer. A representative of that office should confer with the affected employee to review all options, ascertain the wishes of the employee with respect to continued employment, and determine the physical and mental ability of the employee to perform all of the essential duties of the position or job in question. The human resource office shall also analyze the threat, if any, of having the employee continue working in a particular job on the health or safety of fellow employees, customers, or others. Finally, the human resource office should consider the threat to the health of the infected employee who, at least in the situation of being HIV positive, could contract debilitating and fatal medical conditions from other personnel or the public while at work.

E. If the employee wishes to continue in his or her regular job, an analysis must be made of whether he or she is qualified to perform the essential duties of that position, with or without reasonable accommodation. If accommodation is necessary, a review of all potential accommodations will be made and discussed with the employee; those which are unreasonable will be rejected. Further, those which are reasonable will be rejected if their implementation places an undue burden upon the Employer. Any recommendations of the human resource office with respect to these issues will be submitted to the General Manager, who will make all final decisions.

F. All documents and records pertaining to the infectious or communicable disease shall be confidentially maintained with limited access.

G. If legally required, information on the infectious disease shall be communicated to the state or city health department.

Document 3
Sample Policy: AIDS Conditions

A. Any employee who learns that he or she is HIV positive, regardless of whether there are symptoms of ARC or AIDS, is required to report that condition to the personnel office, where a special form will be completed and signed. That completed form will be retained in a special, sealed file, and will be treated on a confidential basis. Any employee who continues working at this facility with knowledge of positive HIV status, but without reporting that fact to the Employer is in violation of this policy and subject to disciplinary action.

B. Whenever the Employer is informed that a particular employee has an AIDS condition, the proper representative of the Employer shall discuss the entire matter with the employee. All medical reports and records concerning the AIDS condition, including a copy of the HIV antibody test, shall be presented and shown to the Employer's representative; any evaluation or opinion by the employee's personal physician concerning that employee's present ability to perform the essential duties of the job in question shall be presented to the Employer. Further, the employee's wishes and desires with respect to continuing to work in the job in question, being transferred to another position, or being placed on leave of absence, or some other action or option, shall be thoroughly explained to the Employer. The Employer has the right to have its physician examine and confer with the infected employee; any report by the Employer's physician as to the present ability of the employee to perform the essential duties of his or her job, or the essential duties of any other position, shall be revealed to and discussed with the employee.

C. Normally, an asymptomatic employee (one who is simply HIV positive) will continue in his or her job without need for accommodation, and without consideration of transfer or leave of absence. However, if and when the employee develops ARC or AIDS, the employee must submit a written statement from his or her physician, explaining that the physician is well familiar with the specific duties of the job in question and stating that the employee is physically and mentally able to perform the essential duties of that particular job. The Employer may accept the opinion and recommendation of the employee's personal physician or the Employer may have its own physician perform a similar evaluation and analysis. If the opinion and recommendation of the Employer's physician conflict with that of the employee's personal physician, the Employer reserves the right to adhere to the evaluation of its own doctor.

D. With special, limited jobs that present possible opportunities for exposing customers, patients, or fellow employees to the blood or other body fluids of the infected employee, the Employer may require a statement from the physician who has examined the infected employee to the effect that his or her presence in the workplace is neither a threat to the health and safety of others nor to the employee, as a condition of continued employment.

E. All reasonable attempts will be made to accommodate an employee with ARC or AIDS. This may mean assigning nonessential duties to other personnel or making practicable changes in the schedule of the affected employee.

F. Any employee with ARC or AIDS returning to work following a medical leave of absence must execute a release certifying that he or she understands the risks and dangers to his or her health associated with the return to work and coming into contact with fellow employees and others, releasing the Employer of all liability and assuming medical and health risks presented by possible damage to his or her immune system, with full knowledge of their implications.

Document 4

Sample Policy: BankAmerica—Assisting Employees with Life-Threatening Illnesses

a. Policy—BankAmerica recognizes that employees with life-threatening illnesses including but not limited to cancer, heart disease, and AIDS may wish to continue to engage in as many of their normal pursuits as their condition allows, including work. As long as these employees are able to meet acceptable performance standards, and medical evidence indicates that their conditions are not a threat to themselves or others, managers should be sensitive to their conditions and ensure that they are treated consistently with other employees. At the same time, BankAmerica seeks to provide a safe work environment for all employees and customers. Therefore, precautions should be taken to ensure that an employee's condition does not present a health and/or safety threat to other employees or customers.

b. Personnel Relations—Consistent with this concern for employees with life-threatening illnesses, BankAmerica offers the following range of resources available through Personnel Relations:
   1) Management and employee education and information on terminal illness and specific life-threatening illnesses.
   2) Referral to agencies and organizations that offer supportive services for life-threatening illnesses.
   3) Benefit consultation to assist employees in effectively managing health, leave, and other benefits.

c. Guidelines—When dealing with situations involving employees with life-threatening illnesses, managers should:
   1) Remember that an employee's health condition is personal and confidential, and reasonable precautions should be taken to protect information regarding an employee's health condition.
   2) Contact Personnel Relations if you believe that you or other employees need information about terminal illness, or a specific life-threatening illness, or if you need further guidance in managing a situation that involves an employee with a life-threatening illness.
   3) Contact Personnel Relations if you have any concern about the possible contagious nature of an employee's illness.
   4) Contact Personnel Relations to determine if a statement should be obtained from the employee's attending physician that continued presence at work will pose no threat to the employee, co-workers or customers. BankAmerica reserves the right to require an examination by a medical doctor appointed by the company.
   5) If warranted, make reasonable accommodation for employees with life-threatening illnesses consistent with the business needs of the division/unit.
   6) Make a reasonable attempt to transfer employees with life-threatening illnesses who request a transfer and are experiencing undue emotional stress.

7) Be sensitive and responsive to co-workers' concerns, and emphasize employee education available through Personnel Relations.
8) Not give special consideration beyond normal transfer requests for employees who feel threatened by a co-worker's life-threatening illness.
9) Be sensitive to the fact that continued employment for an employee with a life-threatening illness may sometimes be therapeutically important in the remission or recovery process, or may help to prolong that employee's life.
10) Encourage employees to seek assistance from established community support groups for medical treatment and counseling services. Information on these can be requested through Personnel Relations or Corporate Health Programs #3666.

Document 5

Sample Policy: ABC Restaurant

Rules, Policies, and Procedures Regarding Infectious Diseases

1. RULES

A. Employees must notify either the corporate human resource office or the General Manager of their Restaurant, in writing, if either they or members of their immediate family contract an infectious disease. All such communications shall be confidential. Examples of infectious diseases include hepatitis A and B, the HIV virus, ARC, AIDS, tuberculosis, German measles (Rubella), and chicken pox. Employees who fail to so notify the Company, in violation of this rule, are subject to disciplinary action.

B. A medical evaluation of whether the employee is a threat to the health and safety of customers, fellow employees, or others will be made. Any reports of the employee's personal physician should be presented to the Company, which may have its doctor examine the employee and determine whether performance of the duties of the job in question would constitute a health problem.

C. As long as an employee is capable of performing all the essential duties of the particular job, or as long as he or she maintains eligibility for disability or illness plans, an employee with an infectious disease will not be terminated. It is incumbent upon infected employees to keep the Company fully apprised of all medical developments in their condition and any impairment of their ability to perform all of the essential duties connected with the job in question. Employees unable to perform all of the essential duties of his or her job and no longer eligible for company illness and disability plans are subject to termination without prejudice to their right to reapply at a later time. Other options include possible transfer to a position the infected employee is presently capable of performing and medical leave of absence.

2. POLICIES AND PROCEDURES FOR HANDLING EMPLOYEES WITH INFECTIOUS OR COMMUNICABLE DISEASES

A. The Company recognizes its duty to comply with all health and sanitation laws and regulations and to take appropriate action to protect the health and safety of its customers at all restaurants.

B. The Company also recognizes its duty to protect and promote the health and safety of all employees at all restaurants.

C. The health and safety of both the public (potential and actual customers) and the employees are threatened when either an employee or a member of his or her immediate family contracts an infectious or communicable disease.

D. Employees are to be periodically informed and reminded of the Rule that they must notify appropriate managers if either they or ommediate members of their family contract an infectious disease. The communication of this Rule shall be by bulletin board announcement, employee handbook, and employee meetings.

E. The definition of infectious or communicable disease includes hepatitis A and B, the HIV virus, ARC, AIDS, tuberculosis, German measles (Rubella), and chicken pox.

B, the HIV virus, ARC, AIDS, tuberculosis, German measles (Rubella), and chicken pox.

F. A central manager at corporate headquarters shall be designated to receive all reports from general managers at the various restaurants about an employee or a member of his or her family who has contracted an infectious disease.

1. The central manager or his or her designated representative from the corporate office shall then confer with the employee and the general manager of the restaurant, expressing the Company's concern about the employee's well being, reviewing this policy and medical benefits with the employee, and soliciting the employee's wishes concerning employment.

2. The central manager shall obtain specific information about the various duties of the job in question. He or she shall also review all medical evaluations and reports made by the employee's personal physician. The central manager may have the Company's physician examine the employee, review the valuations of his or her personal physician, and issue a separate report. The central manager may speak directly with the physicians to answer questions and clarify issues.

3. The central manager shall then perform an analysis of the specific medical situation, the duties of the particular job, and the employee's physical and mental ability to perform them, and all other pertinent factors.

4. The central manager has the overall authority for making a decision concerning employment and the employee in question. Possible courses of action include the employee continuing in his or her regular job, with or without accommodation; transferring him or her to another position; placing the employee on paid medical leave of absence; placing the employee on unpaid medical leave of absence; applying the company's sick and disability plans to the employee; and discharge. The decision shall be based upon the analysis of all pertinent factors, including the ability (physical and mental) of the employee to perform all the essential duties of the position in question, the burden of possible accommodations on the Company, and the availability of other jobs for which he or she may be qualified. If the central manager and employee agree on a course of action, a brief description shall be reduced to writing and signed and dated by both of them.

G. Discharge will not be considered when the employee is able to perform all of the essential duties of his or her particular job or the employee is eligible for a sick pay, disability or other medical leave-of-absence plan. Further, all applicable federal, state, and local laws will be carefully studied to be sure none of them are being violated by the decision that is made.

H. If legally required, information on the infectious disease shall be communicated to the appropriate city or state health department. However, in all other respects, the central manager at corporate headquarters and the general manager of the restaurant will keep the information of the infectious disease on a confidential basis and refrain from communicating it to other employees, customers, or anyone else.

Document 6

Alternative Provisions for Employee Handbooks Concerning AIDS

1. LIFE-THREATENING ILLNESSES AND INFECTIOUS DISEASES

All employees are required to report any life-threatening or infectious illness or disease they may contract to the Personnel Department as soon as they learn of it. Employees must complete and sign a form, and a doctor's statement describing their ability to perform the essential functions of the job in question and assessing the risk of infecting others in the workplace must be submitted.

2. AIDS CONDITIONS

Any employee who has or develops the HIV virus, ARC, or AIDS must report his or her specific condition in writing to the Personnel Department. A medical evaluation will then be conducted to determine the ability and qualifications of the employee to perform the job in question, and the danger—if any—of infecting employees, customers, patients, or others. All reasonable effort will be made to accommodate the employee with the AIDS condition, including assisting him or her with essential duties of the job in question or transferring to another position the infected employee is presently able and qualified to perform. All considerations of accommodation will include an analysis of their burden, if any, on the employer. A medical leave of absence is another option that will be considered if appropriate for the circumstances. The employer shall comply with all applicable laws on this subject in discharging its obligations to both the employee and fellow employees.

3. CONSIDER ADDING THE FOLLOWING TO EITHER OF THE ABOVE PROVISIONS

The employer shall maintain any and all forms and medical records and correspondence on this subject on a strictly confidential basis. Specifically, they shall be reviewed only by the personnel and facility managers, sealed in envelopes marked "confidential," and maintained in a special file cabinet with a secure lock.

Document 7

Checklist: Steps for an Employer to Take Concerning an Employee with an AIDS Condition

1. Appoint a central manager to coordinate all communications and decisions.
2. Check the latest status of all applicable federal, state, and local laws.
3. Disclose the employee's HIV status *only* to managers who have a need to know it. Usually, supervisors, superintendents, and even facility managers do not need to know an employee is HIV positive, while they should be provided with that information for an employee with AIDS who is frequently absent for medical reasons.
4. Have a conversation with him or her, in the presence of a witness, that makes the following points:

    a) the AIDS condition makes him or her vulnerable to health hazards in the workplace, that he or she may contract an infectious disease from co-workers who are successfully fighting it off and perhaps do not even realize they have it.

    b) a statement from the employee's doctor certifying that he or she is released to work, is capable of performing all essential duties of the job in question, and does not threaten the health or safety of customers, patients, or fellow employees is necessary before he or she can continue working.

    c) the employer is very concerned about the employee and solicits the employee's wishes as to continued employment.

5. Consider having the employer's physician examine the person with the AIDS condition and advise him or her of the possibility of picking up an opportunistic disease from coworkers, customers, patients, or others in the workplace; evaluate the employee's mental and physical ability to perform the duties of the job in question; and recommend whether the employee should continue working in the same job, be transferred to another position, or be placed on leave of absence to secure medical treatment.
6. Secure a release from the employee certifying that the employee has had the risk of secondary infections explained to him or her and has voluntarily and knowingly agreed to assume that risk in continuing to work.
7. Carefully document all of these conversations.

Document 8

Employee Consent for HIV Testing

Name of Applicant/Employee _____

Date: _____

I hereby voluntarily authorize and permit a sample of blood to be taken from me and tested in order to detect whether I have antibodies to the HIV virus (human immunodeficiency virus) or any other causative agent of AIDS in my blood. I understand that this test is being performed pursuant to my application for employment or continued employment.

I further understand that the test is performed by withdrawing a sample of blood and conducting laboratory tests to determine the presence of antibodies to HIV. I understand that the result of the HIV antibody blood test will be reported to me. Further, a positive test result will be referred to a physician or family member designated in writing by me and to (public health agency).

I also hereby voluntarily authorize the Employer to obtain a sample of my blood and test it for HIV antibodies at any time it deems it appropriate during the time of my employment. For example, I understand that in the event of a potential exposure to blood or other body tissues contaminated with the virus, several blood samples and tests must be taken over a long period of time to determine if I am positive for HIV virus antibodies.

I have been told that consenting to HIV antibody tests and cooperating in the extraction of blood pursuant to those tests are conditions of my employment. I fully understand that any subsequent refusal by me to so consent or so cooperate would be a violation of the Employer's policies and subject me to disciplinary action, including discharge.

Finally, I understand that, if employed and testing positive, I will be eligible for counseling provided by the Employer.

I have been given an opportunity to read the information on this form and ask questions or make comments. I now freely and voluntarily consent to any HIV antibody testing by the Employer during my period of employment.

_____   _____
Name of Applicant/Employee   Date

Acknowledgements

I wish to express my appreciation for assistance and advice to Ruth Neely, my efficient and skilled secretary; Patti Leggett and Jean Schroeder, our word processors; Dr. Marian Schuda, Program Director, Emergency Medical Residency, Riverside Methodist Hospital, Columbus, Ohio; Steve Humes, Assistant Director of Education, Gay Men's Health Crisis, Inc., New York; Herb Darling, Willis-Knighton Medical Center, Shreveport; the following attorneys: Frederick S. Kullman, Howard S. Linzy, Dwayne Littauer, Robert David, Jeff Hardin; and my editor at Lexington, Beth Anderson.

Index

Behringer v. The Medical Center at Princeton, N. J., 140
Benjamin R. v. Orkin Exterminating Co., Inc., 77
Bergalis, Kimberly, 137, 138
Blood banks
 legal liability for contamination, 131, 151–152
 Look Back policies of, 19
Blood transfusions
 AIDS infection through, 9, 13
 state tort laws and, 84–85
Blum v. Gulf Oil Corp., 55
Breach of confidentiality. *See also* Confidentiality; Privacy
 legal considerations, patient protection, 152
 state tort law and, 84
Brown, Helen Gurley, 12
Buckley, William F., 114
Bush, George, 31, 115
Business concerns, 25–29. *See also* Employers
 AIDS education and, 29
 company policy
 example of testing for HIV, 121–122
 implementation of testing for HIV, 121–122
 government regulation of, avoidance recommendations, 27–28
 health insurance and, 27
 issues facing, 25–26
 labor organizations and, 26–27
 monetary loss argument, 26

C

Cain v. Hyatt, 78
California, laws of, 73, 77
Ceausescu, Nicolae, 7
Centers for Disease Control (CDC)

AIDS education by, 12
health care worker HIV infection and, 138–139, 142–143, 153–154, 158
statements of
 Guidelines for Health Care Workers, 260–265
 Universal Precautions for Prevention of Transmission of HIV, Hepatitis B Virus, and Other Bloodborne Pathogens, 240–244
testing for HIV and, 115, 166
universal and special precautions, 171–175
Chalk, Vincent, 51
Chalk v. U.S. District Court for Central District of California, 51
Chattanooga, Tennessee, municipal laws, 88
China, government policy of, 7
Christian, Marc, 81–82
Chro v. Respondent, Connecticut Human Rights Commission, 78
Chrysler Outboard Corp. v. Wisconsin Department of Industry, 79
Circle K Corporation, 58
Cities. *See* Municipal laws
Citizens for Uniform Laws v. County of Contra Costa, 87
Civil rights
 HIV infection and, 23
 testing for HIV and, 114
Civil Rights Act of 1964, 30, 54–56, 163
COBRA (Consolidated Omnibus Budget Reconciliation Act), 71
Cohn, Roy, 9, 19–20

Lambda Legal Defense Fund, 114
Leckelt v. Board of Commissioners of Hospital District No. 1, 51–52, 182, 183
Legal considerations, 21–25. *See also* Federal law; Municipal laws; State laws
analysis of problems, 193–207. *See also* Analysis of problems
attorney's letter threatening to file suit, 337–338
discrimination and, 21–22
duty to disclose patient status to employees, 178–179
health care and, 130–132
law suits and, 23–24
monetary loss argument, 26
patient protection, 150–152
workplace and, 22–23, 25
Libel, 80, 84
Liberace, 9, 20, 21
Libya, government policy of, 7
Life insurance. *See also* Health insurance; Insurance companies
state and local laws, 95–96
testing for HIV and, 114
Local governments, 87–88. *See also* Federal government; Municipal governments; State governments
constitutional lawsuits and, 71
financial resources of, 17
Local laws, discrimination and, 87–88. *See also* Municipal laws
Louisiana, laws of, 74, 79, 80–81, 93, 115

M

Madonna, 17
Malpractice. *See* Medical malpractice

Mandatory versus voluntary tests (for AIDS), 167–168. *See also* Tests (for AIDS)
Manila, Philippines, 7
Marriage licenses, tests (for AIDS) and, 14, 115
Maryland, laws of, 74
Massachusetts, laws of, 76–77
Masters, William, 115
McCune v. Neitzel, 86
McGann v. M & H Music Company, 57
Media
AIDS education and, 10–11, 12
privacy and confidentiality, ethical considerations and, 20, 21
Medical education, health care provider protection and, 160–161
Medical facts, AIDS, 5
Medical insurance. *See* Health insurance
Medical malpractice
dentistry, 137
health care providers and, 130–132
state tort laws and, 85
Medical records, health care provider protection, 185–188
Mental anguish, state tort law and, 84
Michigan, laws of, 80
Minnesota, laws of, 77–78
Minnesota v. DiMa Corp., 78
Minorities, AIDS infection and, 8
Mortality
infection to death time period, 5
United States rates of, 8
Move v. Schantz, Schatzman, and Aaronson, 85

About the Author

A senior partner with the law firm of Kullman, Inman, Bee, Downing, and Banta, which exclusively represents management in labor and employment matters, Mr. Banta has twenty-five years of experience in the legal and practical aspects of human resource problems.

Much of Mr. Banta's exposure to employment issues involving AIDS has been through health care clients. His firm represents over fifty hospitals and several nursing homes in the Midwest and South; he has been on the board of directors of U.S. Health Corporation, a multihospital system based in Columbus, Ohio, for over five years; and he is a member of the American Bar Association Forum Committee on Health Law and the American Academy of Hospital Attorneys, American Hospital Association.

A graduate of Northwestern University and George Washington University School of Law, Mr. Banta has written two books: *AIDS in the Workplace: Legal Questions and Practical Answers* (1987) and *Complete Handbook for Combating Substance Abuse in the Workplace*, with Dr. Forest Tennant (1989).